PRAISE FOR
GLOBAL LOGISTICS

T0293607

Supply chains are fundamental to the global economy. There is a now a need to rethink the concept of resilience and to tackle the challenges of achieving net-zero emissions and continually evolving consumer demands. This latest edition of *Global Logistics* addresses these issues and provides those in logistics and supply chain operations with valuable and current thinking from which we will all benefit.
Kevin Richardson, Chief Executive, Chartered Institute of Logistics and Transport (CILT), UK

The eighth edition of *Global Logistics* is a testament to its important place in the collections of logistics and supply chain readers seeking a practical approach to a practical industry. This new edition complements underlying basics of logistics and supply chain management with the latest issues challenging our profession from a hands-on perspective. It is not a book for the bookshelf, it is one for the briefcase.
Dr Elizabeth Jackson, Curtin University, Australia, and Regional Editor (Australasia) of *International Journal of Logistics Research and Applications*

This eighth edition of *Global Logistics* is a well-timed publication. Students of SCM will find the well-reasoned arguments in each of the chapters beneficial in gaining greater understanding and discernment of the subject matter of their courses of study. The book is a comprehensive work of merit and will form part the recommended reading list for students of the Institute for Supply Chain Excellence.
Gerard Glynn, Founder and Director, Institute for Supply Chain Excellence, Ireland

Global Logistics brings together insights from over 30 leading supply chain professionals from around the world. The result represents a major contribution to our collective knowledge on the subject of global supply chain management and logistics. I commend Edward Sweeney and his team for making this happen.
Mark Millar, author of *Global Supply Chain Ecosystems* and international supply chain thought leader, Hong Kong

Global Logistics is probably the best book that deals with critical global logistics and supply chain issues. All chapters are from leading scholars in the field and act as a guide for readers to comprehend the complex global environment that affects logistics and supply chain management. It is a must-read for all of those who are interested in understanding the global challenges in the logistics and supply chain field.

Professor Ruth Banomyong, Dean, Thammasat Business School, Thammasat University, Bangkok, Thailand

Global Logistics is a well-researched collection of supply chain topics written by experts with a wealth of knowledge. Their blend of backgrounds provides new directions to 21st-century supply chains that need to be highly innovative. Edward Sweeney's words in relation to 'the critical role of supply chains not just to economic but also to wider social wellbeing' provide a perfect reference point for every responsible supply chain practitioner of tomorrow.

Anshuman Neil Basu, Secretary General, Association of Supply Chain Professionals (ASCP), India

Supply chain management is undergoing a rapid change. The urgency of making the logistics industry sustainable and the development of digital solutions and services are challenging the existing business models and customer relations. I think that this is one of the most important books right now for all who are involved in and want to learn more about this exciting transformation of the area of supply chain management.

Magnus Blinge, Research Manager, Scania AB, and Adjunct Professor, Linköping University, Sweden

8th Edition

Global Logistics

New directions in supply chain management

Edited by Edward Sweeney
and Donald Waters

KoganPage

Sixth edition published in 2010
Seventh edition published in 2014
Eighth edition published in Great Britain and the United States in 2021 by Kogan Page Limited

2nd Floor, 45 Gee Street	122 W 27th St, 10th Floor	4737/23 Ansari Road
London	New York, NY 10001	Daryaganj
EC1V 3RS	USA	New Delhi 110002
United Kingdom		India
www.koganpage.com		

Kogan Page books are printed on paper from sustainable forests.

Hardback   978 1 3986 0002 7
Paperback   978 1 3986 0000 3
eBook   978 1 3986 0001 0

British Library Cataloguing-in-Publication Data
A CIP record for this book is available from the British Library.

Library of Congress Cataloging-in-Publication Data
Names: Sweeney, Edward, editor. | Waters, C. D. J. (C. Donald J.), 1949-
   editor.
Title: Global logistics : new directions in supply chain management /
   edited by Edward Sweeney and Donald Waters.
Description: Eighth edition. | London ; New York, NY : Kogan Page, 2021. |
   Includes bibliographical references and index. |
Identifiers: LCCN 2021016809 (print) | LCCN 2021016810 (ebook) | ISBN
   9781398600003 (paperback) | ISBN 9781398600027 (hardback) | ISBN
   9781398600010 (ebook)
Subjects: LCSH: Physical distribution of goods. | Business logistics.
Classification: LCC HF5415.6 .G55 2021 (print) | LCC HF5415.6 (ebook) |
   DDC 658.7–dc23

Typeset by Hong Kong FIVE Workshop, Hong Kong
Print production managed by Jellyfish
Printed and bound by CPI Group (UK) Ltd, Croydon CR0 4YY

CONTENTS

About the contributors xii
Preface xxi
Acknowledgements xxvi

01   Re-thinking supply chain strategy 1
Martin Christopher
Introduction 1
The search for agility 3
The need for end-to-end planning 4
Building structural flexibility into the supply chain 5
Supply chain orchestration 7
The changing risk profile 8
Achieving resilience 10
Conclusion 12
References 13

02   Linking supply chain management to financial performance 14
Heimo Losbichler and Farzad Mahmoodi
Introduction 14
Financial performance and its drivers 15
Linking supply chain management and financial performance 20
Framework to identify initiatives that create the most shareholder value 24
Difficulties in improving supply chain financial performance 31
References 33

03   Supply chain risk management: finance – the forgotten perspective? 36
Carolyn Somorowsky and Lars Stemmler
Introduction 36
Risk management and the supply chain: an established perception! 37
From operational resilience to financial stability 40

Financing investments collaboratively: reducing the risk of supply chain breakdowns 46

Conclusions 48

Notes 49

References 50

04   Supply chain vulnerability and resilience 52

Alan Braithwaite

Black swans: long tails and unintentional self-harm 52

Probability versus impact 57

Mapping the landscape of risk and vulnerability 57

The evolution of supply chain risk management thinking 60

The financial impact of supply chain disruptions 62

Frameworks for designing for resilience 65

Some examples of disasters and the implications for resilience 72

Digital toolsets and services for risk management 74

In conclusion: supply chain resilience is a capability 77

References 77

05   Fulfilling customer needs in the 2020s with marketing and logistics 79

David B Grant

Introduction 79

Logistics customer service today 82

Logistics customer service elements and issues 83

Logistics customer service strategies 86

Summary 91

References 92

06   New procurement directions in supply chain management 95

Louise Knight, Frederik Vos and Joanne Meehan

Perspectives on procurement 95

Procurement directions for 'improved business-as-usual' 101

New procurement directions for 'business-*not*-as-usual' 108

Contrasting 'improving business-as-usual' and 'business-*not*-as-usual' perspectives 111

References 112

07   **Maximizing capacity utilization in freight transport** 119
Alan McKinnon
Introduction 119
Assessing the utilization of freight transport capacity 120
Factors constraining capacity utilization 125
Measures to improve capacity utilization 129
Conclusion 137
References 137

08   **Retail logistics** 142
John Fernie
Introduction 142
The evolution of the logistics concept 143
Logistics and competitive strategy in retailing 146
The internationalization of the retail supply chain 149
CSR and sustainable supply chains 151
The online revolution 153
The future 158
References 160

09   **Trends and strategies in global logistics and supply chain management** 164
Christian F Durach and Frank Straube
Introduction 164
Research design and research sample 165
Key trends and strategies 168
Strategic delivery reliability 183
Digital transformation in logistics 185
Conclusion and outlook 187
Notes 188
References 188

10   **Global sourcing and supply** 190
Alan Braithwaite
Global trade – economic lifeblood 190
The product economics that have driven global sourcing 193
Sustainability and the UN'S SDGS 197
The key features of 'good practice' in global sourcing 199

Emerging risks and their implications for future sourcing
    strategies 203
Emerging technologies and their impacts 204
Re-shoring, near-shoring and supply chain reconfiguration 206
In conclusion 208
References 208

11   Supply chain relationships: the foundation of
      success 210
      Patrick Daly
      The historical strategic context 210
      The importance of inter-organizational relationships 214
      The importance of clear objectives 217
      Relevant metrics to measure progress towards achieving
          objectives 222
      Summary 227
      References 229

12   Delivering sustainability through supply chain
      management 231
      Maria Huge-Brodin and Edward Sweeney
      Introduction 231
      Sustainability as corporate performance 232
      How supply chains can foster sustainable development 235
      Sustainable supply chains: contemporary and future
          challenges 239
      Some concluding comments 243
      References 244

13   Greening of logistics: cutting pollution and greenhouse
      gas emissions 246
      Alan McKinnon
      Introduction 246
      Emissions from logistics 247
      Managerial and analytical frameworks 252
      Repowering logistics with cleaner, low-carbon energy 255
      Raising the energy efficiency of logistics operations 259
      Increasing the utilization of logistics assets 261
      Shifting freight to greener transport modes 262

Reducing the demand for freight movement 264
Conclusions 265
References 266

14   People powering contemporary supply chains 270
John Gattorna
Introduction 270
Tensegrity: balancing external and internal forces acting on the
    enterprise 271
Segmenting customers versus segmenting supply chains 273
Managing in a parallel universe 275
Digitalization is mandatory 277
From 'static' to 'dynamic' organization designs 280
New focus on the supply side 285
Resilience, delivered 287
A final word 288
Notes 288
References 288

15   Leadership in logistics 289
Richard J Atkinson
What is leadership, and why should we develop leadership
    skills? 289
Better practice, and the law 290
The problem (opportunity) 292
What leadership is not 294
What should we do? 295
Leading innovation 296
Strategy 300
Engagement 301
'How' not 'who' 301
Summary 304
References 305

16   Ethics in supply chains: an illustrated survey 306
Steve New
Introduction 306
Characterizing the field of supply chain ethics 307
Two key issues in supply chain ethics 315

The Boohoo case 320
Concluding comments 327
Notes 328
References 330

17   Humanitarian logistics and supply chain management 338
Yasmine Sabri
Introduction 338
The significance of humanitarian logistics and supply chain management 339
Humanitarian logistics and supply chains phases 341
A framework for managing humanitarian logistics and supply chains 344
Pandemic supply chain: Covid-19 supply chain systems 349
Concluding remarks 352
Notes 353
References 353

18   Digitalization in global supply chain operations 358
Andreas Taschner and Hazel Gruenewald
Introduction 358
Digital technologies and their relevance for global supply chains 359
Current adoption of digital technologies 364
Conclusions 379
Note 380
References 380

19   Digitalization and Industry 4.0 in logistics 382
Pietro Evangelista and Witold Bahr
Introduction 382
The uneasy road to digitalization in logistics: from Industry 4.0 to Logistics 4.0 383
Digitalization in the logistics service industry: challenges towards Logistics 4.0 385
Conclusions 388
References 389

20   Performance measurement and management in the supply chain 391

Alan Braithwaite

Measure to manage 391

Measuring outcomes versus inputs 394

The balanced scorecard: the strategic standard for goal setting and measurement 395

The fundamentals of supply chain performance measurement 399

Mastering the complexity of supply chain and logistics performance management 401

Setting goals across the chain through service level agreements 402

The delivery, recovery and governance model 406

Defining the specific metrics across the chain 408

Control towers: collecting, managing and using data 412

Future directions in performance measurement 414

Conclusion 416

References 417

21   Aligning technology, manufacturing and supply chain: why it matters and how to do it 418

Aristides Matopoulos, Brian Price and Yuchun Xu

Introduction 418

The evolution of concurrent engineering 419

How to align technology, manufacturing and supply chain 421

Conclusion and future research 424

References 425

22   The 'deglobalization' of logistics and supply chains: operating in an increasingly nationalistic and risky world 427

David B Grant, David A Menachof and Christopher Bovis

Introduction 427

Background 428

Research approach 432

Proposed risk framework to address deglobalization 433

Conclusions 440

References 443

Index 447

ABOUT THE CONTRIBUTORS

Richard Atkinson CBE is a Teaching Fellow at Aston University where he teaches leadership, strategy and engagement on executive education programmes. Formerly a fighter pilot, Richard has served as a senior commander of Royal Air Force (RAF) combat forces, a director of NATO operations, and as a deputy director of strategic planning in Whitehall. He has also served as the Director of Media and Communications for the RAF, and for the Chartered Institute of Logistics and Transport (CILT). Richard has a passion for converting theory into practical action to help the next generation lead the creation of a sustainable future for the years ahead.

Witold Bahr is a Lecturer in operations and supply chain management at Coventry University. Prior to a career in academia he worked in all parts of the supply chain. He has also held a full-time academic/research post at Aston University, where he completed his PhD on technology deployment in supply chains. He is a committee member for CILT's Warehouse Technology and Materials Handling Forum. His current work focuses on new and disruptive technologies for supply chains, sustainability, and the divergence between theory and practice.

Christopher Bovis is Professor of International and European Business at the University of Hull. He specializes in all areas of European business law, competition and state aid, intellectual property, transport, telecommunications and infrastructure. He is a leading international authority on public procurement, public–private partnerships and public-sector management. He advises national governments and international organizations on regulatory reforms and has acted on behalf of the public sector and industry on numerous high-profile projects. He is Editor in Chief of *European Procurement and Public–Private Partnerships Law Review*, published by Lexxion Verlagsgesellschaft. His academic work has been translated into several languages, including Chinese, Russian, French and German.

Alan Braithwaite has worked in supply chain and logistics since 1979, forming the specialist LCP Consulting in 1985 which became the leading independent European specialist in supply chain management. During nearly

40 years he has worked with around 400 companies as well in the public sector. Between 1987 and 2018 he was a visiting academic at the Centre for Supply Chain and Logistics Management at Cranfield University and a visiting professor from 2006. He contributed to research and teaching and was Acting Head of Supply Chain Research for 18 months. He has been widely published and is a frequent presenter at conferences. Alan holds an MSc in Business Administration from the London Business School and a BSc in Chemical Engineering from Birmingham University.

Martin Christopher has been at the forefront of the development of new thinking in logistics and supply chain management for almost 50 years. His contribution to the theory and practice of logistics and supply chain management is reflected in the many international awards that he has received. His published work is widely cited by other scholars and has influenced many practitioners. At Cranfield School of Management, one of the world's premier business schools, Martin Christopher helped build the Centre for Logistics, Supply Chain Management and Procurement into a leading centre of excellence. Under his leadership the Centre became one of the foremost focal points for innovative teaching and research in logistics and supply chain management. Now, after leading the Centre for over 20 years, Martin Christopher has become an Emeritus Professor.

Patrick Daly works with many of the top Fortune 500 companies in manufacturing, distribution and logistics services in Europe, Asia and the Americas, helping them to achieve dramatic improvements in their supply chain capabilities and performance through supply chain excellence. In his consultancy assignments, Patrick has worked with clients in China, India, Uruguay, Puerto Rico, Egypt, UAE, United States, UK, Spain, Croatia and others. He is the author of *International Supply Chain Relationships: Creating competitive advantage in a globalized economy* published by Kogan Page in 2019. Patrick is an active member of the National Logistics Forum in Ireland set up by the Department of Transport, Trade and Tourism in April 2020 to advise the Irish government on keeping supply lines open during and after the Covid-19 pandemic.

Christian F Durach (Dr-Ing, Technische Universität Berlin) is full Professor and occupies the Chair of Supply Chain and Operations Management at ESCP Business School, Berlin Campus. His main research activities are related to supply chain risk management, digitization, and the implications of social sustainability on modern operations. He has published several peer-reviewed journal articles (Emerald Outstanding Paper Award, 2018 – *Supply Chain Management: An International Journal*), is Senior Editor of the *Journal of Business Logistics* (Outstanding Reviewer Award, 2019), Senior Associate Editor of the *International Journal of Physical Distribution & Logistics Management* (Emerald Best Reviewer Award, 2017) and Editorial Board Member of the *International Journal of Operations & Production Management* (Emerald Best Reviewer Award, 2020). Christian is the Academic Director of all specialized Master's programmes hosted by the ESCP Berlin Campus.

Pietro Evangelista is Research Director at the Research Institute on Innovation and Services for Development (IRISS) of the Italian National Research Council (CNR). Pietro is a business economist by background and he was awarded a PhD in logistics by Heriot-Watt University (UK) in 2009. He has carried out extensive research into economic and management issues associated with maritime and port logistics, as well as on ICT dissemination in the logistics service industry. His current scientific interest is in decarbonization of freight transport and logistics. Pietro is a member of the editorial board of leading international journals in the supply chain area. He teaches green logistics in Italian and international universities and is a member of the Research Committee of the European Logistics Association (ELA).

John Fernie is Emeritus Professor of Retail Marketing at Heriot-Watt University, Scotland. He has written and contributed to numerous textbooks and papers on retail management, especially in the field of retail logistics. He was the founding editor of the *International Journal of Retail & Distribution Management* and is on the editorial board of numerous marketing and logistics journals. He is a Fellow of the Chartered Institute of Logistics and Transport (CILT).

John Gattorna is a renowned global supply chain 'thought leader' and author. He started his professional life as an engineer, but soon moved into what was then called physical distribution management in the mid-1970s. Over the last four decades John has been a consultant, researcher and teacher in supply chain management. He started the Accenture Supply Chain Practice in Asia Pacific in 1995, and since retiring from that role in 2003 he has focused solely on supply chain 'thought leadership' in an endeavour to give this new field of management science some conceptual horsepower.

He is a prolific author and well respected speaker on the international circuit. He lives in Sydney, Australia. See www.gattornaalignment.com (archived at https://perma.cc/R8XV-VQU4) for further information.

David B Grant is Dean of Research & Societal Impact, Hanken School of Economics, Finland and Bualuang ASEAN Chair Professor, Thammasat University, Thailand. His research interests include customer service quality and satisfaction; retail; and sustainable and societal logistics. Recent research includes retail on-shelf availability and stock-outs; consumer e-commerce fulfilment preferences; and food retail loss and waste. He has over 250 publications and his Kogan Page books *Sustainable Logistics and Supply Chain Management* and *Fashion Logistics* are now in second editions. He was ranked fifth in Economics, Business and Management and first in Industrial Economics and Logistics in a 2019 academic study evaluating Finnish professorial research impact and productivity.

Hazel Gruenewald is Professor of Organizational Behaviour at ESB Business School, Reutlingen University. She received her PhD from the University of Nottingham, UK in 2000. She joined ESB Business School following a nine-year career in industry in various positions spanning global corporate training and development, management development and international programme management. She has acted as an international guest lecturer at universities including SBM ITB (Jakarta, Indonesia), UMP (Kuantan, Malaysia), and, ZSEM (Zagreb, Croatia). Her current research focuses on self-efficacy, motivation, transferrable skills and digitalization.

Maria Huge-Brodin is Professor of Green Logistics at the division of Logistics and Quality Management, and leads the research group Climate Smart Freight Transport, at Linköping University, Sweden. Maria's research interests and current research focus include green logistics and green supply chain management, and its interfaces with related research areas such as consumer behaviour, quality management, and vehicle design and configuration. Maria performs conceptual research, as well as collaborative research with numerous organizations. She is also head of a five-year Master's programme in Energy, Environment and Management at Linköping.

Louise Knight is Professor of Public Sector and Healthcare Procurement at the University of Twente (the Netherlands), and Co-Editor-in-Chief of the *Journal of Purchasing and Supply Management*. Her industry and research experience spans infrastructure, healthcare and government procurement. Louise's research on strategic public procurement, market dynamics and sustainable transitions, the future of procurement (in partnership with the Chartered Institute of Procurement and Supply), and supply network learning is published in a wide range of journals. The unifying theme is the development of a strategic perspective on capacity and capability building in procurement, which are crucial if supply professionals are to play a significant and proactive role in envisioning 'business-not-as-usual' and shaping new directions.

Heimo Losbichler is Professor of Controlling, Head of Studies Controlling, Accounting and Financial Management and Dean of the School of Business and Management at the University of Applied Sciences, Upper Austria. He is Chairman of the International Association of Controllers (Germany) and Chairman of the International Group of Controlling (Switzerland). Dr Losbichler's research interests include controlling, management accounting and financial performance measurement. He has published more than 130 books, book chapters, conference proceedings and articles in a variety of leading German and international academic and professional journals.

Alan McKinnon is Professor of Logistics in Kühne Logistics University, Hamburg and Professor Emeritus at Heriot-Watt University, Edinburgh. A graduate of the universities of Aberdeen, British Columbia and London, he has been researching and teaching in freight transport/logistics for over 40 years and has published extensively in journals and books on many different aspects of the subject. Much of his recent research has focused on the links between logistics and climate change. He has been an adviser to several governments, parliamentary committees and international organizations, including the International Transport Forum/OECD, World Bank, European Commission, World Economic Forum and Intergovernmental Panel on Climate Change.

Farzad Mahmoodi is Joel Goldschein '57 Endowed Chair Professor in Supply Chain Management, and Director of Clarkson's nationally-ranked Global Supply Chain Management Programme. Dr Mahmoodi's research interests are in supply chain systems design and management, and systems modelling and simulation. He has published about 100 articles in a variety of journals, including *Decision Sciences*, *International Journal of Production Research*, *Journal of Operations Management*, and *European Journal of*

Operational Research, as well as edited books and conference proceedings. He serves on the editorial boards of the *International Journal of Industrial Engineering* and *International Journal of Integrated Supply Management*.

Aristides Matopoulos is a Reader in Supply Chain Design & Logistics Systems at Aston University and a visiting professor at the University of Lille. His research on the implementation of the 'Design for Supply Chain/Logistics' concepts led to the development of the Supply Chain Readiness Level Tool which assesses the maturity and capabilities of supply chains. In 2019 he was appointed a Royal Society Short Industry Fellow. His industrial collaborators include Williams Advanced Engineering, Jaguar Land Rover, Saietta, MCTReman, M&S, and many SMEs. His research has been funded by the EC (FP7, Horizon 2020), ERDF and Innovate UK.

Jo Meehan is a senior lecturer in Strategic Procurement at the University of Liverpool Management School. Prior to joining academia, Jo had a long career with ICI working in numerous purchasing and commercial roles. Jo's current research centres on modern slavery, responsible procurement, corporate power and social value. Her research has won numerous awards for its contribution to the procurement field, and she is a regular public speaker on responsible business. Her work is extensively published in leading academic journals and in the professional press. Jo is Associate Editor for the *Journal of Purchasing and Supply Management* and champions the journal's 'business-*not*-as-usual' research.

David Menachof is Associate Professor of Supply Chain and Operations Management at Florida Atlantic University. Previously, he was the Peter Thompson Chair in Port Logistics, based at the Logistics Institute at Hull University Business School. Professor Menachof received his doctorate from the University of Tennessee, and was the recipient of the Council of Logistics Management's Doctoral Dissertation Award in 1993. He is a Fulbright Scholar, having spent a year in Odessa, Ukraine, and was on the designated list of Fulbright Scholars for Global Logistics. His research interests include global supply chain issues, supply chain security, risk and visibility, sustainable supply chain and logistics, financial techniques applicable to logistics, port management, liner shipping and containerization.

Steve New is Associate Professor in Operations Management at Saïd Business School, University of Oxford, and a Fellow in Management Studies at Hertford College. Steve has published extensively in the fields of procurement, supply chain management and quality improvement, with his work appearing in journals ranging from the *Harvard Business Review* to the *British Medical Journal*. Much of his work is interdisciplinary, and he collaborates extensively with colleagues from across disciplines. He regularly works as a consultant with a wide range of clients in the private, public and third sectors.

Brian Price is an academic based at Aston University in the UK, teaching engineering and product design. Active research areas include ultra-low carbon vehicles, engine/transmission design and technology planning. With over 25 years' experience in industry, working worldwide on engine design consultancy, he brings a pragmatic approach to new product development. Previously chief engineer or technical director at a number of major engineering companies, including Lotus Engineering, Cosworth Technology, Mercury Marine, Harley-Davidson and Ricardo Consulting Engineers, he is also a visiting professor at Loughborough University, UK, University of Wisconsin-Madison, USA and Hanyang University, South Korea.

Yasmine Sabri is a Lecturer (Aassistant Professor) in supply chain management at Aston University in the UK. She received her PhD in Management, Economics and Industrial Engineering with distinction from Politecnico di Milano. Her research is centred on designing integrated supply chains that deliver value without compromising the social and humanitarian impact. Yasmine has published articles in *Production Planning and Control*, *International Journal of Logistics Management*, *Journal of Humanitarian Logistics and Supply Chain Management*, and *Journal of Engineering and Technology Management*.

Carolyn Somorowsky has been a researcher at the University of Bremen since 2017. Carolyn holds a Master's degree in information-oriented business administration with specialty in operations research and finance from the University of Augsburg. She studied business administration with a focus on logistics, finance and sustainability. Her research focus is on supply chain management and supply chain finance as well as cooperative game theory. She is currently working on her doctoral thesis entitled 'A Collaborative Approach to Financing Investments in Supply Chains'.

Lars Stemmler is Head of International Projects with bremenports GmbH & Co KG, the infrastructure managers of the ports of Bremen and Bremerhaven. Prior to that, he was deputy head of a credit risk analysis team of a global bank in Germany. Lars has more than 20 years of experience in logistics and finance. He has carried out international projects in port development and transport finance and is visiting professor at various European universities in the field of maritime logistics. Lars holds a PhD in European port policy and a Master of Science in logistics from Cranfield University.

Frank Straube is full Professor for Logistics at TU Berlin since 2004 and MD of the Institute for Technology and Management. He was previously Dean of the School of Business and Management of TU Berlin. Frank studied industrial engineering and received his doctorate in logistics in 1987. He headed an international consulting and planning company for logistics for more than 10 years with projects in Europe, the Americas and Africa. He got his 'habilitation' at the University of St Gallen, Switzerland. Frank is a member of editorial boards of international logistics journals. He founded the International Transfer Center for Logistics (ITCL) and is permanent Visiting Professor at Panthéon-Assas University (Paris) and Tongji University (Shanghai).

Edward Sweeney is Professor of Logistics and Systems and Head of the Department of Engineering Systems & Supply Chain Management at Aston University in Birmingham, UK. He has held full-time academic posts at Technological University Dublin, the University of Warwick and the University of Technology, Malaysia (UTM), as well as visiting positions at several institutions in Asia and North America. Edward's research has been widely published and he sits on the editorial boards of several leading international supply chain journals. He has worked in close collaboration with many of the world's leading companies across many sectors including electronics, food and drink, life sciences and logistics.

Andreas Taschner is Professor of Accounting and programme director of the BSc in International Operations and Logistics Management at ESB Business School, Reutlingen University. He joined ESB Business School from Beuth University of Applied Sciences, Berlin, after 12 years in manufacturing industry, holding various management positions in the marketing and accounting area. Andreas studied Business Administration at Wirtschaftsuniversität Wien and at the University of Illinois at Urbana-Champaign and holds a PhD in social sciences from Wirtschaftsuniversität Wien. Andreas has held various academic management positions and was Dean of ESB Business School from 2016 to 2019. He is also a member of the

German logistics association 'Bundesvereinigung Logistik (BVL)'. Andreas focuses his research and publication activities on management accounting problems in an international manufacturing environment with a special focus on logistics and supply chains and has published various textbooks and journal papers on management accounting topics. He is a reviewer for several peer-reviewed journals.

Frederik GS Vos works as Assistant Professor in Supply Management at the University of Twente and as Senior Consultant at the Public Procurement Research Center (PPRC) in the Netherlands. He is also the Treasurer of the International Purchasing and Supply Education and Research Association (IPSERA), Vice President of the member council of the Dutch association of purchasing professionals (NEVI) and owner of suPlay BV, a serious game company. His areas of expertise include public procurement, public–private partnerships, buyer–supplier relationships, healthcare procurement, data analytics and serious gaming.

Yuchun Xu is Professor of Manufacturing at Aston University. His research expertise lies in the areas of Digital & Smart Manufacturing, and Life Cycle Engineering. Prof Xu's research has close links with industry and has been funded by UK EPSRC, EU H2020, FP7 and Innovate UK. He has had his research published in over 60 peer-reviewed journal and conference papers. Professor Xu is a Member of EPSRC Peer Review College. He regularly serves as a technical and programme committee member and as a session chair at leading international conferences.

PREFACE

The first edition of *Global Logistics and Distribution Planning: Strategies for Management* appeared in 1988. My own supply chain journey has in many ways mirrored developments in the logistics field during the intervening decades. Now in its eighth edition, *Global Logistics: New directions in supply chain management* also reflects the many changes which have taken place in the logistics world during that time. I am writing this preface in late 2020, towards the end of a year during which we have faced unprecedented challenges as a society and as a profession. Our response to the Covid-19 pandemic as a society has highlighted the critical role of supply chains not just to economic but also to wider societal wellbeing. In the early part of the year, many supply chains were reimagined as the lockdown and other restrictions forced radical changes in consumer behaviour, including but not limited to the shift to online shopping. Logistics processes in the healthcare sector proved vital in ensuring reliable supply of personal protective equipment (PPE) and other critical commodities. In addition, the UK's departure from the European Union put our profession at the vanguard in dealing with the many supply chain challenges that Brexit threw up. At the time of writing, the full extent of the economic and other damage caused by Brexit remains to be seen. What is quite clear though is the key role that logisticians and other supply chain professionals will play in dealing with the inevitable fallout.

The underpinning tenets of *Global Logistics: New directions in supply chain management* reflect some key overall drivers. First, the supply chains of 2020 are much more international in complexion than those in which I first worked in the late 1980s and early 1990s. This is a direct result of significant structural changes that have taken place in the international economic and business environment in recent decades. Some recent evidence of 'deglobalization' notwithstanding, the general trend over time has been one of reductions in the many barriers to international trade that have historically existed. It is now possible to move products, services, money, information, knowledge and other resources across international frontiers with relative ease. It is in this context that truly international – sometimes genuinely global – supply chain architectures have been developed. This requires innovation in supply chain processes – ie the identification of new and better ways of carrying out upstream and downstream logistics and other activities. It is the planning and implementation of this innovation that holds the key to improving supply chain capability and performance, thereby enhancing the competitive advantage of firms and the wider supply chains of which they are part. It is these new directions that provide the framework for this book.

Martin Christopher sets the scene for this in Chapter 1 by making the case for the re-thinking – sometimes the quite radical re-thinking – of supply chain strategy. This re-thinking needs to have a clear focus on flexibility and meeting changing customer requirements in the marketplace. There can be little doubt that contemporary supply chain management (SCM) thinking has assumed a more strategic role than in the past when the focus was often largely on short-term cost reductions and service improvements. In this context, it is important to establish a clear link between SCM and financial performance. This is the focus of Heimo Losbichler and Farzad Mahmoodi in Chapter 2, based on the use of economic value added (EVA) as the primary financial metric. The challenges of 2020 sharpened our focus on the risk associated with disruptions of various kinds to business. The concept of supply chain risk management (SCRM) proposed by Carolyn Somorowsky and Lars Stemmler in Chapter 3 aims at minimizing the impact of supply chain disruptions through addressing finance risks. The management of supply chain vulnerability is a capability that is finding its moment in the development of supply chain thinking. 'The downside from supply chain risks is much greater than the upside from perfect supply chains', according to Alan Braithwaite in Chapter 4. In this context, developing a thorough understanding of how supply chain vulnerability can be managed effectively is becoming critically important as organizations strive to build more resilient supply chains.

The next part of the book begins with a discussion of fulfilment of customer needs using both marketing and logistics by David Grant in Chapter 5. My experience suggests that these are two critical but complementary business processes and that their effective engagement is pivotal to the creation and delivery of customer value. Also of critical importance in a supply chain context is procurement – as noted by Louise Knight, Frederik Vos and Joanne Meehan in Chapter 6: 'Procurement is often regarded as one "half" of supply chain management (SCM), with SCM defined as logistics and procurement.' Without doubt, the procurement aspect of SCM has a vital role to play in facilitating competitive differentiation and strategic advantage. The physical movement of product remains a core element of logistics and

SCM. In Chapter 7 Alan McKinnon discusses the critical issue of asset utilization optimization in freight transport systems. The retailing part of the business ecosystem has been changing over a long period of time with recent months having seen particularly rapid changes in response to pandemic pressures. John Fernie explores some of the logistical and supply chain challenges associated with these changes in Chapter 8.

As noted above, this book focuses specifically on those issues that are of most significance in an international or global context. In Chapter 9, Christian Durach and Frank Straube draw on evidence from a number of empirical research projects to highlight some key trends and strategies in global logistics and SCM. A key lesson from this work is that successful companies will strategically integrate their logistics activities into the overall business system. In this context, global sourcing and supply is a central part of the business strategies of most large businesses. In Chapter 10, Alan Braithwaite explores some of the key issues in 21st-century global sourcing. For many firms the reality of global sourcing has required a reassessment and reappraisal of the way in which international relationships are managed. This is the subject of Patrick Daly's discussion in Chapter 11.

Twenty-first-century supply chains need to be sustainable, not only from an economic perspective but also from environmental and social points of view. Chapter 12 by Maria Huge-Brodin and myself provides an overview of the concept of sustainability for businesses and the wider supply chains of which they are part. The anthropogenic impact of logistics activities is now widely understood and the development of more environmentally sustainable logistics practices is a key concern among policy-makers and supply chain professionals. This is the focus of Chapter 13 by Alan McKinnon. It also needs to be recognized that supply chains are fundamentally human or people constructs. In Chapter 14 John Gattorna recognizes that people are the power behind contemporary supply chains. His chapter focuses specifically on the adoption of 'outside-in' mindsets when designing resilient supply chains for the volatile operating environments of the future. Gattorna's signature strategic alignment concept recognizes the critical role of leadership in supply chains. Richard Atkinson uses his many decades of leadership in a variety of logistics settings to provide practical guidance for supply chain professionals in Chapter 15. In the context of social sustainability, there is a wide range of ethical issues that present challenges for logisticians and other supply chain professionals. This is the subject of Chapter 16 by Steve New. Whilst the focus of much of this book is on logistics and SCM issues in commercial businesses, we know that effectiveness in this area is critical in a humanitarian context. Yasmine Sabri provides an overview of this subject in Chapter 17.

The connectivity and integration of global supply chains is fundamentally dependent on our ability to manage information flows efficiently and effectively. In this context, the effective adoption of existing and emerging digital technologies is a critical success factor. In Chapter 18, Andreas Taschner and Hazel Gruenewald explain the digitalization process and its role in global supply chain operations. In a logistics context specifically, the Industry 4.0 concept has and will continue to have a major impact. This is the subject of Chapter 19 by Pietro Evangelista and Witold Bahr.

The final part of the book focuses on some of the key issues that need to be considered in ensuring that supply chain strategies and plans are well executed in practice. Chapter 20 by Alan Braithwaite recognizes that 'what gets measured gets done' and provides a range of valuable insights into performance measurement and management in the supply chain. The proactive design of supply chains depends critically on the effective alignment of technology, manufacturing and the supply chain itself. In Chapter 21, Aris Matopoulos, Brian Price and Yuchun Xu provide some practical guidance on this issue in the context of three-dimensional concurrent engineering (3DCE).

The changing economic and political landscape in the 21st century has fostered discussions about the sustainability of globalization. Hence, any book on global logistics would be remiss if it did not bring this discussion into the supply chain domain. It is in this context that Chapter 22 by David Grant, David Menachof and Christopher Bovis discusses issues related to 'deglobalization', an antithesis to globalization.

The 30 contributors to this book are all acknowledged experts in their fields and each brings a wealth of experience and knowledge to their treatment of the various topics. Some are eminent academics who have undertaken leading-edge supply chain research over recent decades (eg Christopher, McKinnon and New). Others have experience as consultants to leading firms (eg Braithwaite and Daly) while some, myself included, have worked primarily at the academic/business interface and/or in a mix of academic and practitioner roles. This blend of backgrounds brings a rich mix of content to this book. Some chapters present a profile of state-of-the-art research-informed knowledge in areas under consideration, while others provide more practical guidance to those charged with the implementation of this knowledge in a range of practical settings. It is also worth noting that the contributors are based in over a dozen countries across three continents –

this is important in the context of a book that purports to be global in its orientation. Each gives an authoritative view of current thinking. Of course, this does not mean that they present the only view, and we hope that the material will encourage informed discussion.

This edition has been rewritten with new examples to support its theses. The focus is contemporary, data has been refreshed and some of the previous chapters have been replaced. The book continues to evolve, maintaining its focus on current issues that are relevant to an international readership.

The book can be read profitably by anyone with an interest in logistics and the supply chain. This includes: researchers and academics; undergraduate and postgraduate students: supply chain professionals across different industry sectors and in different geographical settings; public policy-makers grappling with myriad logistics-linked challenges; and consultants and others whose work would benefit from an appreciation of current thinking about the supply chain.

As noted by previous editors of *Global Logistics*: 'One of the greatest pleasures of being editor is to be the first to enjoy the riches of the chapters as they are written. I now leave it to new readers to explore the chapters that follow, in the anticipation that they too will benefit, both professionally and personally, from the wealth of knowledge and expertise that they contain.'

Do enjoy reading this book.

Edward Sweeney

ACKNOWLEDGEMENTS

In line with good practice in supply chain management the timely publication of this book has required effective teamwork and collaboration. In this context, there are several people to whom I would like to convey my sincere thanks.

First and foremost, I recognize that an edited volume of this kind is only as good as the team of contributing authors. This book brings together the knowledge and insights of 30 individuals who collectively bring hundreds of years of experience to the endeavour. They represent a mix of academics, consultants and practitioners, thereby ensuring that the book is an effective blend of theory and practice. This is important as we have worked to ensure that this volume can be read equally profitably by those working as supply chain professionals in business and industry, as well as by academics, researchers and students.

This book was written during the Covid-19 period and this in itself brought many unexpected challenges. I am hugely grateful to my friends and family in Ireland, the UK and elsewhere for their support as we have all battled through this difficult period together. The experience has certainly taught us that we can only survive and prosper when we work collaboratively based on a recognition of shared goals and values.

Finally, this book would never have seen the light of day without the unwavering support of Joyce Byrne. As well as providing moral support when I was struggling with various facets of this project during the lockdown period, she brought her many talents – attention to detail and inimitable communication skills in particular – to the onerous task of proofreading and related tasks. I send my love to Joyce as always, as well as my thanks for her practical support.

Edward Sweeney

Re-thinking supply chain strategy

01

Martin Christopher

Introduction

Supply chain management as a concept is not that old. The idea of integrating and managing material and information flows beyond the firm's boundaries began to emerge in the second half of the 20th century. The importance of linking upstream and downstream customers and suppliers through shared information was highlighted in the 1960s in the work of Jay Forester, a professor at MIT in the United States, who developed an approach to business simulation which he called 'Industrial Dynamics'.[1] What Forester demonstrated was that where there was limited visibility of demand or supply across a chain of independent entities, instability in the system rapidly develops. Many readers will be familiar with the 'Beer Game' or variants of it which illustrates how 'bullwhips' of oscillating demand patterns are rapidly created as a result of limited information sharing along the chain.[2] As soon as information is shared amongst the members of the chain the system stabilizes, inventory levels fall and customer service in terms of product availability improves.

Groundbreaking though the work of Forester was, it was several decades later before the principles of supply chain management began to gain traction. In a seminal white paper produced by the consulting firm, Booz Allen and Hamilton, Oliver and Webber articulated the need for a different approach to managing the flow of materials and information across a network and coined the phrase 'supply chain management'.[3]

In the years that followed there was a gradual acceptance of the view that competition was no longer between companies but rather between the supply chains of which they are a part.[4] Alongside this growing awareness of the importance of managing relationships along the supply chain a revolution was taking place in manufacturing with the widespread adoption of 'lean' thinking and a focus on minimizing inventory through the introduction of 'just-in-time' (JIT) delivery practices.[5,6]

Many of these new approaches to operations management originated in Japan and had their roots in the search for the reduction or elimination of waste (*muda*). The goal was to improve efficiencies and capacity utilization and in so doing to reduce cost. As a result the improvement of efficiency was at the heart of most supply chain management initiatives.

In searching for lower costs and greater efficiencies many companies began to outsource some of the activities they once performed themselves and also actively sought to move sourcing and manufacturing to low-cost countries. The result of these actions has been extended supply chains, often with multiple tiers and in many cases a loss of visibility and control.

It can be argued therefore that the dominant business logic of the late 20th century – the period when supply chain management principles were being formulated and practised – was primarily driven by cost and efficiency considerations. Because the global economic climate for much of this time was relatively benign, the tendency was for companies to work on the basis that demand could be forecast and that logistics systems could be optimized. Hence the widespread adoption of ideas such as centralized production and distribution, supplier rationalization and inventory minimization. For the most part these strategies worked and delivered improved profitability and return on assets. As long as supply and demand conditions remained stable and relatively predictable this approach to supply chain design and management was appropriate and fit for purpose.

However, times have very clearly changed. Instead of stability we now have volatility, instead of predictability we have high levels of uncertainty and market growth has in many areas been replaced with decline. In these changed circumstances it is imperative that organizations take a fresh look at their supply chain strategy and the architecture of their network. Clearly in a world of rapid change it is important that the supply chain is flexible and agile enough to adapt to different conditions both on the supply side and the demand side.

The search for agility

Agility, in a supply chain context, can be defined as the ability to respond rapidly to unpredictable changes in demand or supply conditions. The concept of agility was first articulated in the context of manufacturing and was later applied to supply chain management.[7,8] It contrasts with earlier thinking and practice which essentially was based upon the principle of forward planning and was essentially *forecast-driven*. However, as we have suggested earlier, the days have gone when companies could plan ahead with any degree of certainty. Now the risk of relying on forecasts and buying or making products ahead of demand is significant. More than one business has paid the price of inventory obsolescence and write-offs on the one hand or lost sales on the other because of forecast error.

Whilst some might argue that the solution is better forecasts, the reality is that better forecasts are probably not achievable in conditions of increased uncertainty. Instead the challenge is to make the transformation from a forecast-driven business to a *demand-driven* business. Demand-driven organizations strive to respond to known customer requirements and to do this in ever shorter time frames. To achieve this level of responsiveness requires an emphasis on creating agility within the business and across the supply chain.

How might a more agile supply chain capability be created?

Essentially there are two vital elements that underpin supply chain agility: *visibility* and *velocity*. Visibility relates to the ability of the business to see exactly what is happing to demand in as close to real time as possible, as well as having a clear view of upstream supply conditions. In today's volatile business environment being forewarned is to be forearmed when it comes to managing the supply chain. Visibility across the supply chain can only be achieved when there is a high level of collaborative working across company boundaries. Partners in the supply chain must be prepared to share information and to act as if they were a single enterprise.

The second element of agility, velocity, is achieved through time compression – particularly of in-bound lead times. Again this can only be achieved through closer working with key suppliers. In the past there was often a view that suppliers should be held at 'arm's length', and so many opportunities for improving responsiveness may have been missed. Joint supplier/customer teams can be used to explore the many opportunities that exist across the supply chain for the better alignment of key business processes – thus enabling faster throughput times.

Ultimately, supply chain agility can only be achieved by better management of the interfaces between buyers and suppliers – underlining the inescapable fact that today we no longer compete as individual businesses but rather as highly connected supply chains.

A prerequisite for an agile and flexible supply chain is an internal organization structure that has an external focus and that seeks to break down internal functional silos. Traditionally, most organizations have been organized with an internal orientation and with a hierarchical vertical structure. As a result the business has tended to be driven by efficiency targets which emphasize the achievement of departmental targets and thus has lacked the motivation to be truly market-driven. Furthermore, decision-making processes in this type of organization tend to be lengthy and involve multiple hand-offs providing a further barrier to agility.

An agile organization will typically be *team-based* and those teams will be cross-functioned and multidisciplinary. They will also be focused around key value-delivery processes such as procure-to-pay, order-to-delivery and time-to-market. To encourage an outward focus these teams will be measured and guided by metrics that reflect the delivery of value to defined markets including cost-to-serve measures.[9] Driving this horizontal, cross-functional approach will be an effective end-to-end integrated planning process.

The need for end-to-end planning

Whilst many managers would acknowledge the need for some form of integrated planning process across the business, few companies in practice seem to have been able to achieve a real end-to-end (E2E) planning capability. Instead, what often happens is that the business will have many separate planning activities, eg demand planning, materials requirements planning, production scheduling etc, which may not be that well connected. Enterprise planning tools have existed for many years with software packages such as those offered by SAP and Oracle being widely installed. However, the reality is that only rarely have the internal barriers to integration been broken down to enable a 'one-plan' discipline to be made possible.

Even where these enterprise planning tools are working effectively across the business they often do not connect with upstream and downstream partners in the supply chain. E2E planning should allow visibility to be established with information shared on a 'need to know' basis across the supply/demand network. A lack of shared information is a major barrier to supply chain integration and is a key reason for the build-up of inventory buffers at the various interfaces across the network. As was mentioned earlier it has long been recognized that poor visibility exacerbated by inventory buffers is a major cause of supply chain 'bullwhips'.

When supply chain management as a discipline first emerged in the latter part of the 20th century, planning horizons were typically long – often stretching out for several months or longer. These forecast-driven plans, whilst lacking flexibility, worked reasonably well in what was a relatively stable – and hence predictable – business environment. Now however, the turbulence and volatility that characterize today's world means that planning horizons have to be much shorter. The challenge in a fast-changing trading environment means that the process of matching supply and demand has to be dynamic. In other words it must be capable of responding to events as they happen. Hence the physical supply/demand network has to be capable of flexing to meet the peaks and troughs generated by these rapidly changing conditions.

How might supply chains be designed so that they are capable of providing such a level of flexibility?

Building structural flexibility into the supply chain

Flexibility has long been recognized as a positive attribute in business. Certainly in manufacturing management the idea of flexibility has been widely adopted under the umbrella term 'flexible manufacturing systems' (FMS).[10] Here the aim is to develop processes and procedures that will enable the factory to respond rapidly to change in the volume and mix of demand. Thus, if the level of demand increases or decreases the factory can quickly adjust output to meet that change. Likewise if there are changes in the demand for different product variants (eg pack size, colour, flavour, etc) the business can respond accordingly.

Flexibility in the factory can be achieved through focusing on set-up time reduction to achieve quicker change-overs, by eliminating bottlenecks to free up capacity and by multi-skilling on the shopfloor amongst other means. Whilst this type of flexibility will always be desirable, we need to take a wider view. In a world where supply chains are the source of competitive advantage, not just the factory, it is imperative that the concept of flexibility be extended throughout the entire supply/demand network.

The problem is that many companies have invested in specific supply chain solutions which are often fixed for a period of time, eg factories, distribution centres, supply arrangements, etc. As a result they may find it difficult to reconfigure the network as conditions change. Hence, the likelihood is that the network is no longer 'optimal' for current conditions. Indeed it can be argued that because today's highly interconnected global supply/ demand networks are akin to complex systems they can never actually be 'optimized'. All that supply chain decision makers can hope to do is to create solutions that are flexible enough to provide 'satisfactory' solutions in an ever-changing environment. We refer to this ability to quickly change the actual shape of a supply/demand network as *structural flexibility*.[11]

Structural flexibility can be defined as the ability of a firm to reconfigure its supply/demand network in response to changes in the business environment. Companies that lack this vital capability find it difficult or impossible to cope with a fast-changing world. Systems that are rigid and not open to change are susceptible to entropy, ie gradual decay and increasing disorder. The laws of thermodynamics inform us that entropy is the inevitable outcome when a system is closed rather than open. An open system can refresh itself by constantly drawing upon external inputs and resources from new sources.

What does this imply for the design or re-design of our supply chains?

An ideal basis for the creation of a structurally flexible supply chain is the adoption of a 'real options' approach to decision making. Whilst the idea of real options originated in financial planning, it applies also in supply chain decision making. Put simply, it is based on the view that states that the best decisions are the decisions that keep the most options open. So rather than choosing a course of action that leads to, say, the lowest cost outcome we should adopt a strategy which would lead to least regret if circumstances in the future were to change. Almost certainly keeping the options open will not be the cheapest solution but longer term it will provide an insurance against the impact of uncertainty.

The journey to gaining structural flexibility in the supply chain should begin with a review of the assets that are needed across the supply chain to achieve the firm's strategic goals. These assets are not only physical facilities such as factories or distribution centres but also knowledge, technology, data and management capabilities. The question to be asked is 'what assets are required to achieve our corporate goals?'

The second question is who should own these assets? Conventionally organizations usually preferred to own the assets themselves. They would own factories, warehouses and even retail outlets. They would hire employees and perform most activities in-house. Research and development and product innovation would be an internal activity. Similarly all the functional activities such as procurement, distribution and information systems management would be conducted by internal departments. However, such arrangements clearly limit flexibility and are often 'set in concrete' and are difficult to change quickly.

The alternative is to see the issue not so much as being about owning the asset but rather as having *access* to it.

Having access to an asset when we need it, rather than owning it when it is not required, provides real flexibility. Increasingly many consumers are becoming a part of what has been called the 'sharing economy'. Thus rather than own a car many people will rent one when they need it or use ride-sharing providers such as Uber. This principle can be applied to the need for access to the assets that the business will need to successfully compete in its chosen markets. So rather than owning a factory the business may choose to use a contract manufacturer. Or rather than owning distribution centres they may choose to use a third-party logistics provider's facilities. It could be argued that the only assets we might wish to own are those that give us some unique advantage over competitors. This would be true not just for physical assets but for intangible assets too.

Supply chain orchestration

Clearly if we outsource critical business activities and create a wider, more complex supply/demand network the question of how that network should be managed and controlled becomes crucial. There is always a danger that through outsourcing an activity we lose control of it. A classic example of the consequences of such a case is that of the Boeing 787, the so-called 'Dreamliner' aeroplane. Boeing outsourced the design and manufacture of almost every part of the aircraft – the wings, the fuselage, the landing gear, the tail fin, the engines – to globally dispersed specialist businesses. There were something like 50 of those subcontractors who were responsible for the design, manufacture and delivery of their part of the aircraft – Boeing then doing the final assembly.[12]

Perhaps not surprisingly things went badly wrong. Major time slippages and cost over-runs were building up as well as quality problems with some of the delivered modules. Whilst there were a number of reasons for these issues it seemed that the fundamental cause was the lack of control that

Boeing was able to exert across the supply chain. In those critical early stages of the project there was no 'control tower' in place to provide visibility across the extended supply chain. Boeing had failed to understand the fundamental principle that whilst a company might outsource the execution of activities they should never outsource their control.

For dispersed global supply/demand networks to operate in a reliable and coordinated way a high level of what might be termed 'orchestration' is clearly required. The focal firm – Boeing in the case just cited – needs to be firmly in the driving seat utilizing information based upon as near to real-time visibility across the supply chain as can be achieved.

The keys to successful supply chain orchestration are control and co-ordination – just like the conductor of an orchestra bringing together many different musicians playing diverse instruments to produce a polished and integrated interpretation of the score. In the same way it can be argued that the role of the supply chain manager is ultimately to utilize the information and intelligence flowing into the control tower to enable the many entities across the supply/demand network to work together seamlessly and synchronously.

The challenge is to understand what information is required to ensure an effective control tower operation and to find ways to capture that information in a timely way. Fortunately today, using modern technology such as the Internet of Things (IoT) and Artificial Intelligence (AI), it is becoming increasingly possible to dramatically improve the connectivity of the supply chain. Capturing and interpreting information from multiple sources in real time significantly enhances the ability to control the network and to create a more responsive and resilient capability.

The changing risk profile

We have observed several times in this chapter that volatility and turbulence have become the constant backdrop to supply chain operations today. This new normal, as some have termed it, contrasts with the more stable business environment that previous generations of supply chain managers were accustomed to. Today supply chain risk – in the sense of exposure to disruption – is probably as great as it ever has been.

Many forces have been at work in the opening decades of the 21st century to create these disruptive conditions. Catastrophic climate-related events seem to be on the increase and the impact of geopolitical actions can be considerable. The global financial crisis of 2008/9 and the Covid-19 pandemic of 2020 created seismic economic shocks. Whilst these forces are clearly beyond the control of the individual business there have also been a number of decisions taken by managers that perhaps have exacerbated the effect of these external forces.

Here are just a few of the decisions that businesses have taken over the last 40 or so years that might possibly have increased the vulnerability of supply chains to severe disruption:

- **Lean supply chains and just-in-time practices:** Many companies have actively sought to improve the efficiency of their supply chains by introducing JIT arrangements and have sought to 'lean' down their operations. Often this has led to reduced levels of safety stock and less spare capacity. In its extreme version there will be no buffers available – either of inventory or capacity – to absorb unexpected shocks.

- **Reduction of the supplier base:** Partly to benefit from a JIT delivery capability when moving to vendor-managed inventory (VMI) and also to gain economies of scale (and hence a lower price) companies have moved in many instances to single sourcing. In other words, rather than having several suppliers for the same item they have chosen to create what some have termed 'strategic' suppliers where those suppliers are solely responsible for the supply of an item.

- **The trend to outsourcing:** One of the biggest changes in business thinking over the last 50 years has been the view that organizations should focus on their core competencies and outsource everything else. Previously many companies were 'vertically' integrated, often owning upstream supply facilities and/or downstream distribution outlets. Today some companies are closer to a 'virtual' business model where all non-core activities have been outsourced to specialist third-party providers. As a result dependency upon external entities has increased dramatically.

- **The globalization of supply chains:** There has been a dramatic shift away from the predominantly 'local-for-local' manufacturing and marketing strategies of the past. Now as a result of offshore sourcing, manufacturing and assembly – often driven by a search for lower cost – supply chains extend from one side of the globe to the other. As a result there is an exposure to a diversity of risk sources such as political actions, exchange-rate changes and longer and more variable lead times.

- **Focused factories and centralized distribution:** In an attempt to capture economies of scale many companies have rationalized their production facilities and centralized their distribution. Thus, instead of many smaller and often local factories and warehouses serving local markets, those companies now seek to serve global markets from fewer, bigger facilities. Often too the factories are 'focused', ie producing a limited number of products or variants but in greater volume. As a result the risk to the system as a whole increases if one of those facilities becomes inoperable.

Underpinning each of the above trends is a strong economic logic. However, put them all together and a potent recipe for potential supply chain vulnerability emerges. As we previously observed many companies have taken decisions on supply chain design based on a search for lower costs and greater efficiency – with a consequential reduction in their resilience.

Achieving resilience

Resilience in a supply chain context may be defined as the ability of a system to return to its original or desired state after being disturbed by an unexpected event.[13] One way to look at supply chain resilience is to consider it as having two key components: resistance and recovery. *Resistance* refers to the robustness of the supply chain which enables it to cope with the shocks that inevitably will impact it. Think of it as a feature akin to a shock absorber in a vehicle. We might hit a rut in the road whilst driving a car but the effect on the driver and the passengers is mitigated by the shock absorber. *Recovery* relates to the ability of the supply chain to get back on its feet quickly after the occurrence of a disruptive event. For example, if a key supplier were no longer able to supply us – for whatever reason – could we rapidly access an alternative source?

Resilient systems have a number of characteristics chief amongst which are:

1 Adaptivity/flexibility

As we have observed earlier, systems that are not able to adapt in response to changed conditions are unlikely to survive. To be able to change in the face of new challenges, supply chains need to be capable of reconfiguration in the shortest possible time frames. In essence this is the idea of 'structural flexibility' previously discussed in this chapter. Unfortunately, so many supply chain arrangements are inflexible – thus for example we might have legacy manufacturing or procurement processes driven by the goal of low unit cost – the effect of which is to make it difficult to switch to alternative solutions if market or supply conditions change.

Ultimately, the key to enabling a more adaptive and flexible supply chain is the way we organize it and manage it. It was suggested earlier that too many businesses exhibit a 'silo' mentality – both internally and externally. What this means is that managers are focused on achieving narrow departmental goals and fail to see the bigger picture. Markets may be changing rapidly but the ability of the organization to respond is hampered by an unwillingness to alter behaviours within the silos to enable the system as a whole to change.

2 Inter-operability/modularity

Achieving the previous attribute of adaptivity/flexibility is greatly aided by having a supply chain that can be 'taken apart' and 'reassembled' easily. A good analogy is with a box of Lego bricks. The bricks in the box can be used to build a particular shaped structure but those same bricks can just as easily be used to create a totally different structure. Imagine now that one Lego brick represents a factory, another Lego brick represents a distribution centre, this one a supplier and so on. So for a particular market requirement we might put together a particular sequence of bricks, but for another market need we might use different bricks creating a different architecture.

In the real world the problem is that these entities (factories, distribution centres, suppliers, etc) are not like Lego bricks – once they have been put together in a certain way it is not easy to subsequently rearrange them.

What is required is for supply chains to be designed on a 'modular' basis and for a high level of 'connectivity' to be achieved between these modules. By modular we mean that the various entities in a supply chain are capable of being 'plugged in' or 'detached' from the network relatively easily to provide the flexibility that changing conditions demand. The key to achieving this level of inter-operability is *digitalization*.

The use of a digital platform makes it possible to easily link any number of entities in a network. A number of commercial organizations now provide access to cloud-based platforms to enable data from any source to be shared in real time across the supply chain.

3 Visibility/transparency

Many businesses, even in today's hi-tech world are still reliant on information systems that only provide limited visibility of what is happening across the supply/demand network. The data that is generated is often historical, ie it relates to the past, not to the present or the future. To achieve true resilience in the supply chain requires the ability to capture data in as close to real time as possible and to translate that data into meaningful information and insight. The old saying 'to be forewarned is to be forearmed' very much applies in the context of supply chain risk management.

To achieve this level of visibility and early warning will require the construction of what we earlier called a 'control tower'. The idea behind the control tower is that complex global supply chains need to be constantly monitored in a systematic and formal way to ensure that intended events and outcomes are spotted as soon as possible so remedial action can be taken. Information on inventory levels, delivery lead times, supplier performance and so on will be available through the supply chain control tower.

Increasingly artificial intelligence (AI) and machine learning will enable the better interpretation of the data flowing into the control tower and will provide a basis for faster and more effective decision making.

Conclusion

Supply chain management is now acknowledged as a critical activity in today's uncertain and turbulent world. All organizations need to recognize that they are dependent upon myriad external and independent entities for the sustained functioning of their operations. The argument advanced in this chapter is that the solutions that worked well in yesterday's world may no longer be fit for purpose in the changed conditions we are experiencing now and, probably, for some time to come.

Those companies that are prepared to invest in re-engineering their supply chains and their business processes, to create more agile and flexible capabilities, will have a greater chance of success in tomorrow's world than those who choose to stay with yesterday's ways of doing things.

References

1 Forrester, J (1964) *Industrial Dynamics*, MIT Press, Cambridge, MA
2 Senge, P (1990) *The Fifth Discipline*, Doubleday, New York
3 Oliver, K and Webber, M (1982) Supply chain management: logistics catches up with Strategy, *Outlook*, Booz Allen Hamilton
4 Christopher, M (1992) *Logistics and Supply Chain Management*, 1st edn, Pearson
5 Womack, J and Jones, D (1996) *Lean Thinking*, Simon & Schuster
6 Schonberger, R (1982) *Japanese Manufacturing Techniques*, The Free Press
7 Goldman, S and Preiss, K (1991) *21st Century Manufacturing Enterprise Strategy: An industry-led view*, Iacocca Institute at Leigh University
8 Christopher, M (2000) The agile supply chain: Competing in volatile markets, *Industrial Marketing Management*, **29**, pp 37–44
9 Braithwaite, A and Semakh, E (1998) The cost-to-serve method, *International Journal of Logistics Management*, **9** (1), pp 69–84
10 Chryssolouris, G (2005) *Manufacturing Systems – Theory and Practice*, Springer Verlag
11 Christopher, M and Holweg, M (2011) Supply Chain 2.0: Managing supply chains in the era of turbulence, *International Journal of Physical Distribution and Logistics Management*, **41** (2)
12 Tang, C and Zimmerman, J (2009) Managing new product development and supply chain risks: The Boeing 787 case, *Supply Chain Forum: An International Journal*, **10** (2)
13 Christopher, M and Peck, H (2004) Building the resilient supply chain, *International Journal of Logistics Management*, **15** (2), pp 1–13

Linking supply chain management to financial performance

02

Heimo Losbichler and
Farzad Mahmoodi

Introduction

Intense global competition, short product life cycles, disruptions in the healthcare system and shortages of critical items due to the Covid-19 pandemic, and the need to create shareholder value have resulted in significant interest in supply chain management. More recently, the force and speed of the global downturn due to the Covid-19 pandemic has further reinforced the importance of supply chain excellence as a key to unfreeze cash, reduce operating cost and meet rapidly changing customer behaviour. Against a backdrop of economic uncertainty and rising supply chain risk, it is more critical than ever to select the supply chain initiatives that result in superior financial performance.

This chapter describes the link between supply chain management and financial performance. We first define Economic Value Added (EVA) as the primary financial metric and conduct an analysis of two global companies that are generally perceived to be among the supply chain leaders. We also link supply chain management to financial performance and propose a comprehensive five-step framework to identify supply chain initiatives that create the most shareholder value by utilizing EVA. Finally, we describe the difficulties and pitfalls in creating shareholder value along the supply chain.

Financial performance and its drivers

The typical goal of a corporation and its top executives is to maximize the long-term financial performance of the company and its value to shareholders. Financial performance and shareholder value are measured by utilizing a variety of metrics. In today's global equity markets, companies are expected to generate competitive returns for the investors. For publicly traded companies, the total shareholder return (TSR) is measured by the increase in stock price plus the dividends. It is the external financial performance of a company and a very critical view of shareholder value (fuelled by stock option programmes) that can easily divert management's focus to short-term strategies which might be rewarded by the financial markets but turn out to be a drain in the long term.

Although shareholders can only increase their individual wealth from an increase in stock price and dividends, TSR is an inappropriate metric because it is not always clear what drives a company's stock price. In the long run, stock prices are driven by company profits or cash flows. Thus, we refer to shareholder value in this chapter from the perspective of the internal financial performance of a company. Even from this internal perspective, shareholder value goes by many names. Over the years two basic concepts related to either discounted cash flow or economic profit (eg EVA) have been proposed to measure shareholder value. Despite the ongoing debate about which metric is best suited for determining the value of a firm, EVA is considered to be a superior performance metric (Al Mamun and Abu Mansor, 2012; Kumar, 2016; Obaidat, 2019).

The key performance metric: EVA

Economic value added (EVA) is defined as the residual wealth calculated by subtracting the total cost of doing business (ie operating costs, taxes and cost of capital) from the revenues. EVA is a comprehensive measure that enables managers to determine whether they are earning an adequate return (Stewart, 1991). While accounting profits measure profits earned, EVA defines the difference to what should have been earned in other investments of similar risk. If EVA is positive, the operational business can cover total costs including the cost of the capital (ie equities and liabilities). Thus, if the company is earning a higher return than other investments of similar risk, the stock price should increase and shareholder value is created. However, if EVA is negative, value is being destroyed and the company faces the flight of capital and a lower stock price.

As illustrated in Figure 2.1, EVA is a measure of net operating profit after taxes, less cost of capital. EVA is also the spread between a company's Return on Capital Employed (ROCE) and the Weighted Average Cost of Capital (WACC), multiplied by the Capital Employed (CE):

$$EVA = (ROCE - WACC) \times CE$$
$$ROCE = NOPAT / CE$$
$$(NOPAT = \text{net operating profit after tax})$$

The key point is that value is only created when revenues exceed all costs, including cost of capital (ie ROCE has to exceed WACC). Management guru Peter Drucker described EVA as follows: 'There is no profit unless you earn the cost of capital. Alfred Marshall said that in 1896, Peter Drucker said that in 1954 and in 1973, and now EVA has systematized this idea, thank God' (Schlender, 1998).

Drivers of financial performance

As indicated above, the return on the capital that is required for doing business has to be higher than the interest rate paid for the capital to lenders and shareholders. Thus, the return of capital employed (ROCE) is EVA's major driver and ROCE can easily be mapped to its basic drivers: revenues, costs and capital employed (assets). Note that it is better to break down capital employed into fixed assets and working capital, allowing trade-offs between lower inventory and higher equipment efficiency. As a result, ROCE and EVA have four basic value drivers which all can be impacted by supply chain management initiatives:

- higher revenues measured by revenue growth;
- lower cost measured by profit margin;
- lower fixed assets measured by fixed asset turnover; and
- lower working capital measured by cash-to-cash (C2C) cycle time.

The C2C cycle time is a composite metric describing the average days required to turn a dollar invested in raw material into a dollar collected from

Figure 2.1 Calculating EVA

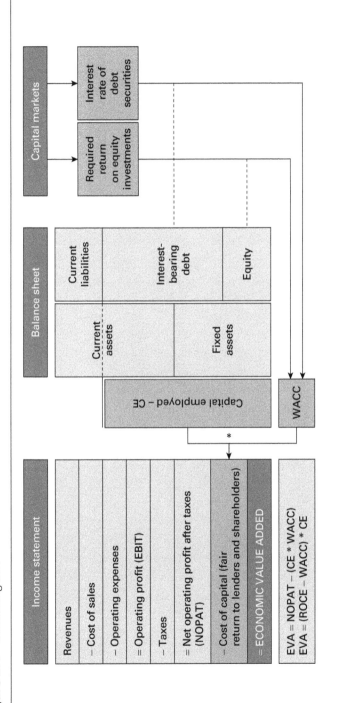

Income statement

Revenues	
– Cost of sales	
– Operating expenses	
= Operating profit (EBIT)	
– Taxes	
= Net operating profit after taxes (NOPAT)	
– Cost of capital (fair return to lenders and shareholders)	
= ECONOMIC VALUE ADDED	

EVA = NOPAT – (CE * WACC)
EVA = (ROCE – WACC) * CE

Balance sheet

Current assets	Current liabilities
Fixed assets	Interest-bearing debt
	Equity

Capital employed – CE

WACC

Capital markets

Required return on equity investments	Interest rate of debt securities

Figure 2.2   Cash-to-cash (C2C) cycle time calculation

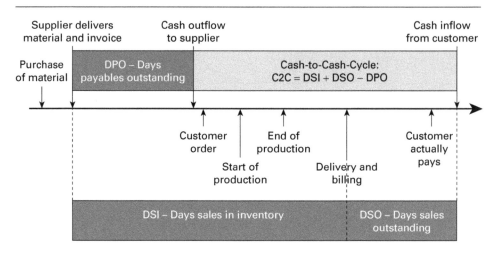

a customer. The C2C cycle time is equal to Days Sales in Inventory (DSI), plus Days Sales Outstanding (DSO), minus Days Payables Outstanding (DPO), as illustrated in Figure 2.2.

Figure 2.3 illustrates the basic link between supply chain management and shareholder value: supply chain initiatives can affect all four value drivers of a company's internal financial performance measured by EVA. This financial performance enables companies to pay dividends to shareholders and drives companies' stock price, in the long term. Thus, supply chain management can create shareholder value.

Note that EVA is a comprehensive metric that accounts for the trade-offs between income statement and balance sheet. Supply chain decisions often simultaneously affect more than one driver of financial performance. In fact, they involve trade-offs between revenues, costs and assets. For instance, lower unit costs as a result of offshoring can be offset by higher transportation costs, an increase in the lead time and higher inventory carrying costs due to increased safety stock requirements. Thus, the source with the lowest unit cost may not have the highest impact on shareholder value (Ferreira and Prokopets, 2009). Utilizing EVA can help managers make better decisions and extract greater value from supply chain initiatives.

Figure 2.3 Link between supply chain management and shareholder value

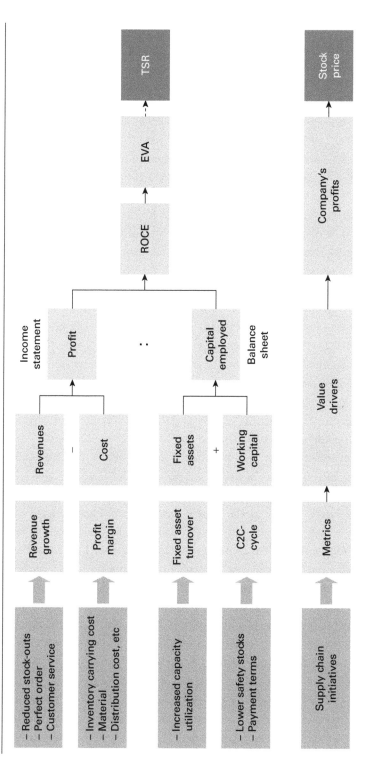

Linking supply chain management and financial performance

With the increasing importance of supply chain management, the question of how to measure its financial impact became the focus of much research in the early 2000s. In the period from 2000 to 2003 important research results were published (ie Timme and Williams-Timme, 2000; Lambert and Pohlen, 2001; Ellram and Liu, 2002; Singhal and Hendricks, 2002; D'Avanzo *et al*, 2003). Today, there is no doubt that supply chain excellence ultimately improves financial performance. The following section provides a brief overview of the research that has emerged after 2003.

Supply chain management competency has been cited as playing a critical role in creating shareholder value by directly impacting revenue growth, operating costs, working capital and customer satisfaction (Camerinelli, 2009). In addition, numerous studies have examined the supply chain management competency as a means of creating competitive advantage (eg Cook *et al*, 2011; Christopher, 2011). Research has shown that supply chain effectiveness can lead to increased firm financial performance (eg Craighead *et al*, 2009). Such outcomes have been primarily attributed to lower cost and increased supply chain efficiency.

Greer and Theuri (2012) investigated the linkages between firm supply chain leadership, as determined by Gartner's Top-25 supply chain ranking and overall financial performance. The goal of this study was to determine the overall financial health of supply chain leader firms and whether they demonstrated more financial health compared with firms not identified as supply chain leaders in the same industry sector. Their results indicated that firms recognized as supply chain leaders consistently outperformed their non-supply chain leader peers in accounting-based costs and activity and liquidity ratios. They also concluded that the decisions made by supply chain managers have an impact on the financial health of the firm.

Ellinger *et al* (2012) examined the influence of supply chain management competency on customer satisfaction and shareholder value (as measured by EVA). Utilizing data from Gartner Group's Top-25 supply chain ranking, they assessed the supply chain management competency. The results indicated that firms recognized by peers and experts for superior supply chain management competency exhibited higher levels of customer satisfaction and shareholder value than their respective industry averages. Based on the study of the Top-25 companies over the years, Gartner reported that supply chain leaders as a group carried 15 per cent less inventory, were 60 per cent faster to market, had 35 per cent shorter cash-to-cash cycle time and had 5 per cent higher profit margins (Ravindran and Warsing, 2016).

Hartmann *et al* (2012) utilized a performance measurement model to empirically validate whether purchasing and supply management contributes to the company's financial success, and whether the financial value contribution is mediated by benefits of cost, quality and innovation performance. Their survey results indicated that a comprehensive implementation of purchasing and supply management activities contributed to an improvement in purchasing and supply management outcomes, which in turn mediated company success.

According to a McKinsey study (Constantine *et al*, 2009), companies with high-performing supply chains enjoy lower distribution and logistics costs, better customer service and better inventory performance than ordinary performers. This study, based on in-depth interviews with more than 60 company operations executives across Europe and North America, assessed the performance of companies in more than 50 aspects of supply chain management, including business processes, corporate culture, network configurations, organizational structures, supporting infrastructure and the capabilities of personnel.

Leuschner *et al* (2013) conducted a meta-analysis to determine the impact of supply chain integration on firm performance. Their results indicated that there is a positive and significant correlation between supply chain integration and firm performance.

Feng *et al* (2018) investigated the mediating effects of environmental and operational performance on the relationship between Green Supply Chain Management (GSCM) and financial performance, using data from a sample of 126 automobile manufacturers in China. The results suggested that GSCM, as an integral supply chain strategy, is significantly and positively associated with both environmental and operational performance, indirectly leading to improved financial performance.

Finally, Kalyar *et al* (2020) examined how individual dimensions of GSCM practices affect firms' financial performance. Furthermore, they investigated the contingent role of institutional pressures on the direct link between GSCM practices and environmental performance and GSCM practices and financial performance, using a convenience sampling technique by collecting data from 238 textile firms in the province of Punjab, Pakistan. They demonstrated that GSCM practices have a significant direct impact on firms' financial performance, as well as through environmental performance.

Major challenges in supply chain integration

According to Camerinelli (2009), supply chain competency plays a critical role in improving profitability and creating shareholder value by directly impacting revenue growth, operating costs and working capital. However, the benefits of supply chain initiatives are notoriously difficult to quantify due to supply chain integration issues.

Supply chain integration, which involves the strategic alignment of various functions and processes within an organization, has emerged as a major field of interest (Kumar *et al*, 2017). Information integration, coordination and resource sharing, and organizational relationship linkage are identified as three major dimensions of supply chain integration (Alfalla-Luque *et al*, 2013). A recent study investigating the effect of information, operational and relational integration on the overall supply chain performance claim that information and operation integration has a positive effect on supply chain performance (Som *et al*, 2019).

Major challenges in supply chain integration include:

1 Many supply chain-related expenses cut across organizational units; the practice of grouping expenses into natural accounts such as salaries, rent, utilities and depreciation fails to identify or assign operational responsibility. In addition, budgeting processes generally lack a systems perspective by viewing requirements in any specific activity on a unit-cost basis, resulting in efficiency in one area without full appreciation of the impact on other areas.

2 Traditional accounting practice fails to assign appropriate inventory carrying costs by primarily focusing on the cost of capital (ie understate the carrying costs by not including insurance, taxes, obsolescence, damage, spoilage, shrinkage, overhead, etc).

3 The two largest individual supply chain expenses (ie transportation and inventory) are generally reported in a manner that obscures their importance and are not meaningful to other senior executives. For example, utilizing metrics such as transportation costs per mile, or warehouse picking costs per unit versus more systemic and comprehensive supply chain metrics that relate supply chain activities to the overall financial objectives of the organization.

As a result, companies focus on what they can see and measure rather than what is relatively invisible and hard to measure. For example, since lost revenue does not appear on the income statement, companies tend to focus on supply chain solutions that are slow and cheap rather than more agile and expensive.

What supply chain leaders do in practice

In this section we describe the supply chain characteristics, practices and strategies pursued by two global companies that are perceived to be among the supply chain leaders in their respective industries: Zara and Walmart.

The unique supply chain management practices of Spanish garments retailer Zara has enabled it to gain competitive advantage over other global fashion retailers (Loeb, 2013). Zara's parent company (Inditex) has been opening an average of more than a store a day for the past few years, leveraging its centralized distribution infrastructure to rapidly expand its online presence. Zara brings a large variety of high fashion apparels to the market very quickly, based on customer feedback at a relatively reasonable price by utilizing a responsive supply chain. Zara's vertically integrated, aligned and agile supply chain enables it to place the latest designs in any store across the world in two to three weeks. The company produces thousands of fashionable designs a year in a limited quantity, with new designs appearing in the stores twice a week. Such small and frequent shipments have kept inventories fresh and scarce, compelling customers to frequently visit the store in search of what's new and to buy now, because it *will* be gone tomorrow (O'Marah, 2016).

Their quick turnaround on merchandise helps generate cash that eliminates the need for significant debt. Potential bottlenecks are avoided because Zara is vertically integrated. For short lead times, 60 per cent of the manufacturing processes are outsourced in countries close to the Zara headquarters, and the postponement strategy is utilized effectively. Finally, Zara maintains a strong relationship with its contractors and suppliers, viewing them as part of the company.

Walmart, the largest retailer in the world, is perceived to be one of the best supply chain operators of all time. Many analysts attribute Walmart's leadership status in the retail industry and its phenomenal growth to its pursuit of a hybrid supply chain strategy that focuses on both efficiency and responsiveness (Gilmore, 2012; Rubin, 2020). The company has been able to offer a large variety of products at the lowest cost. Two major factors have contributed to this success: efficient and responsive distribution and transportation systems (resulting in reduced logistics costs and lead time), and its computerized inventory system, which has shortened replenishment cycles, speeded up the checking-out time and recording of transactions, as well as minimizing inventory carrying and stock-out costs.

Furthermore, Walmart has been able to reduce its sourcing costs by procuring directly from manufacturers, bypassing all intermediaries, as well as utilizing its enormous purchasing power to obtain more favourable terms from its suppliers. Finally, Walmart has utilized sophisticated technology and information systems to track sales and merchandise in its facilities and to communicate effectively both internally and with its supply chain partners across the globe. The benefits of such supply chain practices include lower costs, shortened lead times, higher inventory turnover, increased warehouse space, reduced safety stocks, better customer service and improved working capital utilization.

There are clear trade-offs between possessing a responsive and an efficient supply chain. While agile supply chains create shareholder value by primarily increasing revenue growth and shortening C2C cycle time, efficient supply chains create shareholder value by increasing a company's profit margin and fixed asset turnover. It is critical to view supply chain management as a powerful tool to pull all the financial levers.

Framework to identify initiatives that create the most shareholder value

A framework is required to help supply chain managers create value and achieve supply chain excellence. While the SCOR (supply chain operations reference) model advocates a set of supply chain performance indicators as a combination of reliability, cost, responsiveness and asset measures, it does not guide managers to identify the supply chain initiatives that create the most shareholder value. We propose a five-step framework that spans from identifying value gaps to defining the business case for selecting specific supply chain initiatives, as depicted in Figure 2.4.

Step 1: Identify value gaps

Management's attention first needs to be directed to the areas where the potential for value creation is high. Therefore, the first step is to conduct a high-level financial performance gap analysis. The four value drivers – revenue growth, profit margin, fixed asset turnover and cash-to-cash cycle time – should be benchmarked with a peer group. Value gaps can be identified

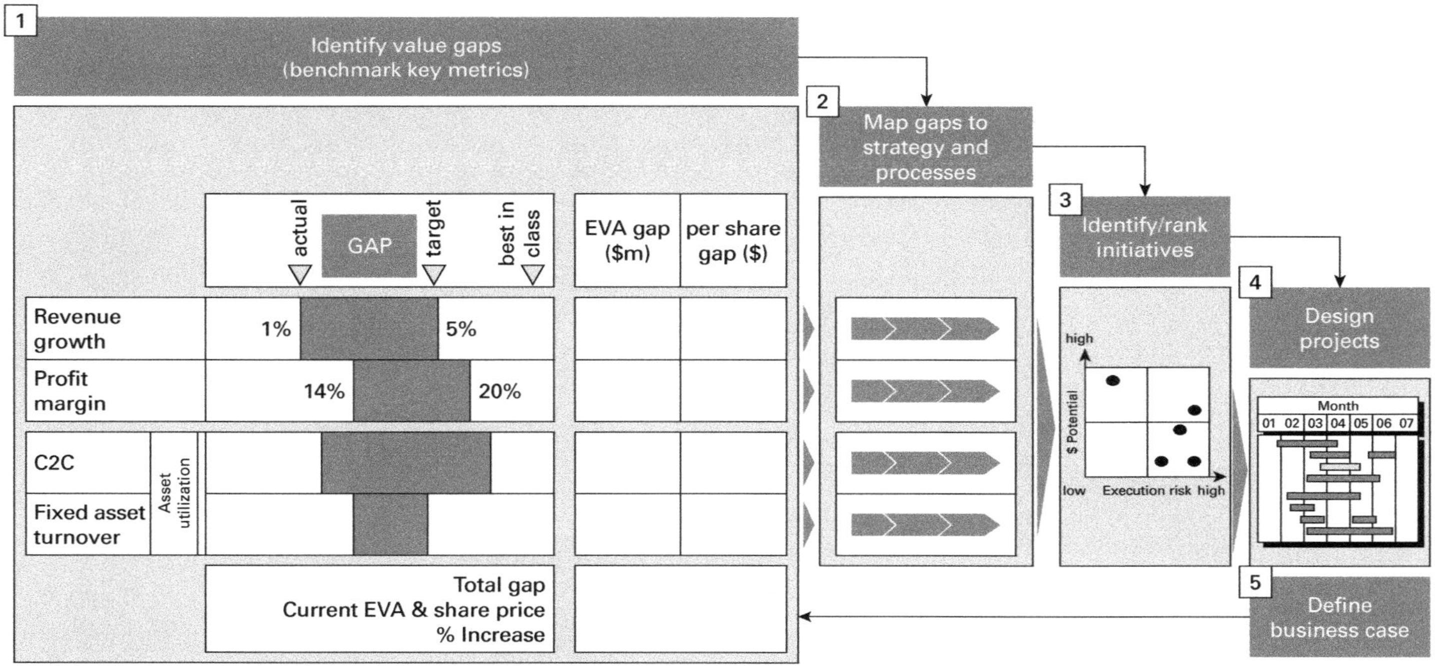

Figure 2.4 Proposed framework to create value and achieve supply chain excellence

and targets can be set. For example, if a company's revenue growth rate is 1 per cent per year while its peer group is experiencing a 5 per cent growth rate per year (and the best-in-class is growing by 8 per cent), then the gap of this value driver (compared to the peer group) is 4 per cent. Subsequently, the improvement in ROCE and EVA (ie EVA gap) can be calculated by applying 4 per cent additional growth to the company's current growth rate (see Step 1 in Figure 2.4). The gaps can be converted into ROCE, EVA or stock price gaps. The size of these gaps helps to identify those supply chain drivers that offer the greatest leverage on shareholder value and ensure that managers only consider the supply chain initiatives that can create the most value.

We have already analysed the financial leverage of the four value drivers for the two supply chain leaders discussed above ('What supply chain leaders do in practice'). The financial impacts we present rely on numerous assumptions. For example, which liability accounts are deducted from current assets to determine working capital? This task is critical, as it has a significant impact on the outcome and requires accounting expertise. A detailed presentation of the balance sheets and description of these assumptions would go beyond the scope of this chapter.

Figure 2.5 illustrates the impact of the four value drivers on ROCE for Walmart and Zara in 2020. Cost reduction by far provides the highest leverage to improve financial performance. For Walmart, a 5 per cent reduction of total operating cost (cost of sales plus operating expenses) would boost ROCE by about 16 per cent (from 13 to 29 per cent), assuming everything else remains unchanged. In contrast, a 5 per cent reduction of fixed assets would only account for a minor ROCE improvement of 0.7 per cent. Note that these figures rely on certain assumptions. For instance, we assumed an 80 per cent variable cost model for determining the impact of revenue growth. Comparing Walmart and Zara, we can see that increasing the fixed asset turnover is more attractive than revenue growth. Finally, Figure 2.5 illustrates the limited potential of working capital improvements for Walmart and Zara because they have optimized working capital over many years. Walmart's cash-to-cash cycle time equals 2.6 days, while Zara already has a negative cash-to-cash cycle time of minus 30.9 days (these figures are based on the 2020 annual reports).

Determining EVA-gaps and analysing the leverage of the value drivers at the beginning guarantees that managers only consider supply chain initiatives that can create the most value.

Figure 2.5 The impact of the four value drivers on ROCE for Walmart and Zara

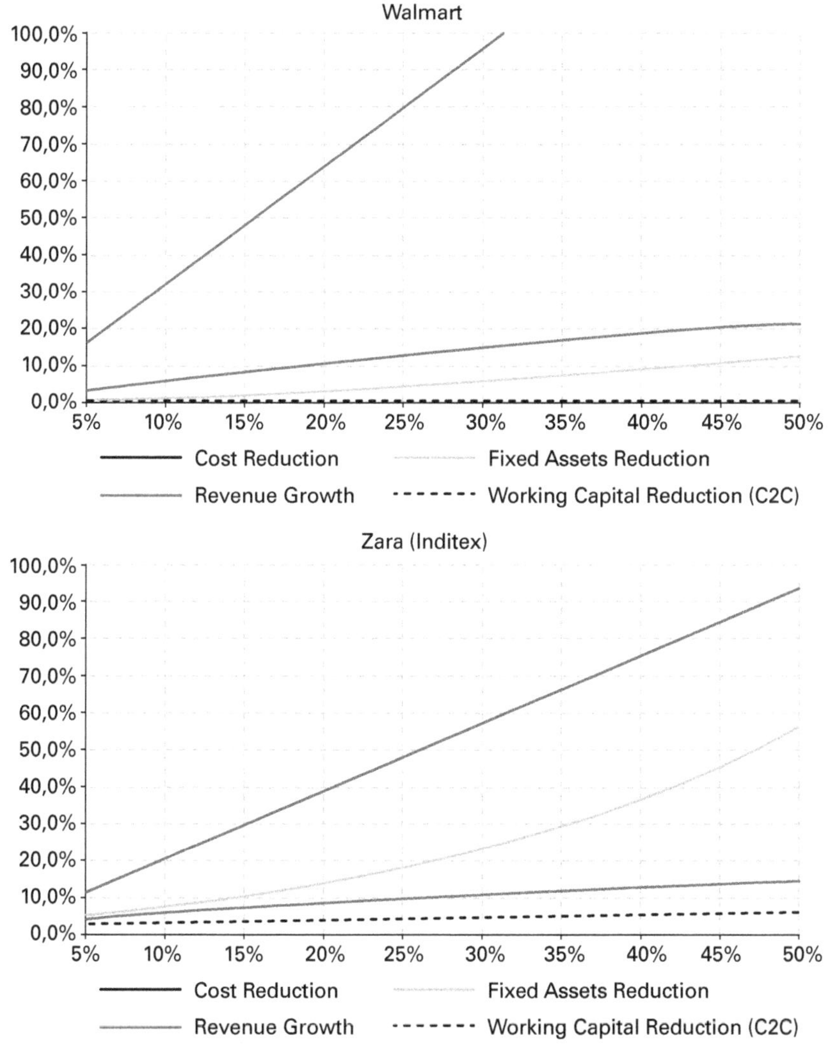

Step 2: Map gaps to supply chain processes

In the second step, the identified gaps have to be mapped to the company's strategy and its supply chain processes. For instance, if the company desires shorter cash-to-cash cycle times and its unique selling proposition is short delivery times, the company may carry significant amount of inventory re-sulting in a longer cash-to-cash cycle time. Upon comparison of the company's cash-to-cash cycle time with its peer group in Step 1, the company will realize that its cash-to-cash cycle time is longer. Subsequently, in Step 2, the company is required to justify this choice rather than blindly reducing inventory and potentially losing customers. However, if the value gap is simply due to supply chain inefficiencies, then the company should address root causes and make process improvements.

Step 3: Identify and select supply chain management tools

The goal of this step is to identify and select appropriate supply chain initiatives that can improve the identified business processes and close the value gap. An EVA impact matrix, categorizing supply chain initiatives based on their level of execution risk and their corresponding financial leverage (ie EVA improvement), such as the one depicted in Figure 2.6, can help evaluate the estimated EVA improvement and its difficulty of implementation. This would offer a systematic framework to unveil and rank supply chain initiatives according to their attractiveness in terms of financial leverage and likelihood of success. Note that at this stage it is not necessary to quantify the financial impact precisely.

To be successful, it is important to distinguish between the potential financial leverage and the difficulty of achieving the expected improvements. For instance, in Figure 2.5 the great leverage of cost reductions is illustrated. If Zara were able to reduce total cost by 20 per cent it could boost ROCE

Figure 2.6   Financial leverage versus execution risk matrix

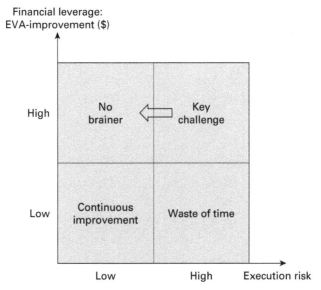

from 37.8 per cent to an amazing 75.1 per cent. But how likely is such an improvement? Most companies' supply chain initiatives are designed to reduce stockouts, lead times, purchase prices, transportation costs, warehousing costs, inventory carrying costs, fixed costs, as well as increasing service levels. Despite all these efforts, according to data from Bloomberg, the majority of large US and European companies (Dow Jones Industrials and Euro Stoxx 50 companies, excluding the financial sector) were not able to make sustainable improvements in the four value drivers from 2009 to 2019, as illustrated in Figure 2.7. Note that the profit margins and cash-to-cash cycle times have remained fairly flat, their revenue growth has been inconsistent, while their fixed asset turnover has deteriorated. Thus, they have not been able to improve their financial performance from 2009 to 2019. The median ROCE of the Euro Stoxx 50 companies decreased slightly from 7.0 to 6.5 per cent, while the median ROCE of the Dow Jones Industrial companies decreased from 17.5 to 12.8 per cent.

Step 4: Design projects

This step transforms the alternatives for optimizing the supply chain into specific projects. For each project, the scope, targets and resources should be defined. These project plans are needed to develop the business case, as discussed in Step 5.

Step 5: Define the business case

For each individual project a business case has to be developed to determine the value created. Therefore, the impact on the four financial value drivers (ie growth, profitability, fixed asset turnover, and cash-to-cash cycle time) must be determined. Because of the complex nature of supply chain initiatives (ie they typically impact several corporate functions), managers should be aware that developing the business case for each project independently can lead to double counting of benefits or ignoring synergies. Business cases should be determined for the portfolio of initiatives. Clearly, using scenarios created in interdisciplinary teams can be very helpful. Then, the potential value created for each project and required investment is evaluated to determine which projects should be accepted and rank the accepted projects. Finally, the EVA improvement as a result of the business case should be compared with the identified EVA gap.

Figure 2.7 Long-term development (2009–2019) of the value drivers of Dow Jones Industrials and Euro Stoxx 50 companies (excluding the financial sector)

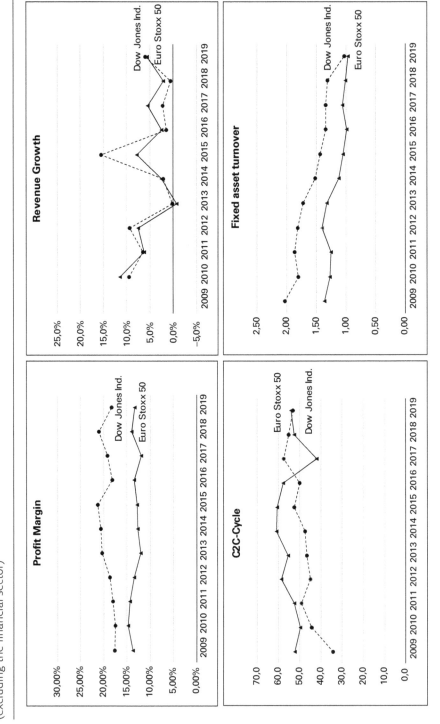

Difficulties in improving supply chain financial performance

While very few executives question the relevance of supply chain management as a tool to improve a company's financial performance, many remain sceptical about its ability to achieve major improvements across the entire chain. This may seem to be a paradox, but it is the nature of supply chain management that is diminishing the power beyond a firm's border. Many supply chain management efforts to improve the financial performance in one area of the chain will actually be offset by a decline in other downstream or upstream areas. For example, lower purchase prices will reduce the buyer's cost, but will also lower the supplier's revenues and profits. Lowering working capital by shortening the cash-to-cash cycle time through longer payment terms to suppliers will be correspondingly offset by an increase in the supplier's cash-to-cash cycle time. In such a scenario, the supply chain cash-to-cash cycle time will not change at all, as illustrated in Figure 2.8.

Good intentions can produce poor results, as improvements in one area of the supply chain may be offset by the decline in other areas of the supply chain. In fact, improvements in one area can actually lower the overall financial performance of the supply chain. Consider a company that shifts raw material inventory to its supplier in order to relieve its balance sheet.

Figure 2.8 Company's C2C cycle time versus supply chain C2C cycle time

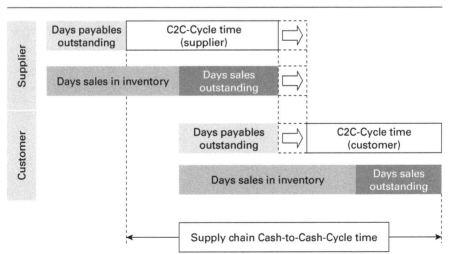

Figure 2.9   Win–win versus win–lose initiatives

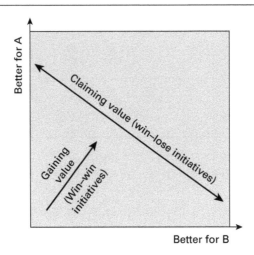

This shift would reduce its working capital and its associated inventory carrying cost. If suppliers have higher cost of capital than the company does, total supply chain carrying cost will actually increase. Someone in the supply chain will have to absorb these higher costs. Depending on the company's bargaining power, it is fairly common to shift working capital to suppliers. For example, Apple stretched out its days payables outstanding (DPO) from 76.6 days in 2013 to 124.6 days in 2018.

To unfold the power of supply chain management, companies have to be aware of the supply chain initiatives' impact across the supply chain, and differentiate between 'win–win' and 'win–lose' initiatives. While 'win–lose' initiatives usually involve 'shifting' or 'claiming' financial performance, 'win–win' initiatives involve 'gaining' financial performance for the different parties in the supply chain, as illustrated in Figure 2.9. Increased liquidity by lowering inventory based on increased synchronization and visibility, or cost savings by perfectly aligning business processes, are examples of win–win initiatives.

Improving the financial performance across the supply chain

To take full advantage of supply chain management, companies need to consider supply chain initiatives' financial impact across the entire supply chain, resulting in win–win scenarios. This would require overcoming supply chain integration issues discussed in Section 2.1. Possible strategies to overcome these challenges, and to better align the supply chain include:

1 Use of modern information technology. Big data analytics, artificial intelligence, cloud services, blockchain, robotics or the Internet of Things enable us to map, visualize, coordinate and optimize supply chain networks. Early explorations by leading corporations demonstrate that current technology provides data-driven insights and better visibility across the supply chain, increased traceability, as well as enhanced coordination among partners (Gaur and Gaiha, 2020).

2 Utilizing comprehensive supply chain metrics such as cash-to-cash cycle time or supply chain days of supply. Note that such metrics are impacted by multiple functional areas (eg logistics, marketing, sourcing, manufacturing, etc), resulting in a systems perspective.

As supply chains have become more extended in recent years, coordination and information sharing among supply chain members to improve system efficiency has become more common. Such collaborative relationships among supply chain members are gradually replacing the more self-serving and opportunistic behaviour of individual firms. Although such collaborative relationships among supply chain members are not commonplace, a number of exemplary companies have begun to practise them with their best suppliers.

References

Al Mamun, A and Abu Mansor, S (2012) EVA as superior performance measurement tool, *Modern Economy*, **3** (3), pp 310–18

Alfalla-Luque, R, Medina-Lopez, C and Prasanta K (2013) Supply chain integration framework using literature review, *Production Planning and Control*, **24** (8–9), pp 800–17

Camerinelli, E (2009) *Measuring the Value of the Supply Chain: Linking financial decisions with supply chain performance*, Gower Publishing, Burlington, VT

Christopher, M (2011) *Logistics and Supply Chain Management*, 4th edn, Financial Times Series, Prentice Hall, London

Constantine, B, Ruwadi, B and Wine J (2009) Management practices that drive supply chain success, *The McKinsey Quarterly*, February

Cook, LS, Heiser, DR and Sengupta, K (2011) The moderating effect of supply chain role on the relationship between supply chain practices and performance:

An empirical analysis, *International Journal of Physical Distribution & Logistics Management*, **41** (2), pp 104–34

Craighead, CW, Hult, GT and Ketchen, DJ (2009) The effects of innovation-cost strategy, knowledge, and action in the supply chain on firm performance, *Journal of Operations Management*, **27**, pp 405–21

D'Avanzo, R, Von Lewinski, H and Van Wassenhove, L (2003) The link between supply chain and financial performance, *Supply Chain Management Review*, **7** (11–12), pp 40–47

Ellinger, AE, Shin, H, Northington, WM and Adams, FG (2012) The influence of supply chain management competency on customer satisfaction and shareholder value, *Supply Chain Management: An International Journal*, **17** (3), pp 249–62

Ellram, LM and Baohong Liu (2002) The financial impact of supply chain management, *Supply Chain Management Review*, November/December Issue, pp 30–37

Feng, M, Yu, W, Wang, X, Wong, C, Xu, M and Xiao, Z (2018) Green supply chain management and financial performance: The mediating roles of operational and environmental performance, *Business Strategy and the Environment*, **27**, Issue 7, pp 811–24

Ferreira, J and Prokopets, L (2009) Does Offshoring Still Make Sense?, *Supply Chain Management Review*, **13**, Jan–Feb, pp 20–27

Gaur, V and Gaiha, A (2020) Building a transparent supply chain, *Harvard Business Review*, May–June Issue, pp 94–103

Gilmore, D (2012) 50 years of Walmart's supply chain, *Supply Chain Digest*, 26 July

Greer, BM and Theuri, P (2012) Linking supply chain management superiority to multifaceted firm financial performance, *Journal of Supply Chain Management*, **48** (1), pp 97–106

Hartmann, E, Kerkfeld, D and Henke, M (2012) Top and bottom line evidence of purchasing and supply management, *Journal of Purchasing and Supply Management*, **18**, pp 22–34

Kalyar, M, Shoukat, A and Shafique, I (2020) Enhancing firms' environmental performance and financial performance through green supply chain management practices and institutional pressures, *Sustainability Accounting, Management and Policy Journal*, **11**, Issue 2, pp 451–76

Kumar, J (2016) Synoptic view on economic value added (EVA): Literature review summary, *Wealth: International Journal of Money, Banking and Finance*, **5**, Issue 2, pp 34–57

Kumar, V, Chibuzo, E, Garza-Reyes, J, Kumari, A, Rocha-Lona, L and Lopez-Torres, G (2017) The impact of supply chain integration on performance: Evidence from the UK food sector, *Procedia Manufacturing*, **11**, pp 814–21

Lambert, D and Pohlen, T (2001) Supply chain metrics, *International Journal of Logistics Management*, **12** (1), pp 1–19

Leuschner, R, Rogers, DS and Charvet, FF (2013) A meta-analysis of supply chain integration and firm performance, *Journal of Supply Chain Management*, **49** (2), pp 34–57

Loeb, W (2013) Zara's secret to success: The new science of retailing, *Forbes*, 14 October

O'Marah, K (2016) Zara uses supply chain to win again, *Forbes*, 9 March

Obaidat, AN (2019) Is economic value added superior to earnings and cash flows in explaining market value added? An empirical study, *International Journal of Business, Accounting and Finance*, **13**, Issue 1, pp 57–69

Ravindran, R and Warsing, D (2016) *Supply Chain Engineering: Models and applications*, Taylor & Francis, Boca Raton, FL

Rubin, C (2020) Walmart supply chain 2020: Why it continues to dominate, Skubana.com, www.skubana.com/blog/walmart-leading-way (archived at https://perma.cc/PZ27-RVZ8)

Schlender, B (1998) Peter Drucker takes the long view. The original management guru shares his vision of the future with Fortune's Brent Schlender, *Fortune Magazine*, 28 September, money.cnn.com/magazines/fortune/fortune_archive/1998/09/28/248706/index.htm (archived at https://perma.cc/JZQ4-QGDD)

Singhal, V and Hendricks, K (2002) How supply chain glitches torpedo shareholder value, *Supply Chain Management Review*, **6** (1), pp 18–24

Som, J, Cobblah, C and Anyigba, H (2019) The effect of supply chain integration on supply chain performance, *Proceedings of the 9th International Conference on Engaged Management Scholarship*, ssrn.com/abstract=3454081 (archived at https://perma.cc/2E84-DCVG)

Stewart, BG (1991) *The Quest for Value*, HarperCollins

Timme, S and Williams-Timme, C (2000) The financial-SCM connection, *Supply Chain Management Review*, **4** (2), pp 32–43

Supply chain risk management

03

Finance: the forgotten perspective?

Carolyn Somorowsky and Lars Stemmler

Introduction

Supply chain risk management (SCRM) is an established element of supply chain management (SCM). SCM can be described as inter-organizational collaboration to achieve the objective of and, thus, the improvement of the profit of each organization and the supply chain as a whole (total payoff). Since risk management has its origin in finance, SCRM cannot be limited to operational and natural risks. Supply chains are also prone to interruptions following the occurrence of financial risks. But the integration of financial risks in SCRM shows the conceptual shortcomings of some approaches to supply chain risk management.

These conceptual shortcomings can be remedied by modelling investments along supply chains as cooperative games. The concept proposed here aims at minimizing the impact of supply chain disruptions through addressing finance risks. This can be achieved through risk reallocation amongst partners so as to maximize the payoff of the total supply chain. The objective of this chapter is to underpin this importance and to offer a conceptual approach of how to evaluate the risk of defaulting supply chain partners. At the core of the concept is cooperative game theory. A supply chain is a cooperative game aimed at maximizing the outflow to all participants rather than the separate optimization of each partner's activities.

Recent examples illustrate that manufacturers invest in their suppliers to ward off illiquidity and, as such, a supply chain interruption due to default of a partner. This kind of inter-company investment implicitly assumes a supply chain approach. In economic terms, a supply chain is nothing other than the cycle 'money – commodities – more money', which micro-economists assume to describe a firm. This means that funds (money) are turned into assets (long-term eg warehouses, and short-term, ie working capital, such as inventory), which again are transferred into more money to compensate the investor for the risk and to provide a return. In financial terms, the specific objective of a supply chain (ie satisfying the end-customer) becomes one of maximizing the payoff of such a collaboration – but not the payoff of an individual company along the supply chain.

Risk management and the supply chain: an established perception!

Operations, risk and resilience as building blocks

The identification, assessment and controlling of risks are inherent to managing commercial undertakings. Risk management was developed in the financial services industry before it spread to other sectors. In 2002, the Sarbanes–Oxley Act introduced systematic risk management in finance in the United States driven by the accounting manipulations of Enron. The statutory requirement to establish a formal risk management system also took hold in Europe. For example, the German commercial code stipulates the development of an early-warning system in order to identify risks that threaten the existence of the company at an early stage.

A number of companies have realized the potential of risk management in improving planning processes and helping to mitigate potential and actual sources of risk, in the sense of proactive risk management (Hopkin, 2013). It is not just banks that actively pursue risk management. Companies in other sectors have increasingly become aware of the potential value-added of an integrated risk management.

SCM has adopted (and adapted) the concept of risk management. One of the decisive moments proved to be the 'Ericsson' mishap:

> The effect on Ericsson, a Swedish mobile-phone company, of a fire in a New
> Mexico chipmaking plant belonging to the Dutch firm Philips, has become a
> legend. The fire, in March 2000, was started by a bolt of lightning and lasted
> less than 10 minutes but it caused havoc to the super-clean environment that

chipmaking requires. Ericsson, unable to find an alternative source of supply, went on to report a loss of over US $2 billion in its mobile-phone division that year, a loss that left it as an also-ran in an industry where it had once been a leader.

SOURCES The Economist (2006); Walker (2013)

Other examples include the Fukushima disaster where a melting nuclear power plant caused severe supply chain disruptions in Japan.

What do we associate with the term 'risk'? Risk denotes the chance of danger, loss or injury. In a commercial environment, the chance of a good bargain must also be summarized under this term. Risk is to be differentiated from the term 'uncertainty'. Whereas risk assumes that the probabilities of the possible results of an event are known, this is not the case with uncertainty. Hence, risk is measurable uncertainty.

General risk management includes activities to identify, analyse and assess, as well as to communicate and control, risks (Müller, 2003). In an ideal case, risk management is directly assigned to the top management, providing continuous support to ensure the company's ability to survive in the marketplace (Burger and Buchhart, 2002). Risk management is governed by the internal risk policy, making the enterprise in extreme cases either a risk taker or a risk avoider. The risk management process describes systematically the framework and methods from initially identifying the risks to finally controlling them (Holzbaur, 2001).

Ensuring supply chain integrity

A supply chain is basically a sequence of processes with inherent risks – however, the processes are owned and managed by different legal entities. This requires inter-organizational cooperation. Conflicting interests due to the legal and economic independence of the supply chain partners need to be aligned to a single supply chain objective. If successful, the competitive advantage of these partners increases considerably.

SCM can be described as a holistic management approach to integrating and coordinating the material, information and financial flows along a supply chain (Handfield and Nichols, 1999). Further, this includes the management of the interfaces between the partners involved in this chain, particularly from an information management and technology point of view (Schary and Skjøtt-Larsen, 2001).

There are a number of implications of SCM on risk management. As already said, risk management is an important tool to ensure the economic integrity of an organization. This holds particularly true if the boundaries of this organization are clearly set, for example by means of arm's length transactions. In a supply chain management environment these boundaries become blurred, which does not mean that they no longer exist legally, but operations-wise it becomes very difficult to identify the separating line between any two companies. Just consider employees of a logistics provider doing packaging work on the premises of the shipper. The implications on the risk management system are obvious – the scope of 'traditional risk management' needs to be extended to integrate a supply chain. At the same time, having to ensure process quality, risk management evolves into logistics.

Consequently, Christopher (2002) suggests defining supply chain risk management as 'the integration and management of risks within the supply chain and risks external to it through a coordinated approach amongst supply chain members to reduce supply chain vulnerability as a whole'. The vulnerability of the chain stems from external and internal risks to it. The objectives of SCRM are clearly laid out by Kajüter (2003). He sees risk management in the supply chain as 'a collaborative and structured approach to risk management, embedded in the planning and control processes of the supply chain, to handle risks that might adversely affect the achievement of the supply chain goals'.

The Ericsson example, as well as the Fukushima event mentioned earlier, highlight a necessary shift in perception regarding risk management. This shift has been driven primarily by logistics, but it goes beyond the established perception of risk management (see Figure 3.1):

- The logistics function provides a clear competitive advantage to a company regardless of which strategy it pursues. With either of Porter's (1999) strategies of cost leadership or of differentiation, logistics helps to fulfil the company's objectives and to deliver added-value to the customer. The Ericsson example of a disrupted supply chain is clearly the tip of the iceberg.

- SCM aims at integrating partners along the supply chain, reducing interfaces and smoothing the flow of material, information and finance. However, the higher the level of integration the higher the probability of dependency on single partners. In addition, global sourcing adds a further dimension of uncertainty in terms of long transport legs, unstable political environments and different levels of commitment to quality and reliability.

- A closely-knit international supply chain results in complex processes of coordinating and administering the partners along the chain. Different levels of accountability of staff and partners, as well as different legal environments, have to be taken into account. The focus of risk management necessarily shifts from an enterprise-only to a supply chain perspective.

Figure 3.1   Risk management in the supply chain: an established perception

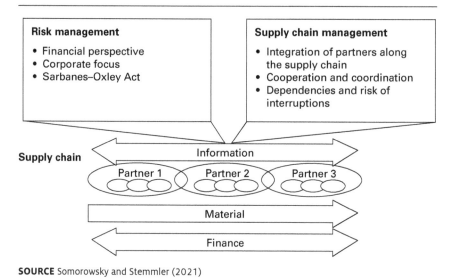

SOURCE Somorowsky and Stemmler (2021)

From operational resilience to financial stability

Two pillars of SCRM

The adoption of risk management into the supply chain context has become an established perception. However, the example of Ericsson suggests a focus on supply chain resilience and operational aspects. A more recent example widens the perceived scope of supply chain risk management. It is about Bosch, a medium-sized German automotive supplier.[1] Bosch invested in their sub-suppliers in order to avoid a supply chain disruption due to insolvency of one of the supply chain partners. This example shows that financial aspects play an important role in supply chain risk management. The latter not only needs to adopt, but also to adapt and widen, its risk perception.

The conceptual shortcomings are obvious. Financial risk management was and still is inherently corporate-centric. Nevertheless, it provides an important understanding of risks. Further, it offers tools taken up by supply chain risk management and applied towards an integrated value chain. Financial risk management addresses investor interests that are focused on individual entities. A central issue is the avoidance of a default of this entity. By contrast, supply chain management uses a collaborative and/or cooperative approach to design and operates integrated value chains. SCRM needs to exploit this overlap, ie it needs to address the interdependencies of the partners along value chains.

Consequently, there must be two complementary pillars of SCRM (see Figure 3.2). First, supply chain risk management of recent understanding has only adopted the general idea of risk management from financial management and applied it towards supply chains. The focus appeared to be on operations and business resilience. Most prominent are the examples of Ericsson and the Fukushima accident. Second, the adaption of risk management in supply chains needs to go beyond merely copying risk management as a general concept to operations and to include a methodical element.

This observation implies two questions:

- What does this adaption look like?
- To what extent does this concept make sense in a holistic supply chain perspective?

The Bosch example clearly illustrates the interdependencies of supply chain partners, including on a financial level. Bosch investments were driven by a likely default of one of its sub-suppliers. Such a probability of default is expressed as a 'rating' of a firm. A rating is an established element of corporate financial risk management. Consequently, for supply chain risk management and the objective of supply chain integrity, the integration of financial risks triggers the notion to think along similar lines, such as a supply chain 'rating'.

Supply chain interdependencies reflected in financial risks

Finance is an inherently corporate-driven function: investors fund organizations rather than supply chains; banks have to review the creditworthiness of their borrowers by law; and rating agencies assign probabilities of default to corporations rather than to supply chains. The prime objective of supply

Figure 3.2 Two pillars of supply chain risk management

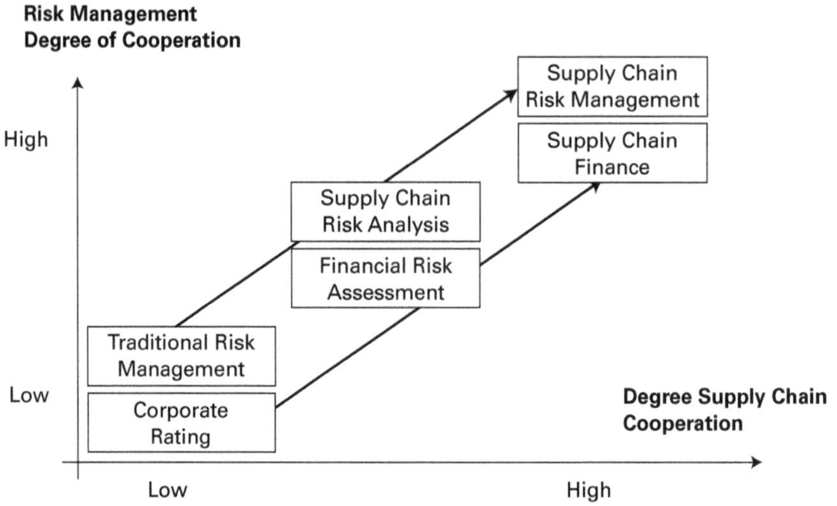

**Risk Management
Degree of Cooperation**

SOURCE Based on Kajüter (2003) with major additions

chain risk management is to identify those risks posing a major threat to the supply chain.

Finance and operations are two sides of the same coin. Financial funds are turned into investments in long- and short-term assets. These are managed to yield distributable cash flows and returns back to the initial investors. In logistics, this is reflected in the concept of the 'cash-to-cash' cycle, whereby trade liabilities and receivables, as well as inventory, are estimated in days of supply (or demand) and used to calculate the time it takes for a corporation to turn short-term investments into operational cash flows.

An investor makes assumptions about the probability of those returns: what is the probability of an initial investment being turned into a return that not only covers the investment but additionally yields a profit in order to cover the risk of failure (ie no or a smaller return than anticipated)? In financial terms this is measured in the probability of default (PD) of a corporation (ie the 'rating').[2] Financially stable companies, related to the probability of default, are less likely to file for bankruptcy during a crisis (Muscettola and Naccarato, 2013; Tate, Balse and Ellram, 2019) and thus reduce the risk of supply chain breakdown (Babich, 2010). Credit risk, which refers to the probability of default, especially relates to long-term investments. Short-term obligations also need to be taken into account. The more loans that are taken out and the higher the short-term obligations, the higher the risk of a default. Just changing a supplier is often combined with

Figure 3.3   From a corporate rating to an integrated supply chain probability of default

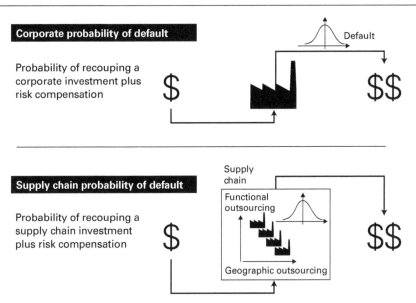

SOURCE Somorowsky and Stemmler (2021)

high costs or other problems due to specialization or due to the absence of alternative suppliers. Default risk obtained by financial institutions is a good indicator of risk (Hernandez and Wilson, 2013). Of course, successfully implemented risk management can improve the default risk of a company. However, risk management cannot mitigate unsound business cases in the first place.

What is described here for a single corporation (and hence integrated operations) applies also in a wider supply chain context (see Figure 3.3). Decreasing costs of transportation and information exchange led to geographically and functionally fragmented supply chains. Such a chain has been spread out over various organizations that in the past used to be a single, vertically integrated corporation. Nevertheless, the key concept of the duality of finance and operations remains unchanged.

Outside of a supply chain environment, commercial interactions are mostly done at arm's length. A specific characteristic of a supply chain is the collaboration amongst all partners along the chain. Along a supply chain, commercial interactions are planned and executed in a collaborative way.[3] Therefore, endogenous operational risks can be clearly assigned to specific partners, even if it is a risk-on-risk situation. However, taking all partners together, and specifically their supply chain-related investments, we can also talk about 'collaborative investments'. Consequently, the investors in a particular supply chain should not only be interested in the risk of default by the individual partners (and hence in their respective corporate probabilities of default) but also in the total probability of the supply chain yielding the required return on their investments. Thus, 'collaborative investments' distribute financial risks along the respective supply chain (Jüttner and Maklan, 2011).

These considerations clearly have an impact on the scope and functionality of a company-focused risk management system. However, the concept of risk management can actively be employed along a supply chain. It enables all partners contributing to a supply chain to limit adverse risks to the chain. For this objective to be achieved, risk management along the supply chain has to address the following issues:

- All three flows – ie material, information and finance – along a supply chain and its associated processes.
- The boundaries of the system have to be pushed beyond a single organization to cover the full length of the chain.
- The challenge of covering not only the strategic but also the operational level, turning the risk management system from a statutory reporting function into a planning function, as well as a function providing operational responsiveness.

Accordingly, associated risks can be structured into risk coming from within the supply chain (endogenous risks) as well as from external sources (exogenous risks) (see Figure 3.4).

The endogenous risks can be divided into the category of organizational risks (those of individual partners) and specific risks from integrating, co-operating and coordinating along the supply chain, as well as risks stemming from the financial stability of the relevant supply chain partners. Company-specific risks are adequately described in traditional risk management maps. Specific supply chain risks can now be identified – for example, the risks of a sharing of information on integrated platforms (integration), the risks of a high level of interdependence amongst the partners (cooperation), and the risks stemming from interwoven processes (coordination).[4] Finance risks are included in cooperation risks as a sub-category of endogenous risks. Of particular importance are bankruptcy risks of supply chain partners. Category-wise it is open for discussion whether a liquidity risk warrants a separate, exogenous category; exogenous because liquidity risks

Figure 3.4 Risk categories extent into supply chain specific risks

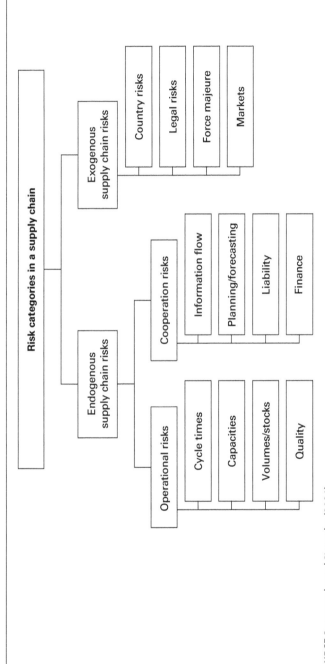

SOURCE Somorowsky and Stemmler (2021)

describe market-driven (ie external) impacts on the liquidity of the supply chain partners.

Financing investments collaboratively: reducing the risk of supply chain breakdowns

Risk management must provide tangible benefits to managers, particularly on an operational and on a financial level. Coming back to our earlier example of Bosch, simply insisting on an answer to the question of what ensures business contingency is too broad as an approach. However, financial tools such as credit rating can be used as an indicator to predict the likelihood of business contingency, especially in times of crisis.

Financially stable corporates with good credit ratings and thus, lower probabilities of default, are more likely to survive a crisis and to recover. In terms of financial benefit, it is not just about securing the operational flow. The overall goal is to make profit – from the perspective of the supply chain as well as from the perspective of the individual company. A collaborative approach needs to be applied where everyone is benefiting (see Figure 3.5). The collaborative concept for financing investments in supply chains can be subdivided into four parts: appraisal of a network investment; determination of the financial situation of the supply chain operator; determination of the financial contribution; and profit allocation.

For all supply chain actors, the profitability of an investment should be evaluated. A particular investment can affect the profitability of one or more supply chain actors. For this purpose, the profits of the individual actors would have to be assessed, where the output of one supply chain operator is the input of the successor. Only profitable investments for the supply chain should be selected. The determination of the financial situation can be observed by the credit rating, which is an observable signal to all parties. On the basis of the credit rating, the level of capital cost can be determined, which is defined by the capital cost rate in combination with volume and duration. Further, the credit rating is an indicator of the probability of default. It is assumed that a default results in a disruption of the material and financial flow, which can be observed from practical examples. A default of a supply chain actor can therefore compromise the supply of its customers as well as the payment to its suppliers. Given the financial

Figure 3.5 Collaborative supply chain investment

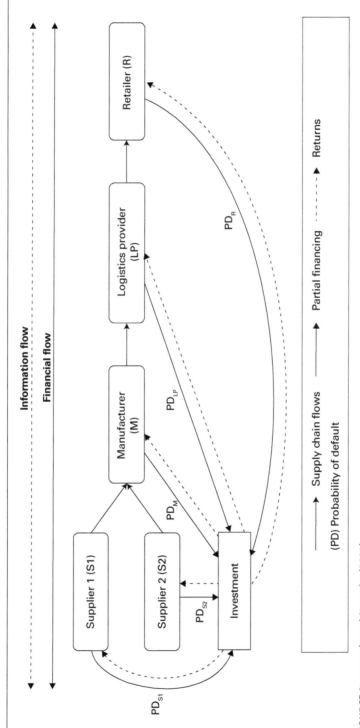

SOURCE Somorowsky and Stemmler (2021)

structure, the profitability of the investment, and the cost of investment, the optimal financial contribution can be calculated for each supply chain operator. The overall value is assumed to be optimal since it includes the profits obtained by individual supply chain operators. The payoffs for the supply chain operators depend on their marginal contributions obtained through their financial and operational capabilities. Members with higher contributions get more of the total profit compared to members with lower contributions. This presupposes transfer payments between supply chain operators (Somorowsky and Haasis, 2020).

This concept might be a mechanism for financing investments in supply chains while reducing the likelihood of supply chain breakdown. Further, this concept might be used as an incentive scheme since financial stability improvement and the optimization of operations would lead to higher contributions and, therefore, higher payoffs. Obviously, no partner would like to be worse off with the cooperation than on its own. Cooperative game theory analyses the mutual basis required for all partners in the cooperation to be satisfied. More specifically, it examines the problem of profit allocation and the determination of a stable coalition, which is clearly of interest in supply chains. As cooperation is voluntary, an incentive has to be provided to support it. The behaviour of the partners will be according to the joint payoff that can be achieved and is self-enforcing, eg by making binding agreements or commitments (Brânzei, Dimitrov and Tijs, 2008; Meca and Timmer, 2008).

Conclusions

The overall objective of supply chains is to gain competitive advantage and improve profits of the individual company as well as the profit of the whole supply chain. A high degree of collaboration is necessary to underpin the sources of competitive advantage and to ensure supply chain resilience, especially during a crisis. Due to the distributed nature of a supply chain not all operational risks can be shared. However, financial risks can be shared among the members of the supply chain, if they are subject to supply chain-wide risk management. Since supply chains are prone to interruptions following the occurrence of financial risks, they should be taken into account.

Those conceptual limitations of traditional SCRM can be remedied by modelling investments along supply chains as cooperative games. The concept proposed here aims at minimizing the impact of supply chain disruptions through addressing finance risks. Financial risk is reflected in a credit rating or the probability of default by a commercial entity. A probability of default is a good predictor of the risk of bankruptcy. However, it is inherently corporate-focused. In a supply chain context it is no longer all about company-specific investments, assessed by those default measures. Moreover, investors should also adopt a supply chain focus.

In economic terms, a supply chain is nothing other than the cycle 'money – commodities – more money', which micro-economists use to describe a firm. In financial terms, the specific objective of a supply chain of satisfying the end-customer becomes one of maximizing the payoff of such a collaboration, ie rather than the payoff of individual companies along the supply chain. Individual and collaborative goals need to be aligned and incentives need to be set on operational and financial levels, requiring some form of transfer payment system. The challenge here is that the concept proposed requires transparency, commitment and trust. However, the effective implementation of supply chain management already requires this type of co-operation, thereby helping to ensure a great leap forward.

Notes

1 www.reuters.com/article/us-bmw-production-bosch-idUSKBN18S5FJ (archived at https://perma.cc/AW33-WD77)
2 There are various PDs. A rating corresponds to the PD of debt capital. However, a similar PD can be assigned to equity. In addition to the nominal value of the financing (a loan is only repayable up to the nominal amount), an equity-PD needs to consider the market value of the financing as well. Apply WACC-mechanism of weighted capital costs also towards capital type-specific PDs = capital ratio-weighted PDequity+PDdebt.

   Otherwise, according to the trade-off theory, capital structure matters as it increases the financial risk, which usually is associated just with debt financing. A trade-off between the tax shield, achieved with debt financing, and the cost associated with bankruptcy, which increases with debt financing, is to be taken into account. The WACC-approach should be extended with the cost of bankruptcy.
3 Or 'cooperative'.
4 Supply chain finance (SCF) is a research field within the SCM located on the interface between finance and logistics. Due to past crises affecting the financial position of companies and triggering a wave of insolvencies, SCF aims to align the financial flows with the flows of information and goods to maximize profit,

share risk, avoid bankruptcy, and reach financial stability along the supply chain with the benefit of fewer supply disruptions.

References

Babich, V (2010) Independence of capacity ordering and financial subsidies to risky suppliers, *Manufacturing and Service Operations Management*, **12**, pp 583–607

Branzei, R, Dimitrov, D and Tijs, S (2008) *Models in Cooperative Game Theory*, Springer Verlag, Berlin

Burger, A and Buchhart, A (2002) Risiko-Controlling (Risk controlling), Oldenbourg Wissenschaftsverlag GmbH, München

Christopher, M (2002) *Supply Chain Vulnerability*, Executive Report, Cranfield University, Cranfield

Handfield, RB and Nichols, EL (1999) *Introduction to Supply Chain Management*, Prentice Hall, Upper Saddle River, New Jersey

Hernandez Tinoco, M and Wilson, N (2013) Financial distress and bankruptcy prediction among listed companies using accounting, market and macro-economic variables, *International Review of Financial Analysis*, **30**, pp 394–419

Holzbaur, UD (2001) *Management*, Kiehl, Ludwigshafen

Hopkin, P (2013) *Risk Management*, Kogan Page, London

Jüttner, U and Maklan, S (2011) Supply chain resilience in the global financial crisis: An empirical study, *Supply Chain Management: An International Journal*, **16**, pp 246–59

Kajüter, P (2003) Risk management in supply chains, in *Strategy and Organization in Supply Chains*, eds S Seuring, M Müller, M Goldbach and U Schneidewind, Springer Verlag, Heidelberg

Meca, A and Timmer, JB (2008) Supply chain collaboration, in *Supply Chain, Theory and Applications*, eds K Al-Mutawah and V Lee, I-Tech Education and Publishing, Vienna, Austria, pp 1–18

Müller, S (2003) *Management-Rechnungswesen: Ausgestaltung des externen und internen Rechnungswesens unter Konvergenzgesichtspunkten (Management accounting: Developing a convergent management accounting system)*, Deutscher Universitäts-Verlag, Wiesbaden

Muscettola, M and Naccarato, F (2013) Probability of default and probability of excellence, an inverse model of rating: One more tool to overcome the crisis: an empirical analysis, *Business Systems Review*, **2** (2), pp 71–93

Porter, ME (1999) *Wettbewerbsstrategie (Competitive Strategy): Methoden zur Analyse von Branchen und Konkurrenten*, 10th edn, Campus Verlag, Frankfurt am Main

Schary, PB and Skjøtt-Larsen, T (2001) *Managing the Global Supply Chain*, 2nd edn, Copenhagen Business School Press, Copenhagen

Somorowsky, C and Haasis, H-D (2020) Financing investments in a landlord port, in *Data Science in Maritime and City Logistics: Data-driven solutions for logistics and sustainability*, eds CM Ringle, W Kersten and C Jahn, epubli GmbH, Berlin, pp 409–40

The Economist (2006) When the chain breaks: Being too lean and mean is a dangerous thing, 17 June

Tate, W, Bals, L and Ellram, LM (2019) *Supply Chain Finance: Risk management, resilience and supplier management*, p 43, Kogan Page, London

Walker, R (2013) *Winning with Risk Management*, World Scientific, New Jersey

Supply chain vulnerability and resilience

04

Alan Braithwaite

Black swans: long tails and unintentional self-harm

This chapter is an update on the previous chapter for this book that was prepared in 2014. It has been written in the middle of the Covid-19 pandemic which is proving to be a bigger and more lasting shock than the financial crash in 2008/9, albeit with different impact and mitigation measures, some of which are as yet unknown. The research for the update has exposed a significant shift in outlook and language over just six years.

In 2014 the idea of black swan events was not common language in government departments. The UN had not proposed its 17 Sustainable Development Goals for 2030. The world had dusted its hands of the SARS virus (2002–4). The financial crash was history, resulting in new regulatory regimes around the world. By 2018, the overwhelming concern for global security had become global warming based on CO_2 emissions from fossil fuels and the implications of air quality on health. The geopolitical implications of some countries' leadership 'choices' was also a rumbling concern.

And then the pandemic arrived, unexpected and unannounced. Was this indeed a black swan event? When that term was first coined it was used to convey the idea of something that does not exist. Black swans do, of course, exist in Australia and were discovered in 1697 by Dutch explorers led by Willem de Vlamingh. The term subsequently changed to become a metaphor for the idea of a perceived impossibility proving to be a reality.

Black swan events were discussed by Taleb in his 2001 book *Fooled By Randomness*, which focused on financial events.[1] His 2007 book, *The Black*

Swan, extended the metaphor to events outside financial markets.[2] Taleb concluded that major discoveries, events in history and artistic accomplishments are black swans – undirected and unpredicted. For him this would include the development of the internet, personal computing, world wars and the break-up of the USSR.

It is proposed that there are three characteristics of a black swan. First, it is not part of normal or regular expectations since it is outside previous experience and the realms of possibility; second, it brings an extreme impact; and third, it is the subject of a considerable 'after the event' explanation. This 'post hoc' rationalization may provide some psychological comfort and self-exoneration but does nothing to mitigate the impact.

Another perspective on black swans or unexpected events comes from that famous quote of Donald Rumsfeld. In December 2002, he observed at a press conference:

> Reports that say that something hasn't happened are always interesting to me, because as we know, there are known knowns; there are things we know we know. We also know there are known unknowns; that is to say we know there are some things we do not know. But there are also unknown unknowns – the ones we don't know we don't know. And if one looks throughout the history of our country and other free countries, it is the latter category that tend to be the difficult ones.

Returning to the pandemic, the question is whether, or not, it was truly a black swan or indeed a Rumsfeldian 'unknown unknown'?

The answer to that question, a resounding 'no', can be found in two sources. First is the 2018 Global Risk Report from the World Economic Forum.[3] Table 4.1 shows that pandemics were clearly identified as one of the top likelihoods and impacts in 2008/9/10 and emerged again as a high potential impact event in 2015. Second is the author's personal experience of discussions with UK civil servants in the 2010–14 time frame that stressed the concern in government of the potential for a pandemic and the fact that planning was underway.

Table 4.1 has been extracted and adapted from the WEF report to show how the idea of public health and pandemic issues have moved in and out of focus since the SARS epidemic in 2003. The table was constructed by the WEF researchers through polling, so this is the compiled thinking of many practitioners. That explains why the terminology moves slightly under the same general heading. There is no point in being critical of the failure to track pandemics as an issue. Perception of the contributors was their reality

Table 4.1 Rankings of likelihood and impact of top five global risks

Likelihood

Rank\Year	2008	2009	2010	2011	2012	2013	2014	2015	2016	2017	2018
First	Asset price collapse	Asset price collapse	Asset price collapse	Storms and cyclones	Severe income disparity	Severe income disparity	Severe income disparity	Interstate conflict with regional consequences	Large-scale involuntary migration	Extreme weather events	Extreme weather events
Second	Middle East instability	Slowing Chinese economy	Slowing Chinese economy	Flooding	Fiscal crises	Fiscal crises	Extreme weather events	Extreme weather events	Extreme weather events	Large-scale involuntary migration	Natural disasters
Third	Failed and failing states	Chronic disease – PANDEMIC	Chronic disease – PANDEMIC	Corruption	Rising greenhouse gas emissions	Rising greenhouse gas emissions	High structural un-/under-employment	Failures of national governance	Failure of climate change mitigation/adaptation	Natural disasters	Cyber-attacks
Fourth	Oil and gas price spike	Global governance gaps	Fiscal crises	Bio-diversity loss	Cyber attacks	Water supply crises	Climate change	State collapse or crisis	Interstate conflict with regional consequences	Large-scale terrorist attacks	Data fraud or theft
Fifth	Chronic disease – PANDEMIC	Retrenchment from globalization	Global governance gaps	Climate change	Water supply crises	Mismanagement of population ageing	Cyber attacks	High structural un-/under-employment	Natural disasters	Data fraud or theft	Failure of climate change mitigation/adaptation

Impact

Rank\Year	2008	2009	2010	2011	2012	2013	2014	2015	2016	2017	2018
First	Asset price collapse	Asset price collapse	Asset price collapse	Fiscal crises	Major systemic financial failure	Major systemic financial failure	Fiscal crises	Water crises	Failure of climate change mitigation/adaptation	Weapons of mass destruction	Weapons of mass destruction
Second	Retrenchment from globalization	Retrenchment from globalization	Retrenchment from globalization	Climate change	Water crises	Water crises	Climate change	Chronic disease – PANDEMIC	Weapons of mass destruction	Extreme weather events	Extreme weather events
Third	Slowing Chinese economy	Oil and gas price spike	Chronic disease – PANDEMIC	Geopolitical conflict	Food shortage crisis	Fiscal crises	Water crises	Weapons of mass destruction	Water crises	Water crises	Natural disasters
Fourth	Oil and gas price spike	Chronic disease – PANDEMIC	Fiscal crises	Asset price collapse	Chronic fiscal imbalances	Weapons of mass destruction	Unemployment and under-employment	Interstate conflict with regional consequences	Large-scale involuntary migration	Natural disasters	Failure of climate change mitigation/adaptation
Fifth	Chronic disease – PANDEMIC	Fiscal crises	Fiscal crises	Extreme energy price volatility	Extreme volatility in energy and agri prices	Failure of climate change mitigation/adaptation	Cyber attacks	Failure of climate change mitigation/adaptation	Severe energy price shock	Failure of climate change mitigation/adaptation	Water crises

SOURCE Adapted from the World Economic Forum Global Risk Report at the time and would likely be different if they were asked the same questions at the time of writing.

So the conclusion from this analysis is that the Covid-19 pandemic was not a black swan; it was a 'known known' (or perhaps slightly unknown) that had slipped from focus in the crowd of potential risks. The reason in perhaps terming it a 'known unknown' is that the exact impact could not have been predicted; after all, SARS was relatively contained.

The WEF risk report goes on to say:

> Future shocks is a warning against complacency and a reminder that risks can crystallize with disorienting speed. In a world of complex and interconnected systems, feedback loops, threshold effects and cascading disruptions can lead to sudden and dramatic breakdowns. We present 10 such potential breakdowns – from democratic collapses to spiralling cyber conflicts – not as predictions, but as food for thought: what are the shocks that could fundamentally upend your world?

A chapter in the report also warns against cognitive bias in making assessments of risks. It points out how difficult it is to reach a balanced assessment of the exposure that may exist to particular hazards. Two quotes from this chapter help to set the scene for an alternative argument that is the core of this chapter:

> Risk management starts with estimating the probability and impact of a given threat. We can then decide whether a risk falls within our tolerance limits and how to react to reduce the risk or at least our exposure to it. Time and again, however, individuals and organizations stumble during this process – for example, failing to respond to obvious but neglected high impact 'grey rhino' risks while scrambling to identify black swan events that, by definition, are not predictable.

And...

> In deliberative situations... anchoring and confirmation biases can distort perceptions by assigning more weight to information and views presented early on.

In simple terms, 'group think' is prevalent when considering such a difficult and complex set of potential issues.

Given that the author's experience and the WEF chronology showing that pandemics were on the radar, the experience in the West of Covid-19 must be considered a failure of risk management. In contrast, the relative success of countries like Japan and South Korea can be attributed to their protecting the learning from SARS; mask wearing is culturally habitual, and the test and trace capability is organizationally embedded in public health programmes. While Covid-19 would have been an unwelcome surprise, they could respond quickly, even if the exact nature of the illness was not known. The investments had been made and protected.

Probability versus impact

The WEF report invites teams with responsibility for risk assessment and planning to consider both probability and impact. This chapter will argue that any attempt to estimate and then base decisions on probability is a fool's errand. By definition, such risks are remote and unquantifiable; so, the combination of cognitive bias and huge margin for error makes any effort in that direction a distraction. As the WEF tracking of pandemics shows, it hinders thoughtful planning on the possibilities.

Risk or vulnerability management leading to better resilience is ultimately about a willingness to invest in covering potential hazards. Depending on your role in the 'system', that investment may take the form of well-rehearsed contingency plans with some potentially redundant investment or re-designed operations to anticipate or eliminate potential risks. Such investment may involve higher running costs. and therein lies the choice. Invest now to mitigate a possible impact and accept the cost and potential competitive disadvantage compared to others who may not have taken that action. Alongside that is the possibility that the specifics of your mitigation measures may not be exactly effective when called on.

Goethe wrote in the 18th century: 'The dangers in life are infinite and among them is safety.' So while 'failing to plan is like planning to fail' and is a potential act of self-harm by omission, the risk remains that the plans may not be perfect.

Mapping the landscape of risk and vulnerability

Companies, organizations and governments face myriad hazards. It is useful to set out a taxonomy to capture the diversity of potential issues and their implications for resilience.

Figure 4.1 Risk source probability versus mitigation controllability

SOURCE Manuj and Mentzer (2008)

Figure 4.1 provides one taxonomy perspective from Manuj and Mentzer.[4] It uses four general areas of risk and once again it reaches for probability as a factor, alongside classifications of mitigation. It is interesting to note that pandemics were part of this assessment but considered low probability and influenceable.

The question that this figure raises is whether the impact, potential mitigation and improvement of an ICT disruption or a border delay can fairly be considered on the same page as the effects of climate change. There are important distinctions which are time- (onset and recovery), scope- and impact-related. Figure 4.2 offers an alternative view and shows the diversity of potential hazards faced.

The boxes with arrows show the key questions at each stage. Threading a risk across this diagram can help to provide a perspective on any particular risk and vulnerability. It is useful to contrast some issues from Table 4.1 and Figure 4.1. Questions of political stability have international system impact, take months and years to manifest themselves, can last a long time, may never lead to a full recovery and cost billions of dollars. Shipping delays across borders can take a week or two to become a reality, last for a month, recovery (once resolved or an alternative route put in place) will be fast and the impact is a budget adjustment. They are clearly not on the same page in terms of who deals with them and their criticality.

And risk can span organizational boundaries and 'ownership'. For example, a business or industry may experience a risk such as Brexit but be forced to accept outcomes and timing based on government actions.

Figure 4.2 Mapping the taxonomy of any given risk event

Risk Area	System impact	Onset time	Duration	Recovery time	Impact
➤ Geo-political	❑ International	❖ Months – years	○ 5–10 years	⌘ Never	⊙ Existential
➤ Environmental	❑ Governmental	❖ 1 month to 6 months	○ Years	⌘ Years	⊙ $ Billions
➤ Economic	❑ Industry	❖ 1 week – 4 weeks	○ Month – 1/2 year	⌘ Months	⊙ $ Millions
➤ Technological	❑ Supply chain	❖ 1 day – 1 weeks	○ Weeks	⌘ Week	⊙ Profit warning
➤ Operational	❑ Company	❖ Hours – 1 day	○ Days	⌘ Day	⊙ Budget adjustment
	Who is in control of any response?	Could it have been seen coming sooner and an improved response made?	Could it have been cleared up faster?	After the immediate shock – how long did it really take to recover?	What was the scale of the impact on the organization

SOURCE Braithwaite (2020)

An article by John Collingridge for the *Sunday Times* (15 November 2020) drew attention to the risks of solar flares wiping out the electrical transmission and digital grids; this was not on the WEF radar at all. He also observed that inspection of the pre-pandemic annual reports of many of the UK's biggest businesses for their risk assessments showed remarkable contrasts:

> For Whitbread, the owner of the Premier Inn hotels chain, a pandemic or terrorism was relatively high on its list of risks, with regular crisis management exercises held. But for Heathrow, the word pandemic did not make an appearance in the risk section of its 2019 annual report, which was instead concerned about climate change and the threats to its third runway.

Using the model in Figure 4.2, the ownership of the pandemic risk is with government, onset was one to six months, duration is likely to have been a year, recovery time for Premier Inns will be months and for Heathrow will be years. The impact for both businesses will be millions of dollars. The reality for both businesses is that planning any contingency and mitigation measures would have been likely to have limited effect; at the company level this was out of scope. However, the same question for personal protective equipment (PPE) suppliers, toilet-roll manufacturers and e-retailers would have been a story of planning for growth!

It should be clear that effective planning for risk and designing for resilience is the most difficult endeavour. The balance of the chapter provides some insights into tools and techniques.

The evolution of supply chain risk management thinking

More than 90 per cent of organizations surveyed by the World Economic Forum in 2012 indicated that supply chain risk management had become a greater priority in the prior five years.[5] The 2018 report referenced earlier confirms that this focus is unchanged and likely to have intensified.

The academic literature is equally affirming of the trend and focus. Analysis of the EBSCO and Proquest academic publication databases shows a huge surge in publications.

The Master's thesis project by Dionne Reid at Manchester Metropolitan University in 2012/13 commissioned by the author exposed in the systematic literature review that much of the focus was on risk management as opposed to disruption resilience.[6] Some gaps in thinking and practice that were found to need further work were identified as:

- *Criteria for monitoring risks*: Since there are multiple risk sources and multiple ways of categorizing them, there is a requirement to understand how organizations are actually monitoring their risk sources. Work by Christopher *et al* in a 2011 study revealed that although using a number of informal approaches to cope with risk sources, most companies did not have a structured supply chain (SC) risk management and mitigation system.[7] This suggests there is opportunity for firms to improve their approach to managing SC disruptions.

- *Ensuring adequate supply chain visibility*: Reid's literature review demonstrates that the complex nature of modern SCs impedes visibility and that visibility is a key barrier to the implementation of tools for resilience. However, there is not sufficient information in the literature as to whether organizations truly understand how their SC networks extend or what they are doing to enhance their visibility in the face of multiple sources of potential disruption.

- *Staff management and training*: Another barrier to tool implementation was identified as staff training. In the literature, the focus is on the tools and strategies that organizations could employ; however, there was little information on the training required for staff to manage events and use the tools effectively.

- *Appropriate levels of bureaucracy and organizational culture*: Organizational culture in relation to SC disruption resilience featured the least in literature. Although Christopher and Peck's (2004) resilience framework encompasses the dimension of culture, it does not highlight the core values to drive appropriate behaviour.[8] There was also no evidence on the appropriate level of bureaucracy required to deal with disruptions swiftly; this is even though professionals acknowledge the potential economic loss if they do nothing about disruption. Supply chains are interactive systems, whose operational efficiency allows risks to propagate fast and efficiently (Zurich, 2011).[9]

There are companies that have now addressed these gaps. The availability of digital solutions to improve visibility, monitor events and model options has transformed the potential to identify and respond as hazards occur; we will return to the cases and the tools that are being deployed.

But tools are simply an aid to decision making which is the essence of managing vulnerability and resilience. The classic case of Nokia, Ericsson and the Philips Microchip factory fire is worth mentioning at this point. It is one of the most often quoted stories of supply chain risk but the telling of the story often ignores the key point of Nokia's competitive response. Nokia's VP of Purchasing and Supply was alerted to the fire at the time it happened. He activated the response instantly, knowing that a fire in a clean manufacturing site will disrupt output for months. He instructed his team to travel to the site and also to other suppliers on the same night and to contract for their capacity within hours or days. In contrast, Ericsson delayed their response believing that the fire was minor and then, when they did respond, found that Nokia had locked up all the spare capacity in the market. The damage for Ericsson was existential; the company withdrew from the market segment – a major financial blow.

The financial impact of supply chain disruptions

The reality of supply chain disruption is that the downside is invariably faster and more dramatic than the competitive upside from growth in sales, margin and market share from optimizing supply chains. There are two measures that serve to illustrate this point.

At the national level, stock markets generally fall, but not consistently, in response to natural and economic disasters. Figure 4.3 shows a WEF and Accenture chart of how markets responded to some events.

Inspection of the markets' response to the pandemic shows a greater decline and longer recovery; but at the time of writing the big indices have shaken off the shock and are close to their former levels. There will of course have been big winners and losers inside these numbers, as shown in Figure 4.4.

Both charts point to a surprising resilience at the 'system level' – probably assisted by government and international measures. They have a strong vested interest in supporting the system to avoid total collapse.

But at the company level, there are more prosaic risk events that are not normally linked to natural and economic disasters. Individual share prices are much more severely affected by disruptions from risk events and the observation is that recovery of value is more prolonged. Singhal and Hendricks evaluated the impact of what they quaintly called supply chain

Figure 4.3   Stock market responses to global events

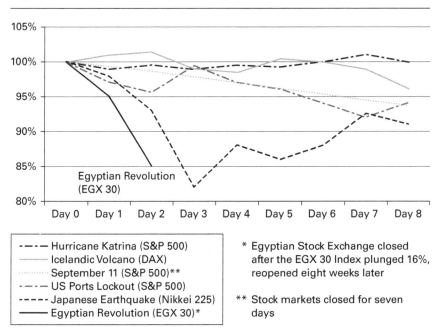

Egyptian Revolution
(EGX 30)

Day 0   Day 1   Day 2   Day 3   Day 4   Day 5   Day 6   Day 7   Day 8

-- - -- Hurricane Katrina (S&P 500)
———— Icelandic Volcano (DAX)
.... September 11 (S&P 500)**
-- - -- US Ports Lockout (S&P 500)
-- -- -- Japanese Earthquake (Nikkei 225)
———— Egyptian Revolution (EGX 30)*

* Egyptian Stock Exchange closed
after the EGX 30 Index plunged 16%,
reopened eight weeks later

** Stock markets closed for seven
days

SOURCE WEF (2012)

Figure 4.4   Stock market responses to the pandemic

FTSE 100 Index

S&P 500 Index

Jan   Feb   Mar   Apr   May   Jun   Jul   Aug   Sept   Oct   Nov   Dec

SOURCE Index data extracted from Yahoo Finance

Figure 4.5   Plot of average share price in relation to public announcement of a supply chain 'glitch'

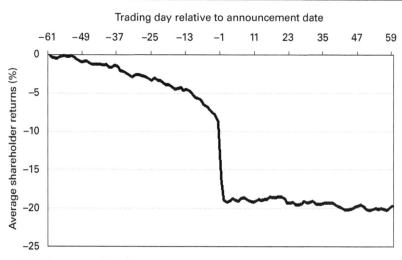

SOURCE Singhal and Hendricks (2000)

'glitches' on shareholder value; to do this they analysed a sample of 861 profit warning announcements associated with supply chain difficulties.[10] They found that announcing these glitches was associated with an 8.62 per cent market adjusted reduction in shareholder value and that, if a period of 60 days before and after the announcement is included, the total effect is about minus 20 per cent. This is illustrated in Figure 4.5 which shows an average for the data sample.

Glitches are classified as including: parts shortages; changes by customers; ramp and roll-out problems; production problems; development problems; quality problems.

Clearly, from this data we can conclude that so-called 'foul ups' are not isolated problems, and they destroy shareholder value. They affect customers and suppliers alike, often with equally disastrous results. Observations of how companies actually mitigate risk in supply chain design, planning and execution point to the fact that many do not adequately govern the relationship between their corporate strategy and supply chain management. In these circumstances disruption is inevitable as risk events crystallize for which supply chain design was inadequate and/or mitigation responses were insufficient.

However, the landscape of governance has evolved and continues to change as a result of the enacting of the Sarbanes–Oxley Act (SOX) in 2002. This was a direct response to the financial and accounting scandals of a number of major corporates including those affecting Enron, Tyco International, Adelphia, Peregrine Systems and WorldCom. These scandals cost investors billions of dollars when the share prices of affected companies collapsed, shaking public confidence in the US securities markets.

The law has set new or enhanced standards for all US public company boards, management teams and public accounting firms. Top management must now individually certify the accuracy of financial information. This covers a whole swathe of requirements including auditor independence, corporate governance, internal control assessment and enhanced financial disclosure. In supply chain terms the effect of the SOX Act is seen in rather detailed assessments of corporate risk in the US Stock Exchange Commission (SEC) filings. The levels of disclosure and analysis in the SEC 10K documents are increasing; risks are enumerated and described and their consequences and mitigations are set out.

Such legislation is now also found in many other countries such as Japan, Germany, France, Italy, Australia, Israel, India, South Africa and Turkey. In the UK it is not a legal requirement but is becoming standard practice because of the international markets in listed companies. The same does not apply to smaller companies and the suppliers' suppliers and customers' customers of these major corporates.

Frameworks for designing for resilience

Strategic decisions are made for most businesses (certainly manufacturing businesses) on a long-term horizon, at least two years out. These decisions are about where to produce or source, how the business will interact with its sources and markets and the associated economics and social responsibility. Once a decision is made to source in a particular way, some of the outcomes are 'hard-wired' and adverse events will have predictable outcomes. As an example, if we single source product from a supplier on an earthquake fault, we have created a disruption waiting to happen. The President of Honda is on record following the tsunami and Fukushima disaster that his company would dual source in future.

Tactical decisions can be varied in shorter time frames but still not instantly. These decisions include the form of contracts, the incentives that might be paid for specific performance and the balance of supply and levels of inventory that will be made or held. Here the information that might be used to inform a tactical decision would be the capacity utilization of a facility or supplier; the greater the utilization, the more will be the risk of disruption if anything goes wrong. Equally, if there are expected peaks or troughs in demand or specific events, the business may make tactical decisions to ensure that risks are minimized and resilience is increased. The extended horizons of the S&OP (sales and operational planning) processes can deal with expected supplier shutdowns, market peaks and seasonal events. An example would be the application of intelligence that a supplier was financially stressed and might not survive; in such a situation the creation of additional tooling or putting in place shadow contracts would be key decisions. Land Rover failed to make such a decision in 2002 when its body supplier called in the receiver. If they had been aware of the situation and/or acted on it, the company might have been able to mitigate lost production and the investment in buying the assets from the receiver.

At the *operational* level, the decisions are quite short term, working within the strategic and tactical frameworks that have been established. Here it is about responding to events that may occur inside or outside the business. Examples might include plant breakdowns, transport disruptions, quality failures, or second- and third-tier supply chain failures. An example would be the Icelandic volcanic disruption which hampered airfreight in northern Europe and required that routes through southern Europe were quickly opened. Another would be supplier non-conformance leading to airfreight to keep the supply chain running without failure.

Management teams need to be thinking on all three levels simultaneously. But if the strategy and tactics are not correctly framed, the team will inevitably be forced into operational recovery from time to time.

The first step on this journey is to understand and map the chain across the many tiers of supply and demand. Each tier will have its inherent risks of failure based on capacity, utilization, reliability, environmental risk, social issues and conflicts with other markets; the tiers will interact with each other and it is important to understand this in as much detail as possible.

Figure 4.6 illustrates how risks can occur at every point in the extended chain: suppliers' suppliers to customers' customers. These risk profiles are generally additive rather than self-compensating which means that the experience at the final customer is invariably badly skewed to lateness and poor service.

Work by the author with Cranfield School of Management created a supply chain risk and vulnerability handbook in 2003.[11] This work has been revisited in the preparation of the original chapter and this revision. It has not been found to be wanting in any core respect. It provides a structured

Figure 4.6 The scope of supply chain risk

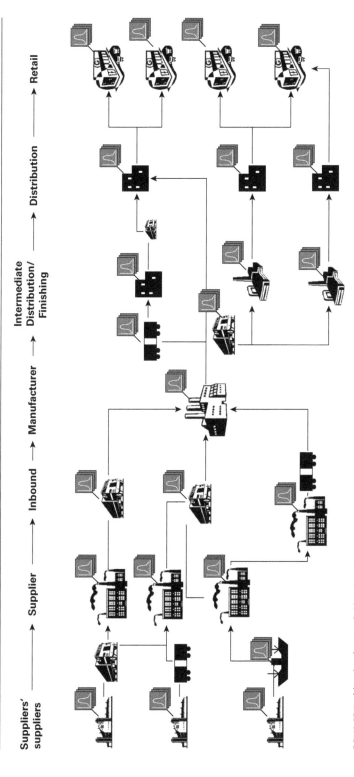

Suppliers' suppliers ⟶ Supplier ⟶ Inbound ⟶ Manufacturer ⟶ Intermediate Distribution/Finishing ⟶ Distribution ⟶ Retail

SOURCE Braithwaite, for Cranfield University

Figure 4.7   The honeycomb of supply chain resilience

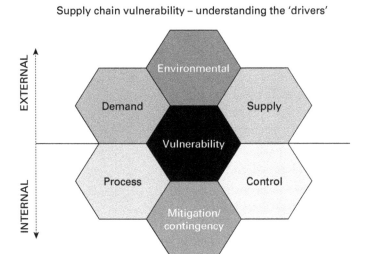

Supply chain vulnerability – understanding the 'drivers'

EXTERNAL

INTERNAL

Environmental

Demand

Supply

Vulnerability

Process

Control

Mitigation/
contingency

SOURCE Cranfield (2003)

framework to think through and plan for strategic and tactical supply chain risk. Figure 4.7 shows the conceptual model – which we call the honeycomb of resilience.

The underlying principle is that there are external determinants of risk that relate to the business environment of demand and supply. Also, there are internal determinants that relate to how the organization is aligned to its external environment. Design for risk mitigation and resilience is the third internal determinant and is how companies can address the risks in the other five areas.

The following points step through the segments and how they fit together.

The external drivers are the risk areas that are most commonly considered by managers. For the reason that they are external, these risks may be perceived as 'unmanageable'. The risks of unpredictable demand, unreliable supply and the effects of external shocks in the business, social and climatic environment are all the areas that can easily be used as scapegoats for unexpected outcomes. These are the risks picked up by the WEF reports. Based on the 'threading of risks' proposed in Figure 4.2, many can be planned with contingencies.

The internal drivers of processes and control are more tightly under the direction of the firm itself and are therefore less obvious as being sources of vulnerability. The segment that deals with mitigation/contingency is where the business can take positive action to embed resilience: effectively altering the dynamics of the honeycomb.

Working through the structured process set out in the risk and resilience handbook to step through the vertical and diagonal connections between the external and internal dimension areas can bring a conceptual break-through in understanding how risk is uniquely embedded in the individual firm's supply chains. It is designed to take people away from their instinctive focus on probability. Supply chain risks are improbable and random, other-wise nothing would ever work. We should be most interested in the impact, the duration, the recovery measures and the cost implications of building in resilience. With that information compiled in a 'war room', strategic and tactical decisions can be made. The discovery from using this process is that many impactful and damaging issues are relatively easy and cheap to address; Singhal and Hendricks' catalogue of disasters is consistent with this observation.

But the analysis will surface for many firms the inherent vulnerability of 21st-century supply chains based on their scale, distance and complexity. The dilemma is that these designs have been strategies from which great benefits in price competitiveness have flowed, notwithstanding their inherent risks. For many, taking the safe course of action of avoiding such extended, complex global supply chains would have been equally risky, even to the point of being terminal.

There is increasing commentary on strategies that involve some combina-tion of re-shoring, near-shoring and dual sourcing. In this context it is important to note that not just the risk conditions have changed but also the economic fundamentals. Since many extended supply chains were hard-wired in companies' operating models, the costs in China have risen, tooling and economic lot sizes have declined across the world and digital tools and techniques have enabled multiple sourcing options. It is possible that for many the perceived insurmountable economic gap has closed significantly.

The easiest way to learn and experience how the risk elements are con-nected is to work through the process in the handbook, for which there is not enough space in this chapter. The following points provide an entry level platform for understanding the approach.

Demand risk

- Many companies in manufacturing and distribution are dependent on a small number of customers for a large part of their revenue; the loss of these customers, highly volatile ordering patterns or delays in new product call-offs represent serious risks for these firms.

- The first step is to map your customers' and their customers' demand, understand your dependency on the big ones and think through what might disrupt their behaviours and practices.
- These risks can be at least partially offset and managed through the existence of good controls for account management, for collaborative forecasting with customers and for commercial terms that recognize the cost of volatility; these controls can extend to the way in which suppliers are managed to connect them to the potential for demand volatility.
- Such risks can also be managed by process measures to reduce lead times and increase supply responsiveness.

Supply risk

- Many companies are equally dependent on just a few suppliers which may provide unique products via specialist tooling or technology, or which may be simply very large in their trading relationships. Typically, firms buy in goods which represent a minimum of 40 per cent and sometimes as high as 80 per cent of revenues, so disruption to supply threatens business continuity.
- Once again map your suppliers and their suppliers, understand your dependency on the big or critical ones and think through what might disrupt their behaviours and practices.
- These risks can be at least partially offset by control processes that monitor supplier capacity, viability and reliability, that share forecasts and plans with suppliers and get visibility of their schedules and the chain that exists behind them.
- Mitigation of supply-side risk could include strategic inventory holding, dual sourcing or arrangements to move tooling; contingency would include the identification of alternative sources of supply and planning for the introduction in the event of failures in the existing base.

Environmental risk

- Environmental risk is the mélange of external risks to the firm, its customers and suppliers that is most difficult to predict of all vulnerabilities as it spans weather, business environment, acts of war, pandemics and so on.

- Here the obligation on the firm is to identify the impacts that could arise based on known hazards: from the very short term of exposure of power failure through to severe business disruption due to natural disasters.

- Environmental risks are likely to impact on both supply and demand and an attempt to identify such events should extend to these communities. Mitigation is less likely in this area than contingency.

- For example, the big retailers have contingency plans to fly in fresh food from around Europe in the event of a port or tunnel blockade, while others have emergency fuel capacity to maintain depot operations in the event of temporary fuel shortages.

- It would be fair to say that few companies could have been prepared for the pandemic in any meaningful way and it would have been incredibly difficult to work through that scenario at the corporate level. Reverting to Figure 4.3, pandemic planning was a task for government and international organizations.

Process risk

- All firms have core processes at their heart. For manufacturers, many of these will be technical; for retailers and distributors they will be in the areas of buying and distribution. Typically, manufacturers are more exposed to process risk than retailers and distributors with issues of yield, plant breakdown, quality, and product safety and health questions.

- For many firms, especially in the areas of food, pharmaceuticals and engineering, these risks are mitigated through standards such as GMP, ISO 9000+.

- They may also be mitigated through safety stock policies and controlled through supply chain visibility and lead time reduction programmes.

Control risk

- The controls that a company applies to its supply chain will impact on its ability to deal with demand, suppliers and to manage the processes by which the firm fulfils demand. Failures in inventory management, demand forecasting, manufacturing scheduling would all be examples of areas where control breakdowns could lead to risks being experienced.

- The existence of programmes of supply chain performance measurement and KPIs, with investments in computer systems to assist in the management of demand and scheduling are mitigating measures.

- Training and people development programmes are equally valuable control mitigation measures as is the existence of standard operating procedures.

Mitigation/contingency

- The lack of mitigation and contingency measures for the major areas of risk that the firm faces is a risk in its own right. The acid test of a firm's preparedness is that it has a risk management programme for its supply chain that has tried to formally identify the risks that could occur and consider its options in relation to them.

The concept behind the workbook is that the process elicits many mitigation and contingency measures that are relatively inexpensive and might be regarded as good management. With the full spectrum set out through the war room process, a management team can decide on their prioritization in terms of change. Only at that stage should probability assessments come into the equation as part of prioritization of actions.

Some examples of disasters and the implications for resilience

It is useful to look at some disasters that have occurred in commercial supply chains in order to show how the specifics of the situation can be understood in the context of the framework. Four recent examples have been selected.

The first is the BP Macondo Well (Deepwater Horizon) disaster. Chapter 4 of the US Government's National Commission on the BP Deepwater Horizon Oil Spill and Offshore Drilling points to serious process and control flaws that lead to the disaster.[12] In summary, some combination of poor processes in the cementing and the installation or supply of the 'blow out preventer' were compounded by overriding or ignoring of management controls and warnings on the rig. The author would contend that the core contracting methods and governance between multiple parties on the rig created an accident waiting to happen; the report appears to support this conclusion. The outcome for BP has been huge costs, measured in billions of dollars, and constraints on its ability to explore, invest and develop its business.

The second example is the Rana Plaza factory collapse in Bangladesh which killed more than 1,000 people, injured about 2,500 and where 332 people are still unaccounted for, assumed dead; it shocked and appalled people around the world. This may sound harsh but this was a failure of suppliers occupying the building. For them it can be classified as a process and control risk, since warnings were ignored as to the state of the building they occupied. For their customers it was both a supply risk and a control risk, since due diligence on the state of the building was clearly lacking. It was expected that there would be severe reputational damage to the brands that were buying from the companies in the factory. However, six months later, this was not evidenced by their trading; they were not dependent on the supplies from the factory and the buying public has not deserted the brands. Nonetheless, it is highly likely that clothing retailers and wholesalers will have stepped up their due diligence controls as a result.

Third is the Japanese earthquake and tsunami which devastated a large area of its industrial heartland. The FT's analysis of how this impacted company profits found that it 'hit a slew of companies both within and outside the country but also created opportunities for many others'. It went on to say 'Asian results for the quarter to the end of June, compared with the same period a year earlier, paint the most complete picture so far of how companies were affected by the disaster, underlining the sharp difference between Japan, where the impact on final production and the supply chain was severe, and other Asian countries, where it was much less marked'.[13] Companies severely affected were Toyota, Nissan, Honda, Nintendo, Toshiba, Panasonic, Sharp and Fujitsu. International businesses impacted included Caterpillar and Coca-Cola. For those companies buying from the affected area, a single source policy had built in supply and control risks. Companies located with production in the area had control and process risk. Both groups had located sole supply in a major earthquake area without suitable contingency; of course, they may have decided that the cost of this safety was too great, taking us back to the economic tension which is a core theme in this chapter.

Finally, there is the case of the Icelandic volcanic ash that closed the skies of Europe for many days and impacted on the movement of people and goods by air. This was an event that was much less easy to anticipate in terms of impact. From the supply chain perspective, companies were in a dilemma in terms of response as to whether to wait for it to 'blow over' or put in place alternative routes from the south of Europe. By the time that course had been adopted, the cloud had passed. At the economic level, the major pain was suffered by the airlines; most companies were able to accommodate the event by operating their way out of it.

Digital toolsets and services for risk management

This chapter should by now have conveyed the scope and complexity of identifying risk and managing vulnerability to secure resilience. Design and execution are required on different horizons with many dimensions to be managed and choices to be made.

In the interval since the earlier version of this chapter, the digital revolution has gathered pace, enabling greater visibility in a variety of ways: design, monitoring and incident management. High speed broadband creates instant anywhere-to-anywhere connectivity and visibility across the world. The Internet of Things allows embedded chips to communicate location and/or status to control points. The 'control towers' concept to assemble incoming information and manage status is now in widespread use, particularly in the logistics sector. The use of artificial intelligence (AI) is increasing as a means to monitor large amounts of 'big data' to identify and interpret trends. Supply chain mapping and visualization to support re-design has also advanced. The change in just six years has been meteoric.

The challenge is to harness these new capabilities, which is itself a capability. The mapping of supply chains and identification of the potential points of failure is a skill that requires research, analytical skills and interpretative experience based on supply chain knowledge. This cannot be automated, and the incorrect application of big data or programming of AI solutions are risks in themselves. An example would be when a company sold off excess stock at a loss and the system spotted a surge in demand leading to an out of stock and re-ordered from the supplier.

It is not the role of this chapter to describe or endorse specific products, so these descriptions are generic to the areas in which products and services fall:

- Supply chain design has traditionally been about optimizing global networks from a cost and inventory deployment point-of-view. Emerging products and solutions are enabling visualization and mapping of chains against both supplier attributes and the environment. This visualization is critical in the context of looking beyond the first tier suppliers and customers to understand where the mostly critical potential points of failure may be. In the context of the honeycomb model, this visualization with supporting data allows inductive thinking around the scenarios for vulnerability. From this the business can frame the big choices.

- Monitoring is about both reviewing performance against plan and sensing for events that might impact on the performance of the supply chain. Reviewing performance against plan is generally known as event or work flow management. Successful introduction of such systems requires a huge effort in underlying data accuracy, recording due dates and tolerances; for that reason, their adoption has proved difficult. Large logistics and shipping companies such as the AP Moller–Maersk group have implemented systems that capture orders and monitor supplier and shipping performance against them, data that they have easily. Now this information can be captured and analysed for systemic characteristics, taking their application on from the operational to the strategic.

- The idea of sensing is likely to be more significant since it harnesses incomplete information from within the firm that is available over the internet. There are a number of companies in India that provide such services. In this context, the case of BMW is particularly interesting and is described in more detail below. It is important to note that such solutions may contribute at the strategic, tactical and operational levels.

- Disaster recovery is about coordinating the whole network once a full blown incident is encountered. There are solutions available now that are, in effect, virtual war-rooms; they enable the compilation of data from different sources that allow the centre to review and take decisions, communicate actions and get feedback. These are purely operational and short term in nature.

The case of BMW provides a valuable insight into how visualization and sensing can be used to identify and respond to potential risks in the supply chain. Even BMW in Germany experienced fallout from the Fukushima earthquake but it took weeks to reach their headquarters in Munich. Like many vehicles, the electronics in the entertainment, navigation and control systems in their cars are fitted with parts from Japanese companies. BMW did not face any immediate stoppages following the earthquake; eventually it emerged that a tier one supplier would not be able to deliver because of just one minor part that was made in the Fukushima area. The company found only after many days that its second- and third-tier suppliers had been affected as shortages cascaded through the system. They realized they needed to be able to proactively identify where they might be impacted by delivery failures that would affect production across the group.

Figure 4.8   An illustration of the BMW tool on Google Maps

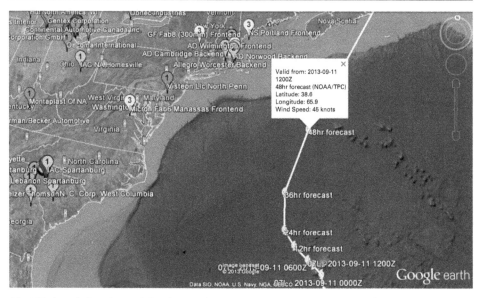

SOURCE Alex Scholz and Tom Kirchmaier, Manchester Business School/London School of Economics

BMW needed greater visibility and increased speed of sensing of issues. This led to a collaboration between BMW's Alex Scholz and Tom Kirchmaier from Manchester Business School and the London School of Economics.[14] This team has built an early-warning system that scans the internet to sift and coordinate information about its suppliers and the areas in which they are based.

Dr Kirchmaier is on record as saying that it is about 'marshalling unstructured information of which there is an enormous wealth on the internet. Astonishingly, companies make very little use of it because it's difficult to know how to source and then condense it in a way that is useful and meaningful.' The information can be used with Google Maps and an example is shown in Figure 4.8 on which Tier 2 and 3 suppliers can be clearly shown in the face of an incoming storm.

Mr Scholz says that BMW needs to understand more about its chain of about 10,000 suppliers, which manufacture components worth €30bn a year for the carmaker. They have built tools that can read, search, sort and select large amounts of information in a systematic way to build up interactive profiles of each supplier and sub-supplier.

Information from earthquakes, other natural disasters and other threats to the supply chain can then be added, flagged and displayed within Google Maps on a large screen.

Information from this analysis is condensed, sorted and delivered to managers as text in an app. While it started as a tactical response tool, the realization has emerged that it can be part of the strategic design and procurement thinking.

In conclusion: supply chain resilience is a capability

The management of supply chain vulnerability is a capability that is finding its moment in the development of supply chain thinking. The downside from supply chain risks is much greater than the upside from perfect supply chains. This means that companies need to be more alert to the tensions and build in resilience through formal processes of strategy and design. The tools are emerging, as the BMW case showed, that allow sensing and feedback to operational, tactical and strategic decision-making horizons. In the six years since this chapter was first prepared, the technical capabilities have improved beyond recognition but it cannot be said that they are commonplace. As Brexit has shown, too few businesses have a robust strategic overview of how their chains actually work. What is needed is a combination of management resolve to invest in the capabilities and the skills to do the job.

References

1 Taleb, NN (2001) *Fooled by Randomness: The hidden role of chance in life and in the markets*, Random House
2 Taleb, NN (2007) *The Black Swan: The impact of the highly improbable*, Random House
3 World Economic Forum (2018) The Global Risks Report, 13th edn, www3.weforum.org/docs/WEF_GRR18_Report.pdf (archived at https://perma.cc/9XYL-GGRK)
4 Manuj, I and Mentzer, JT (2008) Global supply chain risk management strategies, *International Journal of Physical Distribution and Logistics Management*, 38 (3), pp 192–223

5 World Economic Forum (2012) Global Risks, 7th edn, www3.weforum.org/docs/WEF_GlobalRisks_Report_2012.pdf (archived at https://perma.cc/PPF4-7S3S)

6 Reid, DE (2011–12) *Categorising Supply Chain Disruption: Managing risk and designing for resilience*, Manchester Metropolitan Business School, MSc thesis

7 Christopher, M, Mena, C, Khan, O and Yurt, O (2011) Approaches to managing global sourcing risk, *Supply Chain Management*, **16** (2), pp 67–81

8 Christopher, M and Peck, H (2004) Building the resilient supply chain, *International Journal of Logistics Management*, **15**, Issue 2, pp 1–13

9 Wildgoose, N (2011) Avoiding the pitfalls of supply chain disruptions, Zurich Insights [online], *Supply Chain Risk*, 2011 Issue

10 Singhal, VR and Hendricks, K (2000) Report on supply chain glitches and shareholder value destruction, Dupree College of Management, Georgia Institute of Technology

11 LCP Consulting (2003) *Understanding Supply Chain Risk: A Self-Assessment Workbook*, prepared by LCP Consulting in conjunction with the Centre for Logistics and Supply Chain Management, Cranfield School of Management, supported by the Department for Transport, ISBN 1 861941 03 X

12 *Deep Water, The Gulf Oil Disaster and the Future of Offshore Drilling: Report to the President by the National Commission on the BP Deepwater Horizon Oil Spill and Offshore Drilling*, January 2011, Chapter 4

13 Brown, K (2011) Tsunami impact on profits less severe than feared, FT.com (archived at https://perma.cc/QM2K-NTJP)

14 From discussions with Alex Scholz, BMW AG, and Tom Kirchmaier, Manchester Business School and London School of Economics

Fulfilling customer needs in the 2020s with marketing *and* logistics

05

David B Grant

Introduction

This chapter discusses how firms can fulfil customer needs using both marketing and logistics in the second decade of the 21st century. The notion that both are related first appeared at the turn of the 20th century when Weld (1915) discussed distributive trade practices and the increasing significance of 'middlemen' performing specialist functions between producers and consumers. These specializations included logistical activities still prevalent today such as assembling, storing, risk bearing, financing, rearrangement, selling and transporting. These activities provide place and time utility, ie products are in the right place through movement and transport or the 'Go' aspect of logistics, and at the right time through storage and availability or the 'Stop' aspect of logistics (Grant, 2012). The operative instrument for middlemen was the channel of distribution.

From a firm's marketing perspective, business logistics systems and the physical distribution or 'place' component are part of its marketing mix and thus the interface between logistical activities and marketing's demand creation process. The measure of how well a logistical system creates time and place utility for customers is essentially a customer's perception of service and their resultant satisfaction (Grant, 2012). However, a segregation of physical distribution from the other three marketing mix variables of product, price and promotion began in the 1950s with the introduction of the marketing concept. Physical distribution activities were reduced to only physical supply and distribution functions and the notion of physical distribution customer service was misplaced (Bartels, 1982).

A move to reintegrate physical distribution and marketing began when LaLonde and Zinszer (1976) initiated a refocus on logistics customer service with their major study, *Customer Service: Meaning and measurement*, published almost half a century ago. Their definition of logistics customer service was presented as:

> a process which takes place between buyer, seller and third party. The process results in a value added to the product or service exchanged. ...the value added is also shared, in that each of the parties to the transaction or contract is better off at the completion of the transaction than they were before the transaction took place. Thus, in a process view: Customer service is a process for providing significant value-added benefits to the supply chain in a cost-effective way.
>
> **SOURCE** LaLonde and Zinszer (1976, p 15)

This 'customer service process' concept suggests logistical activities can be considered services as they exhibit the fundamental characteristics of services as opposed to products. There are five characteristics of services that distinguish them from products or goods: services are generally intangible; service provision can be inconsistent or heterogeneous; services are perishable and cannot be inventoried; the production and consumption of a service are inseparable; and services cannot be owned in the same manner as a physical product (Grant, 2012).

Customers have become more sophisticated and demanding since LaLonde and Zinszer's work, and their expectations of suppliers' abilities to meet their needs have subsequently increased. Further, the logistical landscape has significantly changed, for example, they now include stakeholders within a firm's wider supply chain and incorporate various technological and online or e-commerce processes that expand a customer's frame of reference. Accordingly, many suppliers, retailers and service organizations have striven to improve logistics customer service processes to establish or maintain a competitive advantage. Desired outcomes are satisfied customers, increased customer loyalty, repeat and increased purchases, and improved corporate financial performance (Grant and Philipp, 2014).

What is less clear is how customers and indeed consumers view how inseparable logistical or supply chain activities are from other marketing activities, particularly in today's online or e-commerce world. Customers have traditionally been involved primarily in the ordering and receiving stages and thus passive throughout the provision of logistical activities, provided service variability is within accepted bounds.

However, common definitions of logistics discuss the efficient and effective flow of goods, services and related information from point-of-origin to point-of-consumption, ie not simply to point-of-sale, in order to meet customer needs (Grant, 2012). Hence, such definitions imply customers and consumers are involved in the logistics process to some degree, for example, when importing goods manufactured abroad in today's global supply chain network, or when scheduling online deliveries to home (or an alternative location such as a pick-up point, another retailer or parcel locker) (Aspara, Grant and Holmlund, 2020).

At a basic household level, when consumers set out for their weekly grocery shop to a retail supermarket, which can be considered a massive 'cash and carry' warehouse, they pick and pack goods, transport the goods to their homes, and put away the goods as inventory in their own personal cupboards or storage centres (Grant, Fernie and Schulz, 2014). Consumer logistics has therefore received some attention in recent years (Teller, Kotzab and Grant, 2006; 2012), and has become more important with the advent and growth of online retailing where the consumer initiates and has more control over the purchasing process (Philipp and Grant, 2015). Consumers now have a choice between undertaking their own physical distribution during a weekly grocery or other non-grocery shop and outsourcing that task to the retailer or a third-party logistics service provider.

Products and prices are relatively easy for competitors to duplicate. Promotional efforts also can be matched by competitors, except for a well-trained and motivated sales force. A satisfactory service encounter, or favourable complaint resolution, is one important way that a firm can really distinguish itself in the eyes of the customer or consumer. Logistics can therefore play a key role in contributing to a firm's competitive advantage by providing excellent customer service and should form part of its logistics and supply chain performance measurement system (Grant, 2012).

Thus, the application of logistics customer service would be well served by using concepts and tools from the services marketing area. However, theories and techniques in the marketing discipline have not found huge acceptance in logistics research, notwithstanding calls for reintegration with logistics and calls for other interdisciplinary applications in logistics (Stock, 1997; 2002).

The foregoing raises practical questions regarding logistics customer service and its application within firms. For example, what is the current state of the art? What are important elements of logistics customer service? And how can firms establish appropriate customer service strategies and policies for both traditional and online or e-commerce activities? These issues are explored in the following sections.

Logistics customer service today

Firms attempt to meet various shareholder/stakeholder requirements in the ordinary course of their business. Profitability, calculated from sales revenue (or turnover) minus expenses, is one of those requirements and is by no means assured for firms that do not consider both factors carefully. Without profits, shareholder capital and retained profits will erode and bankruptcy might result.

Logistics costs such as inventory, warehousing, transportation and information/order processing contribute to a firm's expenditure on customer service. Further, a firm's objective is to maximize profits and minimize total logistics costs over the long term, while maintaining or increasing customer service levels. Such an objective might be considered a 'mission impossible' and firms must carefully choose among the various trade-offs to satisfy customers' needs and maximize profits while minimizing total costs and not wasting scarce marketing mix resources. Thus, there is a necessity to evaluate trade-offs between determining/providing additional customer service features sought by customers and the costs incurred to do so.

However, customer service levels may be higher than a customer would set them and thus choosing when to meet and when to exceed customer expectations is a key factor for firms. Not all service features are equally important to each customer and most customers will accept a relatively wide range of performance in any given service dimension.

Further, most firms in the supply chain do not sell exclusively to endusers, except perhaps in online or e-commerce contexts. Instead, they sell to other intermediaries who in turn may or may not sell to the final customer. For this reason, it may be difficult for these firms to assess the impact of customer service failures, such as stock-outs, on end-users. For example, an out-of-stock situation at a manufacturer's warehouse does not necessarily mean an out-of-stock product at the retail level. However, the impact of stock-outs on the customer's behaviour is important.

These observations reinforce the notion that firms must adopt a customer-orientated view and seek out customer needs. Firms also must ask customers the right questions to ensure important and relevant criteria are captured. And yet, despite almost 50 years of research and application of logistics customer service, the correct questions may still not be asked. This suggests that a customer's product and service needs, and their subsequent supplier selection criteria for logistics services, go beyond usual business-to-business criteria such as product quality, technical competence and competitive prices. Customer evaluation of logistics suppliers may include several intangible factors related to the service being provided as the customer seeks added-value or utility from it.

Finally, both customers and consumers are nowadays more aware of wider issues surrounding their purchases and related logistical activities, such as sustainability (Shaw, Grant and Mangan, 2020) related to a firm's environmental credentials and subsequent loyalty (Dabija, Bejan and Grant, 2018) or the sourcing of products including social aspects regarding production (Blechingberg-Kilpi and Grant, 2020) and attendant risks (Rafi-Ul-Shan *et al*, 2018).

A firm must therefore be able to recognize and respond to customer needs if it is to have any chance in satisfying them and achieving the benefits of loyalty and profitability. But to do that it must initially determine what the customer's needs are, both from its own perspective and from that of the customers. The next section discusses possible logistics customer service elements and strategies.

Logistics customer service elements and issues

LaLonde and Zinszer (1976) suggested that logistics customer service contains three distinct constructs – pre-transaction, transaction and post-transaction – which reflect the temporal nature of a service experience. Other studies since then, from the customer's perspective as opposed to the supplier's perspective, have found similar constructs of logistics customer service as well as relationship elements in the post-transaction construct. A set of customer service elements or variables related to these constructs is shown in Table 5.1.

84   Global Logistics

Table 5.1 Elements of logistics customer service and relationships

Construct	Variable Name
Pre-Order **(Pre-Transaction)**	Availability Appropriate OCT Consistent OCT
Order Service and Quality **(Transaction)**	Accurate Invoices On-Time Delivery Complete Orders Products Arrive Undamaged Accurate Orders Consistent Product Quality Products Arrive to Specification
Relationship Service **(Post-Transaction)**	After Sales Support Delivery Time Helpful CSRs Customized Services
Relationship Quality **(Post-Transaction)**	Trust Commitment Integrity
Global Satisfaction (*The outcome...*)	Overall Supplier Quality Feelings towards Suppliers Future Purchase Intentions

SOURCE Adapted from Grant (2012, p 18)

Firms can use this list of elements to develop their own customer service features; this list is by no means exhaustive but does provide an appropriate starting point for firms to develop logistics customer service strategies. Firms will likely have to add or delete some elements to service their own sectoral and local requirements.

Since the turn of the millennium the internet has created a retail revolution by providing a new, convenient channel for consumer shopping. The e-commerce or online retail market is growing rapidly and now covers a large assortment of products and services. Throughout this period retailers have had to ensure they offer consumers appropriate customer service and a pleasant online shopping experience, including the order fulfilment process.

The responsibility for many physical aspects in the fulfilment process, previously done traditionally with the consumer in-store and beyond, is now taken on by the retailer. This final extension to usual definitions of logistics management from 'point-of-origin to point-of-consumption' is referred to as the 'last mile' process and means greater complexity now attaches to a retailer's distribution system. This has major implications for a retailer as the efficient management of distribution and fulfilment in the last mile can reduce costs, enhance profitability and thus provide competitive advantage.

Online purchases involve the handling and transferring of physical products, ie packing, picking, dispatching, delivering, collecting and returning. Further, a product purchased online or 'virtually' cannot be used by the consumer until it is delivered to them at the right place, at the right time, in the right quantities and in the right condition.

Thus, from a consumer's perspective fulfilment is generally considered to be of the utmost importance and a crucial attribute affecting their judgement of service quality and satisfaction. Thus, fulfilment is a major challenge facing internet retailers and possibly a major barrier preventing consumers from purchasing online.

What is missing in many organizations regarding their services is an appreciation for aspects at the end of the service process, ie post-transaction or service recovery if there is a service failure or 'event' (Grant, 2012), particularly in an online context (Fernie and Grant, 2019). However, service failures are not failures of the service per se. Instead, the propensity for service failure is in the service system design built on assumptions derived from other business models such as manufacturing where human resources are not encouraged or incentivized to deal with a potentially failure or event. This suggests a temporal nature to services, particularly failure and recovery.

Regarding online recovery, Marimon, Yaya and Fa (2012) found that efficiency is the most important construct of online quality regarding its effect on customer loyalty and is slightly more important than service recovery. The implication here is that providing a service free of failures is the best way to enhance customer loyalty, rather than responding to a failure. Nevertheless, when service failure does occur the responsiveness dimension of e-commerce recovery has a significant effect on loyalty. This is in line with the temporal model of pre-, trans- and post-transaction service activities.

Complaints are also an issue that derive from a 'moment of truth' between supplier and customer that is considered a 'critical incident' which has been defined in psychology as:

> any observable human activity that is sufficiently complete in itself to permit inferences and predictions to be made about the person performing the act.
> To be critical, an incident must occur in a situation where the purpose or intent

of the act seems fairly clear to the observer and where its consequences are sufficiently definite to leave little doubt concerning the effects.

SOURCE Flanagan (1954, p 327)

In a business context a 'critical incident' is that 'moment of truth' which becomes representative in a customer's mind.

In summary, firms should categorize customer service elements into dimensions related to pre-transaction, transaction and post-transaction events when facilitating operations design and customer service planning, whether traditional or online. This categorization will enable firms to determine critical events in their service and allow them to monitor and follow up on service failures and provide appropriate recovery.

The next section discusses various customer service strategies to do so.

Logistics customer service strategies

The impetus to develop traditional logistics customer service strategies can be either proactive, reactive or a combination of both. A proactive impetus follows from a firm's desire to satisfy its customer's needs, while a reactive impetus results from a service failure.

It is important that a firm establishes customer service policies based on customer requirements and that are supportive of the overall marketing strategy. What is the point of manufacturing a great product, pricing it competitively, and promoting it well, if it is not readily available to the consumer? At the same time, customer service policies should be cost efficient, contributing favourably to the firm's overall profitability. A proactive customer service strategy allows a firm to consider all these factors.

One popular method for setting customer service levels is to benchmark a competitor's customer service performance. One major question is what to benchmark, and the Supply Chain Council's supply chain operations reference (SCOR) model provides a framework to analyse internal processes – plan, source, make, deliver and return (Shaw, Grant and Mangan, 2010).

There are several issues about the effectiveness of benchmarking; for example, it may promote imitation rather than innovation; best practice operators may refuse to participate in any benchmarking exercise; it focuses on particular activities and thus there is a failure to allow for inter-activity trade-offs; and there is difficulty in finding well-matched comparators.

Further, while it may be interesting to see what the competition is doing, this information has limited usefulness. In terms of what the customer requires, how does the firm know if the competition is focusing on the right customer service elements? Therefore, competitive benchmarking alone is insufficient. Competitive benchmarking should be performed in conjunction with customer surveys that measure the importance of various customer service elements (Shaw, Grant and Mangan, 2010).

Opportunities to close the difference between customer requirements and the firm's performance can be identified so the firm can then target primary customers of competitors and also protect its own key accounts from potential competitor inroads. The service quality model developed from the services marketing discipline and presented in the next section enables a firm to identify such differences and follows the call to use more interdisciplinary techniques in logistics customer service.

Customers evaluate services differently from goods due to their different characteristics. One popular method to investigate such evaluations is the seminal service quality or 'gaps' model (Parasurman, Zeithaml and Berry, 1985). Customers develop a priori expectations of a service based on several criteria such as previous experience, word-of-mouth recommendations or advertising and communication by the service provider.

Once customers 'experience' a service they compare their perceptions of that experience to their expectations. If their perceptions meet or exceed their expectations, they are satisfied; conversely if perceptions do not meet expectations, they are dissatisfied. The difference between expectations and perceptions forms the major 'gap' that is of interest to firms.

Figure 5.1 presents this model and includes the customer's and firm's positions. The 'gap' between expectations and perceptions is affected by four other 'gaps' related to the firm's customer service and service quality activities that are for the most part invisible to the customer.

Firstly, the firm must understand the customer's expectations for the service. Gap 1 is the discrepancy between consumer expectations and the firm's perception of these expectations. Secondly, the firm must then turn the customer's expectations into tangible service specifications. Gap 2 is the discrepancy between the firm's perceptions of consumer expectations and the firm's establishment of service quality specifications. Thirdly, the firm must provide the actual service according to those specifications. Gap 3 is the discrepancy between the firm's establishment of service quality specifications and its actual service provision. Lastly, the firm must communicate its intentions and actions to the customer. Gap 4 is the discrepancy between the firm's actual service provision and external communications about the service to customers.

Figure 5.1 Service quality or 'gaps' model

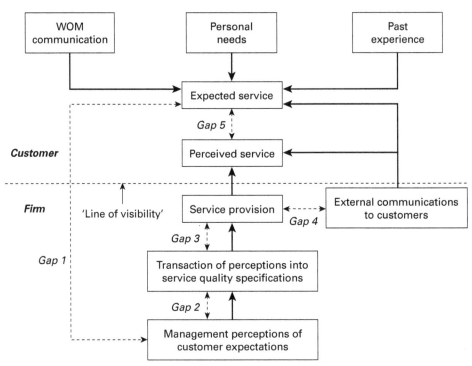

SOURCES Adapted from Parasuraman, Zeithaml and Berry (1985, p 44) and Grant (2012, p 30)

Gap 5 is associated with a customer's expectations for a service experience compared with their perceptions of the actual event, and is the sum of the four gaps associated with the firm, ie Gap 5 = (Gap 1 + Gap 2 + Gap 3 + Gap 4). The firm must minimize or eliminate each discrepancy or gap that it has control over in order to minimize or eliminate the customer's discrepancy or gap related to the service experience. Using the service quality model forces a firm to examine what customer service and service quality they provide to customers in a customer-centric framework and is particularly important in an online retail setting as retailers try to fulfil consumer needs. This is particularly important in the fast-growing online retail sector, which is considered in the next section.

Understanding and obtaining information about customer requirements necessitates an exchange of information between customers and firms. As introduced in the last section, complaint analysis is one such exchange concerning perceived customer dissatisfaction resulting from a customer service experience or critical incident.

The critical incident technique (CIT) was developed as a process to investigate human behaviour and facilitate its practical usefulness for solving practical problems (Flanagan, 1954). CIT procedures consist of collecting and analysing qualitative data to investigate and understand facts behind an incident or series of incidents. Some uses of CIT applicable to business include training, equipment design, operating procedures, and measurement of performance criteria or proficiency and – as will be discussed in the next section – can be a useful strategy.

Complaint handling is significantly associated with both trust and commitment (Tax, Brown and Chandrashekaran, 1998). These concepts are important for supplier–customer relationship development. Complaint analysis thus has a role as part of a post-transaction process but is not a complete form of information for firms when used in isolation. However, such information does not provide an understanding about what customer service features provide customer satisfaction.

Complaint analysis can be considered a defensive strategy since its focus is directed at aggressively protecting existing customers rather than searching for new ones. Therefore, firms using only complaint analysis or CIT techniques might find it difficult to determine current and future success factors and establish a competitive advantage.

Strategies for logistics customer service in an online context are different and challenging (Abrudan, Dabija and Grant, 2020), particularly when providing them for different generations of customers and consumers who may have different motivations and experiences in purchasing online (Popa, Dabija and Grant, 2019). Xing and Grant (2006) developed an electronic physical distribution service quality (e-PDSQ) framework from the consumer's perspective to address the foregoing issues facing retailers who sell on the internet. The framework consists of four constructs – availability, timeliness, condition and return, and related variables, as shown in Table 5.2 – and was tested to ensure its veracity and validity (Xing *et al*, 2010).

This e-PDSQ framework was empirically tested in a survey of online consumers in Edinburgh, UK and confirmed the framework's appropriateness. Price was the most important online purchasing criteria, which suggests it is the principal motivator in the online market that is getting more price-transparent with consumers that are becoming more price-sensitive.

The four variables most important to consumers in an online delivery context were: order condition, reflecting its role in demonstrating a retailer's reliability; order accuracy, considered important for repeat business; order confirmation, which demonstrates consumers' unwillingness to wait and

Table 5.2 E-PDSQ framework constructs and variables

Constructs	Variables
Timeliness (T)	Choice of delivery date Choice of delivery time slot Deliver on the first date arranged Deliver within specified time slot Can deliver quickly
Availability (A)	Confirmation of availability Substitute or alternative offer Order tracking and tracing system Waiting time in case of out-of-stock situation
Condition (C)	Order accuracy Order completeness Order damage in-transit
Return (R)	Ease of return and return channels options Promptness of collection Promptness of replacement

SOURCE Adapted from Xing and Grant (2006, p 285)

their intolerance with out-of-stocks; and easy return and prompt replacement, which reflect consumers' concerns over product returns.

The study provided a parsimonious set of e-PDSQ variables and constructs for retailers to use to design and operate their online offerings, based on the seminal service quality model (Parasuraman, Zeithaml and Berry, 1985) and thus demonstrates how firms can adapt and use models and ideas from other disciplines to provide effective customer service in a logistics context.

However, from a logistics perspective the study also highlighted challenges for retailers and their third-party logistics service provider (3PL) who is responsible for the fulfilment process, particularly multi-channel retailers as opposed to 'pure play' online retailers such as Amazon and ASOS (Xing et al, 2011). Between 25 and 30 per cent of online purchasers do not remain at home to collect their goods when they are delivered. Leaving aside these apparent bad manners, the non-delivery of goods to consumers imposes extra costs on the retailer and its 3PL to try and deliver again, deliver to a pick-up point, or cancel the order.

To overcome this issue, many retailers are now looking to implement 'unattended delivery' as an option for consumers to choose when purchasing online. Examples include leaving in a safe place at the home or with a neighbour, 'click-and-collect' for products at retail stores, post offices or from parcel lockers that can be at determined locations including petrol stations or public transport stations, 'drones' or 'octocopters' that have electric motors to deliver to home (Vakulenko *et al*, 2019). However, while the latter solutions conjure up a 'Jetsons-style' future, they don't address the issue of no one being at home. What would the drone or octocopter do in that case and would it be economically feasible to man them with operators to drop in a safe location?

Further, what additional strategies should retailers adopt to ensure consistent fulfilment, handle seasonal peaks and ensure cyber-Christmas stockings are filled? Unipart Logistics (2013) considers planning is critical and suggests setting up a cross-functional 'seasonal team' under a single manager to forecast potential seasonal activity using previous years' data, plan necessary changes to infrastructure, processes and manpower for the season, trial capabilities and resources in advance of the season, and plan for increased levels of returns during and after the season.

Summary

Customer service is a necessary requirement in logistics activities and is affected by various environmental factors shaping today's marketplace, including increasing online purchases by consumers. Logistics customer service has its roots in the marketing discipline and logisticians can use and learn from marketing techniques and methodologies to investigate customer service.

A strategy for logistics customer service requires a basic trade-off between costs incurred and enhanced profit received. Each industrial sector will also have its own unique needs and issues that further complicate such considerations. However, while the importance of individual customer service elements varies among firms there is a common set of elements presented above that should provide a useful starting point for most firms.

A global perspective focuses on seeking common market demands worldwide rather than cutting up world markets and treating them as separate entities with very different product needs. However, different parts of the world have different customer service needs such as information availability, order completeness and expected lead times. Local infrastructure, communications and time differences may make it impossible to achieve high levels of customer service. Also, management styles in different global markets may be different to those prevalent in the firm's 'home' environment.

Although customer service may represent the best opportunity for a firm to achieve a sustainable competitive advantage, many firms still do not implement logistics customer service strategies or do so by simply duplicating those implemented by competitors. The service quality framework discussed above can be used by firms to collect and analyse customer information, determine what is really important to customers, and thus enhance their customer service initiatives. Globally, customer services provided by the firm should match local customer needs and expectations to the greatest degree possible. A successful output of such customer service considerations will be a satisfied customer, which should lead to increased profitability for the firm.

References

Abrudan, IN, Dabija, D-C and Grant, DB (2020) Omni-channel retailing strategy and research agenda, in *Perspectives on Consumer Behaviour: Theoretical aspects and practical applications*, ed W Sroka, pp 261–80, Springer International, Cham, CH

Aspara, J, Grant, DB and Holmlund, M (2020) Consumer involvement in supply networks: A cubic typology of C2B2C and C2B2B business models, *Industrial Marketing Management*, in press at doi.org/10.1016/j.indmarman.2020.09.004 (archived at https://perma.cc/4YUL-HHQA)

Bartels, R (1982) Marketing and distribution are not separate, *International Journal of Physical Distribution and Materials Management*, **12** (3), pp 3–10

Blechingberg-Kilpi, P and Grant, DB (2020) Corporate and social responsibility perspectives of Finnish fashion retailers and consumers, in *Essential Issues in Corporate Social Responsibility: New insights and recent issues*, eds SO Idowu and C Sitnikov, pp 55–71, Springer International, Cham, CH

Dabija, DC, Bejan, BM and Grant, DB (2018) The impact of consumer green behaviour on green loyalty among retail formats: A Romanian case study, *Moravian Geographical Reports*, **26** (3), pp 173–85

Fernie, J and Grant, DB (2019) *Fashion Logistics*, 2nd edn, Kogan Page, London

Flanagan, JC (1954) The critical incident technique, *Psychological Bulletin*, **51** (July), pp 327–58

Grant, DB (2012) *Logistics Management*, Pearson, London

Grant, DB and Philipp, B (2014) A planned study of the impact of B2C logistics service quality on shopper satisfaction and loyalty, *Sinergie Italian Journal of Management*, **95** (4), pp 45–63

Grant, DB, Fernie, J and Schulz, B (2014) Enablers and barriers in German online food retailing, *Supply Chain Forum: An International Journal*, **15** (3), pp 4–11

LaLonde, BJ and Zinszer, PH (1976) *Customer Service: Meaning and measurement*, National Council of Physical Distribution Management, Chicago, IL

Marimon, F, Yaya, LHP and Fa, MC (2012) Impact of e-quality and service recovery on loyalty: A study of e-banking in Spain, *Total Quality Management and Business Excellence*, **23** (7–8), pp 769–87

Parasuraman, A, Zeithaml, VA and Berry, LL (1985) A conceptual model of service quality and its implications for future research, *Journal of Marketing*, **49** (Fall), pp 41–50

Philipp, B and Grant, DB (2015) Does B2C online logistics service quality impact urban logistics? *Logistique and Management*, **23** (2), pp 45–54

Popa, ID, Dabija, D-C and Grant, DB (2019) Exploring omnichannel retailing differences and preferences among consumer generations, in *Applied Ethics for Entrepreneurial Success: Recommendations for the developing world*, eds S Văduva, I Fotea, LP Văduva and R Wilt, pp 129–46, Springer International, Cham, CH

Rafi-Ul-Shan, PM, Grant, DB, Perry, P and Ahmed, S (2018) The relationship between sustainability and risk management in fashion supply chains: A systematic literature review, *International Journal of Retail & Distribution Management*, **46** (5), pp 466–86

Shaw, S, Grant, DB and Mangan, J (2010) Developing environmental supply chain performance measures, *Benchmarking: An International Journal*, **17** (3), pp 320–39

Shaw, S, Grant, DB and Mangan, J (2020) A supply chain practice-based view of enablers, inhibitors and benefits for environmental supply chain performance measurement, *Production Planning and Control*, in press at doi.org/10.1080/09 537287.2020.1737977 (archived at https://perma.cc/9VKC-BGG9)

Stock, JR (1997) Applying theories from other disciplines to logistics, *International Journal of Physical Distribution & Logistics Management*, **27** (9/10), pp 515–39

Stock, JR (2002) Marketing myopia revisited: Lessons for logistics, *International Journal of Physical Distribution and Logistics Management*, **32** (1), pp 12–21

Tax, SS, Brown, SW and Chandrashekaran, M (1998) Customer evaluations of service complaint experiences: Implications for relationship marketing, *Journal of Marketing*, **62** (April), pp 60–76

Teller, C, Kotzab, H and Grant, DB (2006) The consumer direct services revolution in grocery retailing: An exploratory investigation, *Managing Service Quality*, **16** (1), pp 78–96

Teller, C, Kotzab, H and Grant, DB (2012) The relevance of shopper logistics for consumers of store-based retail formats, *Journal of Retailing and Consumer Services*, **19** (1), pp 59–66

Unipart Logistics (2013) White paper: Managing seasonality in the retail supply chain, www.unipartlogistics.com (archived at https://perma.cc/28NU-GULD)

Vakulenko, Y, Shams, P, Hellström, D and Hjort, K (2019) Service innovation in e-commerce last mile delivery: Mapping the e-customer journey, *Journal of Business Research*, **101**, pp 461–68

Weld, LDH (1915) Market distribution, *The American Economic Review*, **5** (1), pp 125–39

Xing, Y and Grant, DB (2006) Developing a framework for measuring physical distribution service quality of multi-channel and 'pure player' Internet retailers, *International Journal of Retail and Distribution Management*, **34** (4/5), pp 278–89

Xing, Y, Grant, DB, McKinnon, AC and Fernie, J (2010) Physical distribution service quality in online retailing, *International Journal of Physical Distribution and Logistics Management*, **40** (5), pp 415–32

Xing, Y, Grant, DB, McKinnon, AC and Fernie, J (2011) The interface between retailers and logistics service providers in the online market, *European Journal of Marketing*, **45** (3), pp 334–57

New procurement directions in supply chain management

06

Louise Knight, Frederik Vos and Joanne Meehan

Perspectives on procurement

Past and present

As a profession and as an academic field, procurement has developed rapidly in recent years, with many organizations across all sectors – commercial, public, health, not-for-profit – shifting from an operational approach to embedding strategic procurement (Mogre, Lindgreen and Hingley, 2017; Knight *et al*, 2020). Strategic procurement is not solely about decision making to secure 'the right materials, from the right suppliers, in the right quantity, in the right place, at the right time, with the right quality' (Monczka *et al*, 2010, p 11). It also generates value through developing a range of competitive options (Ellram and Carr, 1994; Trent and Monczka, 1998; Wynstra, Suurmond and Nullmeier, 2019).

There are three contrasting and complementary views of procurement, each of which highlights the distinct contribution that procurement can make to business and supply chain performance. Procurement is often regarded as one 'half' of supply chain management (SCM), with SCM defined as logistics and procurement (Ellram and Murfield, 2019; Min, Zacharia

Figure 6.1   Three contrasting and complementary views of procurement, linked to operations management, strategy and marketing

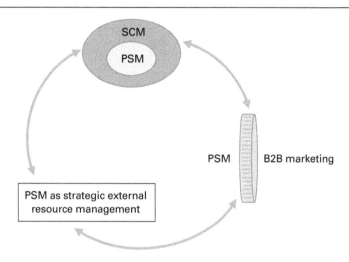

and Smith, 2019; Wisner and Tan, 2000). Another view of procurement places it as the counterpart to B2B marketing, focusing on commercial relationships embedded in business networks (Johnsen, 2018). A third view concerns the strategic management of external resources critical to long-term firm performance (Handfield, 2019; Mogre *et al*, 2017). In this chapter, we consider all three views (Figure 6.1) of procurement which, taken together, define the field of procurement as being about configuring and orchestrating upstream actors, contracts, relationships and systems to acquire products and services effectively, taking account of both short-term business pressures and the longer-term direction of the firm.

Wynstra *et al* (2019) trace procurement's development through an extensive review of academic research, mapping 2,522 articles published from 1995 to 2014 onto four procurement specific categories of variables: enablers, strategic processes, tactical/operational processes and competitive priorities (see Figure 6.2). Modern procurement covers not only the basic procurement process from the specification of need to the payment of orders (bottom of Figure 6.2), but it is also involved in core strategic processes and competitive priorities of organizations (Wynstra *et al*, 2019) (centre of Figure 6.2).

Figure 6.2 Overview of procurement research 1995–2014, based on 2,522 articles

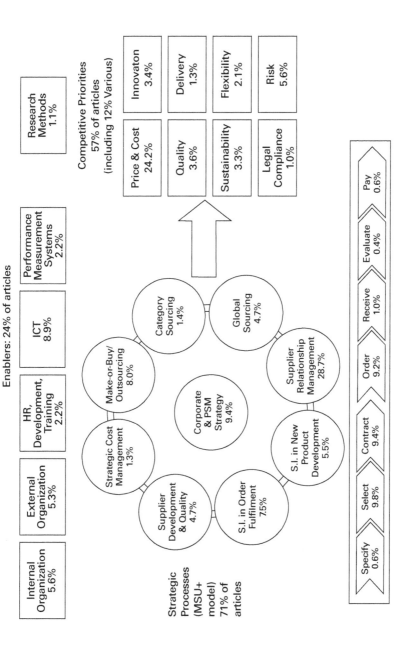

Enablers: 24% of articles

| Internal Organization 5.6% | External Organization 5.3% | HR, Development, Training 2.2% | ICT 8.9% | Performance Measurement Systems 2.2% | Research Methods 1.1% |

Competitive Priorities
57% of articles
(including 12% Various)

Price & Cost 24.2%	Innovaton 3.4%
Quality 3.6%	Delivery 1.3%
Sustainability 3.3%	Flexibility 2.1%
Legal Compliance 1.0%	Risk 5.6%

Strategic Processes (MSU+ model) 71% of articles

- Make-or-Buy/Outsourcing 8.0%
- Category Sourcing 1.4%
- Global Sourcing 4.7%
- Strategic Cost Management 1.3%
- Corporate & PSM Strategy 9.4%
- Supplier Relationship Management 28.7%
- Supplier Development & Quality 4.7%
- S.I. in Order Fulfilment 7.5%
- S.I. in New Product Development 5.5%

Tactical/Operational Processes (Van Weele); 32% of articles (including 1.3% Various)

| Specify 0.6% | Select 9.8% | Contract 9.4% | Order 9.2% | Receive 1.0% | Evaluate 0.4% | Pay 0.6% |

SOURCE Wynstra et al (2019, p 8)

The review reveals a clear emphasis on supplier relationship management and selection, ordering processes and the price/cost priority. Other areas have also drawn researchers' attention: organization, ICT, risk, order fulfilment and make-or-buy/outsourcing. Future-oriented topics, such as sustainability (3.3 per cent), ICT (8.9 per cent), innovation (3.4 per cent), and global sourcing (4.7 per cent) were rather under-represented in research in the 2000s and early 2010s. Notably, Wynstra, Suurmond and Nullmeier's (2019) analysis revealed that, although the total number of publications has risen over time, the proportion relating to strategy has diminished. This possibly reflects mutually reinforcing shifts in research priorities:

- now that – in many quarters – the argument that procurement should be regarded as a strategic (as well as operational) function is won, researchers have moved on to other themes such as innovation; and,

- the rise of research on supply chain management and the role of ICT in enabling integration leads to a focus on operational processes.

However, rising resource scarcity and rapid changes in the business landscape imply there is much still to learn about the opportunity for procurement to both generate, and destroy, value. Advanced practices not only improve profitability, but also underpin effective governance, delivery of organizations' environmental and social commitments, and secure the organization's long-term future. Procurement decisions generate the network of organizations that constitute the supply chain (Ulkuniemi, Araujo and Tähtinen, 2015; Vurro, Russo and Perrini, 2009), signalling the need to consider the impact of strategic procurement beyond outcomes for the firm or tier one suppliers only.

What's driving change?

Procurement research over the last decades makes a strong case for the positive impact of advanced procurement on achieving organizational priorities. Most obviously, effective procurement influences economic success through lowering costs and assuring quality. Beyond this, procurement professionals contribute to risk and innovation management, and lead initiatives to improve the environmental and social outcomes of key suppliers (Goebel et al, 2018; Guarnieri and Gomes, 2019; Tate, Ellram and Dooley, 2012). Most of this research concludes with commentary on future directions. Only a small proportion of procurement research specifically focuses on the future of the field (Bals et al, 2019; Cheng et al, 2018; Ghadimi et al,

Figure 6.3   Four megatrend clusters

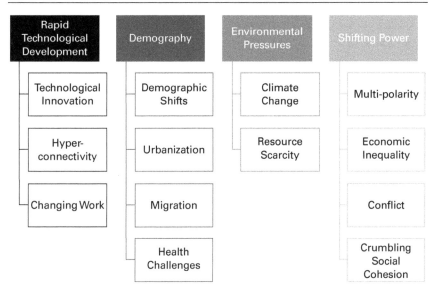

SOURCE Artuso and Guijt (2020, p 12)

2016; Khripunova *et al*, 2014; see summary in Knight *et al*, 2020; Mogre *et al*, 2017; Schneider and Wallenburg, 2013; Schoenherr and Speier-Pero, 2015; Spina *et al*, 2013; Zheng *et al*, 2007). Nevertheless, the case for the continued development of procurement is strong. Below, we discuss what this might look like, first elucidating key changes and their drivers and the current development pathways for procurement, then considering an alternative view – 'new directions' – of how procurement might need to change if it is to support radical change ('business-*not*-as-usual') in the coming decades.

Whilst we will signpost some of this research here, this chapter is not designed as a review of research on the future of procurement. Rather, we build on that research and combine it with visions of, and calls for, transformational change as widely discussed in the mainstream media, to address critical macro-environmental challenges, illustrated in Figure 6.3 from a recent report commissioned by Oxfam. These globally-oriented, transformative goals are captured in the United Nation's 17 Sustainable Development Goals (SDG) (UN, 2020). These challenges and goals have the potential to change the trajectory of the global economy and business priorities, impacting how organizations operate. We asked ourselves: 'What could it mean for procurement if the radical change envisioned in these calls were realized and organizations were fundamentally transformed?'

Radical change brings new opportunities, threats and uncertainties that require new thinking and novel approaches. The acceleration of transformative change is leading organizations to recognize the need to develop foresight and experimental scenario work. (We recommend Future Agenda as a valuable resource [futureagenda.org/ (archived at https://perma.cc/48VW-258J)], published under Creative Commons Non-Commercial Share-Alike.) We adopt a similar thought experiment to allow us to 'step back' from current procurement practice and research, reflect on aspirations for future change, and critically consider whether, and how, current developments in procurement align with those aspirations. These reflections reveal what we term here *new* procurement directions for 'business-*not*-as-usual'. By the very nature of the process, the results are not definitive. They are intended to stimulate critical thinking, surface assumptions about the role and contribution of procurement, promote diverse debate within the profession, and encourage readers to identify new procurement directions in their own context.

Differentiating 'improved business-as-usual' and 'new procurement directions for business-not-as-usual'

With the interactions and uncertainties of megatrends and SDGs in mind, two contrasting perspectives on new directions for procurement can be sketched out. The first assumes that procurement will continue on its current development pathway, with the aim of improving organizational performance measured in familiar terms and for familiar goals, the pursuit of (cost) efficiency while reducing direct environmental and social harm – ie incremental improvement on business-as-usual. The second perspective is based on contrasting assumptions centred on widespread and enduring radical change in business systems (which we take to include also the public/ health/non-profit sectors interacting with commercial firms, not only B2B). In this business-*not*-as-usual scenario, recognition of the need to build resilient, socially just and inclusive, and environmentally sustainable business systems would require fundamental strategic reorientation for many firms which would, in turn, place new demands on procurement.

Procurement directions for 'improved business-as-usual'

The megatrends and aspirations for change (as captured, for example, in the SDGs) lead to a complex web of political, economic, social, environmental and technological influences on the goals of procurement, what is procured, how procurement is undertaken, and from which suppliers. Mapping the consequences for procurement outcomes (in terms of availability/access to resources, prices, transaction costs, social and environmental outcomes, resilience, long-term competitiveness of supply markets, dependence on suppliers) shows equally complex patterns, and no single, clear direction of development for the field of procurement.

We derive several themes, that are drawn from our own research (Knight and Meehan, 2018), the limited body of research which specifically addresses the future of procurement (see above), and the numerous, broad-ranging but fragmented views expressed in research articles. The themes are clustered using the 5W1H method (also sometimes called the Kipling method), a problem-solving method to activate creative thinking, finding and developing new ideas (Burtonshaw-Gunn and Salameh, 2009; Hamborg *et al*, 2018; Hart, 1996). The 5W1H method implies that the questions why, what, where, when, who and how are addressed when analysing or describing a problem. We addressed the 'where' (ie procurement in organizations) and the 'when' (ie in future) above. The remainder of this section presents future procurement themes around the remaining four core questions:

What changes will occur in...

- procurement strategic priorities? (why)
- what is bought? (what)
- procurement practices and processes? (how)
- the supply-side landscape? (who)

Procurement's strategic priorities

Increasingly the (relatively) simple framing of procurement as a cost-reducing role is complemented by the need to consider the social and environmental outcomes of procurement decisions. Initiatives such as those requiring suppliers to reduce their carbon footprint, or to hire staff from disadvantaged groups, are now commonplace in sourcing strategies

(Lăzăroiu *et al*, 2020; Loosemore, Alkilani and Mathenge, 2020; Yu, Yang and Chang, 2018).

Also, in light of growing uncertainties and change in business environments, supply chain resilience is an emerging strategic priority for many organizations. Research on supply chain resilience draws on diverse fields including psychology, ecosystems, humanitarian logistics and risk management, covering a range of issues including capabilities, agility, visibility, structure, and collaboration (Ali and Gölgeci, 2019; Jain *et al*, 2017). Much attention has been paid to supply chain failures caused by natural disasters (Dixit, Verma and Tiwari, 2020; Papadopoulos *et al*, 2017; Wong *et al*, 2020). Often these failures are seen as a logistics problem, but the Covid-19 pandemic has highlighted procurement's role in resilience, with many health and public contracting authorities seeking new, geographically proximate suppliers (Tip *et al*, 2021).

How these goals fare when in tension with cost drivers remains a critical question, especially in times of recession (Goebel *et al*, 2018). Looking at how to scale up, and speed up, change highlights two key challenges. The first is how buyers can promote and monitor improvements beyond first-tier suppliers, especially if the buyers are not themselves powerful. Second, there is growing recognition that such initiatives are about doing less harm (Boersma, 2017; Hughes, Morrison and Ruwanpura, 2019; Montabon, Pagell and Wu, 2016), rather than genuine sustainability (Ehrenfeld and Hoffman, 2013). They are necessary but their impact is not sufficient. The climate emergency and deepening inequalities require more fundamental change (Pagell and Shevchenko, 2014); change which organizations could foster by reducing their resource requirement and reforming the configuration and performance of upstream supply chains.

Supply chain resilience requires consideration of ecological and social vulnerability alongside commercial considerations. Yet crucially, risks beyond costs are externalized by organizations and often mitigated rather than being fully integrated into strategic priorities. If organizations are to learn to rebuild supply chain systems that are 'better' than their pre-failure position, further consideration is needed on their accountabilities and impacts.

Changes in what is being procured

Just as consumers increasingly lease goods and buy services on subscription, so it is often attractive for businesses to buy integrated product–service bundles from a single supplier (Kohtamäki, Einola and Rabetino, 2020).

Servitization (Paschou *et al*, 2020; Raddats *et al*, 2019) is common business strategy among large manufacturing/engineering firms, but it is also attractive to start-ups as a means of capturing more supply chain value (Lafuente, Vaillant and Vendrell-Herrero, 2017). From the buyer's perspective, the benefits are much as with outsourcing – reduced capital expenditure, leveraging suppliers' expertise, and greater focus on core activities (Sasse *et al*, 2019).

Lindberg and Nordin (2008) contrast the servitization agenda with *objectification*. While some companies are moving to higher-value and complexity integrated products/services, others follow a business model which is about simplifying the item on offer. Likewise, modularization and systems integration (Rajala *et al*, 2019) lead to the reconfiguration of supply chains. Rather than buying components, organizations source more complex, integrated systems from their first-tier suppliers. The network of contracts and suppliers supporting the business is reduced, whilst the value of transactions rises.

Increasing dependence on suppliers also arises when organizations buy products benefiting from materials innovation (Yeniyurt, Henke and Yalcinkaya, 2014). Whilst product performance may be much enhanced, there are important trade-offs (Noordhoff *et al*, 2011). For example, a high-cost, innovative product may lead to savings in deployment and maintenance costs, but also new technical interdependencies and power asymmetry based on intellectual property. As with servitization, lock-in is an important risk (Ford, Verreynne and Steen, 2018).

Another aspect to consider regarding what is bought is rooted in the environmental agenda. Many natural resources are becoming increasingly scarce, motivating firms to find substitutes in the form of alternative materials, which may be innovative materials, or recovered/reused materials as part of circular economy initiatives (Bell, Mollenkopf and Stolze, 2013; Svensson, 2007). At best, a firm may find ways to stop using a scarce material as part of a demand reduction technique (Kalaitzi *et al*, 2018).

Changes in procurement practices and processes

The most high-profile development affecting the 'how' of procurement is digitalization. As highlighted in Legenvre, Henke and Ruile (2020), the digitalization agenda affects procurement departments both in what they buy – in supporting digitalization of other organizational processes – and in changing procurement processes. Blockchain, Industry 4.0, big data and artificial intelligence are all expected to play a significant role in reforming procurement practice (Culot *et al*, 2020; Schiele and Torn, 2020).

Improved processes yield better data which can then in turn be deployed for better procurement. Higher quality and new types of data can enable transparency of transactions, underpinning better spend analysis, transaction visibility and supply chain governance. Discussions on the impact of these developments on procurement practice pivot on three interconnected uncertainties:

- The rate of adoption – whilst enthusiasm for digitalization is high, there is much uncertainty about timing. Srai and Lorentz (2019) identified the gap between practice and the rhetoric. Very long implementation lead times exist for implementing digital solutions.

- The scope of adoption – will digitalization be more limited, focusing on more operational/transactional processes, or will it extend to more strategic activities influencing practice in, for example, supplier development and relationship management?

- Leveraging the data advantage – whether and how organizations will make effective use of the large volumes of data yielded by new systems (Elgendy and Elragal, 2016).

Dealing with powerful suppliers, whether they leverage data or some other form of advantage, is an increasingly important capability. Especially in the United States, many supply markets are increasingly consolidated (Philippon, 2019). Recent hearings of the US Congressional House Anti-trust Subcommittee have focused on the business practices of Alphabet (Google), Amazon, Facebook and Apple. Of particular concern was their acquisition and use of data to restrict competition and capitalize on their dominant position. Although this was considered with respect to consumers, the issues raised relate to many more B2C markets and to industrial buyers in many sectors (see, for example, the extensive list of sectors published by the Open Markets Institute, www.openmarketsinstitute.org/learn/monopoly-by-the-numbers (archived at https://perma.cc/F7PC-Q89S)). Conversely, some very small firms also exercise disproportionate power in relation to their corporate customers, thanks to controlling critical intellectual property.

One approach buyers adopt in such circumstances is to collaborate. Since the 1990s, buyer–supplier partnerships have received much attention (Lamming, 1993). This was followed by interest in buying groups, notably in public-sector contexts, where organizations combine their buying power to reduce prices and transaction costs on commonly purchased items (Hezarkhani and Šošić, 2018; Saha, Seidmann and Tilson, 2019; Schotanus and Telgen, 2007; Walker *et al*, 2013). New systems and better data open further opportunities for looser forms of cooperation based on exchange of information, and not necessarily collaborative purchases. These same systems reduce coordination costs and risks, and open up the possibility of larger-scale, more geographically dispersed cooperation. Conversely, warnings of increasing natural resource scarcity and the shifts towards more open innovation draw procurement experts' attention to how to acquire (innovative) goods and services in increasingly competitive environments. New strategies are needed to secure supply and facilitate buyer–supplier relationships, and can include developing a position as a preferred customer (Schiele, Calvi and Gibbert, 2012; Vos, 2017) or actively managing factor market rivalry (Ellram, Tate and Feitzinger, 2013; Schwieterman and Miller, 2016).

Changes in the supply-side landscape

Too often, the issues described above are debated by procurement experts without direct acknowledgement of the associated consequences for the supply-side business landscape. For example, on their current development pathways, servitization and digitalization are mutually reinforcing, and tending to drive market consolidation. Further, the rise of platforms is a critical driver of change in the procurement field. B2C platforms, notably Amazon, are diversifying into B2B markets, offering much the same advantages and risks to organizational buyers as they provide consumers – much reduced prices and transaction costs in the short term, and risks associated with reduced competition in the longer term, exacerbated by information asymmetry (Broekhuizen *et al*, 2021). Of course, not all platforms operate at a large scale. Platform applications can be deployed by local/regional networks, for example to facilitate building a circular economy (Silvestri, Spigarelli and Tassinari, 2020; Virtanen *et al*, 2019).

Changes in manufacturing processes also have consequences for the long-term configuration of supply networks. The rise of 3D printing and decentralized manufacturing (Singh *et al*, 2020) drives new patterns of procurement, either with more suppliers (printers) for lower volumes, or delegating sourcing activities to specialist intermediaries (Braziotis, Rogers and Jimo, 2019; Kunovjanek and Reiner, 2020). Switching from labour-intensive to highly automated suppliers also places new demands on procurement to follow the changing emphases on technologies, cost structures and supplier location. Similarly, automation within service operations presents both new risks and opportunities. For example, artificial intelligence may significantly reduce operating costs but may also present greater risks around legal liability and supply chain governance (Baryannis *et al*, 2019).

High-impact disasters, such as the Covid-19 pandemic, and associated supply chain failures, highlight the risks of global supply chains and encourage politicians and business leaders to reduce dependence on geographically remote suppliers. This recognition adds momentum to a longer-term transition towards regionalization, linked to sustainable and socially responsible sourcing, and to re-shoring (Li *et al*, 2020; Nassimbeni *et al*, 2019). This translates to reduced international sourcing and, for global firms, to decentralizing procurement activities.

Business-as-usual: the interaction of factors and factors over time

As described in the previous sections, directions for improving procurement within the current business frame concern deepening knowledge and enhancing capabilities on established development pathways. For improved supply chain management, procurement digitalization is critical. The procurement function will need to strengthen its technical capabilities to drive change within procurement processes, but also to be a competent partner with key stakeholders. To enhance external resource management, procurement leaders need to sustain their progress in increasing their contribution to business strategy deliberations. Advanced relationship strategies and management skills are essential to ensure sustained access to the best suppliers. With continued focus on efficiency and globalization, developing expertise in securing supplies in the face of rising rivalry will predominate, but that will also depend on collaboration capability. This will include longer-term contracting, vertical integration, enhancing supply chain visibility through the network of contracts and shared data. The upstream reach and scale of environmental and social initiatives need attention.

Some of the aforementioned influences can counteract one another's effects. For example, technologies such as 3D printing, and goals such as reducing environmental impact, encourage the decentralization of production (and consequently procurement activity), whereas other influences such as rising natural resource scarcity, market dominant suppliers, and factor market rivalry point to the need to centralize procurement to maximize buying power.

Several influences have short-term, beneficial effects on some outcomes, but longer-term detrimental impacts on other outcomes. For example,

Table 6.1   Highlighting key, interconnected themes of improved procurement for 'business-as-usual'

Procurement strategic priorities (Why?)	What is bought (What?)	Procurement practices and processes (How?)	Supply landscape (Who?)
Focus on efficiency – cost/ price drivers	From product to service	Digitalization of operational processes	Concentration of supplier/factor markets
Supply chain resilience as a procurement issue	Modularization	Data for performance improvement	New intermediaries
	Performance and cost improvements		Re-shoring
Influencing beyond first tier suppliers	Innovation and competitiveness risks	Dealing with powerful suppliers	Distributed manufacturing
Doing less (environmental and social) harm	Rising resource scarcity	Supplier partnering	Supplier automation
		Collaborative purchasing	
Supporting genuine sustainability	Sourcing others' waste	Securing scarce resources	
		Competing for limited market capacity	

servitization and modularization reduce the need for buy-side technical know-how and improve performance in the shorter term. Over time, however, loss of knowledge and intellectual property lock-in builds dependency and increases the risk of higher prices and reduced innovation. The benefits and advantages are yielded when the system is in transition/at the time of initial implementation. The disadvantages of new dependencies may play out over a much longer term – eg loss of agility becomes more apparent at times of crisis. Such risks could be – at least in part – offset by increased competence in buying services and better market intelligence, which in turn could be improved through effective use of data generated by digitalization.

The summary of the key themes regarding improving 'business-as-usual' procurement is presented in Table 6.1. The list reveals the complex interconnections between the factors, across categories and over time.

New procurement directions for 'business-*not*-as-usual'

Returning to the question framing this chapter, this section sketches some ideas for what procurement could be about if the radical changes envisioned in the calls to address the grand challenges (as represented, for example, in the United Nations SDGs (UN, 2020)) were realized. We set out some critical activities around three themes: digitalization, ecosystems and resources. These themes reflect the three views of procurement illustrated in Figure 6.1. More specifically, we considered: 'What would it take for procurement to effectively support organizations that are: oriented towards achieving long-term economic performance; committed to effective governance to radically reduce resource consumption and reverse environmental degradation, and to increase social equity?' Recognizing their interconnectedness, we propose these activities should be considered together as (tentatively) describing new directions for procurement.

Below, we envision procurement aligned with, and enabling, 'business-not-as-usual'. A series of bullet points, clustered according to the three key themes of digitalization, ecosystems and resources, illustrate its various facets.

Digitalizing for good governance and sustainability, not just efficiency

Digitalization beyond process improvements

Digitalizing procurement to deliver new functionality, extending much beyond more efficient operational processes to leverage better supply chain visibility and business intelligence. This includes using new data sources and techniques to deepen knowledge of market capacity and dynamics, including leveraging data across organizational boundaries.

Artificial intelligence as decision support

Developing new ways of making sourcing decisions/determining sourcing criteria with the capability to make effective use of artificial intelligence in advanced applications (eg related to sustainability).

A new age of accountability

Use digitalization to help secure deep change in environmental and social outcomes, through more open and accountable governance.

Open data initiatives

Managing data value appropriation in the supply chain, to avoid market consolidation and promote market dynamism and diversity. An emphasis on open data-exchange and shared accountability for data (eg via the use of blockchains and similar technologies).

Adopting a long-term, ecosystem-centred view

The ambitious ecosystem

Supporting system-level innovation – bringing commercial/contractual expertise to brokering change across organizational ecosystems, with an ambitious agenda (mission-driven in the public sector; sustainability transitions across all sectors).

Improved long-term decision making

Influencing decision-making processes and criteria to build in a preference for long-term, systemic outcomes. This will be especially challenging with increased automation, given the difficulties of designing suitable algorithms to assess more nuanced, complex, distributed, long-term benefits rather than short-term, private financial advantage.

Vertical and horizontal chain collaboration

Building resilience through agility/flexibility through an ability to monitor developments and respond rapidly via shifting coalitions, engaging horizontally with other buyers, as well as vertically with suppliers and customers.

Coopetition for change

Partnering with other buyers to jointly foster long-term consumption reduction and capacity building. Finding novel ways to align incentives and balance private, shared and common goods arising from collective action. This includes competitors working together towards the same long-term goals (eg towards sustainability, see https://spp.earth (archived at https://perma.cc/BH7Q-U7AT) for an example of such a collaboration).

Managing critical resources in the very long term, and regarding supply markets (not just products and services) as critical resources

A strategy for environmental/social impact

Focusing on securing environmentally and socially sound resources for the long-term future of the organization and, if that is not possible, then helping to re-design the organization vision/strategy within its resource constraints.

From private consumption to collective capacity

Finding ways to engender a shift in focus from firm-level resource consumption to building collective capacity, facilitated by private and public supply chain initiatives. This requires moving from exploitative, non-cooperating strategies to reciprocal cooperation, enhancing the shadow of the future in decision making (Axelrod, 1984; Heide and Miner, 1992) and including consumers in the shift towards more effective resource management. The inclusion of consumers is essential to achieving this shift.

Going beyond 'green at the edges'

Transitioning from 'greening at the edges' to a circular economy to reduce resource consumption, with associated approaches for better alignment of long-term incentives in the system.

A 'power-view' on resource and market management

Monitoring market dynamics and taking account of buyers' influence on the 'market health' (Government Commercial Function, 2019), recognizing the middle path needed between concentration and control versus fragmentation and instability. Requires new tools, effective use of new tech, and a preventative/precautionary approach when evaluating anticipated shifts in market power.

Contrasting 'improving business-as-usual' and 'business-*not*-as-usual' perspectives

Within the business-*not*-as-usual scenario, the procurement developments sketched out above are not substitutes to those described in the previous section; they are complements. Our aim is to promote critical debates, challenge assumptions within existing trajectories, and explore additional ways to extend procurement's value proposition, whilst being cognizant of future landscapes that can risk value destruction. Table 6.1 summarizes developments in procurement which are necessary, but not sufficient. By considering more radical changes for procurement, current blind spots and new opportunities emerge. Among the effective organizations imagined in our business-*not*-as-usual thought experiment, these developments would be deepened and broadened to help organizations pursue wider, collective goals, as well as maintain their long-term economic viability – what we term here 'sustainability advantage'.

By setting out these changes, we propose some new directions for procurement. Necessarily, these are conjectural. They are designed to draw attention to the need for ambitious visions for procurement, and to encourage reflection on the gaps between our ambitions and current trajectories (see Figure 6.4).

Figure 6.4   Contrasting familiar, 'business-as-usual' directions with new procurement directions

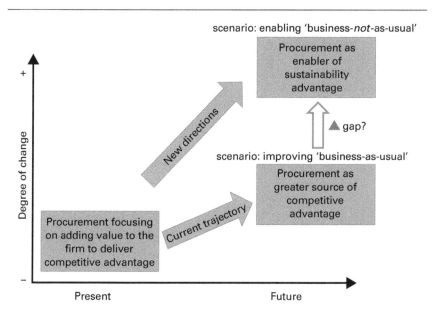

This chapter has been written in the midst of the Covid-19 pandemic, when questions are being asked across the world of how global, national and local economies can rebuild on stronger, more equitable foundations. Yet, these aspirations bring new tensions. While our ecological systems had a temporary reprieve from the demands of the modern world, economic and societal fault lines have been exposed. Business survival is frequently pitted against health and human freedoms in government decisions related to lockdowns and opening up the economy, highlighting the interconnection of economic, environmental and social systems. Success in one system should not be at the expense of another. New ways to collaborate to humanize and harmonize our supply chains need to be developed for our post-Covid world.

The debates on what type of future we want to experience raise fundamental questions about the role and impacts of business in society and, for procurement, about the impacts of our sourcing decisions. Interestingly, what is not so apparent in these debates is 'how did we get here'? Exploring this question forces us to consider the misalignment of our economic, environmental and social systems. The consequences of past inattention to the 'why, what, where, when, who and how' of our sourcing decisions have not been neutral (that is, just a failure to 'add value'); rather, they have often destroyed value.

There is no doubt that procurement has always had the potential to contribute to broader agendas in delivering value to firms, supply chains and wider global concerns. Procurement can continue to play a vital role in enabling transformative change in organizations and business ecosystems, but only by paying close attention to wider trends and external priorities beyond the organization's immediate competitive arena.

References

Ali, I and Gölgeci, I (2019) Where is supply chain resilience research heading? A systematic and co-occurrence analysis, *International Journal of Physical Distribution and Logistics Management*, **49** (8), pp 793–815

Artuso, F and Guijt, I (2020) *Global Megatrends: Mapping the forces that affect us all* (Oxfam Report), Oxfam discussion paper, retrieved from oxfamilibrary. openrepository.com/handle/10546/620942 (archived at https://perma.cc/5J5S-Y5FK)

Axelrod, R (1984) *The Evolution of Cooperation*, Basic Books, New York

Bals, L, Schulze, H, Kelly, S and Stek, K (2019) Purchasing and supply management (PSM) competencies: Current and future requirements, *Journal of Purchasing and Supply Management*, **25** (5), pp 1–15, doi.org/10.1016/j. pursup.2019.100572 (archived at https://perma.cc/Z8B8-S3PF)

Baryannis, G, Validi, S, Dani, S and Antoniou, G (2019) Supply chain risk management and artificial intelligence: State of the art and future research directions, *International Journal of Production Research*, **57** (7), pp 2179–202

Bell, JE, Mollenkopf, DA and Stolze, HJ (2013) Natural resource scarcity and the closed-loop supply chain: A resource-advantage view, *International Journal of Physical Distribution and Logistics Management*, **43** (5–6), pp 351–79

Boersma, M (2017) *Do no harm? Procurement of medical goods by Australian companies and government*, retrieved from opus.lib.uts.edu.au/ bitstream/10453/95576/1/Do_No_Harm_Report.pdf (archived at https://perma.cc/KZ5K-L7ZX)

Braziotis, C, Rogers, H and Jimo, A (2019) 3D printing strategic deployment: The supply chain perspective, *Supply Chain Management: An International Journal*, **24** (3), pp 397–404

Broekhuizen, T, Emrich, O, Gijsenberg, M, Broekhuis, M, Donkers, B and Sloot, L (2021) Digital platform openness: Drivers, dimensions and outcomes, *Journal of Business Research*, **122**, pp 902–14

Burtonshaw-Gunn, S and Salameh, M (2009) *Essential Tools For Organisational Performance: Tools, models and approaches for managers and consultants*, John Wiley and Sons, London

Cheng, W, Appolloni, A, D'Amato, A and Zhu, Q (2018) Green public procurement, missing concepts and future trends: A critical review, *Journal of Cleaner Production*, **176**, pp 770–84

Culot, G, Nassimbeni, G, Orzes, G and Sartor, M (2020) Behind the definition of industry 4.0: Analysis and open questions, *International Journal of Production Economics*, **226**, pp 1–14

Dixit, V, Verma, P and Tiwari, MK (2020) Assessment of pre and post-disaster supply chain resilience based on network structural parameters with CVaR as a risk measure, *International Journal of Production Economics*, **227**, pp 1–15

Ehrenfeld, JR and Hoffman, AJ (2013) *Flourishing: A frank conversation about sustainability*, Stanford University Press, Stanford, CA

Elgendy, N and Elragal, A (2016) Big data analytics in support of the decision making process, *Procedia Computer Science*, **100**, pp 1071–084

Ellram, LM and Carr, A (1994) Strategic purchasing: A history and review of the literature, *International Journal of Purchasing and Materials Management*, **30** (1), pp 9–19 doi.org/10.1111/j.1745-493X.1994.tb00185.x (archived at https://perma.cc/3B4R-UJXH)

Ellram, LM and Murfield, MLU (2019) Supply chain management in industrial marketing – Relationships matter, *Industrial Marketing Management*, **79**, pp 36–45

Ellram, LM, Tate, WL and Feitzinger, EG (2013) Factor-market rivalry and competition for supply chain resources, *Journal of Supply Chain Management*, **49** (1), pp 29–46

Ford, JA, Verreynne, M-L and Steen, J (2018) Limits to networking capabilities: Relationship trade-offs and innovation, *Industrial Marketing Management*, **74**, pp 50–64

Ghadimi, P, Azadnia, AH, Heavey, C, Dolgui, A and Can, B (2016) A review on the buyer–supplier dyad relationships in sustainable procurement context: Past, present and future, *International Journal of Production Research*, **54** (5), pp 1443–462

Goebel, P, Reuter, C, Pibernik, R, Sichtmann, C and Bals, L (2018) Purchasing managers' willingness to pay for attributes that constitute sustainability, *Journal of Operations Management*, **62**, pp 44–58

Government Commercial Function (2019) *Market Management: Guidance Note*, HM Government: London, retrieved from assets.publishing.service.gov.uk/ government/uploads/system/uploads/attachment_data/file/816636/20190710-Market_Management_Guidance_Note.pdf (archived at https://perma.cc/3EV8-6GFH)

Guarnieri, P and Gomes, RC (2019) Can public procurement be strategic? A future agenda proposition, *Journal of Public Procurement*, **19** (4), pp 295–321

Hamborg, F, Lachnit, S, Schubotz, M, Hepp, T and Gipp, B (2018), *Giveme5W: main event retrieval from news articles by extraction of the five journalistic w questions*, Paper presented at the International Conference on Information, 15 March, Sheffield, UK, pp 356–66, Springer, Cham

Handfield, R (2019) Shifts in buyer-seller relationships: A retrospective on Handfield and Bechtel (2002) *Industrial Marketing Management*, **83**, pp 194–206

Hart, GJ (1996) The five W's: An old tool for the new task of audience analysis, *Technical Communication*, **43** (2), pp 139–45

Heide, JB and Miner, AS (1992) The shadow of the future: Effects of anticipated interaction and frequency of contact on buyer-seller cooperation, *Academy of Management Journal*, **35** (2), pp 265–91

Hezarkhani, B and Sošić, G (2018) Who's afraid of strategic behavior? Mechanisms for group purchasing, *Production and Operations Management*, **28** (4), pp 933–54

Hughes, A, Morrison, E and Ruwanpura, KN (2019) Public sector procurement and ethical trade: Governance and social responsibility in some hidden global supply chains, *Transactions of the Institute of British Geographers*, **44** (2), pp 242–55

Jain, V, Kumar, S, Soni, U and Chandra, C (2017) Supply chain resilience: Model development and empirical analysis, *International Journal of Production Research*, **55** (22), pp 6779–800

Johnsen, TE (2018) Purchasing and supply management in an industrial marketing perspective, *Industrial Marketing Management*, **69**, pp 91–97

Kalaitzi, D, Matopoulos, A, Bourlakis, M and Tate, W (2018) Supply chain strategies in an era of natural resource scarcity, *International Journal of Operations and Production Management*, **38** (3), pp 784–809

Khripunova, A, Vishnevskiy, K, Karasev, O and Meissner, D (2014) Corporate foresight for corporate functions: Impacts from purchasing functions, *Strategic Change*, **23** (3–4), pp 147–60, doi.org/10.1002/jsc.1967 (archived at https://perma.cc/YK3V-YSN3)

Knight, L and Meehan, J (2018) *The Future of Procurement and Supply Management*. Stamford, UK: Chartered Institute of Procurement and Supply Management (available to CIPS members at the CIPS website, or on request to the authors)

Knight, L, Meehan, J, Tapinos, E, Menzies, L and Pfeiffer, A (2020) Researching the future of purchasing and supply management: The purpose and potential of scenarios, *Journal of Purchasing and Supply Management*, **100624**, pp 1–9

Kohtamäki, M, Einola, S and Rabetino, R (2020) Exploring servitization through the paradox lens: Coping practices in servitization, *International Journal of Production Economics*, **226**, pp 1–15

Kunovjanek, M and Reiner, G (2020) How will the diffusion of additive manufacturing impact the raw material supply chain process? *International Journal of Production Research*, **58** (5), pp 1540–554

Lafuente, E, Vaillant, Y and Vendrell-Herrero, F (2017) Territorial servitization: Exploring the virtuous circle connecting knowledge-intensive services and new manufacturing businesses, *International Journal of Production Economics*, **192**, pp 19–28

Lamming, R (1993) *Beyond Partnership: Strategies for innovation and lean supply*, Prentice-Hall, Hemel Hempstead

Lăzăroiu, G, Ionescu, L, Uță, C, Hurloiu, I, Andronie, M and Dijmărescu, I (2020) Environmentally responsible behavior and sustainability policy adoption in green public procurement, *Sustainability*, **12** (5), p 2110

Legenvre, H, Henke, M and Ruile, H (2020) Making sense of the impact of the internet of things on purchasing and supply management: A tension perspective, *Journal of Purchasing and Supply Management*, **26** (1), pp 1–14

Li, T, Sahu, AK, Talwalkar, A and Smith, V (2020) Federated learning: Challenges, methods, and future directions, *IEEE Signal Processing Magazine*, **37** (3), pp 50–60

Lindberg, N and Nordin, F (2008) From products to services and back again: Towards a new service procurement logic, *Industrial Marketing Management*, **37** (3), pp 292–300

Loosemore, M, Alkilani, S and Mathenge, R (2020) The risks of and barriers to social procurement in construction: A supply chain perspective, *Construction Management and Economics*, **38** (6), pp 552–69

Min, S, Zacharia, ZG and Smith, CD (2019) Defining supply chain management: In the past, present, and future, *Journal of Business Logistics*, **40** (1), pp 44–55

Mogre, R, Lindgreen, A and Hingley, M (2017) Tracing the evolution of purchasing research: Future trends and directions for purchasing practices, *Journal of Business and Industrial Marketing*, **32**(2), pp 251–57

Monczka, RM, Handfield, RB, Giunipero, LC, Patterson, JL and Waters, D (2010) *Purchasing and Supply Chain Management*, South Western Cengage Learning, Boston, MA

Montabon, F, Pagell, M and Wu, Z (2016) Making sustainability sustainable, *Journal of Supply Chain Management*, **52** (2), pp 11–27

Nassimbeni, G, Sartor, M, Wan, L, Ancarani, A, Di Mauro, C, Mascali, F, Barbieri, P, Di Stefano, C, Fratocchi, L, Lapadre, L and Orzes, G (2019) *Future of manufacturing in Europe. Reshoring in Europe: Overview 2015–2018.* Luxembourg: Publications Office of the European Union

Noordhoff, CS, Kyriakopoulos, K, Moorman, C, Pauwels, P and Dellaert, BG (2011) The bright side and dark side of embedded ties in business-to-business innovation, *Journal of Marketing*, **75** (5), pp 34–52

Pagell, M and Shevchenko, A (2014) Why research in sustainable supply chain management should have no future, *Journal of Supply Chain Management*, **50** (1), pp 44–55

Papadopoulos, T, Gunasekaran, A, Dubey, R, Altay, N, Childe, SJ and Fosso-Wamba, S (2017) The role of Big Data in explaining disaster resilience in supply chains for sustainability, *Journal of Cleaner Production*, **142**, pp 1108–118

Paschou, T, Rapaccini, M, Adrodegari, F and Saccani, N (2020) Digital servitization in manufacturing: A systematic literature review and research agenda, *Industrial Marketing Management*, **89**, pp 278–92

Philippon, T (2019) *The Great Reversal: How America gave up on free markets*, Harvard University Press

Raddats, C, Kowalkowski, C, Benedettini, O, Burton, J and Gebauer, H (2019) Servitization: A contemporary thematic review of four major research streams, *Industrial Marketing Management*, **83**, pp 207–23

Rajala, R, Brax, SA, Virtanen, A and Salonen, A (2019) The next phase in servitization: Transforming integrated solutions into modular solutions, *International Journal of Operations and Production Management*, **39** (5), pp 630–57

Saha, RL, Seidmann, A and Tilson, V (2019) The impact of custom contracting and the infomediary role of healthcare GPOs, *Production and Operations Management*, **28** (3), pp 650–67

Sasse, T, Guerin, B, Nickson, S, O'Brien, M, Pope, T and Davies, N (2019) *Government Outsourcing: What has worked and what needs reform?*, Institute for Government, London

Schiele, H, Calvi, R and Gibbert, M (2012) Customer attractiveness, supplier satisfaction and preferred customer status: Introduction, definitions and an overarching framework, *Industrial Marketing Management*, **41** (8), pp 1178–185, doi.org/10.1016/j.indmarman.2012.10.002 (archived at https://perma.cc/BC8U-24V7)

Schiele, H and Torn, RJ (2020) Cyber-physical systems with autonomous machine-to-machine communication: Industry 4.0 and its particular potential for purchasing and supply management, *International Journal of Procurement Management*, **13** (4), pp 507–30 doi:10.1504/IJPM.2020.108627

Schneider, L and Wallenburg, CM (2013) 50 years of research on organizing the purchasing function: Do we need any more? *Journal of Purchasing and Supply Management*, **19** (3), pp 144–64, doi.org/10.1016/j.pursup.2013.05.001 (archived at https://perma.cc/RP3K-8CU9)

Schoenherr, T and Speier-Pero, C (2015) Data science, predictive analytics, and big data in supply chain management: Current state and future potential, *Journal of Business Logistics*, **36** (1), pp 120–32, doi.org/10.1111/jbl.12082 (archived at https://perma.cc/99MR-7L95)

Schotanus, F and Telgen, J (2007) Developing a typology of organisational forms of cooperative purchasing, *Journal of Purchasing and Supply Management*, **13** (1), pp 53–68

Schwieterman, M and Miller, J (2016) Factor market rivalry: Toward an integrated understanding of firm action, *Transportation Journal*, **55** (2), pp 97–123

Silvestri, F, Spigarelli, F and Tassinari, M (2020) Regional development of circular economy in the European Union: A multi-dimensional analysis, *Journal of Cleaner Production*, **255**, 120218

Singh, J, Graham, G, Lorentz, H, Phillips, W, Kapletia, D and Hennelly, P (2020) Distributed Manufacturing: A new form of localized production?, *International Journal of Operations and Production Management*, **40** (6), pp 697–727

Spina, G, Caniato, F, Luzzini, D and Ronchi, S (2013) Past, present and future trends of purchasing and supply management: An extensive literature review, *Industrial Marketing Management*, **42** (8), pp 1202–212

Srai, JS and Lorentz, H (2019) Developing design principles for the digitalisation of purchasing and supply management, *Journal of Purchasing and Supply Management*, **25** (1), pp 78–98

Svensson, G (2007) Aspects of sustainable supply chain management (SSCM): Conceptual framework and empirical example, *Supply Chain Management: An International Journal*, **12** (4), pp 262–66

Tate, WL, Ellram, LM and Dooley, KJ (2012) Environmental purchasing and supplier management (EPSM): Theory and practice, *Journal of Purchasing and Supply Management*, **18** (3), pp 173–88

Tip, B, Vos, FGS, Peters, E and Delke, V (2021) *A Kraljic and competitive rivalry perspective on hospital procurement during a pandemic (Covid-19): A Dutch case study*, Paper presented at the 30th Annual Conference of the International Purchasing and Supplier Education and Research Association, Online

Trent, RJ and Monczka, RM (1998) Purchasing and supply management trends and changes throughout the 1990s, *International Journal of Purchasing and Materials Management*, **34** (4), pp 2–11

Ulkuniemi, P, Araujo, L and Tähtinen, J (2015) Purchasing as market-shaping: The case of component-based software engineering, *Industrial Marketing Management*, **44**, pp 54–62

UN (2020) Take Action for the Sustainable Development Goals, retrieved from www.un.org/sustainabledevelopment/sustainable-development-goals/ (archived at https://perma.cc/G8RE-5E9M)

Virtanen, M, Manskinen, K, Uusitalo, V, Syvänne, J and Cura, K (2019) Regional material flow tools to promote circular economy, *Journal of Cleaner Production*, **235**, pp 1020–25

Vos, FGS (2017) *Preferred Customer Status, Supplier Satisfaction and their Contingencies*, Netzodruk, Enschede

Vurro, C, Russo, A and Perrini, F (2009) Shaping sustainable value chains: Network determinants of supply chain governance models, *Journal of Business Ethics*, **90** (4), pp 607–21

Walker, H, Schotanus, F, Bakker, E and Harland, C (2013) Collaborative procurement: a relational view of buyer–buyer relationships, *Public Administration Review*, **73** (4), pp 588–98

Wisner, JD and Tan, KC (2000) Supply chain management and its impact on purchasing, *Journal of Supply Chain Management*, **36** (3), pp 33–42

Wong, CW, Lirn, T-C, Yang, C-C and Shang, K-C (2020) Supply chain and external conditions under which supply chain resilience pays: An organizational information processing theorization, *International Journal of Production Economics*, **226**, pp 1–15

Wynstra, F, Suurmond, R and Nullmeier, F (2019) Purchasing and supply management as a multidisciplinary research field: Unity in diversity? *Journal of Purchasing and Supply Management*, **25** (5), pp 1–17

Yeniyurt, S, Henke, JW and Yalcinkaya, G (2014) A longitudinal analysis of supplier involvement in buyers' new product development: working relations, interdependence, co-innovation, and performance outcomes, *Journal of the Academy of Marketing Science*, **42** (3), pp 291–308

Yu, F, Yang, Y and Chang, D (2018) Carbon footprint based green supplier selection under dynamic environment, *Journal of Cleaner Production*, **170**, pp 880–89

Zheng, J, Knight, L, Harland, C, Humby, S and James, K (2007) An analysis of research into the future of purchasing and supply management, *Journal of Purchasing and Supply Management*, **13** (1), pp 69–83, doi.org/10.1016/j.pursup.2007.03.004 (archived at https://perma.cc/XDB2-R9QE)

Maximizing capacity utilization in freight transport

07

Alan McKinnon

Introduction

In an ideal world all freight vehicles would run fully laden on every kilometre travelled. While this vision of complete asset utilization is unattainable, the potential does exist to raise vehicle load factors well above their current level. This would reduce the distance that vehicles travel to deliver a given quantity of freight. In the short term, this would translate into lower transport costs, less fuel consumption and fewer emissions. In the longer term, it would allow companies to reduce fleet sizes, ease pressure on transport infrastructure and labour markets and offer a cost-effective means of decarbonizing freight transport.

This chapter examines the various ways in which the utilization of freight transport capacity can be assessed, considers the reasons why there is so much empty running and under-loading of vehicles and outlines a series of measures that companies can take to achieve higher levels of vehicle fill.

Research on this subject has been seriously constrained by a chronic lack of data. Very few governments or international organizations collect the data required to assess under-utilization at a macro level. Almost all the available statistics relate to road freight movements. This has made the efficiency of trucking operations the focus of academic research and the target for criticism, particularly from environmental groups, that hauliers do not do enough to fill their vehicles. Freight operators in the rail, maritime and aviation sectors escape similar scrutiny and censure, mainly because there is little hard evidence in the public domain of the under-utilization of their capacity. Anecdotal evidence, however, suggests that it is also substantial and endemic.

The wide disparity in the amount of utilization data available for road and other freight transport modes is reflected in the content of this chapter. This partly explains its primary concern with the loading of trucks. The focus on road freight can also be justified on the grounds that this mode accounts for roughly two-thirds of all CO_2 emissions from freight transport worldwide (OECD/ITF, 2019a) and that improved vehicle loading has been identified as one of the most cost-effective ways of reducing them (McKinnon, 2018; ALICE, 2019). It should also be noted that many of the causes of under-loading and of the opportunities for overcoming them apply to freight transport in general and not simply to road haulage. When the word 'vehicle' is used in this chapter it is often in a generic, cross-modal sense, also referring to the movement of freight in rail wagons, ships and planes as well as trucks and vans.

Assessing the utilization of freight transport capacity

Different indices can be used to measure the utilization of this capacity, each giving a different impression of transport efficiency. It is important to draw a distinction between 'productivity' and 'capacity utilization' as the two terms are sometimes confused. In a seminal review of logistics efficiency metrics, Caplice and Sheffi (1994, p 18) define productivity as a measure of 'transformational efficiency typically reported as the ratio of actual outputs produced to actual inputs consumed'. The productivity of a freight transport system is usually measured with respect to input variables such as labour, energy use, infrastructure and vehicle fleet size. It assesses how efficiently the system converts these inputs into an output of freight movement, typically measured in tonne-kilometres. Measured in this way the productivity of some freight transport systems has greatly improved over particular time periods. For example, the number of revenue tonne-kms moved annually per rail wagon in the United States rose 2.4 times between 1980 and 2008 (Martland *et al*, 2011). In the UK there was a five-fold increase in average tonne-kms per lorry per annum between the early 1950s and late 1990s (Department of Transport, 2005). While both trends were

Table 7.1 Comparison vehicle productivity and utilization measures

Gross weight	Max payload (tonnes)	Annual distance travelled (km)	Average load tonnes	Productivity Tonne-kms / veh / year	% Capacity utilization Actual t-km/ max t-km
32 tonnes	20	100,000	16	1,600,000	80%
40 tonnes	26	100,000	18	1,800,000	69%

very impressive, the indices used do not show how much of the productivity gain was due to better use of available carrying capacity. For example, the maximum gross weight of lorries in the UK increased by 83 per cent over a 40-year period, increasing the total amount of freight that could be carried by a lorry per annum, but this still left much available carrying capacity unused.

A vehicle with greater capacity can record higher productivity despite having inferior utilization, as illustrated in Table 7.1. Capacity utilization therefore needs to be separately monitored. Caplice and Sheffi (1994) defined it as the 'percentage of an input used to some norm value'. In a freight context this can be the ratio of the amount of carrying capacity actually used to the total amount available. Broadly speaking, this carrying capacity is measured in terms of weight, volume or both.

Weight-based measurement

Almost all the available statistics on freight loading, across all transport modes, is weight-based. This is because consignment weight is easily measured and usually has to be recorded for commercial, operational or legal reasons. Often data on payload weights is aggregated and averaged but without reference to the available carrying capacity of the vehicle. For example, Eurostat (2020) publishes statistics showing variations in average truck payload weights by EU country and through time, but in the absence of capacity data this does not permit analysis of percentage utilization. Even if it did, however, it would provide only a partial view of vehicle utilization because it would take no account of the proportion of space within the vehicle occupied by the load.

Volumetric measurement

Many low-density products fill the available vehicle space (or to use the jargon 'cube-out') long before the maximum permitted weight is reached. In sectors characterized by low-density products, weight-based load factors tend to underestimate the true level of utilization. Where there are tight limits on the stacking height of the product, loading is usually constrained much more by the available floor (or deck) area than by the cubic capacity. This deck area, for example, can be covered with pallets stacked to a height of 1.5 metres, leaving a metre or more of wasted space above them. So space utilization can be measured in both two and three dimensions.

It is generally acknowledged that the average density and 'stackability' of freight are declining. Table 7.2 lists the major reasons for these trends. This is increasing the relative importance of volumetric measures of vehicle utilization. Despite this, few attempts have been made to collect volumetric data on road freight flows, partly because it is often not required for operational reasons, but also because it is difficult to do on an accurate and consistent basis. In the case of unitized freight, moving in standardized handling units such as pallets or roll-cages, the ratio of actual units carried to the maximum that could be transported can be used as a proxy measure of space utilization. At the next level down, however, the internal utilization of these units can be highly variable, making this a very approximate indicator of cube fill at a vehicle level.

Very little research has been done on the volumetric utilization of freight vehicles. One of the first, conducted in the Netherlands and Sweden by Samuelsson and Tilanus (1997) asked a panel of industry experts to estimate the average utilization of trucks engaged in less-than-truckload deliveries, with reference to a series of space-related indices. This revealed that cube utilization was typically very low at around 28 per cent. On average, however, just over 80 per cent of deck area was occupied and 70 per cent of the available pallet positions filled. It was therefore mainly in the vertical dimension that space was being wasted, with average load heights reaching only 47 per cent of the maximum. A series of 'synchronized audits' of road freight efficiency in the UK between 1997 and 2009 shed much more light on the loading of vehicles with seven different categories of commodity, measuring capacity utilization by deck area, load height and weight (McKinnon, 2009). These studies not only revealed substantial under-loading of vehicles relative to the theoretical maxima; benchmarking of carrier data found wide variations in utilization within particular industry sectors.

Table 7.2 Reasons for the declining density and stackability of road freight

1. **Change in the nature of the products:** Many consumer products have become lighter through time, as plastic and other synthetic materials have increasingly replaced metal, wood and leather.

2. **Increase in packaging:** As packaging is relatively light, increases in the ratio of packaging volume to product volume reduces the average density of freight consignments.

3. **Greater use of unitized handling equipment:** This handling equipment takes up space in the vehicle and reduces the average weight / volume ratio for the overall payload.

4. **Declining rigidity:** In some sectors the increasing fragility of the product and weakening of packaging material is limiting the height to which it can be stacked. In the food and drink industry, for instance, cans have become thinner and rigid cardboard, plastic, or even wooden boxes have been replaced by cardboard trays, which offer little vertical support.

5. **Order-picking of palletized loads at an earlier stage in the supply chain:** The mixed pallet-loads that this produces tend to be lower, have an irregular profile and offer less opportunity for stacking.

6. **Tightening health and safety regulations:** These regulations have restricted the height to which pallets can be stacked to minimize the risk of injury to operatives during loading and unloading.

Combined weight and volume measurement

High density loads 'weigh-out' before they 'cube-out' while the opposite applies to products with a low density. Where possible it is therefore beneficial to combine products of differing density so that the mixed load comes closer to reaching both the weight and space limits. This requires companies to adopt a composite vehicle loading metric that takes account of both weight and volume. One company which has successfully done this is Procter & Gamble, taking advantage of wide variations in the density of the products it manufactures. Incorporating a 'cubefill' index into its calculations has enabled it to increase its truck utilization in Europe by 10–15 per cent (McKinnon and Petersen, 2021).

Empty running

The concept of empty running varies by freight transport mode. For example, in the rail freight sector it can be a locomotive running on its own to reposition motive power capacity, a trainload of empty wagons being returned as a complete set or a mixed load of empty and loaded wagons on the same train. In the maritime sector, it can be an empty bulk tanker on its way to collect a new load, empty slots on a container ship or roll-on roll-off ferry or the repositioning of empty containers either by sea or across port hinterlands. No published data is available on the various forms of empty running on the rail network, though it is possible to compile data on the movement of empty ships. One study has also analysed the annual global cost and carbon footprint of repositioning empty shipping containers at $15–20 billion and 19 million tonnes of CO_2 (Boston Consulting Group, 2015).

The amount of data available on the empty running of other freight modes is paltry by comparison with that available for road haulage. Many governments, particularly in Europe, track empty running as a performance metric in their annual surveys of road freight operations, generally expressing it as the percentage of truck kilometres run empty.

The proportion of empty running tends to vary with length of haul, type of vehicle, industrial sector and the nature of the delivery operation (McKinnon, 1996). It generally occurs when an operator is unable to find a suitable or commercially viable return load and must reposition its vehicle empty. Unlike passengers, who usually return to their starting point, most freight only travels in one direction. Finding backloads for otherwise empty trucks generates extra revenue and reduces total vehicle-kms, fuel consumption and emissions. The resulting economic and environmental benefits can be substantial. For example, without the drop in empty running by lorries in the UK from 33 per cent in 1980 to 27 per cent in 2004, road haulage costs in 2004 would have been £1.2 billion higher and CO_2 emissions 1 million tonnes greater (McKinnon and Ge, 2006). Unfortunately, since 2004 empty running in the UK has rebounded to 30 per cent (Department for Transport, 2020a) sharply contrasting with the results of a Delphi poll of expert opinion in 2008 which predicted that the proportion of empty running would drop to 21 per cent by 2020 (Piecyk and McKinnon, 2010).

Statistical evidence that 25–30 per cent of truck-kms are run empty can give the impression that there is huge inefficiency in road haulage and enormous potential for increasing backloading. On the contrary, a retrospective analysis of just under 9,000 road deliveries in the British food supply chain over a period of 48 hours revealed relatively few opportunities for backloading after allowance was made for a series of operational constraints (McKinnon and Ge, 2006). It may not be possible to extrapolate this result to other sectors and countries, though it does cast doubt on claims that empty running can be drastically reduced.

Factors constraining capacity utilization

There are many reasons for the under-loading of freight vehicles:

- *Demand fluctuations:* Variability of demand over daily, weekly, monthly and seasonal cycles is one of the main causes of the under-utilization. Vehicles that are acquired with sufficient capacity to accommodate peak loads inevitably spend much of their time under-used. Companies subject mainly to seasonal fluctuations can hire additional vehicles or outsource more of their transport at peak periods, allowing them to carry a regular base-load of traffic on their own vehicles during the year. For those exposed to demand volatility on a daily basis, the efficient management of transport capacity presents a more formidable challenge. Figure 7.1, for example, shows fluctuations in the daily demand for trucks experienced by a major distributor of metal products in the UK over the period of one month. The average daily requirement was for 150 vehicles, but on particular days it varied between 96 and 190 vehicles. The company in question was often only informed at 4 pm on Day 1 how many vehicles would be required for deliveries by noon on Day 2. It is clearly very difficult to maintain high load factors across a vehicle fleet when service demand is so variable and uncertain (Sanchez-Rodrigues *et al*, 2010).
- *Just-in-time (JIT) delivery:* The replenishment of supplies in smaller quantities more frequently within shorter lead times has tended to depress vehicle load factors. Companies are often prepared to accept lower vehicle utilization and higher transport costs in return for large reductions in inventory and other productivity benefits accruing from JIT. By reconfiguring their inbound logistics, however, companies, particularly in the automotive sector, have been able to mitigate the adverse effects of JIT on transport efficiency.
- *Unreliability of delivery schedules:* Where schedules are unreliable transport managers are naturally reluctant to arrange backhauls or more complex collection and delivery routes within which higher degrees of load consolidation can be achieved. Companies understandably prioritize distribution to customers and fear that a vehicle engaged in backhauling may not return in time to handle the next outbound delivery.

Figure 7.1 Variations in the daily demand for trucks experienced by a major distributor of metal products

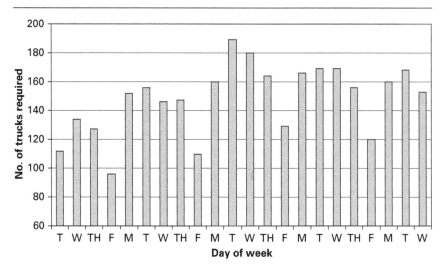

- *Vehicle size and weight restrictions:* As noted above, some loads 'cube-out' while others 'weigh-out' within current vehicle size and weight restrictions. If either or both of these restrictions are eased then a more balanced utilization of vehicle capacity by space and weight can be achieved. This is discussed in more detail in a later section.

- *Handling requirements:* Many companies sacrifice vehicle utilization for handling efficiency. For example, by using roll-cages rather than wooden pallets, supermarket chains can substantially reduce handling times and costs but at the expense of around 15–20 per cent lower cube utilization of shop delivery vehicles.

- *Incompatibility of vehicles and products:* It is clearly not possible to transport a return load of bulk liquids in a box van or to consolidate part-loads of fertilizer and hanging garments. Some companies use cross-contamination matrices to show which products cannot be combined in the same vehicle. The need for specialist handling and/or refrigeration can also restrict the proportion of the truck fleet that can be used for particular commodities.

- *Health and safety regulations:* The weight and dimensions of loads are partly constrained by health and safety regulations designed to ensure the welfare of employees.

- *Capacity constraints at company premises:* Often the size of load is constrained by the available storage capacity at either the origin or the destination of the trip, more commonly the latter. Tanks and silos at farms or factories, for example, may not be able to hold a full truckload, while many retailers have compressed back-storeroom areas to maximize the front-of-shop sales floor. Warehouse racking systems, particularly in the fast-moving consumer goods (FMCG) sector, have a standard slot height for pallets of 1.7 metres. This limits pallets to a height significantly below the vertical clearance of at least 2.4 metres in most articulated trucks.

- *Lack of information about backloading and load consolidation opportunities:* Many of these opportunities are missed because carriers are simply unaware of them. In the past companies relied on informal methods of finding backloads, most commonly 'word-of-mouth', or local brokerages. As discussed later, the internet has transformed the search for available loads, making the lack of market transparency much less of a constraint on backloading than in the past.

- *Geographical imbalances in the pattern of freight flow:* It is very difficult to maintain high levels of vehicle utilization when much more freight flows in one direction than the other. This is a problem that afflicts all freight transport modes. At a global scale, for example, in 2015 roughly 87 per cent more containerized trade moved eastbound on trans-Pacific sea routes than westbound (UNESCAP, 2018). At least in the maritime sector, the empty boxes have to be returned. A practice known as 'triangulation' has traditionally been used by carriers, across all modes, to maximize average loading where freight flows are unbalanced on particular corridors. Online freight procurement has made it easier, cheaper and more effective to apply this practice.

- *Poor coordination of the purchasing, sales and logistics functions:* Possible opportunities for backloading are often overlooked when procurement and sales managers are negotiating trading links. For example, purchasing departments typically regard inbound delivery as the responsibility of the supplier and fail to explore with logistics managers possible synergies with the transport operations of vendor companies. This reflects the silo structure that still exists in many businesses.

These 11 constraints can be classified into five general categories: regulatory, market-related, inter-functional, infrastructural and equipment-related

Figure 7.2   Five-fold classification of the constraints on vehicle utilization

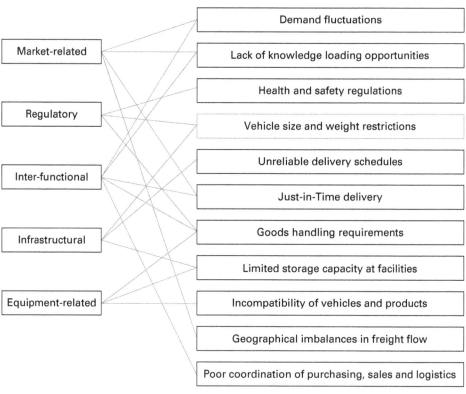

SOURCE McKinnon (2015)

(Figure 7.2). This network diagram shows how the same constraint can belong to more than one category, illustrating how complex and multi-dimensional the under-utilization problem can be.

The inter-functional category is particularly important as it relates to the relationship between transport and other activities such as production, pro-curement, inventory management, warehousing and sales. Companies often quite rationally give these other activities priority over transport efficiency. For example, inventory savings from JIT replenishment or reductions in handling costs accruing from the use of roll-cages may exceed the additional cost of running a truck only part loaded. It can also be economically justifi-able to deliver small orders to important customers in an effort to secure their longer-term loyalty. In under-utilizing their vehicles companies can therefore be behaving rationally and achieving higher-level logistics optimi-zation and/or profit maximization.

Much under-utilization of vehicle capacity, however, is not based on careful analysis of logistical cost trade-offs and explicit calculations of any related sales benefits. It is often unplanned and reflects the relatively low status given to transport within corporate hierarchies dominated by production, finance, marketing and sales. Often the most that a logistics manager can do is to optimize transport within the targets and constraints set by other departments. This may not always be in the best interests of the company, however. Ideally the costs, and increasingly the environmental impacts, of reduced vehicle utilization should be quantified and objectively weighed against the benefits derived from those activities that regularly impair transport efficiency. Santén (2016, p 65) also argues that logistics providers could do more to make their clients, the shippers, aware of 'their negative influence on load factor... for example, by demanding shorter lead times and delivering smaller shipments with a higher frequency'.

Measures to improve capacity utilization

This section outlines a range of measures that companies can adopt, individually and collaboratively, to make better use of vehicle capacity. It groups them under five headings:

- changes to business practice;
- adoption of more transport-efficient order cycles;
- changes to the vehicle;
- changes to the handling system and unitized loading;
- digitilization.

Changes to business practice

There is a limit to how much any company can do on its own to improve transport utilization. To reach high levels of utilization it is often necessary to collaborate with other companies. In supply chain terms, this collaboration can occur either horizontally or vertically.

Horizontal collaboration

This practice, which in more recent literature (eg Vanovermeire *et al*, 2014; Sanchez-Rodrigues *et al*, 2015) is called horizontal logistics collaboration, occurs where companies at the same level in the supply chain coordinate their freight demands to consolidate loads and/or create additional back-loading opportunities. There are many examples of two or more companies sharing transport capacity to their mutual benefit. Kellogg's and Kimberly-Clark, for example, firms with similarly low-density products and complementary transport demands, jointly saved around 430,000 vehicle-kms per annum by doing so (Anon, 2008). A much-cited collaboration between United Biscuits and Nestlé was more radical in that these companies were direct competitors in the biscuit/confectionery market. They nevertheless took the view that they 'competed on the shop shelf and not in the back of a lorry' and were able to achieve transport savings of around 280,000 vehicle-kms per annum mainly through eliminating empty journey legs (Hastings and Wright, 2009).

Several surveys have been conducted in the UK as part of a longer-term 'Starfish' project to assess the potential efficiency gains from 'multilateral' horizontal collaboration among a group of manufacturers, retailers and wholesalers in the FMCG sector. Using large company data-sets these studies have assessed the benefits of a series of collaboration scenarios. The most basic scenario, in which part-loads would be combined locally within existing facilities, when modelled with a sample of 27 companies, yielded cost and CO_2 savings of 4 to 5 per cent (Palmer and McKinnon, 2011). In a more recent survey of 10 companies (Palmer et al, 2016), the two most easily implementable scenarios were found to offer cost savings of between 7 and 9 per cent and CO_2 reductions of 5 to 10 per cent.

Despite a wealth of research evidence and numerous company case studies showing the economic and environmental benefits of horizontal collaboration, it is still the exception rather than the rule. It is inhibited by a range of factors including management culture, lack of trust and concerns about data privacy and legality. The supply chain conditions have also to be conducive for companies to coordinate their transport operations (Sanchez-Rodrigues et al, 2015). Following an exhaustive analysis of 'cross-chain logistical collaboration' Cruijssen (2020) outlines what businesses, government policy-makers and academics should do to promote its wider uptake. An investigation of logistical collaboration undertaken for the UK government (White et al, 2017, p 3) concluded that many of the 'easy wins' had been taken and recommended that a Collaboration Promotion Programme be introduced to raise awareness of the subject 'among key targeted audiences'.

Vertical collaboration

This involves collective action by trading partners at different levels in a supply chain, often with the assistance of logistics service providers. It can help to ease the first three constraints on vehicle utilization listed earlier, namely demand fluctuations, lack of information and JIT pressures. The term *collaborative transportation management* (CTM) is sometimes used to describe the sharing of information and coordination of transport planning between manufacturers, retailers and carriers to cut delivery costs while improving service quality. As Browning and White (2000, p 3) explain: 'CTM... re-engineers the whole process so that the carrier is now part of the larger, more focused buyer/seller team.' This can help to reduce the amount of uncertainty in the management of carriers' operations which is a major cause of capacity under-utilization (Sanchez-Rodrigues *et al*, 2010). By giving carriers an 'extended planning horizon' some were able to increase the utilization of their regional truck fleets in the United States by between 10 and 42 per cent, mainly as a result of improved backloading (Esper and Williams, 2003). Later simulation modelling demonstrated the wider supply chain benefits of CTM as well as its positive effect on vehicle load factors (Chan and Zhang, 2011).

Another initiative relating to the management of product flow through the vertical channel is *vendor-managed inventory* (VMI). This gives suppliers control over the replenishment process, enabling them to phase the movement of products in a way that makes more efficient use of vehicle capacity. Simulation modelling demonstrated the potential transport benefits of VMI over a 'traditional supply chain' (Disney, Potter and Gardner, 2003). Sometimes it is also necessary to increase storage capacity at the customer's premises to accommodate the delivery of supplies in full truckloads.

Cooperation between suppliers and retailers has also been rationalized in other ways to reduce empty running and improve vehicle fill. It is now common for supermarket chains to backload their returning shop delivery vehicles, many of which would otherwise have been empty, with inbound orders collected from suppliers' premises. In an 'onward delivery' system suppliers' vehicles on their way back from a retailer's distribution centre deliver loads to its shops on or near the return routes. These practices eliminate empty journey legs and, where the amount of deviation from the direct routes is small, the net saving in vehicle-kms, fuel and emissions can be substantial.

Adoption of more transport-efficient order cycles

The nature of the order-fulfilment process can have a significant impact on the efficiency of the transport operation. There are ways in which this process can be modified to allow firms to increase the degree of load consolidation and hence improve transport efficiency. For example, firms operating a 'nominated day delivery system' (NDDS) inform customers that a vehicle will be visiting their area on a 'nominated' day and that to receive a delivery on that day they must submit their order a certain period in advance. The advertised order lead time then becomes conditional on the customer complying with the order schedule. By concentrating deliveries in particular areas on particular days, suppliers can achieve higher levels of load consolidation, drop density and vehicle utilization. This practice can weaken the competitiveness of a company's service offering and possibly result in sales losses in excess of the transport cost savings. The experience of many businesses that have applied NDDS suggests that this rarely occurs.

Many companies invoice their customers at the end of each month, giving them an incentive to order at the start of the month and thereby obtain a longer period of interest-free credit. This can induce wide monthly fluctuations in freight traffic levels, making it difficult for firms to manage their vehicle capacity efficiently. By relaxing the monthly payment cycle and moving to a system of 'rolling credit', in which customers are still granted the same payment terms but from the date of the order rather than the start of the month, suppliers can significantly improve the average utilization of their logistics assets. This, however, can breach long-established practices in sales and finance departments.

Reverse logistics

As the principles of the circular economy become more widely applied, the proportion of products moving back along the supply chain for repair, reuse, recycling or remanufacture will increase (Weetman, 2020). This creates new opportunities for the backloading of vehicles in many industrial and retail sectors. It has been common practice for many years for retailers to use their shop delivery vehicles for the return of packaging waste and surplus stock to distribution centres and 'resource recovery units' (Cherrett *et al*, 2015). The challenge for all businesses is now to integrate the strengthening flow of 'returns' into their logistics systems in a way that maximizes vehicle loading within organizational and operational constraints.

Changes to the vehicle

Vehicles can be re-designed to permit greater load consolidation. For example, the compartmentalization of trucks has enabled grocery retailers and their logistics providers to combine the movement of frozen, chilled and ambient-temperature products on the same trip. Foldable ISO containers can be collapsed when empty to allow four or five to be transported on a single trailer, greatly reducing the amount of traffic generated by the repositioning of empty boxes across port hinterlands (Goh, 2019). Some companies, such as the UK supermarket chain Waitrose, have even adjusted the height of their vehicles downward to match the typical height of the loads they carry, reversing the usual principle of taking vehicle capacity as a given and maximizing the load within it. Much more common is the enlargement of freight vehicles to permit higher levels of load consolidation.

As discussed earlier, very few loads simultaneously reach vehicle weight and volume limits. In the UK in 2001, only 7 per cent of lorry loads simultaneously reached the vehicle weight and volume limits. In that year the legal limit on the maximum gross weight of lorries was raised from 41 to 44 tonnes. According to annual surveys by the Department of Transport over the following seven years, the proportion of loads weighing-out and cubing-out at the same time increased to 37 per cent. Over the first three years of the new limits the resulting load consolidation was estimated to have cut traffic levels, road haulage costs and CO_2 emissions by, respectively, 290 million vehicle-kms, £240 million and 530,000 tonnes (McKinnon, 2005). This was a good demonstration of the infrastructural, commercial and environmental benefits that can flow from this type of regulatory change.

It was noted earlier that the average density and stackability of freight appear to be declining. As a consequence, many road freight operators have greater need for extra cubic capacity than for heavier weight limits. Truck dimensions are constrained, among other things, by the geometry of road layouts, bridge and tunnel heights and the loading facilities at industrial and retail premises. Where transport infrastructure permits, extra space can be gained by lengthening vehicles or making them taller. In most countries, height clearances over the road network limit the latter option, making lengthening of the vehicle the only practical solution.

In an increasing number of countries, vehicle length and weight limits have been relaxed to allow companies to run so-called 'longer and heavier vehicles' (LHVs) (also known as 'high capacity vehicles (HCVs)'), typically 25 metres or more in length and with maximum gross weights in excess of

50 tonnes. The benefits and costs of legalizing such vehicles have been thoroughly researched. Some studies have been based on simulation modelling; others on the extensive real-world experience of operating these vehicles in Scandinavia, North America, Australia and New Zealand, South Africa and an expanding group of EU member states that have permitted these vehicles since 2012, including the Netherlands, Denmark and Spain. This research was comprehensively reviewed by Steer Davies Gleave (2013) for the European Parliament and by the International Transport Forum (OECD/ITF 2010 and 2019b). The ITF's most recent report concludes that, with 'well-crafted policy instruments' HCVs can 'promote a blending of improved road freight productivity and safety... including reduced fuel use and carbon emissions per unit of cargo transported, without any significant additional stress to infrastructure' (OECD/ITF, 2019b, p 81). It allays concerns about the displacement of freight to lower cost LHVs from other less environmentally damaging modes, particularly rail, and the possibility that the consequent cost savings might generate more freight movement overall.

The lengthening of trucks in the UK has been more modest and done on a trial basis. It permits articulated vehicles with semi-trailers one or two metres longer than the 13.6 metre standard, the latter extension offering 15 per cent more cubic capacity. After eight years this relaxation of the vehicle length limit was reckoned to be reducing vehicle-kms by 8 per cent for those companies using them, eliminating roughly one journey in 12 (Department for Transport, 2020b). In the UK, however, the cubic capacity of road trailers has mainly increased vertically, taking advantage of the unusually generous height clearances of up to 5 metres across most of the UK road network (by comparison with 4.0–4.2 metres elsewhere in Europe). This allows companies to double-deck their trailers, increasing volumetric carrying capacity by 80 to 90 per cent depending on the trailer configuration and density of the product, almost halving vehicle-kms, delivery costs and CO_2 emissions (Freight Best Practice Programme, 2007).

It is also possible to increase the maximum weight-carrying capacity of a truck within legal restrictions by reducing the weight of the empty vehicle (or 'tare' weight). This can be done by building vehicles with more lightweight materials such as aluminium, plastic and carbon fibre. In a UK study, Galos *et al* (2015) found that cutting the weight of trailers carrying 'mass-constrained' loads by 30 per cent could reduce the energy intensity of deliveries by between 11 per cent and 18 per cent. In guidance to US trucking companies, however, NACFE (2015) suggests that lightweighting can be a relatively expensive way of cutting fuel consumption, except for companies whose vehicles run close to the weight limit on most trips.

Changes to handling systems and unitized loading

The space-efficiency of handling equipment can be improved to allow companies to pack more product into the available vehicle cube. Companies always have to reconcile the desire to maximize vehicle fill with the need to protect consignments from damage in transit and to minimize loading/ unloading times and costs. The following examples illustrate the effects that changes to handling systems can have on the transport operation:

- *Choice of loading method:* one large mail order company managed to improve vehicle cube utilization and cut vehicle-kms by 6 per cent by loading parcels loose rather than in bags. Manually stacking loose product on the floor of a vehicle or container (a practice sometimes called 'deadpiling') can substantially increase fill, but is much slower and more labour-intensive than the mechanized loading and unloading of handling units such as pallets, roll-cages and stillages. It is common, however, where labour costs are low and containers moved long distances as in the case of container traffic from the Far East to Europe and North America.

- *Dimensions of handling units:* standardizing on more efficient sizes and shapes of handling equipment that correspond more closely to vehicle and container dimensions offers the potential to significantly improve load factors. For example, a New Modular Loading Unit (NMLU) proposed by the Clusters 2.0 (2020) project could improve 'load efficiency' by 13–38 per cent depending on the density of the freight.

- *Stacking height:* the height to which goods are stacked on pallets is often constrained by the slot height in warehouse racking systems (typically 1.7 metres) whereas articulated trailers commonly have internal heights of 2.4 metres. As a result, vehicles transport a lot of air above the load. Better coordination of vehicle and warehouse design can help to improve vehicle fill.

- *Use of slip sheets:* the use of these narrow sheets, rather than wooden pallets, can increase the available payload and cubic capacity of a 40-tonne articulated truck in Europe by, respectively, 3 per cent and 16 per cent (ECR Europe, 2000).

- *Load-building software tools:* These software packages help companies optimize the loading of freight vehicles and containers using data on the dimensions of individual consignments to show how they should be positioned to maximize cube fill.

Digitalization

In the late 1990s there was a proliferation of start-up businesses offering internet-based load-matching services and web-enabled procurement of freight services (Lewis, 2002). This made it easier to match supply with demand in the road freight sector on both a short- and medium-term basis. One online freight exchange estimated that companies using its procurement services were able to cut their transport costs by an average of 8 per cent by increasing 'carrier's asset utilization while protecting their margins' (Mansell, 2006, p 27). The functionality, diversity and uptake of online platforms for the buying and selling of freight capacity have all greatly increased over the past 20 years:

- Visibility of the freight market has improved, particularly with the advent of big data and cloud computing and a huge growth in the proportion of the truck fleet that can be tracked in real-time.

- Higher levels of carrier and shipper participation have increased the probability of load-matches that meet operational and commercial criteria.

- Performance of the algorithms used by the online platforms has been substantially upgraded, partly with the use of artificial intelligence and machine learning.

- Use of mobile devices has decentralized the load-matching process and made it more accessible to the large population of small operators that account for a large share of the road freight market in most countries. This has been described as the 'Uberisation of freight' (LEK Consulting, 2017).

- Online trading of freight capacity has spread to other transport modes, particularly with the development of a new generation of 'digital freight forwarders' and the digital transformation of 'legacy' forwarders, much of whose business is in the shipping and air cargo markets.

- Online freight procurement has diffused into emerging markets, such as India and China, characterized by rapidly rising freight traffic levels and high levels of empty running.

While these digitalization processes are already well underway, their full impact on the utilization of freight capacity has yet to be felt. In a recent

European survey, three-quarters of a sample of senior executives indicated that they expect digitalization to have a transformational impact on logistics over the next five years (McKinnon and Petersen, 2021). They expect its main impacts to be felt through improved supply chain visibility, vehicle telematics, advances in transport management systems, online logistics platforms and innovations in vehicle routing, all of which can enhance capacity utilization.

Looking well beyond a five-year horizon, the development of a 'physical internet' 'based on the interconnection of logistics networks by a standardized set of collaboration protocols, modular containers and smart interfaces' (Ballot *et al*, 2014) offers the prospect of much higher levels of asset utilization being achieved in warehouses and terminals as well as vehicles. While digitalization lies at the heart of this ambitious vision of the future of logistics, its realization will also depend on fundamental changes in organizational structures, business practice and materials handling.

Conclusion

The utilization of freight capacity has always to be optimized within a range of constraints. This chapter has examined these constraints and recommended a series of actions that companies and governments can take to help overcome them. Achieving a substantial improvement in the average loading of freight vehicles will require a combination of technological, operational, behavioural and regulatory changes. One of the main drivers of this improvement will be the mounting pressure to decarbonize freight transport operations over the next few decades. Unlike many other decarbonization options for the freight sector (discussed in Chapter 13), measures which increase vehicle utilization can be implemented in the short-to-medium term and offer economic as well as environmental benefits. They therefore merit their reputation as 'low hanging fruit' to be harvested in the pursuit of sustainable logistics.

References

ALICE (2019) *Roadmap towards Zero Emissions European Logistics by 2050*, Brussels, retrieved from: www.etp-logistics.eu/wp-content/uploads/2019/12/ Alice-Zero-Emissions-Logistics-2050-Roadmap-WEB.pdf (archived at https://perma.cc/7V99-HY9Y)

Anon (2008) Collaboration brings savings for Kellogg's and Kimberly-Clark, *Logistics Manager*, 13 October

Ballot, E, Russell, M and Montreuil, B (2014) *The Physical Internet: the Network of Logistics Networks*, Paris: PREDIT

Boston Consulting Group (2015) *BCG launches platform that could save the container industry billions of dollars*, press release, 17 November, BCG, retrieved from: www.bcg.com/d/press/17november2015-bcg-launches-xchange-22133 (archived at https://perma.cc/3HAQ-WT9Q)

Browning, B and White, B (2000) *Collaborative transportation management: A proposal*, White Paper, Logility Inc, Atlanta

Caplice, C and Sheffi, Y (1994) A review and evaluation of logistics metrics, *International Journal of Logistics Management*, 5 (2), pp 11–28

Chan, FTS and Zhang, T (2011) The impact of collaborative transportation management on supply chain performance: A simulation approach, *Expert Systems with Applications*, 38 (3), pp 2319–329

Cherrett, T, Maynard, S, McLeod, F and Hickford, A (2015) Reverse logistics for the management of waste, in *Green Logistics*, 2nd edn, ed AC McKinnon, M Browne and Whiteing, Kogan Page, London

Clusters 2.0 (2020) *NMLU a Clusters 2.0 Innovation: Fast, efficient and smart*, retrieved from: www.clusters20.eu/wp-content/uploads/2020/07/20200702_NMLU-webinar_final_compressed-2.pdf (archived at https://perma.cc/98YR-ASJK)

Cruijssen, F (2020) *Cross-chain Collaboration in Logistics: Looking back and ahead*, Springer, Cham

Department for Transport (2005) *Transport Statistics Great Britain*, The Stationery Office, London

Department for Transport (2020a) *Road freight: domestic and international statistics*, DfT, London, retrieved from: www.gov.uk/government/collections/road-freight-domestic-and-international-statistics (archived at https://perma.cc/GD35-LMNH)

Department for Transport (2020b) *GB Longer Semi-Trailer trial: 2019 Annual Report*, Department for Transport, London

Disney, S, Potter, A and Gardner, B (2003) The impact of VMI on transport operations, *Transportation Research part E: Logistics and Transportation*, 39, pp 363–80

ECR Europe (2000) *Transport Optimisation Report*, Brussels

Esper, TL and Williams, LR (2003) The value of collaborative transportation management (CTM): Its relationship to CPFR and information technology, *Transportation Journal*, 42 (4), pp 55–65

Eurostat (2020) *Road Freight Transport Statistics*, Luxembourg, retrieved from: ec.europa.eu/eurostat/statistics-explained/index.php/Road_freight_transport_statistics

Freight Best Practice Programme (2007) *Focus on double decks*, Department for Transport, London

Galos, J, Sutcliffe, M, Cebon, D, Piecyk, M and Greening, P (2015) Reducing the energy consumption of heavy goods vehicles through the application of lightweight trailers: Fleet case studies, *Transportation Research Part D: Transport and Environment*, **41** (Supplement C), pp 40–49

Goh, SH (2019) The impact of foldable ocean containers on back haul shippers and carbon emissions, *Transportation Research Part D*, **67**, pp 514–27

Hastings, R and Wright, R (2009) *Working with your competitor to remove empty trucks from the roads*, presentation to IGD Sustainable Distribution conference, London, 10 June

LEK Consulting (2017) *The Uberization of Freight: Perhaps but it will be a long haul*, retrieved from www.lek.com/sites/default/files/insights/pdf-attachments/1908_Uberization_for_Freight.pdf (archived at https://perma.cc/2CW8-TKFZ)

Lewis, CN (2002) Freight exchanges: How are the survivors faring, *e.logistics magazine*, **16**

Mansell, G (2006) Transport tendering comes of age, *Transport and Logistics Focus*, **8** (4), pp 26–28

Martland, CD, Lewis, P and Kreim, Y (2011) *Productivity Improvements in the US Rail Freight Industry 1980-2010*, Massachusetts Institute of Technology, Boston, MA

McKinnon, AC (1996) The empty running and return loading of road goods vehicles, *Transport Logistics*, **1** (1), pp 1–19

McKinnon, AC (2005) The economic and environmental benefits of increasing maximum truck weight: the British experience, *Transportation Research Part D*, **10** (1), pp 77–95

McKinnon, AC (2009) Benchmarking road freight transport: review of a government-sponsored programme, *Benchmarking: An International Journal*, **16** (5), pp 640–56

McKinnon, AC (2015) Opportunities for improving vehicle utilisation, in *Green Logistics: Improving the environmental sustainability of logistics*, eds AC McKinnon, M Browne, MI Piecyk and A Whiteing, 3rd edn, Kogan Page, London

McKinnon, AC (2018) *Decarbonizing Logistics: Distributing goods in a low carbon world*, Kogan Page, London

McKinnon, AC and Ge, Y (2006) The potential for reducing empty running by trucks: A retrospective analysis, *International Journal of Physical Distribution and Logistics Management*, **36** (5), pp 391–410

McKinnon, AC and Petersen, M (2021) *Measuring Industry's Temperature: An environmental progress report on European Logistics*, Center for Sustainable Logistics and Supply Chains, Kühne Logistics University, Hamburg

North American Council for Freight Efficiency (2015) *Trucking Efficiency Confidence Report: Lightweighting*, retrieved from: nacfe.org/technology/lightweighting-2/ (archived at https://perma.cc/L9Y6-4ZS8)

OECD/ITF (2010) *Moving Freight with Better Trucks*, OECD, Paris

OECD/ITF (2019a) *Transport Outlook 2019*, OECD, Paris

OECD/ITF (2019b) *High Capacity Transport Towards Efficient, Safe and Sustainable Road Freight*, OECD, Paris

Palmer, A and McKinnon, AC (2011) An analysis of the opportunities for improving transport efficiency through multilateral collaboration in FMCG supply chains, in *Proceedings of the Logistics Research Network Annual Conference*, ed T Cherrett *et al*, University of Southampton

Palmer, A, Dadich, P and Greening, P (2016) *Project 3D: Reconfiguring logistics networks (STARFISH II)*, Centre for Sustainable Road Freight, Heriot-Watt University, Edinburgh

Piecyk, MI and McKinnon, A C (2010) Forecasting the carbon footprint of road freight transport in 2020, *International Journal of Production Economics*, **128** (1), pp 31–42

Samuelsson, A and Tilanus, B (1997) A framework efficiency model for goods transportation, with an application to regional less-than-truckload distribution, *Transport Logistics*, **1** (2), pp 139–51

Sanchez-Rodrigues, V, Harris, I and Mason, R (2015) Horizontal logistics collaboration for enhanced supply chain performance: An international retail perspective, *Supply Chain Management: an International Journal*, **20** (6), pp 631–47

Sanchez-Rodrigues, V, Potter, A and Naim, MM (2010) The impact of logistics uncertainty on sustainable transport operations, *International Journal of Physical Distribution and Logistics Management*, **40** (1/2), pp 61–83

Santén, V (2016) *Towards environmentally sustainable freight transport: Shippers' logistics actions to improve load factor performance* (Doctoral thesis), Chalmers University of Technology, retrieved from /publications.lib.chalmers.se/publication/243257-towards-environmentally-sustainable-freight-transport-shippers-logistics-actions-to-improve-load-fac (archived at https://perma.cc/5NGX-SF9Q)

Steer Davies Gleave (2013) *A Review of Megatrucks*, Transport and Tourism Committee, Directorate General for Internal Policies, European Parliament, Brussels

UNESCAP (2018) *Regional Shipping and Port Development*, Chapter 5, retrieved from: www.unescap.org/sites/default/files/pub_2484_CH5.pdf (archived at https://perma.cc/69TD-3GLY)

Vanovermeire, C, Sörensen, K, Van Breedam, A, Vannieuwenhuyse, B and Verstrepen, S (2014) Horizontal logistics collaboration: Decreasing costs through flexibility and an adequate cost allocation strategy, *International Journal of Logistics: Research and Applications*, **17** (4), pp 339–55

Weetman, C (2020) *Circular Economy Handbook for Business and Supply Chains*, 2nd edn, Kogan Page, London

White, M, Willis, S, Douglas, C and Walker, R (2017) *Freight Industry Collaboration Study*, TRL, Crowthorne

Retail logistics   08

John Fernie

Introduction

Retailers were once effectively the passive recipients of products, allocated to stores by manufacturers in anticipation of demand. Today, retailers are the active designers and controllers of product supply in reaction to known customer demand. They control, organize and manage the supply chain from production to consumption. This is the essence of the retail logistics and supply chain transformation that has taken place during the last 25–40 years (Fernie and Sparks, 2018, p 9). On writing this two years earlier, little would we know that the world would be gripped by a pandemic that would cause the closure of shops and hospitality facilities for months. High streets and cities were eerily quiet and supply chains were either severely stretched or barely ticking over.

It was always the intention to completely revise this chapter from the earlier edition in 2014 but the 'new normal' has added another dimension to the work. Some of the earlier material has the same broad structure, discussing the evolution of the logistics concept and logistics and competitive strategy in retailing. The remaining sections are new and reflect the most significant developments in retail logistics this century. So we discuss the internationalization of the retail supply chain with particular reference to fashion supply chains. This conveniently links into corporate social responsibility (CSR) and sustainability issues that have arisen from offshore sourcing and outsourcing to third-party intermediaries in Asian and other more distant geographic markets. Fashion is one of the most resource-intensive industries in the world in terms of its use of water and chemicals although most attention tends to focus upon social responsibility issues such as wages, working hours and working conditions. The penultimate section deals with the impact of the online revolution on retail supply chains, discussing the costs of providing a range of options from home delivery, click-and-collect and dealing with returns. Finally, the section on 'the future' tries to forecast a future faced with so much uncertainty. However, we review how retailers have responded to the pandemic and the likely scenarios for the post-pandemic environment.

The evolution of the logistics concept

The roots of supply chain management as a discipline are often attributed to the management guru Peter Drucker and his seminal article in *Fortune* magazine in 1962. At this time he was discussing distribution as one of the key areas of business, where major efficiency gains could be achieved and costs saved. Then, and through the next two decades, the supply chain was still viewed as a series of disparate functions. Thus, logistics management was depicted as two separate schools of thought, one dealing with materials management (industrial markets), the other with physical distribution management (consumer goods markets). In terms of the marketing function, research has focused upon buyer–seller relationships and the shift away from adversarial relationships to those built upon trust – see the work of the IMP group, for example (Ford *et al*, 2011). At the same time, a body of literature was developing, mainly in the UK, on the transformation of retail logistics from a manufacturer-driven to a retail-controlled system (McKinnon, 1989; Fernie, 1990; Fernie and Sparks, 2018). (See also Fernie, Sparks and McKinnon (2010) for a review of the development of retail logistics in the UK.)

In both industrial and consumer markets, several key themes began to emerge:

- the shift from a push to a pull, ie a demand-driven supply chain;
- the customer is gaining more power in the marketing channel;
- the role of information systems to gain better control of the supply chain;
- the elimination of unnecessary inventory in the supply chain; and,
- the focus on core capabilities and increasing the likelihood of outsourcing non-core activities to specialists.

To achieve maximum effectiveness of supply chains, it is imperative that integration takes place by 'the linking together of previously separated activities within a single system' (Slack *et al*, 1998, p 303). This means that companies have had to review their internal organization to eliminate duplication and ensure that total costs can be reduced rather than allowing separate functions (including marketing) to control their costs in a sub-optimal manner. Similarly, supply chain integration can be achieved by establishing ongoing relationships with trading partners along the supply chain.

Throughout the 1970s and 1980s, attention in industrial marketing focused upon the changes promulgated by the processes involved in improving efficiencies in manufacturing. Total quality management, business process re-engineering and continuous improvement brought Japanese business thinking to Western manufacturing operations. The implementation of these practices was popularized by Womack, Jones and Roos's (1990) book on the machine that changed the world. Not surprisingly, much of the literature on buyer–seller relationships focused upon the car-manufacturing sector. The update by Womack and Jones (2005) of the state of 'lean solutions' put retailing (or at least some retailers) at the heart of the changes underway. In this retail context it is claimed that food retailers such as Tesco have increasingly embraced such lean principles for parts of their business (eg Jones 2002; Leahy 2012; Evans and Mason, 2015).

During the 1990s, this focus on lean production was challenged in the United States and in the UK because of an over-reliance on efficiency measures rather than innovative responses. Harrison, Christopher and Van Hoek (1999) have therefore developed an agile supply chain model that is highly responsive to market demand. Agility as a concept was developed in the United States in response to the Japanese success in lean production. Agility plays to US strengths of entrepreneurship and information systems technology. Harrison, Christopher and Van Hoek (1999) argue that the improvements in the use of information technology to capture 'real-time' data mean less reliance on forecasts and the creation of a virtual supply chain between trading partners. By sharing information, process integration will take place between partners who focus upon their core competences. The final link in the agile supply chain is the network where a confederation of partners structure, coordinate and manage relationships to meet customer needs.

Both approaches have their proponents. There is, however, no reason why supply systems may not be a combination of both lean and agile approaches, with each used when most appropriate – the so-called 'leagile' approach (Mason-Jones, Naylor and Towill, 2000; Naylor, Naim and Berry, 1999; Towill and Christopher, 2002). Table 8.1 provides a summary comparison of lean, agile and leagile supply chains (Agarawal, Shanker and Tiwari, 2006). It can be seen that they have value in particular circumstances.

Table 8.1   Comparison of lean, agile and leagile supply chains

Distinguishing attributes	Lean supply chain	Agile supply chain	Leagile supply chain
Market demand	Predictable	Volatile	Volatile and unpredictable
Product variety	Low	High	Medium
Product life cycle	Long	Short	Short
Customer drivers	Cost	Lead time and availability	Service level
Profit margin	Low	High	Moderate
Dominant costs	Physical costs	Marketability costs	Both
Stock-out penalties	Long-term contractual	Immediate and volatile	No place for stock-out
Purchasing policy	Buy goods	Assign capacity	Vendor-managed inventory
Information enrichment	Highly desirable	Obligatory	Essential
Forecast mechanism	Algorithmic	Consultative	Both/either
Typical products	Commodities	Fashion goods	Product as per customer demand
Lead time compression	Essential	Essential	Desirable
Eliminate muda (waste)	Essential	Desirable	Arbitrary
Rapid reconfiguration	Desirable	Essential	Essential
Robustness	Arbitrary	Essential	Desirable
Quality	Market qualifier	Market qualifier	Market qualifier
Cost	Market winner	Market qualifier	Market winner
Lead time	Market qualifier	Market qualifier	Market qualifier
Service level	Market qualifier	Marker winner	Market winner

SOURCE After Agarawal *et al* (2006)

Logistics and competitive strategy in retailing

Many of the current ideas on supply chain management and competitive advantage have their roots in the work of Porter (1985) who introduced the concept of the value chain in relation to competitive advantage. These ideas have been further developed by academics such as Martin Christopher in the UK (see Christopher and Peck, 1997). In essence, we have a supply chain model whereby at each stage of the chain, value is added to the product through manufacturing, branding, packaging, display at the store and so on. At the same time, at each stage cost is added in terms of production costs, branding costs and overall logistics costs. The trick for companies is to manage this chain to create value for the customer at an acceptable cost. The managing of this so-called 'pipeline' has been a key challenge for logistics professionals in the 1990s, especially with the realization that the reduction of time not only reduced costs but gave competitive advantage.

According to Christopher and Peck (2003) there are three dimensions to time-based competition that must be managed effectively if an organization is going to be responsive to market changes. These are:

- *time to market* – the speed at bringing a business opportunity to market;
- *time to serve* – the speed at meeting a customer's order; and
- *time to react* – the speed at adjusting output to volatile responses to demand.

In the current Covid-19 crisis the last principle has been particularly relevant as companies have had to respond to exceptional changes with a slump in demand for many non-essential goods and an increase in demand for online grocery services.

Christopher and Peck (2003) used these principles to develop strategies for lead time management. By understanding the lead times of the integrated web of suppliers necessary to manufacture a product they argue that a 'pipeline map' can be drawn to represent each stage in the supply chain process from raw materials to customer. In these maps it is useful to differentiate between 'horizontal' and 'vertical' time: *horizontal time* is time spent on processes such as manufacture, assembly, in-transit or order processing; *vertical time* is the time when nothing is happening, no value is added but only cost and products/materials are standing as inventory.

It was in fashion markets that the notion of 'time-based competition' had most significance (Fernie and Grant, 2019), in view of the short time window for changing styles. In addition, the prominent trend in the last 20 years has been to source products offshore, usually in low-cost Pacific Rim nations, which lengthened the physical supply chain pipeline. These factors combined to illustrate the trade-offs that have to be made in supply chain management and on how to develop closer working relationships with supply chain partners, whether local or distant. The fast fashion retailers that have embraced time-based competition have fallen into two categories: those without factories (eg H&M, Top Shop) and the well documented vertically integrated firms (eg Zara and Benetton) with their unique business models (Tokatli, 2008; Lopez and Fan, 2009; Fernie and Perry, 2011; Bhardwaj and Fairhurst, 2010).

Zara broke the traditional four-seasons collections and 'slow' fashion that dominated the high street. By the 1990s it had invested heavily in an information and logistics infrastructure that allowed it to respond quickly to the latest fashion trends (Ferdows, Lewis and Machura, 2004). New ideas and fashion trends were evaluated so that around 11,000 items were selected from 30,000 designs. These were then produced in-house with the labour-intensive finishing stages being contracted to nearby Spanish and Portuguese suppliers. Lead times were three to six weeks and stores received product twice a week from its 500,000-square-metre distribution centre based at its headquarters in La Coruna. More importantly, store managers monitored sales through hand-held monitors so that the correct quantities of stock could be allocated across the store portfolio. This meant that Zara offered a wider range yet a lower inventory than its competitors. It played upon the notion of freshness and originality, thereby creating a feeling of exclusivity. It is not surprising, therefore, that customers visited Zara's stores more frequently than the competition. The international retailer, ASOS, has replicated Zara's time-based model to an online market environment.

Another catalyst for many of the initiatives in lead time reduction came from work undertaken by Kurt Salmon Associates (KSA) in the United States in the mid-1980s. KSA were commissioned by US garment suppliers to investigate how they could compete with Far East suppliers. The results were revealing in that the supply chains were long (one year three months from loom to store), badly coordinated and inefficient (Christopher and Peck, 1998). The concept of quick response was therefore initiated in order to reduce lead times and improve coordination across the apparel supply chain. In Europe, quick response principles have been applied across the clothing retail sector. Supply base rationalization has been a feature of companies' strategies as they have dramatically reduced the number of suppliers in order to work much closer with the remaining suppliers to ensure more responsiveness to the marketplace.

The resource-based perspective also builds upon Porter's models by focusing upon the various resources within the firm that will allow it to compete effectively. Resources, capabilities and core competences are key concepts in this theory. As a supply chain perspective to competitive advantage increases the resource base within which decisions are taken, this theory links to transaction cost analysis and network theory. Thus, firms have to make choices on the degree of vertical integration in their business, to 'make or buy' in production and the extent of outsourcing required in logistical support services. Building upon Williamson's (1979) seminal work, Cox (1996) has developed a contractual theory of the firm by revising his ideas on high-asset specificity and 'sunk costs' to the notion of core competences within the firm. Therefore, a company with core skills in either logistics or production would have internal contracts within the firm. Complementary skills of medium-asset specificity would be outsourced on a partnership basis, and low-asset specificity skills would be outsourced on an 'arm's-length' contract basis.

The nature of the multiplicity of relationships has created the so-called network organization. In order to be responsive to market changes and to have an agile supply chain, flexibility is essential. Extending the resource-based theory, the network perspective assumes that firms depend on resources controlled by other firms and can gain access to these resources only by interacting with these firms, forming value chain partnerships and, subsequently, networks. Network theory focuses on creating partnerships based on trust, cross-functional teamwork and inter-organizational cooperation.

Benetton has been hailed as the archetypal example of a network organization (Camuffo, Romano and Vinelli, 2001). Along with Zara, it has applied just-in-time principles to retailing whereby the capital-intensive parts of the operation (dyeing, weaving, knitting, cutting) are retained in-house and the labour-intensive parts of production (sewing, tailoring, finishing) are carried out by a network of subcontractors. The success of Zara and Benetton with this business model built up expectations that the drift to offshore sourcing could be reversed and create a revival of production in industrialized economies. This has not been the case, as will be shown in the next section.

The internationalization of the retail supply chain

In the 1970s and 1980s most retail supply chains were domestic in nature. Retailers tended to buy from local markets within a decentralized buying structure. In the last 40 years, however, the supply chain has been transformed as the larger retailers began to diversify and expand beyond their national boundaries. At the same time retailers began to source further afield. In food this was due to consumers acquiring more sophisticated tastes and demanding products all year round. In non-food the key driver was cost as companies were willing to manage longer lead times for lower prices.

In the case of the large multinational groups they entered new markets and tended to transform the logistics support for the stores that they inherited or developed. In a previous edition of this book it was noted that distribution cultures vary across markets according to, *inter alia*, geography, land and labour costs and the nature of buying power in any given market (Fernie, 2014). It was shown that one of the reasons for Walmart's failure in Germany was their attempt to centralize distribution across two chains and a large geographical area. In most cases, however, retailers have adapted their distribution models to the countries that they entered. For example 'Tesco in a box' was the approach that Tesco took to implementing its successful UK model to international markets (see Sparks, 2018; Wood *et al*, 2016).

These large companies also had a strong non-food offering in their merchandising mix and this necessitated the development of international buying hubs for sourcing products such as Tesco's head office in Hong Kong. It is on non-food sourcing, in particular for fashion goods, that much academic attention has focused in recent years. The two main trends that have occurred in the fashion sector have been the offshore sourcing and outsourcing of the production function to a global network of independent subcontractors. These trends were facilitated by a combination of geopolitical reasons (end of quotas), market needs (increased competition) and technological advancements (information technology and transport improvements) (Fernie and Azuma 2004; Djelic and Ainamo, 1999). The discussion on whether to outsource and/or seek to produce offshore relates to the degree of control that a company wishes to exert across the supply chain and the cost/quality trade-off in terms of product category.

Table 8.2 Typology of fashion retailer supply chain relationships

---

Vertically integrated or strong control of supply network
- Luxury fashion houses or those with a unique business model (eg Zara/Benetton/American Apparel)
- But as these companies have developed a greater international store network, more offshore sourcing has occurred

Mid-market retailers with collaborative relationships
- QR concepts applied offshore
- Development of international sourcing and distribution hubs
- Use of full package intermediaries (eg Li & Fung)

Fast fashion retailers
- Strong emphasis on sourcing from cheapest supplier
- Relationships can be short and variable
- Markets classified into short and long lead times
- For Western European retailers, a gradual shift from China to Vietnam; Turkey to Egypt, and Romania to Moldova in terms of sourcing patterns

---

The conceptual arguments with regard to these decisions were discussed in the previous section; however, it should be noted that most companies moved from a vertically integrated model to one of design, source and distribute. This meant that the design and marketing were controlled in the 'home' market but production was devolved to independent contractors. Table 8.2 shows the different typologies of supply chains in the fashion sector. The luxury companies have been the champions of the vertically integrated model in order to retain control over quality and promote the artisan skills that are required to make bespoke luxury items. This has been an important part of French luxury houses' strategies to enhance brand values (and prices!). However, as many luxury companies moved into new markets, especially in Asia, they began to outsource production to offshore markets for diffusion products, ie those aimed at a more mass market. This meant that their core products for which they were famous continued to be produced domestically. Some Italian brands such as Prada and Tod's, in addition to the UK brand Burberry, have brought back production to their home market – in the latter case because of criticism of the company's branding of its British credentials whilst making product in offshore markets.

As mentioned earlier, Zara and Benetton were also heralded as the saviours of domestic production but this has changed over the last decade as both companies faced increasing competition and the need to reduce costs. Benetton, in particular, now only manufactures around 10 per cent of production in Italy with a third outsourced to suppliers in China, India and southeast Asia while retaining in-house production in nearby, lower cost markets of Hungary, Croatia and Tunisia (Filieri, 2015).

In the other two segments identified in Table 8.2 the main driver for change has been cost as companies seek out cheaper sources of supply for the labour-intensive parts of garment manufacture. So, whereas Hong Kong and Taiwan were the initial sourcing locations, high labour costs meant that these countries had to upgrade to capital-intensive production processes. Basic garment manufacturing has subsequently become 'a race to the bottom' as new areas were targeted, initially China, Vietnam and Indonesia, now Bangladesh, Myanmar and Cambodia. Another major supply chain challenge in relation to an increasingly complex global network has been the ethical and sustainable issues of such a network. The Rana Plaza disaster, when a factory building collapsed killing 1,100 people in Bangladesh in 2013, highlighted the plight of workers in an unsafe environment. The Covid-19 crisis and the closure of retail outlets will not help the plight of workers in these manufacturing areas.

CSR and sustainable supply chains

The terms 'CSR' and 'sustainability' are often used interchangeably in that social and environmental issues are intertwined and difficult to separate in practice. On the one hand, environmental issues of pollution relate to the high use of natural resources, especially that of water and toxic chemicals at the fabric production and processing stage, in addition to textile waste issues in the consumer disposal of used garments (Perry and Wood, 2018). The United Nations Economic Commission for Europe (2018) reports that the textile sector is the second highest user of water worldwide, producing 20 per cent of global water waste – for example, producing one cotton shirt requires 2,700 litres – and the worldwide sector emits 10 per cent (or 1.2 billion tonnes) of global CO_2 emissions. Regarding waste, over 85 per cent of textiles, ie 21 billion tonnes or 235 million garments, are sent to landfills each year (Birtwistle and Moore, 2007; Fernie and Grant, 2019).

On the other hand, social issues focus particularly on the implications for workers and associated communities, given the labour-intensive garment manufacturing function. The social issues of CSR can be broken down into three main areas of wages, working hours and working conditions (Perry and Wood, 2018).

Laudal (2010), when discussing the fashion industry, noted that as one of the most global industries in the world the retailer had to balance variations in government regulations, employment, environmental protection and wage levels. In addition to complying with these regulations they also have to adhere to the application of guiding mechanisms and management tools such as codes of conduct and ethical audits to encourage socially responsible practices in the manufacturing process.

CSR implementation may not always conform to the ideal of going beyond minimum legal or regulatory requirements. A rules-based approach to CSR governance does not necessarily lead to improvements on the factory floor or increased worker involvement in the governance process (Raj-Reichert, 2013; Ruwanpura, 2013). Indeed, active worker participation in corporate code implementation is seen as important in securing worker benefits (Yu, 2009). At its worst, the adoption and implementation of codes of conduct may be seen as little more than a PR exercise to deflect further criticism of lead firms, with the monitoring of codes a mere box-ticking exercise that fails to fully address exploitative working conditions for the workers' benefits.

Most companies have been accused of 'greenwashing' in that they highlight selective elements of the CSR agenda to support their green or ethical credentials. Some environmental groups or brand consultancies such as Eco Age would argue that fast fashion and sustainability is an oxymoron in that volume production and consumerism do not go hand in hand with CSR.

There are increasing calls for transparency in supply chains in recent NGO campaigns, including Fashion Revolution (2017), Change Your Shoes (Spetzler, 2016) and Greenpeace (2016), which implies that retailers need to have knowledge of the outer tiers of their supplier networks. On an annual basis the Fashion Revolution produces a transparency index which ranks companies according to how much they disclose publicly on their social and environmental policies. The Corporate Human Rights Benchmark (CHRB) is published each year (see corporatebenchmark.org (archived at https://perma.cc/28F6-35FQ)) and assesses companies on their human rights record based upon the implementation of the UN Guiding Principles of Business and Human Rights and other internationally recognized standards. Rank A Brand is an independent website that assesses and ranks major brands, including fashion brands, according to sustainability and social criteria. It claims to therefore encourage both consumers and companies to act responsibly.

It is important to highlight positive examples where CSR has been the focus of management attention and a core element of corporate strategy rather than the rules-based, box-ticking approach of most companies in the sector. Fernie and Grant (2019) have carried out an analysis of companies with good practice on CSR initiatives. Some common themes emerge. For example, all companies have a commitment from senior management to CSR; indeed in the case of Timberland and Patagonia their mission statements/values embrace social responsibility. Good companies are transparent in their reporting and establish targets to meet environmental and social justice initiatives. Companies that supply these brands have their factories publicly listed and publish their audit performance. It is also important that employees 'buy in' to the CSR agenda, especially with regard to community service.

Fernie and Grant (2019) also highlight how a country like Sri Lanka has taken a strong stance on ethical credentials with its 'Garment without Guilt' initiative. Perry and Towers (2013) show how this initiative may partially overcome the conflict between commercial demands and ethical requirements in fashion supply chains. Perry *et al*'s (2015) research found evidence of long-term partnership relationships between garment manufacturers and mid-market retailers, characterized by trust, commitment and a drive for continual improvement. Collaboration and coordination between buyers and suppliers enabled suppliers to achieve cost reductions as well as improve agility by developing fashion product closer to demand, without a detrimental impact on worker welfare. By collaborating with buyers during product development or by integrating design and product development into the sourcing task, suppliers could reduce lead times and also uncertainty, resulting in less likelihood of order changes or cancellations further down the line. Long-term relationships build trust and facilitate buyer–supplier interactions as the supplier understands the buyer's requirements more quickly and is more willing to move towards those requirements, which support the presence of better working conditions (Starmanns, 2017).

The online revolution

The greatest logistical challenge for retailers in the last 20 years has been the phenomenal growth of online retailing. After a false dawn in the late 1990s when forecasts of massive growth were unrealized and retail sales from online barely reached 1 per cent in most markets of the world, sales are now worth trillions of pounds. China leads the way with $1.5 trillion of sales which was greater than the next 10 markets combined including the United States ($600 billion) and the UK ($135 billion) (Lambert *et al*, 2019).

Table 8.3 The evolution of e-tailing

Hype and experimentation	Retrenchment and sobriety	Sustainability	Focus and fragmentation
Rapid and erratic change	Slower and more predictable change	Stability emerges with predictable cyclical patterns of differentiation	Continued cycle of differentiation by low prices or specialization
Entrepreneurial pioneers with ambitious expansion plans, high start-up and failure rate	E-pioneers forced to adapt or die, physical retailers enter market through various modes of entry	Consolidation, focus strategy through cost leadership or differentiation	Increased business efficiencies, lower prices, integrated multi-channel systems

SOURCE After Williams (2009)

In terms of percentage of online to total retail sales China also leads the way with 25 per cent followed by the UK at 22 per cent. Although Amazon is the largest online global retailer, Chinese companies such as JD.com (archived at https://perma.cc/2JBN-2CS2) and Alibaba have been important entrants to the world stage in the 2010s. More specialist retailers, such as the online fashion companies Zalando from Germany, and ASOS and Boohoo from the UK, are companies founded this century.

According to Williams (2009) there has been a four-stage process in the evolution of e-tailing (Table 8.3). Stage 1 included the hype and experimentation that led to the dotcom boom and bust at the turn of the millennium. This was followed by a stage of retrenchment and sobriety as funding sources for innovators dried up at the same time as the potential of the e-tail market developed and became more apparent for many established retailers. The third stage, sustainability, featured stability in the market and consolidation among e-tailers. A fourth stage of focus and fragmentation is evident as retailers provide shopping opportunities in multiple and mobile platforms, tailor their marketing mixes more precisely to the needs of individual consumers and develop multiple delivery options. Indeed, the 2010s saw a refinement of Williams' model as companies moved from a multi-channel model to an omni-channel model as customers migrated from e- to m-commerce.

The main logistical challenges for mainstream retailers moving into online was how to change the mindset from moving pallet loads of product to regional or national distribution centres to stores for further picking at item level for store delivery. This was an easier transition for some companies than others. For example, the UK fashion retailer Next had established a mail-order presence in the 1980s and was therefore familiar with the operational issues of store and home delivery.

It has been in the non-food sector, especially fashion, that high consumer expectations have driven innovation in the supply chain. As traditional retailers faced increased competition from pure players cited earlier in this section, they have had to take a single integrated view of stock availability. This omni-channel approach means that customers can order, collect and return goods from a number of sites. So a customer can buy online, pick up in-store/collection point or have it delivered to the home and return via the same choice of channels. Managing the return flow of product is a major challenge for fashion retailers in view of the large percentage of goods returned that are purchased online. Fernie and Grant (2019) claim that around 43 per cent of fashion items are returned in the UK and use the examples of ASOS and Schuh to illustrate how these companies manage their returns.

It has been in the grocery sector that the greatest challenges have been encountered by supermarket chains. A typical grocery order comprises 60–80 items across three temperature ranges from a total range of 10,000–25,000 products within 12–24 hours for home delivery or a matter of hours for click-and-collect orders. It will be shown later how retailers have coped with this during Covid-19.

The main two main fulfilment models are the store-based and dedicated order picking model. The former model makes use of existing distribution assets as products pass through distribution centres (DCs) to stores where orders are assembled for delivery to online customers. The advantages of the store-picking model are the low initial investment required and the speed of rolling out the service to a wide geographical market. Customers also receive the same products online as available in stores. This approach also enabled visibility of real-time store stock availability. The problem here was that initially 'out of stocks' and substitutions of products were more prevalent as online shoppers competed with in-store counterparts for products.

The dedicated order picking model utilizes e-fulfilment centres to pick and deliver orders to customers. The advantage of this system is that it is dedicated purely to e-commerce customers so 'out of stocks' should be low and delivery frequencies should be higher. These picking centres, however, may have a smaller product range and need to be working at capacity to justify investment costs.

Figure 8.1   Break-even analysis of switch from store-based to pick-centred fulfilment

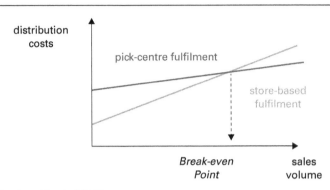

SOURCE Fernie and Sparks (2018)

Ultimately the picking centre model may well be the long-term solution to online grocery fulfilment for some areas, but there will be mixed models (Wollenburg *et al*, 2018). The problem is that the economics of order fulfilment and delivery can be variable and poor in the short run. In the UK in the early 2000s Asda closed two picking centres in London and Sainsbury's developed a hybrid model. So why has the so-called least efficient fulfilment model proven successful? The answer is simple – retailers need to create market demand before investing in costly infrastructure. As illustrated in Figure 8.1, there is a break-even point where sales volumes justify investment in picking centres. Tesco reached this point in 2006 when it opened its first specialist dotcom ('dark store') facility in Croydon and it now has six sites supporting the densely populated south-east of England where volume and order density is high.

Alvarez and Marsal (2014) argue that the current model in use for online grocery fulfilment is unsustainable in the United Kingdom because of the 'last mile' problem, ie the prohibitive costs of picking and delivering to the home. In traditional bricks-and-mortar retailing when customers came to the store, scalability was easy. Retailers engaged in store wars to buy up real estate and logistics costs were kept down as large volumes of product moved from DCs to large stores. The online model is different, and increased scale does not necessarily generate more profit but may increase costs. They maintain that the high picking costs, especially at stores, coupled with a costly number of small drops from 3.5 tonne vans, means that profit margins will be impacted upon as online growth gathers pace. They claim a more radical re-think is needed of how to improve picking rates and number of deliveries per day although the move to click-and-collect, discussed next, will reduce costs.

One of the large changes in recent years has been the expansion of 'reserve-and-collect' and 'click-and-collect' type operations (what the French refer to as the 'drive concept'). It had been thought that internet shopping would be based around home delivery, but consumers have shown that they value where and when they receive the product. In reserve-and-collect type systems consumers seem to be using the internet to check local inventory before going to the store; something valuable in non-food operations where, for example, it is over 50 per cent of sales in Halfords.

Click-and-collect has proven to be popular across all retail sectors. It provides a balance between the conflicting demands of consumer convenience, delivery efficiency and security. Tesco has over 320 locations for grocery pick-up and offers a same-day collection service. Most of Tesco's collection points are in the car parks of their larger stores. In France, lower population densities make home delivery prohibitively expensive so 'click-and-collect' is the favoured distribution channel. Grocery retailers there, led by Leclerc and Auchan, operate over 3,000 drive-through stations (Leroux, 2014; Hubner *et al*, 2016). Colla and Lapoule (2012) also note that most drive-through stations are solitary collection points, unlike those discussed in relation to Tesco earlier. They argue that this is an aggressive marketing strategy to win customers from competitors rather than cannibalizing their own in-store sales. They also note that in the case of Leclerc the elimination of last mile expenses allowed the company to make a profit on its investment in drive-through outlets within two years.

In terms of non-grocery sales, retailers tend to have kiosks or collection points within stores, but many companies, mainly fashion retailers, use collection and delivery points (CDPs) strategically located in or around transport terminals, shopping centres, petrol stations and convenience stores. Collect+, a joint venture between delivery company Yodel and payments group PayPoint, was established in 2009. It utilizes a network of more than 6,000 convenience stores and petrol stations to which orders from retailers can be delivered, returned to and tracked.

In terms of the future, several new technologies have been advocated as solutions to the last mile problem. The use of drones for parcel delivery has been trialled by Amazon and others but the restrictions in terms of weight and distance, not to mention safety considerations, mean that this option is likely to confine drones to a niche sector for the foreseeable future. The very notion of drones and delivery robots, however, points to changing consumer requirements and the extension of supply chains beyond the shop. This also explains the potential use of 3D printing at home for some products, replacing physical by online distribution.

The future

After much of the world has been in lockdown due to the Covid-19 pandemic, it is quite difficult to forecast the implications for retail logistics in the aftermath of the 'new normal'. One thing came over clear – existing supply chains were not flexible enough to respond to a rapid change in circumstances, viz Christopher and Peck's 'time to react' scenario. Even when responding to increased demand for personal protective equipment (PPE) for our health services and key workers, governments were not properly prepared. Individual sectors had to respond in different ways. In terms of meeting demand for food supplies retailers had to respond to a massive increase in online ordering especially as the vulnerable were instructed to stay at home. In non-food, especially fashion products, retailers scrambled to cancel or modify orders with suppliers as their stores remained closed. We will now look at the current and future implications of the new retail environment.

During the pandemic the grocery retailers have received praise from most quarters for their response to feeding the nation in the UK. Perhaps the UK was better positioned in the first place to respond to an increase in online ordering. With 7 per cent of all grocery sales occurring online pre-pandemic the UK was much further down this multi-channel retail offering than any other country in the world. By May 2020 this figure of online sales had nearly doubled to 13 per cent and 10.4 million people shopped for groceries online compared with 4.8 million one year earlier (Armstrong, 2020). Retailers were able to respond to this demand because they could deliver to the home from their larger stores in addition to supplying larger conurbations with picking centres or 'dark stores'. In our debate on which fulfilment model was best in the section on the online revolution, we showed that there was a break-even point when sales could justify picking from a dedicated warehouse (Figure 8.1). In a time of crisis retailers could ramp up supplies through their store network; coincidentally Ocado, the main online-only player, could not meet the surge in demand – their model is based on steady incremental growth whereby new high-tech large warehouses come onstream as demand builds up, but not a surge in demand as witnessed in 2020.

Hence the mainstream retailers could offer more flexibility of choice for their customers.

The question for the future with regard to online grocery is whether these high market share levels can be sustained into the future. It is unlikely, albeit levels will be greater than the 7 per cent pre-pandemic. Consumers had no choice but to eat at home or to get takeaway food. Restaurants, pubs and cafes were closed so demand for groceries inevitably rose considerably. Most online grocery shoppers are couples with young families but the lockdown meant that the so-called vulnerable (the elderly and those with pre-existing medical conditions who were told to stay at home) began to use online shopping. To what extent they will continue to shop this way remains to be seen. However, retailers may not encourage this behavioural change in that the economics of home delivery is an ongoing debate and customers tend to impulse shop more when visiting shops.

In the non-food sector, the closure of shops has only accentuated a trend that has been occurring for the last decade, namely the drift from offline to online shopping. Many of the retailers in traditional sectors such as department stores and middle market fashion were struggling before the pandemic and the crisis has either pushed them into administration (Laura Ashley and Debenhams) or into wholesale store closures (Arcadia group). It is estimated by BOF/McKinsey (2020) that the lockdown has caused financial distress to 80 per cent of US and European fashion businesses. Even companies with an online presence during lockdown have incurred high costs. Indeed Amazon, a clear winner during the pandemic in terms of sales, was due to record its first quarterly loss in five years due to increasing the number of staff and complying with safety measures. The top UK fashion retailer, Next, closed its website for two weeks and only opened up its business slowly as it implemented social distancing at its warehouses.

What can we expect in the 2020s? It is clearly going to be a slow road to recovery with the worst recession forecast in living memory. In China where shops had reopened consumer traffic was down and, in the United States and Europe high rates of unemployment are being experienced. With demand sluggish, retailers have stockpiles of goods that will need to be cleared for new seasonal goods. Prices will be low in the short term until re-adjustments are made as normality is reached. But the new normal may be different. Why? It is likely that patterns of behaviour will change. Having experienced homeworking many businesses will see the benefit of cutting office costs so workers may shop more locally than hitherto. Online retail activity will increase further in that segments of the population who ignored online may now see this as a preferred method of shopping.

In terms of supply, retailers will be re-evaluating their supply chains to build in greater flexibility to meet demand. In the downtime that much of the population has had forced upon them consumers have been able to reflect upon where their goods are sourced and how much the environment has improved with less economic activity. Sourcing local may not only be a grocery phenomenon but for CSR and security of supply reasons the shift to some form of re-shoring or near-shoring may also be accelerated for fashion goods. This was already happening in the luxury sector with Prada and Burberry bringing back to their domestic market secondary lines that had been sourced in China. The top-quality labels such as Hermes and Louis Vuitton have always made their core lines in the *maisons* in France and will be less affected than most fashion retailers that are driven by the offshore sourcing/outsourcing model. It is interesting to note that one of the major success stories during the pandemic has been the online fast fashion retailer, Boohoo.com (archived at https://perma.cc/A23M-EN5K). Why? It has a flexible supply chain and sources 40 per cent of its product from UK suppliers.

References

Agarawal, A, Shanker, R and Tiwari, MK (2006) Modelling the metrics of lean, agile and leagile supply chains: an ANP-based approach, *European Journal of Operational Research*, **173** (1), pp 211–25

Alvarez and Marsal (2014) *Home Delivery Fulfilment in UK Grocery: Opportunities and threats from market growth*, Alvarez and Marsal, London

Armstrong, A (2020) Supermarkets shaken by consumers' seismic shift online, *The Times*, 2 June

Bhardwaj, V and Fairhurst, A (2010) Fast fashion responses to changes in the fashion industry, *International Review of Retail, Distribution and Consumer Research*, **20** (1), pp 165–73

Birtwistle, G and Moore, CM (2007) Fashion clothing – where does it all end up? *International Journal of Retail and Distribution Management*, **3**, (3), pp 210–16

BOF/McKinsey (2020) *The State of Fashion: Coronavirus Update*, Business of Fashion/McKinsey & Company

Camuffo, A, Romano, P and Vinelli, A (2001) Back to the future: Benetton transforms its global network, *MIT Sloan Management Review*, Fall, pp 46–52

Christopher, M and Peck, H (1997) *Marketing Logistics*, Butterworth-Heinemann, Oxford

Christopher, M and Peck, H (1998) Fashion logistics in *Logistics and Retail Management*, eds J Fernie and L Sparks, Kogan Page, London

Christopher, M and Peck, H (2003) *Marketing Logistics*, 2nd edn, Butterworth-Heinemann, Oxford

Colla, E and Lapoule, P (2012) E-commerce: Exploring the critical success factors, *International Journal of Retail and Distribution Management*, **40** (11), pp 842–64

Cox, A (1996) Relationship competence and strategic procurement management: Towards an entrepreneurial and contractual theory of the firm, *European Journal of Purchasing and Supply Management*, **2** (1), pp 57–70

Djelic, ML and Ainamo, A (1999) The coevolution of new organizational forms in the fashion industry: A historical and comparative study of France, Italy, and the United States, *Organization Science*, **10** (5), pp 622–37

Drucker, P (1962) The economy's dark continent, *Fortune*, April, pp 265–70

Evans, B and Mason, R (2015) *The Lean Supply Chain: Managing the challenge at Tesco*, Kogan Page, London

Fashion Revolution (2017) Fashion transparency index 2017 [Online] Fashion Transparency Index 2017 by Fashion Revolution, issuu.com/fashionrevolution/docs/fr_fashiontransparencyindex2017 (archived at https://perma.cc/752Q-9XH3)

Ferdows, K, Lewis, MA and Machura, AD (2004) Rapid-fire fulfilment, *Harvard Business Review*, **82** (11), pp 104–10

Fernie, J (1990) *Retail Distribution Management*, Kogan Page, London

Fernie, J (2014) Retail logistics, in *Global Logistics*, eds D Waters and S Rinsler, 7th edn, Kogan Page, London

Fernie, J and Azuma, N (2004) The changing nature of Japanese fashion: Can quick response improve supply chain efficiency? *European Journal of Marketing*, **38** (7), pp 790–808

Fernie, J and Grant, D (2019) *Fashion Logistics*, 2nd edn, Kogan Page, London

Fernie, J and Perry, P (2011) The international fashion supply chain, in *Case Studies in International Management*, eds Z Zentes, B Swoboda and D Morchett, Gabler, Wiesbaden

Fernie, J and Sparks, L (2018) *Logistics and Retail Management*, 5th edn, Kogan Page, London

Fernie, J, Sparks, L and McKinnon, AC (2010) Retail logistics in the UK: past, present and future, *International Journal of Retail and Distribution Management*, **38** (11/12), pp 894–914

Filieri, R (2015) From market-driving to market-driven: An analysis of Benetton's strategic change and its implications for long term performance, *Marketing Intelligence and Planning*, **33** (3), pp 238–57

Ford, D, Gadde, L-E, Hakansson, H and Snehota, I (2011) *Managing Business Relationships*, John Wiley, Chichester

Greenpeace (2016) The Detox Catwalk 2016 [Online] www.greenpeace.org.cn/site/toxics/2016/catwalk/download/Detox_Catwalk_Explained_2016 (archived at https://perma.cc/32KT-Y69J)

Harrison, A, Christopher, M and van Hoek, R (1999) *Creating the Agile Supply Chain*, Institute of Logistics and Transport, Corby

Hubner, A, Kuhn, H and Wollenburg, J (2016) Last mile fulfilment and distribution in omni-channel grocery retailing, *International Journal of Retail and Distribution Management*, **44** (3) pp 228–47

Jones, DT (2002) Rethinking the grocery supply chain, in *State of the Art in Food*, eds J-W Grievink, L Josten and C Valk, Elsevier, Rotterdam

Lambert, B, Wang, J, Wang, KW and Zipser, D (2019) *China Digital Consumer Trends 2019*, McKinsey Digital

Laudal, T (2010) An attempt to determine the CSR potential of the international clothing business, *Journal of Business Ethics*, **96** (1) pp 63–77

Leahy, T (2012) *Management in Ten Words*, Random House Business Books, London

Leroux, M (2014) Trials and tribulations of real and virtual worlds, Raconteur Future of Retail, supplement in *The Times*, 24 June, pp 12–13

Lopez, C and Fan, Y (2009) Internationalisation of the fashion brand Zara, *Journal of Fashion Marketing and Management*, **13** (2), pp 279–96

McKinnon, AC (1989) The advantages and disadvantages of centralised distribution, in *Retail Distribution Management*, ed J Fernie, Kogan Page, London, pp 74–89

Mason-Jones, R, Naylor, B and Towill, DR (2000) Lean, agile or leagile? Matching your supply chain to the marketplace, *International Journal of Production Research*, **38** (17), pp 4061–070

Naylor, JB, Naim, MM and Berry, D (1999) Leagility: Integrating the lean and agile manufacturing paradigms in the total supply chain, *International Journal of Production Economics*, **62** (1), pp 107–18

Perry, P and Towers, N (2013) Conceptual framework development: CSR implementation in fashion supply chains, *International Journal of Physical Distribution and Logistics Management*, **43** (5/6), pp 478–501

Perry, P and Wood, S (2018) Exploring the international fashion supply chain and corporate responsibility: Cost, responsiveness and ethical implications, in *Logistics and Retail Management*, eds J Fernie and L Sparks, 5th edn, Kogan Page, London

Perry, P, Wood, S and Fernie, J (2015) Corporate social responsibility in garment sourcing networks: Factory management perspectives on ethical trade in Sri Lanka, *Journal of Business Ethics*, **130** (3), pp 737–52

Porter, M (1985) *Competitive Advantage: Creating and sustaining superior performance*, Free Press, New York

Raj-Reichert, G (2013) Safeguarding labour in distant factories: Health and safety governance in an electronics global production network, *Geoforum*, **44** (1), pp 23–31

Ruwanpura, KN (2013) Scripted performances? Local readings of 'global' health and safety standards (the apparel sector in Sri Lanka), *Global Labour Journal*, **4** (2), pp 88–108

Slack, N, Chambers, S, Harland, C, Harrison, A and Johnston, R (1998) *Operations Management*, 2nd edn, Pitman, London

Sparks, L (2018) Tesco's supply chain management, in *Logistics and Retail Management*, eds J Fernie and L Sparks, 5th edn, Kogan Page, London

Spetzler, J (2016) Trampling workers' rights underfoot, change your shoes [Online] www.yumpu.com/en/document/view/55775258/trampling-workers-rights-underfoot (archived at https://perma.cc/4XN8-N45U)

Starmanns, M (2017) Purchasing Practices and Low Wages in Global Supply Chains: Empirical cases from the garment industry, ILO, Geneva

Tokatli, N (2008) Global sourcing: Insights from the global clothing industry – the case of Zara, a fast fashion retailer, *Journal of Economic Geography*, **8** (1), pp 21–38

Towill, D and Christopher, M (2002) The supply chain strategy conundrum: To be lean or agile or to be lean and agile? *International Journal of Logistics*, **5** (3), pp 299–309

UNECE (2018) UN Alliance aims to put fashion on path to sustainability, press release, (archived at) perma.cc/XFW9-G22G

Williams, DE (2009) The evolution of e-tailing, *The International Review of Retail, Distribution and Consumer Research*, **19** (3), pp 219–49

Williamson, OE (1979) Transaction cost economics: The governance of contractual relations, *Journal of Law and Economics*, **22**, October, pp 223–61

Wollenburg, J, Hubner, A, Kuhn, H and Tautrims, A (2018) From bricks and mortar to bricks and clicks: Logistics networks in omni-channel grocery retailing, *International Journal of Physical Distribution and Logistics Management*, **48** (4), pp 415–38

Womack, JP and Jones, DT (2005) *Lean Solutions*, Simon and Schuster, London

Womack, JP, Jones, D and Roos, D (1990) *The Machine that Changed the World: The story of lean production*, HarperCollins, New York

Wood, SM, Coe, NM and Wrigley, N (2016) Multi-scaler localization and capability transference: Exploring embeddedness in the Asian retail expansion of Tesco, *Regional Studies*, **50** (3) pp 475–95

Yu, X (2009) From passive beneficiary to active stakeholder: Workers' participation in CSR movement against labor abuses, *Journal of Business Ethics*, **87** (1), pp 233–49

Trends and strategies in global logistics and supply chain management

Christian F Durach and Frank Straube[1]

Introduction

Logistics and supply chain management has long been identified as a key lever for organizational success. At the same time, many companies are still in the process of defining the specific scope of responsibility of the logistics function. Reduced delivery times and adherence to defined delivery dates, as well as complete and accurate deliveries, have become increasingly important for customer satisfaction and organizational competitiveness.

Nevertheless, it remains challenging for managers to develop logistics networks that correspond to their performance aspirations. Worldwide megatrends, such as expanding and increasingly fragmented global sales channels, talent shortages and cost pressure, present difficulties for logistics managers and lead to new and constantly changing demands on the networking competencies of companies. In addition, highly consequential catastrophes, such as the 2011 great East Japan earthquake or the 2020 coronavirus pandemic, posed questions about how firms should react and learn. In summary, more than ever before, today's logistics managers are confronted with dynamic corporate development trends, which are difficult to forecast.

As markets have changed over the past 30 years, in both business-to-business (B2B) and business-to-consumer (B2C) markets, logistics functions have experienced major changes. This trend will continue, given the increasing digitization of businesses and the rapid transmission and analysis of data. A profound understanding of logistics and its trends is of growing importance, since the scope of logistics is likely to expand in the future. Effective preparation depends on companies forecasting future developments and properly identifying such trends in order to build effective logistics coping strategies.

This chapter reports on the study of Handfield *et al* (2013) that aimed to help practitioners to identify key trends and develop strategies for coping with them. Furthermore, we complement these findings with insights from the study 'Pathway of Digital Transformation in Logistics' published in June 2019 by the Logistics Department of the TU Berlin (Straube *et al*, 2019). Finally, we add insights based on our personal experiences, research findings (other than the above) and exchanges with practitioners.

Research design and research sample

The 2013 research project was financed by the German Logistics Association (BVL), as part of their 20-year effort to support research about logistics trends and their impact on the global logistics environment. We are grateful to the authors of the previous study for allowing us to summarize their work (Handfield *et al*, 2013). The research design followed a three-step methodological approach. A comprehensive content analysis of over 200 research reports laid the groundwork for a series of interviews with 62 executives from India, Germany, the UK, France, the United States, China, Brazil and Russia. A subsequent large-scale survey facilitated the confirmation or rebuttal of the key regional trends and strategies identified in the executive interviews. A group of international partners collaborated on the interviews and survey data collection to support the research team from Germany and the United States. In the following text, a more detailed explanation of each of the methodological steps will be given.

The reviewed research reports were categorized, and key issues were analysed and extracted. A content analyser tool was used to compile this information and identify the frequency of major trends and strategies. The tool enabled the scanning of thousands of online research articles to identify relevant publications based on the number of search hits. The tool also

Figure 9.1   Countries represented in the survey

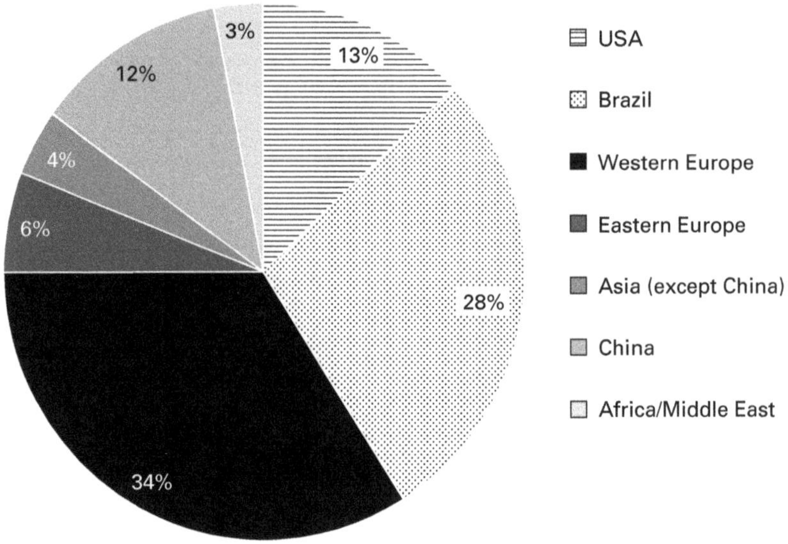

SOURCE Handfield *et al* (2013)

facilitated further validation of the importance of the topics and resulted in a focal set of keywords and themes for further analysis by the team.

A number of databases, such as Business Source Premier, Ibis, Lexis-Nexus and others, were searched. The research team then consolidated and finalized the list of relevant trends and strategies in the literature.

Based on the results of the literature review, the research team developed a preliminary list of logistics trends and strategies, according to which an interview schedule and a protocol for discussions with key industry executives were developed. The interviews were conducted with 62 international supply chain executives at director level or higher, who held positions in logistics services, retail and various manufacturing industries. Subsequently, the interviews were transcribed and coded according to the identified major trends and strategies.

The research team jointly discussed the findings of the interviews and revised the list of trends and strategies as necessary. From this discussion, a survey relating to the key items was developed. The survey was launched in 2013, following the International Supply Chain Conference in Berlin. It was provided in English, German, Portuguese, Chinese and Russian, and posted to an online survey tool (see Figure 9.1).

The online survey targeted global companies from different major regions, in an effort to obtain a global sample of organizations. As shown in Figure 9.1, the research team obtained a wide range of responses from the

Figure 9.2   Industries represented

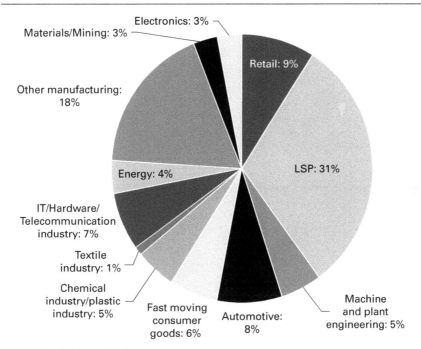

- Electronics: 3%
- Materials/Mining: 3%
- Other manufacturing: 18%
- Energy: 4%
- IT/Hardware/Telecommunication industry: 7%
- Textile industry: 1%
- Chemical industry/plastic industry: 5%
- Fast moving consumer goods: 6%
- Automotive: 8%
- Machine and plant engineering: 5%
- Retail: 9%
- LSP: 31%

SOURCE Handfield *et al* (2013)

United States, Brazil, Western Europe, Eastern Europe, Asia, China, Africa and the Middle East. A total of 1,757 responses were received from various industries, of which 645 were complete for all the questions asked (see Figure 9.2). The number of responses per question varied, based on the structure and response rate of the survey.

The research sample included 39 per cent of organizations with more than $500 (USD) million in annual global sales, a majority (41 per cent) with between $10 million and $500 million, and a strong representation of smaller organizations (20 per cent with less than $10 million). Almost two-thirds (61 per cent) of respondents were from manufacturing industries, 30 per cent from logistics service providers (LSPs), and 9 per cent from retail (see Figure 9.2).

The remainder of this chapter will outline some of the key insights of the study, along with insights drawn from more recent studies by our research team. It describes the major global logistics trends identified in the analysis and discusses the importance of delivery reliability.

The 2019 study 'Pathway of Digital Transformation in Logistics' builds on an online survey and a Delphi workshop (Straube *et al*, 2019). The goal

Figure 9.3   Study panel

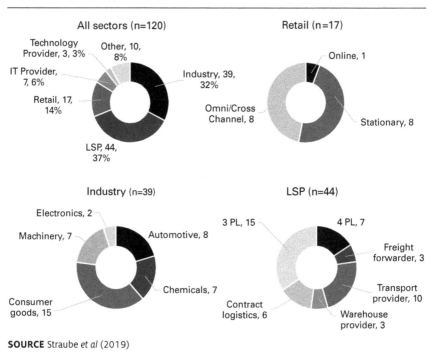

All sectors (n=120)

- Technology Provider, 3, 3%
- Other, 10, 8%
- IT Provider, 7, 6%
- Industry, 39, 32%
- Retail, 17, 14%
- Omni/Cross Channel, 8
- LSP, 44, 37%

Retail (n=17)

- Online, 1
- Stationary, 8

Industry (n=39)

- Electronics, 2
- Machinery, 7
- Automotive, 8
- Chemicals, 7
- Consumer goods, 15

LSP (n=44)

- 3 PL, 15
- 4 PL, 7
- Freight forwarder, 3
- Transport provider, 10
- Contract logistics, 6
- Warehouse provider, 3

SOURCE Straube *et al* (2019)

was to identify concepts of successful companies and future developments in logistics. The group of 120 international participants in the online survey consisted of logistics service providers (37 per cent), industrial companies (32 per cent), trade (14 per cent), IT and technology providers (9 per cent). The Delphi workshop was conducted with 32 participants primarily from industry and logistics service companies (Straube *et al*, 2019). The 2019 study panel is depicted in Figure 9.3.

Key trends and strategies

Trends

The purpose of this section is to summarize the key trends and strategies identified by the 2013 study, and discuss these alongside the 2019 findings, our observations, and our discussions with business executives. Today's global logistics environment is characterized by increasing complexity and a number of important parameters are shaping the global environment. The speed of change of these parameters is breathtaking, driving increasing complexity in logistics ecosystems. Such changes can be labelled 'trends', in that they continue to reshape the logistics landscape, posing a shifting set of environmental risks and limitations that either constrain decisions or, alternatively, present opportunities that agile enterprises can rapidly exploit. Figure 9.4 shows the main identified trends and their relative importance.

The trends reflected executives' perceptions. In the following sections, the top six trends are grouped into two sets of related forces – network and external forces – and briefly discussed.

Network forces

Network forces refer to vertical and horizontal inter-organizational forces operating within networks of customers, suppliers and LSPs that operate across supply systems. The three major network forces are explained in the following sections.

1. Increased customer expectations

As organizations expand, new global customers present a lucrative target, but there are high costs for servicing these customers. A global customer base creates a new set of challenges for organizations that are used to providing standard logistics solutions to a homogeneous regional customer base. Customers not only demand excellent order and delivery reliability, but also require more customized and complex solutions.

The managers' identified top priorities were 'meeting customer expectations', followed by 'on-time delivery', and 'green logistics' (these were ranked as number 1 priorities by 22 per cent, 17 per cent and 13 per cent of respondents respectively). The majority of respondents noted that customers can typically change delivery orders within 10 days of ordering, and a majority (over 50 per cent) indicated that this window could be reduced to one day or even less; therefore, reliability within the supply chain was essential both for meeting consumer demands and allowing flexibility in the customer order process.

2. Networked economy versus localization (the latest trend?)

The second most important trend requires organizations to recognize that their destiny is intertwined with that of others in the network. There has been an explosion of new customer channels that are not well developed but are interlinked with other channels. The networked economy was a key

Figure 9.4 Perceived importance of logistics trends

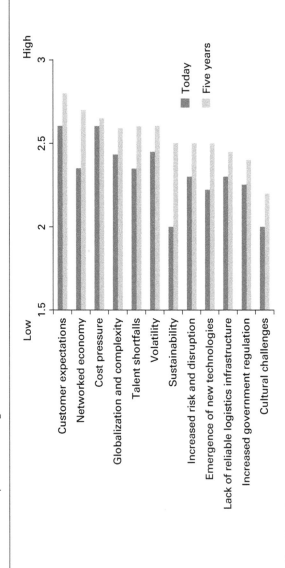

SOURCE Handfield *et al* (2013)

driver for the supply chain crisis that occurred during the coronavirus pandemic. Our recent discussions with practitioners suggest that many companies are now re-thinking their globalization strategies. Localization is becoming increasingly important for companies in two ways: first, it is a key measure for guarding against the risks associated with long lead times and the crossing of country borders; second, localization can be a sales proposition for companies since customers value reliable suppliers during times of increased uncertainty.

In a networked economy, enterprises are expected to have extreme levels of flexibility. Manufacturers have to adapt to new product requirements and/or suppliers; LSPs need to offer flexible services; and retailers must grapple with fulfilling different types of orders and handling the underpinning inventory, since customers are now offered an array of different delivery options (ship to home, store pick-up, etc). E-commerce orders are characterized by high volumes, but smaller, picked orders delivered to homes are more common. The coronavirus crisis revealed that many companies are still struggling to provide such flexibility.

Many of the companies interviewed recognized that they could not operate independently, but needed to become experts at managing global relationships. This was particularly true in regions where sales were at the emerging stage and, in many cases, multinational companies (MNCs) needed to find ways to operate locally. Partnerships were vital for achieving this. Some MNCs sought to outsource their technology design, inventory management, working capital investment, and planning execution to other partners in the supply chain. Experts warned (long before the Covid crisis) that delegating too much responsibility to the supply chain could result in significant risk of companies losing control of the channel (Choi and Linton, 2011).

The most important reasons for collaboration in supply chains, identified by almost 80 per cent of the executives, were to improve coordination and increase trust, as well as to improve synergies and stimulate innovation. In the words of one executive: 'Collaborate or die!' It is clear that organizations are aiming to develop new forms of logistics value and innovation, and that open and trusting dialogues, through which all parties can openly exchange ideas for improvement, are imperative for companies' survival. It is therefore critical for companies to identify reliable partners.

3. Cost pressure
The third most important and unchallenged trend was cost pressure. Customers expected high service levels, strong and fast logistics capabilities,

and innovative products at low prices. The pressure of the last five years has driven many companies to engage in cost saving, and additional savings require more sophisticated approaches. The expediency of moving supply to emerging countries in order to exploit low-cost labour is coming to an end, and savings are not as easy to achieve as they were five to eight years ago. Organizations are finding that they must adopt sophisticated analytical tools in order to design logistics networks that capture multiple cost drivers.

More than one-third of respondents noted that logistics costs increased in 2012, while another one-third stated that they had remained constant. No standardized methods exist in research, or in business practice, to measure logistics costs as a percentage of the overall costs/revenue of a company, due to several factors. First, standards defining what elements of transportation, purchasing, materials handling, quality inspection, and other costs belong in the category of 'logistics' often vary between divisions in the same company. A baseline definition of what is included in logistics costs also varies between companies in the same industry. Despite this limitation, the study showed that the respondents estimated logistics costs as a percentage of overall revenue. Logistics costs exceeded 8 per cent of revenues in industries such as retail, fast-moving consumer goods (FMCG), chemicals, textiles, energy and mining-materials. These industries, not surprisingly, had a strong interest in optimizing their logistics networks. Logistics costs were higher for traditional (ie stationery) retailers than for mail-order or online retailers. Clearly, the pressure to reduce costs and working capital is an aspect of the global landscape that is likely to continue. Organizations must therefore develop innovative solutions for complex customer requirements, without increasing costs.

External forces

External forces represent changes outside the inter-organizational network over which organizations have little or no control. The three major external forces are set out in the following sections.

1. Globalization of logistics networks

Organizations across multiple sectors are continuing to pursue global growth strategies and expand into new regions. In particular, Brazil, Russia, India and China (the BRIC countries) represent major targets for expansion. The research results suggested that Eastern Europe and Russia were the regions that 20 per cent of respondents identified as growth regions. Another

15 to 20 per cent of organizations were expanding into Africa, Central America, India and the Middle East. The expansion into China is now at a much lower rate than in the past. Organizations are finding that the value proposition for many firms in China is disappearing as the competitive cost advantage erodes relative to other countries. Simultaneously, Africa is increasingly being seen as a region for global expansion. All along Africa's Atlantic coast, garment factories are producing scrubs, aprons and laboratory coats. The switch has been due to global suppliers recognizing Africa's low-cost, English-speaking labour force and its convenient ports, which are 10 days closer to the United States eastern seaboard than Asia's garment factories.[2]

Nevertheless, China's Belt and Road Initiative is currently probably the largest infrastructure initiative in the world with far-reaching consequences for international logistics networks. In September 2019, the Competence Center for International Logistics Networks of the TU Berlin hosted a workshop with 16 representatives from industry and services to discuss current challenges and their impact on logistics. In addition to highly volatile prices in rail transport, experts also mentioned capacity constraints in the rail infrastructure to be one of the greatest challenges of the initiative from a European industry perspective. Within the next 10 years, it is assumed that the Silk Road initiative will cause Eastern European industrial production to move further east and that the southern European seaports for goods to and from China will also translate into increasing competitive pressures for the northern European seaports (Nitsche, 2020).

Globalization has nevertheless caused a host of new problems that enterprises are inexperienced in dealing with. As companies continue to expand their global footprints, global networks are faced with challenges due to government regulatory forces, channel fragmentation and poor logistics infrastructure. As mentioned previously, we expect that companies will start localizing their production; that is, even global players operating in multiple countries will adopt local sourcing and production – probably as a key reaction to the coronavirus crisis.

Especially in 2020, the Covid-19 pandemic put international logistics networks to the test. Straube and Nitsche (2020) reveal future potential development paths based on a structured discussion with 23 logistics managers. The authors show that digitalization and the automation of processes are the main levers for efficient risk and volatility management. In addition, more localized, agile logistics networks may play a bigger role in the future.

2. Talent shortages

Each of the executives mentioned the lack of talent as a critical barrier to driving logistics progress and improvement. This was very interesting, considering the recent increase of precarious employment in many industries. Talent shortages were one of the most critical concerns on the horizon for global organizations across all the regions surveyed. This was evident, not only for manual jobs (truck drivers and warehouse operatives), but also for managerial positions (buyers, planners, analysts, schedulers, warehouse supervisors and distribution managers). Supply chains cannot operate without people, but organizations are facing critical shortfalls in labour, with increasing numbers of unfilled jobs, and the shortage is daily becoming more severe.

The study showed that the talent gap was most apparent in the areas of skilled labour and supply chain planning. Both areas were critically short of workers, despite growing unemployment rates in many regions of the world (60 per cent of the firms were experiencing major shortages). The perception was that this shortage of skilled workers and planners would continue to escalate. We assume the greatest shortages are likely to be for certain types of skilled labour (ie warehouse workers). As increasing numbers of experienced workers reach retirement age, there will not be enough skilled replacements to meet the logistical demands and complexities of the global environment.

The root cause of this problem is not simple. Managers from Western European countries noted that young people do not view logistics as an exciting career – students and graduates are often more interested in finance and marketing careers. In Brazil, China and India, the shortage of logistics talent was a very challenging issue, since universities in these countries typically had no logistics subjects on their curricula.

3. Volatility

Volatility is perceived as an increasingly significant phenomenon in the logistics environment (Christopher and Holweg, 2011), and not only due to coronavirus. It refers to major shifts in customer demand volume, product or service mix, government regulations, new competitors, substitute products, short product life cycles, and requirements for rapid network nodal changes and re-design.

Many executives noted that, as their organizations' global footprints expanded, they faced increasingly complex government regulations, especially regarding: logistics regulations; protectionist policies; product mandates; fulfilment of customs, trade and local content obligations; and security requirements. As the private sector expands into emerging countries, there is increasing economic pressure in these countries from import and product restrictions, which are intended to drive national revenue and protect local industries. The barrier of regulatory issues is continually changing, but the fines and penalties for non-compliance are on the rise. These regulations make it more difficult to meet increasing customer requirements for reliable product delivery, and planning becomes challenging.

Nitsche (2019) developed a tool to enable practitioners to perform a case-based evaluation of the state of volatility of a product's logistics network. Using the proposed tool, in a first step, the user can measure the state of volatility management performance for four distinct dimensions of volatility (organizational volatility, vertical volatility, behavioural volatility, market-related volatility). In a second step the peculiarity can be assessed to identify areas to focus on when managing volatility. Eventually the tool enables practitioners to develop strategies dealing with volatility.

Strategies

This subsection will show how high-performing companies prepared themselves to deal with emerging trends (see Figure 9.5) and how some of them managed to exploit various elements to their advantage. The strategies they adopted will be clustered into four different categories: people, processes, technology and networks. Some key insights will be highlighted, based on what these high-performing companies from different sectors did differently.

People

People build the foundation for a company's success. The management of people involves both a talent management strategy that prepares the company for anticipated future skill gaps, and the creation of an organizational culture that supports fast decision-making processes. The deployment of the following people strategies correlated with the occurrence of several trends (global complexity, increased risk, cost pressure, emerging technologies, talent shortages, etc).

Talent management
Talented individuals who join companies may stay for an extended period of time, while others may leave soon afterwards. In order to address

Figure 9.5 Importance of logistics strategies

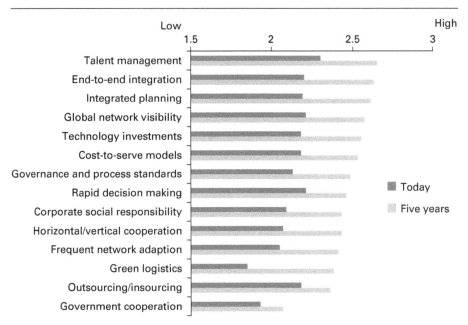

anticipated talent shortfalls, organizations need to deploy a long-term talent management strategy that first identifies and extrapolates talent shortfalls and then develops countermeasures in collaboration with human resources professionals.

According to the principles of supply chain management, people can be seen as a 'product'. As described by Peter Cappelli in his book *Talent on Demand* (Cappelli, 2008), organizations have a choice between 'making' talent (which means developing skills internally) and 'buying' talent (which refers to external hiring) and this view includes an evaluation of the respective costs.

While training was aimed at retaining and motivating good employees, and was offered by 90 per cent of the surveyed companies, engagement with universities was intended to connect students with companies and eventually meet future talent needs. Because many young people are digitally savvy and engaged with social media, building a talent network on this platform is a valid strategy for reaching out to young people. Partnering with universities is also a vital strategy, since they function as 'suppliers' of graduates, and as partners for commercial industry projects, which can be beneficial for organizations.

Case studies can make a significant contribution to training in logistics. For all levels of proficiency, these practice-oriented descriptions of situations can help to develop a more comprehensive understanding of logistics processes. In 2019, the Competence Center for International Logistics Networks of the TU Berlin developed a freely accessible practice-oriented collection of case studies to support education and training in logistics (Nitsche *et al*, 2019). The case studies deal with, among other things, the management of volatility, risks and digital technologies as well as the influence of cultural conditions using the example of European–Asian logistics networks. In cooperation with the CDHK at Tongji University Shanghai and industrial and logistics service companies in Germany and China, case studies were developed that should be of interest to academics, students, practitioners as well as legislators in ministries and international institutions.

Quick decision making

Providing individuals with the authority and ability to make quick decisions is the second component of talent management. Due to the quickly changing environments and demanding challenges in complex global networks, organizations must establish a solid basis for optimal, decentralized decision making. Organizations need to rely on the capabilities of their managers in various locations, who must be able to make quick decisions, independently, with reference to corporate guidelines and the best available data. In this regard, the organizational culture must allow managers to make mistakes as part of their individual development process.

Processes

With the movement toward globalization and localization, it is vitally important for organizations to create the right mix of global governance, process standardization, local production and sourcing, and alignment of internal and external organizational processes. Standardized processes and integrated planning schemes across different actors in the supply chain are a strong basis for a fruitful organizational culture; however, such a culture must embrace the ability to adapt to regional or cultural needs, different logistics and delivery requirements, and diverse transportation infrastructure. A combination of global process standards and governance formats that evaluate whether individuals are meeting established performance standards is seen as an ideal approach for creating a new type of agile logistics structure. One component of this is an integrated planning process to ensure that all individuals in remote places and different positions within the supply chain aim to deliver the same results. This should underpin an organizational ability to adapt the network to different local requirements. These strategies enable companies to cope with trends such as new technologies, networked economies, increased risk and disruption, volatility, poor logistics infrastructure, talent shortfalls and globalization.

Logistics governance and process standards

A process culture is based on an organization's capability to deploy a high level of governance over its logistics processes. While there has always been a need for policies and procedures to determine standards of performance, it remains a challenging task to develop a flexible form of governance that facilitates adaptation to local requirements. Helpful tools to achieve these outcomes are so-called 'maturity models', which can be used to measure outcomes and results.

Regional logistics requirements drive regional logistics design. A centralized Council of Logistics Management manages regional divisions and establishes overall guidelines and structures for the logistics industry. Three components typically build the foundation for developed standards: processes, policies and playbooks. First, processes must be in place and defined by standards (eg transportation planning). Second, standards and associated policies must be followed (eg scheduling). Third, playbooks, as a form of user guide, should be introduced to help workers to understand and carry out processes.

To deal with conflicts between regional requirements, organizations have implemented global sales and operations planning; however, regional divisions may understand, interpret, and act differently regarding the requirements. Global process standardization is neither feasible nor expedient; therefore, a clearly defined organizational structure is required. As organizations with clearly defined roles and responsibilities, and a common understanding of processes, employees are empowered to act independently at the local level in response to local conditions.

A well-functioning logistics environment is key to a country's prospects for trade, growth and employment. This is particularly true in developing countries, where a weak logistics environment often hinders trade. While logistics services are usually provided by private actors, national governments play a key role in ensuring high logistical performance, eg through infrastructure investments and regulatory reforms. Given limited monetary resources, identifying the most critical investments is a crucial task for developing countries. Wiederer and Straube (2019) developed a decision-making framework that prioritizes trade logistics interventions to promote higher-quality exports of perishable food. In addition, this project investigated the requirements and conditions needed for the development of stable export value chains.

Integrated planning and cost analytics

The movement toward global supply planning systems has driven the need for a single planning function, comprising teams of global brand/business planners. Such teams are responsible for market forecasts, inventory management plans, production plans for designated facilities, and distribution models, as well as the development of supply plans. Major goals are to reduce inventory, improve the customer experience and enhance efficiency.

This is an entirely new approach for many companies, since their planning was traditionally conducted on a regional or local level, including finished goods buffers to handle demand and supply deviations from the supply chain to the warehouse. Global supply and demand planning requires a structured process for building, updating and revising plans. To implement and realize such a process, certain organizational and personal prerequisites must be met: roles and responsibilities, as well as positions within the company for regional market planners, must be defined clearly. Inconsistencies in the quality of planning processes across regions can be addressed by training and development. Regional planners need to understand their new roles and responsibilities for global planning. They must also recognize the necessity for common sharing and communication of market forecasts, the development of contingencies, consensus building, capacity planning, supply scheduling, and execution of the plans they develop.

To support decision makers in planning robust international logistics networks, a logistics planning tool was developed at the TU Berlin – the TUB Logistics Navigator. The tool is freely accessible online and enables a co-creation network planning process within the supply chain. Besides the visualization of the entire material and information flow along the supply chain, various analysis functions (including risk and path analysis) support the solution-finding process. In addition, the TUB Logistics Navigator serves as a knowledge management platform, which summarizes a multitude of research works of the Competence Center for International Logistics Networks on the management of international logistics networks between Europe, China and Africa. Among other things, this includes work on measuring and evaluating volatility and risks in logistics networks, the influence of different cultures on logistics management, development scenarios of

European–Chinese logistics networks under the influence of the Belt and Road Initiative and much more. In addition, the TUB Logistics Navigator contains case studies and good practice supply chains of various globally operating companies.

Network adaptation, working capital time frames and logistics network design
Due to increasing complexity and a new view of total cost of ownership, many organizations are restructuring their global expansion by reallocating elements of their supply chains to local actors. Increased requirements for reliable and resilient supply chains, together with volatility, have prompted some organizations to re-evaluate global low-cost country sourcing.

Executives have realized that effective, localized decision making is increasingly important. In addition, suppliers are being forced to make significant capital investments by customers seeking to protect their working capital. The economic downturn has driven many companies to adopt financially conservative measures, and this is expected to remain the overriding trend for some years to come. While earlier capital decisions could have long-term horizons, organizations are now focusing on shorter planning cycles.

Technology

While technology is a great enabler, facilitating the automation of processes and data exchange, its competitive advantage for companies is rather short-lived. High-performing companies use technology to enhance decision-making processes by providing individuals with correct and timely information, thereby driving quicker decision making. By exploiting technology, such companies aim to enhance their future 'what-if' scenario planning and their capability to 'act before others do'.

Aligned technology investments
Technology also supports local sourcing strategies. While, in the past, low-cost country sourcing was necessary, recent advances in hardware (flexible robotics) and software (communication and information) have made formerly cost-intensive locations financially appealing. This could have a major influence on the future of global logistics by changing the imperative for companies to offshore to low-cost countries in order to remain competitive.

The most important trends that drive investments in technology are cost pressure, new mobile and 'big data' technologies, sustainability, the lack of infrastructure in BRIC countries, an increased risk of supply disruption, government regulations, poor infrastructure, and increasing global demand complexity.

Technologies help to simplify complexity and reduce the associated challenges. Information technology (IT)-oriented core technologies are now prevalent and build the foundation for integrated technological solutions. IT cyber security technology, enterprise resource planning systems, warehouse management systems, and 2D (barcode) scanning systems are examples of such core technologies. The integration of these technologies facilitates global material and delivery visibility, as well as business intelligence and correct data capture that make data accessible to all designated individuals. The purposes of such systems are faster responses to global complexity, effective integrated planning, and the provision of a reliable basis for key performance indicators (KPIs) and data to underpin decision making. Business analytics can be built onto this solid quantitative platform. Organizations that drive technological integration must plan their investments with a defined technology roadmap, to provide the basis for future strategic investments in emerging technology that build upon the existing core technology. In this way, solutions can be tailor-made for customers and technological developments elaborated, in cooperation with supply chain partners, in order to achieve better outcomes and reduce time-to-market.

Network visibility

To empower individuals, organizations need to provide real-time data about events, customer requirements, capacity information, and other strategic factors; therefore, they invest in various forms of technology, not only to accumulate and disseminate current data and to increase network visibility, but also to provide network modelling tools. Individuals can then make sound assessments of the projected impacts of certain actions on the network's status. Two key technological enablers have been identified: additive manufacturing (Durach *et al*, 2017) and blockchain technology (Durach *et al*, 2020; Verhoeven *et al*, 2020).

Collaborating with partners within a supply chain is crucial to a company's success. Network optimization technologies provide a collaboration platform for sharing information and scenario analyses, which can be used to model the outcome of possible decisions. To work effectively, this technology gathers data from multiple members of the supply chain, requiring commitment and trust from supply chain partners. Real-time visibility provides the foundation for tactical decision making and enables companies to react quickly to disruptions within the network.

Cost-to-serve analytics

Customer cost-to-serve analytics are an interesting application of so-called 'big data', since they capture the total costs, across the entire supply chain, of fulfilling customers' demands. This data and information offers executives the opportunity to reduce costs, optimize profitability and increase market share. This new and unexploited field of technology has the potential to enhance competitive advantage, and it can enable companies to use social media data and customer feedback in real time and turn them into tactical advantages.

Networks

Companies are often small units within large supply networks. Much of the efficacy of such networks is built on the fact that single players not only strive for their own interests and benefits, but also respect and enable the economic success of their network partners.

End-to-end supply chain integration

Besides integrating processes such as inventory management, warehousing, transportation and customer service, companies aspire to expand their integration back into manufacturing, production scheduling, supplier planning, and product development processes. Since product and system design highly influences the end-to-end supply chain, companies often start such projects in an effort to drive total cost analytics, market intelligence and performance. While information exchange among supply chain partners has been a valid logistics strategy for the last 30 years, end-to-end integration differentiates itself from simple information sharing by its information diversity and depth, its intensity of exchange, and the number of applications it offers.

Outsourcing and near-shoring

Organizations have been deploying outsourcing as a strategy for many years. In the early 21st century, the lure of low wage costs, particularly in China and India, drove a surge in outsourcing. These extended supply chains generated complexity, rising logistics costs (eg in line with fuel prices), and higher demands for supply chain reliability and resilience. The associated risks forced companies to reconsider their outsourcing strategies. As an alternative, near-shoring offers the benefits of shorter reaction times and decreased transportation costs for customers.

Horizontal and vertical cooperation

A strategic component of network strategy is cooperation. Horizontal cooperation describes the collaboration between companies that compete in the same industry sector, while vertical cooperation refers to the upstream and/or downstream extension of cooperation in the vertical supply chain, which enables end-to-end integration. All members of a supply chain must be integrated and included as partners for global logistics design to be successful. The form of collaboration may vary, however, and must be carefully planned, since mistakes cannot only be costly, but can harm the company's reputation and affect future collaboration with other organizations.

Horizontal collaboration with other players in an industry is a powerful tool for influencing government regulations and investment decisions, and/or increasing customer satisfaction. During times of disruption, for example, competitors can assist each other for their mutual benefit; that is, a troubled company can enlist the help of a competitor to serve current customers while it recovers, in order to ensure long-term customer satisfaction (Zeng *et al*, 2012).

Strategic delivery reliability

As mentioned earlier, the study found that logistics performance, as measured by delivery reliability, had deteriorated since the study was first conducted in 2008. Qualitative data suggested that the deterioration was due to developments both upstream and downstream of the focal companies. The purpose of this section is, therefore, to outline the strategic importance of delivery reliability as a major driver of trends and a lever for coping strategies.

In 2008, the BVL research team found that delivery reliability was the most important goal of logistics for all categories of firms (manufacturing, LSP and retail). In 2012, the team found that, downstream from focal companies, increased customer expectations were being driven by consumers or marketing experts down to retailers, who were in turn passing these expectations to manufacturers. This suggested that it was not necessarily the delivery capability of the firms that deteriorated, but rather their ability to keep up with the increasing expectations of the customers. As an FMCG executive stated: 'The biggest challenge we see, by far, is the increased expectation of reliability our major customers are placing on us.' The interviewee also indicated that one of the main reasons for this development was the lack of an adequate logistics infrastructure. Two out of three respondents stated that their company's logistics capability was negatively influenced by poor transportation infrastructure, which was a particular problem in emerging markets.

As an effect of this development, LSPs were being pressured to provide increasingly customer-specific delivery solutions to meet a variety of new demands. E-commerce was also driving a fragmentation of supply chain networks and further undermining the ability of logistics providers to meet customer needs. Customers seemed to be more willing to switch brands and suppliers at short notice if they found a provider that better met their needs in terms of delivery reliability. Furthermore, companies needed high-quality, low-cost and sustainable low-carbon solutions to keep customers satisfied.

An example of an effective coping strategy to ensure enhanced delivery reliability was provided by Symrise: a German global supplier of fragrances, flavours, active ingredients and aroma chemicals, which built a partnership with local vanilla farmers in Madagascar. Symrise is one of the largest buyers of this spice in Madagascar and closely collaborates with over 1,000 vanilla farmers. By collaborating with non-government organizations (NGOs), development organizations and farmers' cooperatives, the company has created sustainable partnerships. It benefits by receiving high-quality vanilla beans from reliable sources.[3]

Customer expectations are not expected to decline any time soon. As mentioned earlier, volatility is the 'new normal' endangering logistics systems, since delivery times can be threatened by such external network forces; it is therefore necessary for companies to create network partnerships in order to increase the reliability of deliveries. As pointed out by a global chemicals executive, there is a 'need to have outstanding processes and reliable systems'. It seems that enterprise transformation is now an ongoing phenomenon, as organizations continuously adapt and reinvent their operating models in the face of rapid global change. The speed and scale of this change in recent decades has been unparalleled.

As discussed, upstream of focal companies, organizations were increasingly being drawn into a networked economy. The delivery reliability of suppliers is essential in such cooperative networks. Product manufacturing and service delivery are no longer stand-alone capabilities, but are increasingly bundled into a single set of capabilities demanded by customers. Since no single company can offer all services and products, companies must find new ways of working with, not only customers and suppliers but, in some cases, competitors. Which leads us to forms of co-opetition.

These given facts are not new. In the 2008 and 2012 studies, German survey participants were asked to estimate the value of delivery reliability in terms of the percentage of goods that were delivered on time. A comparison of the responses from 2008 and 2012 for five selected industries provided a number of important insights. In Table 9.1, a 2008/2012 comparison of delivery reliability is depicted for five German industry sectors. The respondents were grouped into quintiles ranging from 'best-in-class' (BIC) companies to 'latecomers'. The median values for the four indicators remained almost constant, indicating a high degree of industry standardization with respect to delivery reliability. In many countries and industries, logistics delivery reliability did not improve. Conversely, the gap between BIC companies and latecomers increased from 2008 onward. Compared to the top performers, the latecomers in all industries experienced a 3 to 10 per cent decline in their delivery reliability. It seems that many companies were unable to keep pace with the ever-increasing calls for higher delivery reliability. Such companies ran the risk of losing their customers, since customers were, as stated earlier, increasingly willing to switch brands. Executives therefore had to establish logistics as a key value-adding service of their companies, rather than focusing on logistics as a cost-saving measure.

A final point to note is that, in terms of absolute importance, delivery reliability and lead times were evaluated significantly more highly by surveyed logistics managers in countries characterized by poor infrastructure and uncertainty due to government regulations. This was most apparent in the ratings of managers from China and Brazil.

Digital transformation in logistics

The results of the study show that companies are already well advanced when it comes to creating transparency in their value creation networks. Three-quarters of the participating experts stated that they are using solutions to achieve real-time transparency. The step towards cognitive and autonomous logistics processes, on the other hand, is being approached rather hesitantly by companies. Thus, 59 per cent of the surveyed industrial enterprises do not want to invest in artificial intelligence. At the same time, the studies make it clear that best-practice companies especially differentiate through data-driven services from others. It will be a key to success how well these data-driven services will be tailored to individual customer expectations. In the future, customers will no longer be summarized in segments,

Table 9.1 Comparison of delivery reliability

	Year	Latecomer	Catch up	Typical	Advanced	BIC	Median
			Delivery reliability (%)				
German Automotive Industry							
	2012	< 90	≥ 90 – < 97	≥ 97 – < 98	≥ 98 – < 100	≥ 100	98
	2008	< 93	≥ 93 – < 972	≥ 972 – < 98	≥ 98 – < 99.4	≥ 99.4	98
German Chemical and Plastics Industry							
	2012	< 80	≥ 80 – < 95	≥ 95 – 98	≥ 98 – < 99	≥ 99	95
	2008	< 90	≥ 90 – < 94.4	≥ 94.4 – < 95.3	≥ 95.3 – < 98	≥ 98	95
German Electronic Industry							
	2012	< 81	≥ 81 – < 95	≥ 95 – < 98	≥ 98 – < 98	≥ 98	96
	2008	< 90	≥ 90 – < 95	≥ 95 – < 95	≥ 95 – < 98	≥ 98	95
German Machine and Plant Engineering Industry							
	2012	< 85	≥ 85 – < 95	≥ 95 – < 96	≥ 96 – < 98	≥ 98	95
	2008	< 94	≥ 94 – < 95	≥ 95 – < 96.2	≥ 96.2 – < 98	≥ 98	95
Retail							
Stationery	2012	< 81	≥ 81 – < 90	≥ 90 – < 95	≥ 95 – < 98	≥ 98	95
Mail order	2012	< 90	≥ 90 – < 95	≥ 95 – < 95	≥ 95 – < 98	≥ 98	95

but served individually, based on a smaller segmentation down to customer-specific individual profiles. As technology becomes more widespread, over-laps between individual industries and sectors are becoming significantly larger. This requires expertise in a variety of areas in an increasingly competitive environment. This interdisciplinarity requires innovation strategies and a stronger focus on cooperation. The term Open Innovation describes the basic principle that knowledge can enter and leave the innovation process at any time. This can be achieved, for example, by using technologies, investing in start-ups or through the involvement of customers, service providers, suppliers, consulting companies or academic institutions. A look at best-practice companies reveals a number of things. There is agreement that within the innovation process basically every possible stakeholder in future will gain in importance. Companies therefore have to find ways to engage with these stakeholders and to integrate their knowledge into the innovation processes. However, this alone is not enough – innovation management of the future is not process-based, but culture-driven. Employees must be allowed to make mistakes and take risks. It is indispensable that companies not only encourage their employees to test new ideas, but also create a corporate culture in which such behaviour is promoted. For the generation of innovations customers are the most important source, followed by suppliers and competitors.

The introduction of digital transformation in logistics is expected to take place in a stepwise process. The first step to create transparency is already a reality in many companies. The step towards (partially) autonomous processes in logistics networks is in many cases still obstructed – by media breaks, lack of master data quality and missing architectures and standards for data transmission and processing, as well as distrust of innovations within organizations on both the management and the employee sides. Thus, companies should on the one hand create structures to use data profitably, and on the other hand establish an open innovation culture in order to address current challenges in the best possible way (Straube *et al*, 2019; Verhoeven and Junge, 2019).

Conclusion and outlook

Persisting long-term trends create challenges for logistics managers, placing increasing demands on the delivery reliability of today's companies due to trends such as increasing customer requirements, greater volatility and problems with infrastructure. The study revealed that the gap between companies that can provide high delivery reliability and latecomers has increased since 2008. At present, many companies in the manufacturing and retail industries are still focusing their efforts on internal processes and operational goals, but the picture varies between companies and also differs between sectors. Without doubt, these findings have important implications for practitioners in companies that run the risk of missing their chance to be best-in-class. Executives must strengthen the perception of logistics as a key value-adding service for their companies, rather than increasing pressure to save costs in logistics functions.

In future, success in an increasingly networked economy will depend on how successful companies are at collaborating with horizontal and vertical partners in order to meet customers' needs. The successful companies will strategically integrate their logistics activities into the overall business system, recognizing the advantages of logistics and measuring the benefits. This means they will be able to develop better end-to-end scope of responsibility and successfully complete strategic projects.

Notes

1 Disclaimer: The present book chapter is an update of our earlier publication: Durach, CF, Straube, F and Wieland, A (2014) Trends and strategies in global logistics and supply chain management, in *Global Logistics*, 7th edn, eds Donald Waters and Stephen Rinsler, Kogan Page, London. The chapter builds on the findings reported in: Handfield, R, Straube, F, Pfohl, H-C and Wieland, A (2013) *Trends and Strategies in Logistics and Supply Chain Management: Embracing global logistics complexity to drive market advantage*, DVV Media Group, Bremen, Germany.

2 A version of this article appeared on 1 December 2012, on page B1 in the US edition of *The Wall Street Journal*, with the headline: 'Fast-Growing Label: Made in Ghana'.

3 www.symrise.com/newsroom/article/outstanding-excellence-symrise-wins-fi-europe-excellence-awards/ (archived at https://perma.cc/8UM8-2MR5)

References

Cappelli, P (2008) *Talent on Demand: Managing talent in an age of uncertainty*, Harvard Business School Press, Boston, MA

Choi, T and Linton, T (2011) Don't let your supply chain control your business, *Harvard Business Review*, **89** (2), pp 1–8

Christopher, M and Holweg, M (2011) Supply chain 2.0: Managing supply chains in the era of turbulence, *International Journal of Physical Distribution & Logistics Management*, **41** (1), pp 63–82

Durach, CF, Blesik, T, von Düring, M and Bick, M (2020) Blockchain applications in supply chain transactions, *Journal of Business Logistics*, **42** (1), pp 7–24

Durach, CF, Kurpjuweit, S and Wagner, SM (2017) The impact of additive manufacturing on supply chains, *International Journal of Physical Distribution & Logistics Management*, **47** (10), pp 954–71

Handfield, R, Straube, F, Pfohl, H-C and Wieland, A (2013) *Trends and Strategies in Logistics and Supply Chain Management: Embracing global logistics complexity to drive market advantage*, DVV Media Group, Bremen, Germany

Nitsche, B (2019) Development of an assessment tool to control supply chain volatility, *Schriftenreihe Logistik der Technischen Universität Berlin*, Universitätsverlag der TU Berlin

Nitsche, B (2020) Decrypting the Belt and Road Initiative: Barriers and development paths for global logistics networks, *Sustainability*, **12**, pp 1–23

Nitsche, B, Verhoeven, P and Lengeling, C (2019) Navigating international supply chains: A case study collection, in *Schriftenreihe Logistik der Technischen Universität Berlin*, ed Frank Straube, Universitätsverlag der TU Berlin, Berlin

Straube, F and Nitsche, B (2020) Heading into 'The New Normal': Potential development paths of international logistics networks in the wake of the Coronavirus pandemic, *Internationales Verkehrswesen*, **72** (3), pp 31–35

Straube, F (ed), Junge, AL, Verhoeven, P, Reipert, J and Mansfeld, M (2019) Trends and strategies in logistics: Pathway of digital transformation in logistics best practice concepts and future developments, *Schriftenreihe Logistik der Technischen Universität Berlin*, Universitätsverlag der TU Berlin, Berlin

Verhoeven, P and Junge, AL (2019) Digitale Transformation in der Logistik schreitet voran, *Manufacturing Excellence Report 2019*, pp 42–43

Verhoeven, P, Sinn, F and Herden, TT (2020) Examples from blockchain implementations in logistics and supply chain management: Exploring the mindful use of a new technology, *Logistics*, **2** (3), pp 1–19

Wiederer, C and Straube, F (2019) A decision tool for policymakers to foster higher-value perishable agricultural exports, *Transportation Research Interdisciplinary Perspectives*, **2**, pp 1–9

Zeng, AZ, Durach, CF and Fang, Y (2012) Collaboration decisions on disruption recovery service in urban public tram systems, *Transportation Research: Part E*, **48** (3), pp 578–90

Global sourcing and supply   10

Alan Braithwaite

Global trade – economic lifeblood

Adam Smith wrote that 'Every man lives by exchanging'. Today's world of global trade would have been beyond his comprehension, albeit that the port of London was the world's largest at the time. Trade is as old as civilization; the Silk Road and spice routes had their origins before Christ. Since then, the basic concept has changed little: merchants or buyers travel to find goods that are either scarce or competitive in price, or both, in the destination markets. Now, global sourcing and supply is a central part of most large companies' business strategies. It has proved essential to sustaining marketplace competitiveness and maintaining net margins.

Global sourcing and supply has been one of the biggest economic trends of the last 45 years; it has taken advantage of ease of market access, enabled as never before by international travel, sophisticated banking and low-cost and fast logistics. Political initiatives to reduce tariff barriers and deregulate operating environments through the World Trade Organization (WTO) have been a key factor in the growth that we have seen.

Figure 10.1 shows the growth in trade in manufactured goods from 1960 and set alongside the growth in GDP. Until the 2008/9 global downturn, the adoption of low-cost sourcing and supply strategies had displayed an exponential growth trend at around four times the rate of growth in global GDP. This chart was prepared shortly after the 2008 financial crash, showing a short-lived blip in the trend and a forecast that growth would resume at historic rates.

Those forecasts proved over-optimistic as can be seen in Figure 10.2, which shows more recent statistics including the recovery from the 2008/9 financial crisis and the recent Covid pandemic. While the forecast is for continued growth, the rate of increase is predicted to move closer to the trend of GDP.

Figure 10.1 Growth in world trade in manufactured goods versus GDP, 1960 to 2010

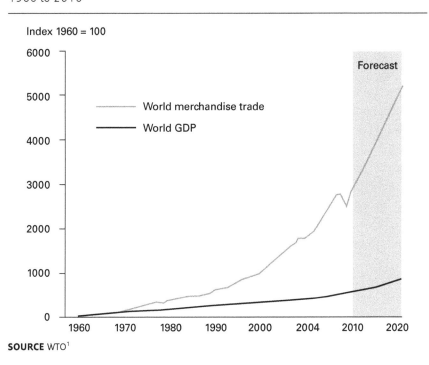

SOURCE WTO[1]

Figure 10.2 Growth in world trade in manufactured goods, indexed 2000 to 2020

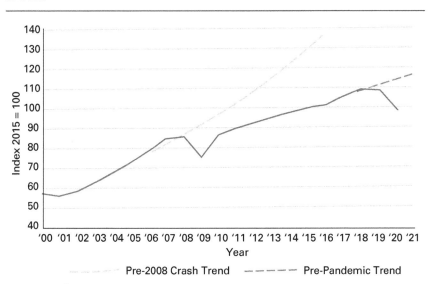

SOURCE WTO[2]

These figures and expert commentary suggest that world trade is reaching some level of saturation in terms of what is practical and viable. The Chief Economist of the Danish shipping giant AP Moller-Maersk is on record as saying that he expects growth in world trade to be much more in line with global growth in GDP. Leading South African academics Jan Havenga and Joubert van Eeden completed a study of the latent potential growth for world trade into their country, concluding that saturation was closer than had hitherto been thought; most commodities were close to maximum potential demand.[3]

The wealth of WTO statistics as well as the author's personal commercial experience working with the shipping line ZIM suggest that the growth is now coming more from intra-regional trade between developing economies rather than between the so-called 'developing' and 'developed' world. The WTO report in 2018 remarked that: 'From 2011, developing economies' exports to other developing economies surpassed its exports to developed economies. "South–South" trade represented an estimated US $4.28 trillion or 52 per cent of total developing economies' exports in 2018.'

With two massive global crises in the last 10 years and the redefining of forecasts, global trade is unlikely to recover its former meteoric growth status. Nonetheless, it is an established geopolitical and economic fact of life; it has been driven by opening markets, reduced trade barriers and low-cost international logistics. The historic growth has both fuelled and enabled the growth in GDP of most countries, both mature and developing markets: exporting jobs to countries with large pools of increasingly skilled and relatively low-cost labour. The capacity of the labour pool in developed countries has been released to higher value work or essentially local activities, particularly the service sector. There can be no turning back – but we are likely to see significant adjustments in mix over the coming 20 years based on sustainability, ethics, technology, product trends and political rejection of internationalism.

This chapter describes the heritage landscape of global sourcing and supply, the areas of 'good practice' that companies need to address to ensure a stable operational and business base and the factors that will come to determine future sourcing strategies. It draws on research conducted at Cranfield School of Management, work with companies on sourcing, supply and logistics, and a consideration of the drivers and trends for the next 20 years. It is a huge subject area – this chapter can only point to the big issues.

The product economics that have driven global sourcing

It is important to understand just how significant global sourcing and supply has been as a strategy for entire industries and specific companies. It has driven low prices for consumers, good margins for retailers and consumer-led economic growth, especially in mature economies.

Let's look first at the global clothing industry. The fashion industry has achieved remarkable growth over the last 20 years. The estimates are that the number of units sold more than doubled between 2000 and 2015 from *c*50 billion units to 106 billion with global revenues reaching $1.3 trillion.[4] This has been driven by a combination of reduced prices, higher disposable incomes and the 'fast fashion' phenomenon driving demand.

The transformation of the fast fashion model can be seen clearly through considering the business model strategy. First, technology enables deep consumer insights and fast response to trends; second, more ranges are designed with more frequent drops to the shopfloor which keeps the market stimulated; and third, the model creates a scarcity value through not replenishing styles – just offering alternative designs. This leaves the consumer no time to consider the merits of the purchase and creates peer pressure.[5] Combined, these strategies have made fashion disposable in the minds of affluent consumers. On a global scale it is possible to infer that the units purchased per person per year has increased from 8 to 14; a classic case of the price elasticity of demand.

The industry has serviced this growth by creating remarkable levels of waste and environmental impact across the extended clothing and textiles supply chains. Global production of textiles was 53 million tonnes in 2017. That production process involved 98 million tonnes of non-renewable resources, including oil and chemicals to produce dye and finish textiles. The amount of water used in production was 93 billion cubic metres. The greenhouse gas emissions from the industry have been estimated at 1.2 billion tonnes of CO_2. This places the end-to-end clothing supply chain as a greater emitter than the combination of air and sea freight in the global rankings, at about 3 per cent of the total.[6] The manufacture of a T-shirt can involve four countries, and four international container shipments from cotton production through spinning and knitting to making and finally to retail. Typical miles covered and the time taken have been mapped at 16,500 miles over up to 700 days.[7]

This huge industry brings major employment across the world. The Ellen MacArthur Foundation estimates that the end-to-end chain employs 300 million including retailing.[8] The conditions of employment across the extended supply chain are now the subject of comment and investigation with modern slavery being commonplace. The industry does not just exploit as it creates products; the landfill and incineration of used clothing is estimated at nearly 39 million tonnes, underlining the societal waste of current consumption and usage patterns.

It can be fairly stated that wealthy people have systematically, albeit unwittingly, exploited the workforce in the developing world and the global environment to indulge their desire for identity through fashion.

Moving from a macro picture to a specific company case helps to drive home how global sourcing became 'transformational magic' in boardrooms. While the following case is historic, it provides a perfect picture of the business dynamic that was put in place by so many companies.

B&Q is a retailer of 'do-it-yourself' (DIY) home improvement products operating primarily in the UK but also in countries such as France (Castorama), China and Poland. It is owned by Kingfisher and at the turn of the century was the group's jewel in the crown. The group provided, at the time, a limited picture of its strategy through presentations to analysts and its report and accounts, which are presented here as a short case study.

In 1999/2000 B&Q embarked on a strategy of Every Day Low Prices (EDLP); this was taken conceptually from the success of Walmart in its categories. The key concept was to sell goods at highly compelling prices all the year round and rely less on promotions and discounting. The strategic objective was and remains to drive top-line growth by selling at slightly lower gross margins with the expectation that the growth would increase overall profitability.

For B&Q the strategy did indeed work and the highlights are:

- By 2003/2004 it had driven revenue up by 70 per cent.
- Volume growth was in the region of 125 per cent.
- To achieve these two numbers together, real prices had to be reduced by around 25 per cent – subject to the mix of sales by category.

This growth was supported by a huge increase in the levels of global direct sourcing, which industry sources suggest went from 5 to 25 per cent in the period. Effectively, by utilizing low-cost supply, the strategy enabled B&Q to sell for less to the consumer while increasing margin.

Table 10.1 Sourcing and selling comparisons for B&Q

	WAS sourced for	NOW sourced for
B&Q knife	88p	40p
Castorama wrench	€8.50	€2.00
	2004 SOLD for	**2005 SOLD for**
B&Q Real wood flooring	£19.98/sqm	£14.07/sqm
Castorama swimming pool	€305.00	€129.00

SOURCE Compiled from company reports by author

Their presentation to analysts gave the product examples shown in Table 10.1, in terms of both buying and selling.

The reductions in the direct buying costs must be partly offset by the cost of shipping, insurance, additional stock and the buying offices that are needed in the sourcing countries. Nonetheless, it is easy from the selling prices to see how the EDLP strategy in conjunction with global sourcing could have driven the market price reductions estimated at 25 per cent.

Analysis of the underlying performance metrics of the business at that time (Table 10.2), with some assumptions to fill data gaps, shows the shift in performance that was achieved. By keeping the net margin rate steady at 10 per cent, the business was able to drive growth in sales and absolute profits. It is also apparent that the company put back a part of the margin gain into service through hiring more employees; this also reflects the increased volumes being handled.

At the time, statements in relation to planned increases in this trend were a regular feature of many corporations' annual reports and analyst briefings. Walmart, the world's largest corporation, made the trend to direct international sourcing a key feature of its 2002 annual report:

> We also are making exciting strides in two other important areas: internal product development and global procurement. Last year we assumed responsibility of global procurement from a third party. This allowed us to better coordinate the entire global supply chain from product development to delivery. In addition, our global procurement programme allows us to share our buying power and merchandise network with all our operations throughout the world.
>
> **SOURCE** Walmart Annual Report (2002)

Table 10.2 B&Q business metrics showing the impact of EDLP and global sourcing

Year	1999/2000	2000/2001	2001/2002	2002/2003	2003/2004	2004/2005
Revenue/Sq ft	143	161	162	175	171	182
Profit/Sq ft	14	15	15	17	16	18
Revenue/employee	75,656	87,375	99,337	112,500	114,815	102,500
Profit per employee	13,154	14,744	11,429	10,571	10,838	10,200
Profit margin	10%	9%	9%	10%	10%	10%
Revenue per sku	66,066	75,051	80,000	92,500	86,667	95,250
Profit per sku	6,420	7,108	7,500	9,000	8,267	8,750

SOURCE Compiled from company reports by author

The trend to global direct sourcing and establishing offices in origin countries for that purpose has not been unique to retailers. The manufacturer, Dyson, closed its entire manufacturing in the UK and moved to Malaysia in 2003/5 as a key element of its entry strategy for the US market.

More recently there have been some strategy adjustments but not wholesale reversal, as the statistics show. The Walmart story is a case in point. In 2010 it entered into a long term contract with Li & Fung to provide buying office services in Asia; Li & Fung is the world's largest buying agent and it committed to setting up a separate business, Direct Sourcing Group (DSG), as a dedicated provider to Walmart. However, by 2013 this arrangement to outsource appeared to be no longer the sole approach. Walmart is reported to have cancelled a deal to buy DSG and is going direct to factories, cutting out the middleman. At that time, Chainamag.com (archived at https://perma.cc/7VV9-5BQ2) reported:

> Li & Fung has, however, set up a new agreement with Walmart. It will remain a primary supplier for Sam's Club in the United States through DSG, while providing buying-agency services to the global retailer's US operations as well as internationally. The new agreement allows Li & Fung to provide higher-margin design and replenishment services, and is set for five years with the possibility to extend by two or more years, according to Bruce Rockowitz, CEO of Li & Fung.

This suggests an organizational search for a few points of margin and improved supply chain performance rather than the dash for the quantum gains that were clear from the B&Q case.

In the context of global trade that is approaching saturation, the strategy of global sourcing and supply is now about 'competitive parity' rather than 'competitive advantage'. Price will always be the single largest buying factor in both personal and corporate purchasing decisions – all other factors such as quality, sustainability and waste are weighed against it.[9] The future will be about how the relative cost structures change and how the perception, or legal imperative, of sustainability benefits moves over time.

Sustainability and the UN'S SDGS

The book titled *The China Price* published in 2006 provides a powerful description of the social and environmental implications of the West's desire for cheap products: exactly the commercial success story described in the section above.[10] The awareness of corporate social responsibility (CSR) has been increasing and was enshrined in the concept of the triple bottom line (TBL) by Elkington to convey the need for companies to focus simultaneously on three goals: people, profit and planet.[11] In 2018 he 'withdrew' the concept in an effort to draw attention to the fact that business and political leaders were paying lip service to the imperative to 'clean up after themselves';[12] some call this 'greenwashing'. But the tensions in boardrooms and government corridors to paper over the challenge are compelling and must be understood. Major brands can put their competitive position at risk by adopting environmentally sound practices if that means they cannot match the prices of those who do not. The issue in boardrooms is whether or not to accept the true costs of the externalities created by exploitative supply chains.

The effect of consumption and resource usage on the planet and society is widely accepted and has been embedded in United Nations policy through its 17 Sustainable Development Goals (SDGs) agreed by 193 countries and set as targets for 2030.[13] With just under 10 years to reach hugely ambitious targets, including the elimination of poverty, analysts for the Social Progress Index, while observing some progress, predict that the world will not attain the SDGs until 2082; this is so far out it should be treated as a polite way of saying 'never'.

In the context of global sourcing practice and the example in the previous section of the clothing industry, attainment of the SDGs requires direct change in numbers 1, 3, 6, 7, 8, 9, 10, 11, 12, 13, 14, 15 and 16 (see Table 10.3).

The argument is now raging as to whether the attainment of these goals will have an ultimate societal cost or whether the cost of inaction will be much greater as natural disasters increase in frequency. The experience of the pandemic in 2020 supports the view that investing in a sustainable future is a wise course of action.

For companies to meet the SDGs requires that they (and their consumers) accept the true societal costs that currently lie outside their supply chains: eg carbon emissions, air quality, pollution, landfill and social exploitation. At present there is no tariff for such damage, no means of imposing such charges and the published 'rates' are likely to understate the true costs or provide sufficient motivation to create a structural shift in working methods.

Politically and economically, driving change to a new global model will be profoundly challenging. But, at some point in the not-too-distant future, the world will have to embrace radical change at a rate that will be as frightening as the pandemic. Only a few countries were prepared for the

Table 10.3 The 17 Goals

GOAL 1:	No poverty
GOAL 2:	Zero hunger
GOAL 3:	Good health and wellbeing
GOAL 4:	Quality education
GOAL 5:	Gender equality
GOAL 6:	Clean water and sanitation
GOAL 7:	Affordable and clean energy
GOAL 8:	Decent work and economic growth
GOAL 9:	Industry, innovation and infrastructure
GOAL 10:	Reduced inequality
GOAL 11:	Sustainable cities and communities
GOAL 12:	Responsible consumption and production
GOAL 13:	Climate action
GOAL 14:	Life below water
GOAL 15:	Life on land
GOAL 16:	Peace and justice strong institutions
GOAL 17:	Partnerships to achieve the goal

pandemic but their responses and experience show how valuable that preparation has proved to be; it also showed that even the well-prepared are part of a global 'system' and had to take some consequences.

The balance of this chapter will look at good practice in global sourcing for companies, key directions for the future and their implications.

The key features of 'good practice' in global sourcing

The operational dynamics of global sourcing and supply has been a fluid and evolving management topic. Global sourcing and supply introduce, by definition, long-distance supply chains, multiple hand-offs, extended lead times and associated risks. There are major implications for companies in how their extended chains are managed; security of supply, demand responsiveness and product life cycle management all take on greater significance.

A systematic literature review on global sourcing and supply was carried out at Cranfield School of Management as a Masters' thesis.[14] The core findings of the work can be summarized in the following points.

First, the work showed the explosion of interest in global sourcing and supply over the previous decades. The volume of publications in the years 2001 to 2005 was more than 3,000 academically accredited papers. Second, the balance of interest over the period analysed moved to a strong focus on the sub-topics of implementation and ongoing control and improvement and away from strategy. This reflects a maturing subject matter area where the question 'why?' becomes less interesting and 'how?' becomes the dominant issue. Third, there was, at the time, a surprisingly low level of attention to the area of sourcing and selection, which probably reflects the commercial confidentiality of the question and hence the lack of good data.

Finally, emerging themes and research gaps were identified. It was found that relationship building (intra- and inter-organizations) and communications are big emerging themes in procurement. This is crucial to successful global sourcing in all its phases.

The work enabled the preparation of a mind-map for the issues in global sourcing and supply and this is shown in Figure 10.3. It is built around the five key themes that emerged from the research: strategy, sourcing and selection, implementation, ongoing control and results. The many petals on the mind-map serve to emphasize the complexity of the endeavour; and each area could be unpacked further into its own specifics. For example, the buying strategies and supply models would include the terms of trade (Incoterms) on which the buying operation will be conducted.

The preparation of this mind-map led to the creation of a 'good practice' model which echoes typical organizational structures. This is shown in Figure 10.4: the 'Layers and Pillars' model.

Interviews on the ground during the course of the Cranfield research found that many companies sourcing globally struggled to create organizational structures that were effective; often silos were erected rather than eliminated. The layers and pillars structure makes clear the need for single roles for the commercial and contractual function, and logistics network management and ICT. Referring to the chapter in this book on performance management and the role of the supply chain team in supply chain governance, there is a role for that team in process design and the facilitation of relationships, capabilities and skills. Those roles are to design, coordinate and integrate. However, the key to success lies in the pillars of capability which truly integrate the extended chain: risk management and cost-to-serve.

Figure 10.3 A mind-map of global sourcing

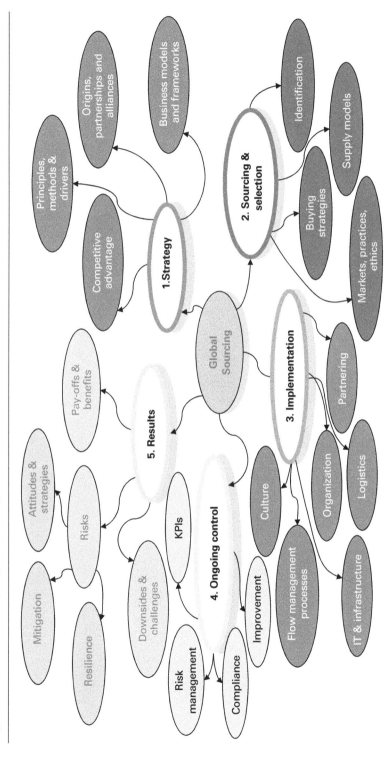

SOURCE Braithwaite (2021)

Figure 10.4   The Layers and Pillars model of good practice in global sourcing

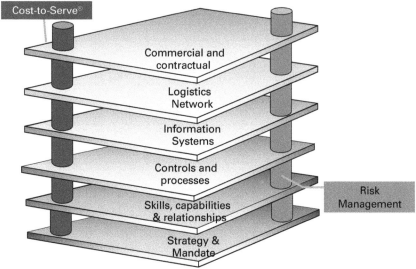

SOURCE Braithwaite (2021)

Risk management is about recognizing and managing for the spectrum of possible factors from supply chain disruption through climate and seismic events to supplier performance including failure and reputational damage. Chapter 4, dealing with supply chain risk and vulnerability, provides a view of the range of potential issues and a process-based approach to identifying and mitigating them. The application of this approach as a discipline is counter-cultural (especially in fast-moving retail organizations) but will invariably repay the effort to put them in place.

The second pillar is about identifying the total cost of acquisition and distribution and ensuring it is viable: the ability to analyse and predict the total cost-to-serve from the source of supply to its final point of sale (the cost-to-serve method).[15] The capability in this analysis is not just to build up the procurement and logistics costs by differentiating the physical characteristics of the freight and the duty and customs regimes that are applicable. It is also important to analyse and build into the costing the inherent margin loss/markdown and lost sales risk of product obsolescence by developing and applying a concatenated profile of market, risk and cost. The inventory holding cost through the chain must also be factored in. Experience has shown that this analysis identifies products that should never be traded on a long lead time, or that should be the subject of a postponement strategy. It is also likely to show that there are some products where actions to reduce lead time and increase flexibility will justify a higher initial purchasing cost: potentially re- or near-shoring.

As global risks and volatility increase (witness the two global shocks in 10 years) and cost structures change in response to environmental and market pressures, these two capabilities will be central to companies being able to identify appropriate change and adjust their global sourcing strategies in a timely and agile way.

Emerging risks and their implications for future sourcing strategies

In looking at emerging risks for global sourcing and supply and their implications, it is important to refer the reader to the chapter in this volume specifically on managing supply vulnerability and then refer to the UN's SDGs described earlier.

The rate at which climatic, seismic, conflict and humanitarian disasters have occurred in the last 20 years has shown a steady increase.[16] On top of that we have warnings (time and scale unknown) of global warming causing irreversible sea level increases, climatic disasters, increasing levels of political trade dispute and protectionism; through the media, we have greater awareness of widespread modern slavery and exploitation.

The devasting economic impact of the 2020 pandemic, which has proved to be more serious and long-lasting than the 2008/9 financial crash, has yet to be fully apparent at the time of writing. The question for management teams is what strategic and tactical responses are appropriate in the short, medium and long term in the context of this dire outlook.

The reality is that global sourcing is deeply embedded in corporate supply chains – quick change is difficult, and the potential may be constrained by capacity. On a horizon of one to four years, the implications will be more about mitigating the impact of potential threats to 'business as usual'. Beyond that there is an opportunity to make structural change; but that too will be constrained by capacity and the cost-to-serve of any possible changes.

Few, if any, businesses will have the courage and margin to completely reconfigure their chains in anticipation of the next possible horror – for that may be a contingency that never occurs. The actions taken may make the company uncompetitive in the short term, before any grim reaper actually arrives. And, finally, the pandemic has thrown up big winners alongside stories of commercial disaster; the risk is that mitigation measures target the wrong events.

So, while we know what might be in store, planning for it and making operational change is a real dilemma. As they say in the United States, this is about 'betting the farm'; you could add that the game is Russian roulette.

Emerging technologies and their impacts

The parallel exponential trend to global sourcing has been the growth of digital technology. The famous Moore's Law shows empirically the logarithmic growth in the power of microchips;[17] but it is not just power that has increased, capacity has also grown exponentially.

The first version of this chapter was prepared in 2013. Its focus on technology was on ICT (information and communications technology) and the use of the internet and GPS to provide visibility of global supply chains. In 2021, the discussion needs to be extended to robotics, automation, Internet of Things (IoT) and additive manufacturing. These technologies have the potential to transform the supply market and help to overcome the wage rate differential for some manufactured goods; opening the possibility of re-shoring.

Extended chains require information technology that can manage the long-distance 'purchase to pay' cycle with all the steps along the way. The key is to make available a single version of the order and its status to every point along the chain; it must allow the appropriate people and organizations to interact with it to make amendments, update status and provide a history of events.

Figure 10.5 illustrates this ICT concept using the idea of an information backbone. The reader should note that this figure is also used in Chapter 20 on performance management. The idea is to have a 'single version of the truth' between all the actors in the extended chain: suppliers, logistics, the company being supplied and potentially its customers. The use of the information is for event tracking, quality, specifications and transactions.

The term 'blockchain' is being used by some as the term to describe this information backbone. In the opinion of the author, blockchain is another step along the technology road map as it has, at its heart, the secure transfer of currency. So the information backbone is a step on from the ERP systems, but a step behind the blockchain concept. At the time of writing the application of the blockchain concept is limited in supply chain and logistics; this

Figure 10.5   The information backbone provides a 'single version of the truth' along the chain

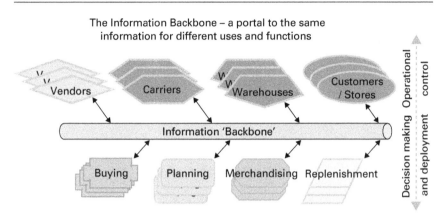

SOURCE Braithwaite (2021)

is because of the difficulty of verifying physical transactions and product quality.

The data architecture needs to be able to handle consignments, waybills, containers, tariffs, providers, VAT and duty as well as orders, SKUs, vendors and locations. Since on-time performance is critically important, systems in international trade need to be able to track time in terms of due dates, key event milestones and any discrepancies between plan and actual. This is much more than conventional ERP where each individual firm in the chain will be holding only some of that data, occasionally with different reference numbers and indexing. Data interchange between systems is essential to provide the visibility needed to achieve flow control. Given the lead times of supply this does not need to be a real-time data feed, but it does require at least daily updates. Internet technology provides the platform on which such many-to-many relationships can be maintained. This includes, 3G, 4G and 5G mobile communications, GPS, scanning and IoT transmissions.

This concept and capability is well established technically but its implementation is challenging, being time-consuming and resource-intensive. The technology is no longer the barrier; it is the resources to define the processes, set up the systems and monitor the outputs. As a result, companies and their logistics providers have tended to invest only where they expect to get the greatest return. It is fair to expect that this process will continue and expertise in the application of such systems will progressively accumulate.

The technologies of robotics, automation, Internet of Things and additive manufacturing were nascent when the earlier version of this chapter was prepared. Their effectiveness and the implications of their application were not clear; neither was the need to anticipate new models of sourcing and supply such an irrefutable fact.

As outlined earlier, we face a world where supply will become more unreliable. And the costs of global sourcing will increase due to higher logistics costs and increases in labour costs in the developing world. That compelling margin gain described earlier will close. The risks of market loss due to non-supply will go hand in hand with the risks of increased obsolescence and write-off; that is what happens when supply chains are unreliable.

This scenario opens the door for supply chain reconfiguration and possible re-shoring or near-shoring. Technology will be the enabler. Automation and robotics will help to close further the cost differential versus lower wage countries. Automation and robotics also help to reduce economic batch sizes and enable shorter product life cycles and reduced lifetime volume goals. Additive manufacturing (aka 3D printing) is part of this landscape and is quickly emerging as a go-to solution in the world of slow-moving spare parts. Some forecasts that it will transform the world of manufacturing contain an element of hype; but the benefits of a 'make-one/sell-one' approach are economically powerful:

- zero stock and obsolescence;
- 100 per cent customer service;
- low logistics costs.

As with implementing the information backbone, it will be the skills and capacity that will be the 'gate' to more widespread adoption of these technologies.

Re-shoring, near-shoring and supply chain reconfiguration

Since the 2008/9 global downturn there has been commentary on, and some evidence of, a reversal in the global sourcing trend. Companies began to think about re-shoring and near-shoring in an effort to increase the demand responsiveness of their supply chains.

The *Financial Times* of London, 23 November 2013, reported increasing evidence that companies are now looking to repatriate their supply. It cited a survey by the UK government's Manufacturing Advisory Service (MAS) that found that one in six small to medium-sized companies has brought production back from overseas. Respondents were taking this decision based on rising costs overseas, including logistics, improving quality and reducing lead times. Steve Barr, the head of MAS is quoted as saying: 'There is a growing desire from companies to take production home. This marks a major change in approach from five years ago when the Far East and Eastern Europe seemed to be the destinations of choice.' Yet it was noted at the time that large global companies were still making the move to the East; for example, Caterpillar of the United States shifted 70 per cent of its small generator production to China with the loss of 760 jobs in Northern Ireland.

The Economist in its issue of 16 December 2020 reflected on the impact of the pandemic on future supply chains and speculated on the efficacy of bringing production closer to consumers. It cited:

- An April 2020 survey conducted by EY, an accounting firm, found that as many as 83 per cent of multinational executives were contemplating so-called 're-shoring' or 'near-shoring'.

- A follow-up survey by EY in October 2020 found that just 37 per cent of executives were still considering re-shoring.

- A recent survey of firms in the United States and Europe by Euler Hermes, a trade-credit insurer, found that less than 15 per cent were contemplating re-shoring because of Covid-19.

It appears that the knee-jerk response to re-shore waned considerably over a six-month period. The article went on to echo the observations of the *Financial Times* quoted earlier that 'for every company re-shoring production, there may be more doing the opposite'. It cited a survey of German manufacturers which found that 2 per cent brought production home between 2010 and mid-2012 while four times as many shifted operations abroad during that time.

This patchy and inconclusive picture is captured by the OECD who found in 2016 that 'the effects of re-shoring on national economies were limited'. Katherine Stapleton of the World Bank and Michael Webb of Stanford University observed that, contrary to expectations, 'the adoption of other technologies can make importing, rather than re-shoring, more attractive.' They found that Spanish firms using robots were more likely to increase their imports from low-income countries, or open affiliates there.

Productivity-enhancing automation led firms to expand output, and so import more parts.

The article from *The Economist*, having pointed to the various contradictory sources on the potential for re-shoring and the potential for governments' intervention through new industrial policies, concludes that history has shown that supply chain networks are resistant to change – in their words, 'sticky'.

It has taken 40 years to transition to the current state, so it may take a similar time to be reversed. For large companies, deciding when to change will require structured vigilance; for some smaller entities, the risks are already high, and they are making the change.

In conclusion

The growth trajectory of global sourcing and supply is close to having run its course. The pressures of sustainability and increased global risks will lead to changes in strategy and operations. But that process will take time unless the economics undergo a seismic shift.

The problem is knowing the timescales and opportunity costs on which change will occur. Move too fast and there will be competitive disadvantage; move too slowly and you may be stranded by events from which you cannot recover. The answer seems to lie in an increasingly vigilant approach focused on identifying the potential risks and the emerging technologies as part of a search for new models.

It will also be appropriate to invest in the intellectual capacity in the pillars of Figure 10.5, cost-to-serve and risk management. Boards will need to listen to those signals and stand ready to embrace rapid change through investment in assets, relationships and skills.

In the meantime, there is a job to do to maintain and improve the reliability of extended global supply chains – the governance role of supply chain managers.

References

1 World Trade Organization (nd), Statistics, www.wto.org/english/res_e/statis_e/statis_e.htm (archived at https://perma.cc/M4ZU-CFQ4)
2 World Trade Organization (nd), Statistics, www.wto.org/english/res_e/statis_e/statis_e.htm (archived at https://perma.cc/M4ZU-CFQ4)

3 Havenga, JH and van Eeden, J (2011) Forecasting South African containers for international trade: A commodity-based approach, *Journal of Transport and Supply Chain Management*, Johannesburg, 5 (1), pp 170–85

4 Ellen MacArthur Foundation (2017) A New Textiles Economy: Redesigning Fashion's Future, static1.squarespace.com/static/5afae80b7c93276139def3ec/t/ 5b07ea5f88251b7468549158/1527245413992/A-New-Textiles-Economy_ Full-Report_Updated_1-12-17.pdf (archived at https://perma.cc/V7XJ-UMWZ)

5 Ferdows, K, Lewis, MA and Machuca, JAD (2004) Rapid-fire fulfilment, *Harvard Business Review*, November, pp 104–10

6 Ellen MacArthur Foundation (2017) A New Textiles Economy: Redesigning Fashion's Future, static1.squarespace.com/static/5afae80b7c93276139def3ec/t/ 5b07ea5f88251b7468549158/1527245413992/A-New-Textiles-Economy_ Full-Report_Updated_1-12-17.pdf (archived at https://perma.cc/V7XJ-UMWZ)

7 NPR (2013) Planet money makes a t-shirt, apps.npr.org/tshirt/#/about (archived at https://perma.cc/A4LM-GA45)

8 Ellen MacArthur Foundation (2017) A New Textiles Economy: Redesigning Fashion's Future, static1.squarespace.com/static/5afae80b7c93276139def3ec/t/ 5b07ea5f88251b7468549158/1527245413992/A-New-Textiles-Economy_ Full-Report_Updated_1-12-17.pdf (archived at https://perma.cc/V7XJ-UMWZ)

9 Braithwaite, A and Christopher, M (2015) *Business Operations Models: Becoming a disruptive competitor*, Kogan Page, London

10 Harney, A (2008) *The China Price: The true cost of Chinese competitive advantage*, Penguin Press

11 Elkington, J (1999) *Cannibals with Forks: The triple bottom line of 21st century business*, Capstone

12 Elkington, J (2018) 25 years ago I coined the phrase 'triple bottom line'. Here's why it's time to re-think it, *Harvard Business Review*, 25 June

13 United Nations Development Programme (2015) *Sustainable Development Goals*, sdgs.un.org/goals (archived at https://perma.cc/ANT8-D6M3)

14 Cranfield School of Management (2005) *Best Practice in Global Sourcing*, MSc thesis project by Julia Xingli Liang, sponsored by LCP Consulting

15 Braithwaite, A and Samakh, E (1998) The Cost-to-Serve® method. Break through the barriers to change: know your supply chain costs, *International Journal of Logistics Management*, 9 (1), pp 69–84

16 The Borgen Project (2015) borgenproject.org/natural-disasters-increasing/ (archived at https://perma.cc/Y2DF-5LM6)

17 Moore, GE (1965) Cramming more components onto integrated circuits, Intel.com, *Electronics Magazine*, 19 April

Supply chain relationships 11

The foundation of success

Patrick Daly

The historical strategic context

Supply Chain Management (SCM) as a discipline emerged in response to the most recent phase of globalization of the world economy that accelerated from the 1970s through to the early 21st century. This wave of globalization was made possible and catalysed by advances in transportation technology, information and communications technology and the deregulation of global trade and finance. In practical terms, these innovations made it possible for businesses to reconfigure themselves to compete in new ways on an international, and in some cases, a global stage.

Previously most companies were highly vertically integrated. Think of the Ford Motor Company in the 1920s for instance (Ford, 2018). In those days, the Ford Motor Company owned and operated power plants, machine shops, foundries, rubber plantations, coal mines, timberland and iron-ore mines, as well as the automobile assembly plants and sales showrooms. In this way, companies like Ford were able to achieve security of supply of the inputs that they needed as well as to directly control quality and price of those inputs. The downside of this highly vertically integrated model was a huge fixed overhead, large capital investment requirements, a lack of flexibility and a high degree of internal complexity within the business.

In the second half of the 20th century, transport innovations such as containerized shipping and airfreight meant that materials, components and ingredients could be sourced more easily and more cheaply from suppliers located far away from the location of production. Information and communications technology advances made it easier and cheaper to communicate and cooperate effectively with distant suppliers and this reduction in trade barriers and financial regulation meant that it was possible to access international markets and to expand sales, access myriad sources of supply, as well as to relocate parts of the value-creation process to lower-cost locations. Companies increasingly began to focus on their core capabilities and they increasingly divested themselves of the ancillary functions that provided many of the inputs and services that they needed to compete.

From vertical to horizontal

With this transformation away from vertical integration, companies' control of supply, quality and price could no longer be exercised through ownership as in the vertically integrated model. They were now faced with managing an increasingly complex array of relationships with external suppliers and service providers. These suppliers and service providers were not subject to the direct control of the firm, and therefore a different approach and set of skills was required to be developed to manage these relationships so that the company could be assured of continuity of supply, quality and competitive pricing. Furthermore, as time went on, and companies began to leverage the deregulation of trade and finance and to take advantage of the advances in transportation and communications technologies, many of these suppliers and service providers came to be located overseas where language, regulations and business cultures were different, as were the fiscal, legal and governance regimes. This led to a veritable explosion in the complexity of the supply chains that needed to be configured and managed by these growing organizations. Supply chains became total production systems spanning the globe.

This new arrangement brought with it the advantage of focus, flexibility and agility and released many enterprises from the asset trap of vertical integration allowing them to be more nimble and more adaptive to changing circumstances. What this change also brought with it was a marked increase in the level of complexity involved in dealing with many more external suppliers of products, materials and services that were essential to the ability of the organization to conduct its business and satisfy the needs of its customers. The types of relationships and interactions required to manage a business based on myriad strategic long- and short-term relationships with a plethora of third-party entities was very different from what had come before. The skills needed and the quality of the relationships and interactions that would bring success were also very different and of a higher order than had previously been the case. The focus on core competences, together with the leveraging of the expertise and experience of outside suppliers and service providers, promised to enhance the overall performance of the business. However, this could only be achieved in practice if new ways of managing the complexity, leveraging the strength of all the partners, and measuring the performance of the supply chain as a holistic system were developed and perfected. Thus emerged through practice, trial and error, the concepts, techniques and tools of the systemic discipline that would eventually be baptized by Keith Oliver, a consultant with Booz Allen Hamilton, as 'supply chain management' (Heckman, Shorten and Engel, 2003) in a 1982 interview with the *Financial Times*. Keith Oliver himself described supply chain management as the management of a chain of supply as if it were a single entity – this was indeed a silo-busting, systems approach to understanding and managing the interconnected production networks that were emerging as firms transformed themselves to cope with an ever more diverse and globalized competitive environment. Since that time, the field has broadened and deepened, and many organizations have taken the concepts and practices and applied them to gain significant competitive advantage over their competitors. In the process, many have created new products and services that deliver consistently high levels of quality at prices that would have been unthinkable in the more constrained economic paradigms of the 1950s, '60s and '70s.

Supply chain management and competitive advantage

Think of the trajectory of organizations such as Apple, Walmart, Tesco, Ryanair, Tata and many others since the time in the 1980s when the concepts and ideas of supply chain management were coalescing into a coherent framework for managing modern business operations internationally. Apple was founded in 1976 by three young men, Steve Jobs, Steve Wozniak and Ronald Wayne to sell the Apple I (Dernbach, 2018) which was essentially an assembled circuit board without a casing, a keyboard or a monitor. Today Apple is a $215 billion dollar business with 116,000 employees and emblematic products such as the iPhone, the Mac and Apple TV. In 1984, Ryanair commenced operations with one 15-seater aircraft flying from the small regional airport of Waterford in the south-east of Ireland to London's Gatwick airport. Today, Ryanair is Europe's largest airline by passenger numbers with 11,000 employees and sales of €6.5 billion (Ryanair, 2018).

Tesco and Walmart, although already decades old in the 1980s, were still essentially regional players in their home countries at that time, Tesco in southern England and Walmart in the southern and midwestern states of the United States. Today both companies are global retailing behemoths that have expanded their operations worldwide and diversified their offerings far beyond their grocery origins. Tesco currently has sales of £55 billion and employs over 475,000 people (Statista, 2017a) while Walmart has sales of $485 billion and some 2.3 million employees (Statista, 2018). Tata, also a company with a long history going back to 19th-century Mumbai, India, has transformed itself into a global industrial conglomerate since the 1980s with divisions producing steel, motor cars, energy and chemicals. Today it has 660,000 employees and sales of $103 billion (Statista, 2017b). What all of these companies have in common is that they have put the diverse aspects of supply chain management relevant to their circumstances into practice to dramatic effect. This has enabled them to build and manage global networks that are bound together by relationships and interactions with myriad suppliers and service providers as well as their own diverse operations in dozens of countries all around the world. This success can be emulated by any business by pragmatic implementation of a supply chain management approach to managing supplier and customer relationships in a way that makes the whole greater than the sum of the parts.

Supply chain management: a systems approach

These networks were systems in a formal and technical sense as conceived of by thinkers such as Karl Ludwig von Bertalanffy (von Bertalanffy, 1968): in the sense that they could be thought of in terms of interconnected components, with boundaries, that had a purpose and that exhibited emergent properties that could only be measured and observed as a whole system and not at the level of the component parts. Consequently, a systems approach to the configuration, management, measurement and improvement of supply chains was required. That systems approach to dealing with the complexity of these new horizontally integrated supply chains or production networks came to be known as supply chain management (SCM).

Why are supply chain interfaces so important to the success and sustainability of supply chain relationships? If the supply chain is thought of as a complex adaptive system, then it will be seen to exhibit emergent properties (Open University, 2016) such as speed, flexibility and cost-effectiveness that will translate to business benefits for the supply chain as a whole that would not have been possible for the components of the system to achieve in isolation. In effect, the whole is greater than the sum of the parts. However, for a supply chain to be a truly effective system, the links and connections at the interfaces between the components need to be effective. To apply the tools and techniques of supply chain management to full effect it is essential to understand that the roots of supply chain management go back to the intellectual framework of systems thinking and its fundamental concepts of components, boundaries, connections, purpose, emergence and sub-optimization (Open University, 2016). Let's first take a look at the key concepts of systems thinking and why it is so important to unlocking the full potential of the supply chain.

Today, practically every business forms part of a supply chain, or more accurately it forms part of multiple supply chains or productive networks, acting as both supplier to its customers and customer to its suppliers. However, while every company is part of the supply chain and carries on a range of supply chain functions including logistics, production, sales, marketing and after-sales service, not every company is doing supply chain management. How can this be you may ask? We are carrying out supply chain activities and we are managing the business therefore we are doing supply chain management, right? No, wrong! So, what is the distinction? The key distinction is that supply chain management requires us to really understand and apply the key concepts of systems thinking (Open University, 2016) and to adopt a systems approach to organizing, managing and measuring the activities of the business. Systems thinking is a way of considering sets of interrelated components and activities as a complex adaptive system with a defined goal or purpose, with clear boundaries between those components that belong to the system and those components that do not. Adopting a systems approach involves looking at the behaviour of this whole system or supply chain, rather than the traditional reductionist approach (Open University, 2016) that breaks the system down into its component parts and analyses the behaviour of each component individually.

The importance of inter-organizational relationships

In the early days, as firms moved away from vertical integration to focus more and more on core competences they began to interact frequently with a greater number of suppliers. Initially, the relationships with many suppliers were adversarial and transaction-based with a narrow focus on price and cost which resulted in frequent changes of supply source as a narrow function of this criterion. In years past, working with companies in the medical devices sector that purchases many commoditized parts and components, we have found that procurement departments acting on the transactional-lowest-price model caused a proliferation of SKU item codes, packaging formats, and variable quality of supplier components that led to an explosion of complexity in the management of transport, warehousing and material flows as well as non-value-added increases in inventory and working capital tied up in that inventory – working capital that could have been put to better use elsewhere in the business. As the process of vertical disintegration unfolded over time, those leading-edge companies that grasped first the systemic nature of supply chain management, and the importance of quality business relationships in that paradigm, began to develop more sophisticated, mutually beneficial relationships with their supplier bases. They realized that there are two sides to managing the supplier base more effectively: one is the reduction in the overall number of suppliers to single or dual supply for most requirements, and the second is a deepening of the supplier relationships with those suppliers that have a critical strategic role to play in the competitiveness and continuity of the business. Through the 1990s and 2000s many companies, such as Boeing, Merck, Intel, Ford and many more, drastically reduced their supplier bases. One early example of the development of supplier–customer relationships designed to deliver benefits to both parties by breaking down inter-organizational barriers, sharing information, developing joint projects and initiatives was the supply chain coordination initiatives between Walmart and one of its major suppliers, Procter & Gamble (Waller, 2013). Prior to this collaboration, the relationship between the two companies had been adversarial, transactional and fragmented among their many divisions and regions. Interactions were limited to day-to-day, buy–sell transactions with no sharing of information, and no visibility of longer-term requirements, planning or coordination. Through the sharing of information, leveraging technologies such as electronic data interchange (EDI) using standardized formats, and working together on the planning and forecasting of replenishment requirements, they were able to achieve benefits that delivered value to both of their businesses as well as to their common customer, the consumer. These benefits included increased inventory turns, decreased inventory levels, increased logistics efficiency in warehousing and transport, and enhanced customer experience.

New ways of thinking about supply chain relationships

These kinds of initiatives require a different kind of relationship and trust between the parties and a different way of thinking about cost and benefit. In some circumstances, it may be beneficial for a customer to invest in the development of a supplier to help them to enhance their knowledge, resources, processes and capabilities in a sort of enlightened self-interest. Toyota and Honda have developed these kinds of initiatives to a significant degree and not just with their supplier bases in Japan within a homogeneous cultural environment but also with their suppliers in the United States, Canada and Mexico for their production requirements in North America. In my own work with multinational pharmaceutical manufacturers, I worked directly on an initiative of this nature. The manufacturing company, my client, operated a long-standing service contract with a logistics service provider to manage inbound flows of raw materials and packaging as well as outbound flows of finished product through the provision of offsite warehousing facilities. In this initiative, I worked on behalf of the manufacturer to develop improved processes and capabilities within the business of the logistics service provider. In effect, the manufacturer invested in improving the service provider's processes and capabilities in order to ensure that they could handle significant increases in the throughput volume on the manufacturer's business while at the same time holding down unit operating costs and the resulting charges for services provided. The logistics services provider, for their part, were able to leverage their new learning in other parts of their business on service contracts with other non-competing manufacturers. This initiative required significant changes in the ways of working of both parties that were challenging for the people involved. These changes ranged from modifications to the timing, content and coordination of activities to the provision and sharing of relevant information, as well as the ongoing measurement and review of performance. These changes took a good deal of purposeful design and implementation in stages that was challenging for all involved but that ultimately established a working relationship that was beneficial to all and that delivered real business benefits to both service provider and customer.

Types of inter-organizational relationships

There are myriad ways in which companies are configuring their operations to compete in this internationalized economy depending on the sector, the products and services they provide and the opposing pressures for global standardization and local responsiveness that they experience. Some adopt more centralized strategies holding value creation at the core in their home markets, while carrying out production and assembly in overseas markets. Others adopt strategies whereby they become truly transnational, with more competences and capabilities devolved to international business units where local responsiveness is important. Additionally, we hear about tools and tactics such as offshoring, outsourcing and global procurement in relation to how enterprises adapt to global threats and opportunities.

These different strategies and approaches have one thing in common. They are leading to a multiplicity of new and complex inter-organizational relationships. In many cases, these are relationships with new and unfamiliar entities, such as government agencies in foreign countries, civic communities, consumer groups and NGOs as well as with myriad suppliers and service providers spread across many countries with different national and business cultures operating in jurisdictions with different governance rules, regulations and legal frameworks. Some of these relationships are situational and short term and are required to respond to specific short-term needs, such as building a production facility in an overseas location, whereas others may be required to become long-term stable relationships and a key part and contributor to the competitive advantage of the organization. Relationships with key suppliers of critical materials and services would fall into the second category. Inter-organizational relationships encounter many challenges, and yet are crucial to the continued success of more and more businesses for reasons that we have already outlined. As business evolves and fragments into myriad specialities, as firms push ever more to a focus on core competences, the requirement to be able to successfully cooperate, collaborate and to form partnerships is becoming ever more a key competence and a differentiator between competitors.

The importance of clear objectives

The difficulties encountered in forming and sustaining successful inter-organizational relationships generally revolve around issues related to clarity on objectives, measures and value (Weiss, 2002). Often, the objectives of the relationship are not made explicit and as a consequence are assumed implicitly by default on the part of the cooperating parties. The trouble is these assumed objectives are often in opposition to each other and inevitably become the source of friction, strife and dissatisfaction.

An example of a long-term inter-organizational relationship

This is an example of a manufacturer of consumer pharmaceutical products that has developed a long-term working relationship with a provider of logistics services for the warehousing and shipping of finished product. From the manufacturer's point of view, this is desirable, because it allows finished product to be moved out of the production plant while quality approval takes place, thus freeing up valuable space within the plant that can be dedicated to other value-added activities such as manufacturing or packaging lines, R&D, laboratories and so on rather than to warehousing. Additionally, this arrangement simplifies the process of despatch at the plant. The product can be loaded onto trailers as it comes off the lines without the need to consolidate and sort by order, batch or customer. These tasks can be carried out later, at the offsite warehouse operated by the logistics service provider, after the Quality department approves and releases the product for shipping. From the manufacturer's point of view, the advantages include the better use of plant facilities, savings in labour costs through simplification and the avoidance of investing valuable capital in warehouse buildings, equipment and technology. From the logistics service provider's point of view the chief benefit is the income stream which provides for the amortization of the investment already made in warehousing and transport infrastructure, systems and personnel and the profit generated by exploiting the economies of scale and process efficiencies that the logistics service provider can provide to the manufacturer. Generally, the charging mechanism in a traditional logistics outsourcing arrangement like this would be built around charge rates for pallet storage per week or month, rates for handling pallets in and out of the offsite warehouse and rates for the transfer of trailer loads between the manufacturing plant and the offsite warehouse facilities operated by the service provider.

Self-interest of the parties

Often, the ostensible objectives for the arrangement are expressed in terms of how many pallets will be stored on average, how frequently they will move and what the times of operation will be. The logistics service provider will calculate the rates to be charged as a function of these parameters and these will generally be at a level that provides a reasonable profit margin to the service provider while at the same time being affordable and competitive from the manufacturer's point of view in terms of the wider business advantages that are being achieved in space saving, capital expenditure avoidance and reduction in complexity.

However, this format is problematic and short-sighted because it sets the self-interest of the manufacturer and that of the service provider in conflict with each other from the outset, and it fails to identify and explicitly express what the true objectives of the relationship are. This will inevitably lead to tension and friction, and an inability of the partners to take full advantage of the potential benefits of the working relationship. For example, if the Quality department of the manufacturer introduces a new process that speeds up the rate of approval and release of product for shipping, the stock will turn faster through the outside warehouse and the average stock-holding will drop. This will have the effect of decreasing the logistics provider's revenue stream for storage on the same overall throughput of stock. So, what is beneficial to the manufacturer, that is, getting product released and out to market sooner, is detrimental to the logistics service provider, who may begin to lose margin due to the fixed overhead component of costs and may begin to agitate with the manufacturer for a storage rate increase to compensate. In effect, the arrangement masked the conflicting underlying objectives of the two parties. Any kind of improvement initiated by the manufacturer to increase stock turns or reduce inventory will be detrimental to the logistics services partner.

In other cases, these outsourced logistics services are charged on a cost-plus margin or management fee basis, with the margin or fee being a percentage of the cost. Perversely then, the higher the cost, the better off the service provider is and the worse off the manufacturer is. Again, the underlying objectives of the two parties are at cross purposes. In outsourced warehousing, for example, there is always scope for process improvement resulting in higher productivity and lower unit costs through changes in the structure of work, planning, communication, equipment and technology. However, a charging mechanism that ensures that the logistics service provider will be worse off if it introduces such productivity gains is simply not fit for purpose. These arrangements are made in good faith on the part of both parties, albeit with lack of real insight into the potential of the arrangement and the opportunities for exploiting mutual business benefits, and often the parties are surprised and disappointed when the relationship tenses and sours over the duration of the term of the contract. The manufacturer is disappointed because the service provider did not bring new ideas and innovation to the table as the supposed expert in the field of logistics and the service provider is disappointed because the volumes and margins did not turn out as projected in the original costing exercise that underpinned their initial proposals. In many instances, the contracts are not renewed at the end of the term and the pattern is repeated with a new outsourced partner in much the same manner.

Making objectives explicit and aligned

To avoid this kind of thing, it is important to make the underlying business objectives explicit from the start of the engagement and then to work very carefully to align them in such a way that the self-interest of both the manufacturing outsourcer and the logistics service provider are oriented in the same direction. This may add time and complexity to the proposal and to the contracting phase of the project but when considered in terms of the return on investment over the lifetime of the contract, it is easily justifiable. What is perhaps more challenging in the face of the traditional way of approaching these inter-organizational relationships is that it requires greater openness and trust than would be customary. Consequently, the skills associated with developing and building frank, open and trustful working relationships become ever more valuable at the interfaces between the partners. Trust will only be established when the first party is confident that the second party is operating with the first's best interest at heart and vice versa, in the firm knowledge and conviction that both will be better off as a result.

By way of example of how this has been achieved in practice among cutting-edge companies, let's look at an example of an international manufacturer of a range of consumer food products who was required to contract with a logistics service provider to receive and store finished product, pick and pack orders for distribution to wholesalers, large multiple retailers and smaller retailers in a regional market, and execute the delivery of orders to all customers. The proposal and contract negotiations were based firmly around the clear and explicit understanding of the objectives, measures and value of the engagement. By 'objectives' we mean a clear expression of the business-relevant outcomes to be achieved. By 'measures' we mean those metrics that will indicate the mutual progress towards achieving those objectives, and by 'value' we mean the business benefits that are provided by reaching those objectives. Typically, in an engagement of this type, the manufacturer is looking to achieve a range of different business outcomes that will include such things as:

- avoidance of capital expenditure in non-core infrastructure, equipment and personnel for logistics activities such as warehousing and transport;

- access to best-in-class knowledge and innovation in logistics practice to drive efficiency in operation and improved service in fulfilment;

- access to economies of scale to deliver operational cost savings on warehousing, transport and distribution;

- reduced specific inventory to support the business and to liberate working capital.

Likewise, the logistics service provider is typically looking at a set of desired business outcomes that include some of the following:

- a predictable revenue stream for an extended period;

- contribution to operational costs;

- amortization of capital investments in buildings, equipment and systems;

- generation of profit;

- experience and exposure to industry sector requirements and standards;

- positive references from reputable and satisfied customers.

If these two sets of objectives are brought to the surface in an explicit manner at the outset of the engagement, they can be explored for mutual alignment. In this specific example of engagement between the manufacturer and the logistics service provider we were working with the manufacturer, and we had determined that because of the large batch sizes, a considerable proportion of the manufacturer's stock profile was suited to a type of racking called 'push-back racking', storing pallets four deep as opposed to conventional pallet racking which stores pallets just one deep. The advantages from the manufacturer's point of view included that the total cubic space and footprint of the building required to hold the stock would be smaller, consequently travel distances for the put-away and retrieval of stock would be shorter, favouring more efficient stock replenishment to order picking locations and shorter overall order picking routes. This all translates into less space, reduced travel time, fewer people and ultimately lower costs and lower rates for storage, handling and order picking.

However, traditionally most logistics service providers favour conventional racking layouts in their facilities. This is because many logistics contracts are short, in the range of one to three years, and these facilities must accommodate different contracts, with different stock profiles and different operational requirements over their lifetime of perhaps 15 to 20 years.

Specialized racking systems such as push-back racks, can be four to six times more expensive per pallet position than conventional pallet racking and consequently it is difficult for the logistics service provider to amortize the investment with a short-term contract, particularly when they may find the system unsuited to the next contract that comes into the facility.

Armed with this knowledge, the two parties were able to negotiate in an informed and frank manner. The manufacturer wanted lower rates over an extended period and the logistics provider wanted a predictable revenue stream for as long as possible. Both were able to align their objectives by establishing a contract for a duration far longer than current industry norms that provided the logistics service provider with a predictable revenue stream over a period sufficiently long to be able to amortize the investment in specialist equipment and at the same time to provide very competitive rates to the manufacturer. Of course, there were other measures agreed to ensure that the productivity, quality standards and ongoing process improvements would be an integral part of the arrangements to ensure that expectations would be met during the lifetime of the agreement.

In the same manner, creative examination of the potential to align each party's explicit objectives will give rise to very beneficial and sometimes unexpected arrangements whereby the relationship can be built on solid foundations that ensure that when one party does well the other does well also. This lays the foundation for sustainable long-term relationships, where trust can be built up over time between the parties, and their best interests are aligned. In our example, the manufacturer knows that it is getting the best deal in terms of service, price and quality and the service provider has a guarantee of long-term revenue stability.

Relevant metrics to measure progress towards achieving objectives

Of course, there is little point in setting objectives that cannot be measured. How else will we know whether we are making progress towards the objective, whether we have reached the objective or whether we have exceeded the objective? To be useful, metrics must be truly indicative of the objective that is of interest, they must be straightforward, and they must be easy to compute and understand. They must provide real insight to those who will use them to guide their actions in making progress towards the objectives, otherwise they can be less than useless and serve only as a distraction, an inappropriate use of resource, or worse, they may drive actions that move the relationship away from the true best interests of both parties. Well-chosen metrics and measures are the cornerstone of all successful inter-organizational relationships that are grounded in mutually beneficial objectives. To do this, they need to be specific and chosen with care.

A quantitative metric to compare global warehouse productivity

I have come across many situations in which a plethora of metrics are computed and reported upon on a regular basis but where these metrics bear little relation to the real business objectives or they are not specified with true insight into the nature of the process being measured. In one case, the supply chain director of a manufacturer with operations in countries across different continents was interested in comparing the productivity of the picking and shipping operations at the finished goods warehouses of the various plants. His desire was to cross-pollenate best practices across the international network and increase the overall productivity of the global network. The finished goods warehouses at the production plants despatched product internationally to another vertical tier within the same organization as well as to third parties who used the finished product as an input to their own production process to produce the final consumer-ready product. The metric chosen had the virtue of simplicity, that is, pallets picked and shipped per man-hour; however it didn't take account of the operational differences between warehouse operations at the various plants, thus giving a misreading of which plants were more productive and which were less productive. In inter-organizational relationships the simplistic specification of metrics in this way can lead to frustration and mistrust, and can call the entire measurement system into disrepute and undermine the ability of organizations to achieve their objectives.

In this case, the difficulty was that, whereas some plants predominantly made and shipped large volume products for big markets, others had a more complex mix of lower consumption products for smaller national markets. Consequently, the former picked and shipped a higher proportion of full pallets. These can be picked and moved to the shipping bays in one single operation using a fork lift truck, whereas the latter required the manual picking of a mix of different items onto pallets that subsequently required checking, wrapping and labelling, which is clearly a far more labour-intensive process. In a situation like this, direct comparison cannot be made between the productivity of the plants based on this metric as it had been specified and calculated. To overcome this limitation, an adjustment factor to allow for the difference could be introduced to enable the productivity of the plants to be compared, but this is often not straightforward. It is more useful in these cases to take a different approach whereby each plant develops a metric based on its own specific process. Its performance against best practice for that type of operation can then be determined. It is then this performance against best practice for their own specific types of operation that can be compared between different sites. This is an example of a situation in which the metric is a quantitative measure and can be calculated mathematically based on data that are collected from the records of movements and transactions within the warehouse operation.

Not all metrics need to be quantitative to be useful, however. Consider for example, a metric designed to measure the effectiveness of inter-organizational communication between those working at the interface between two collaborating organizations. This metric is important because it is an indicator of the quality and sustainability of the working relationship. A metric like this could be defined in terms of distinctions in the subjective experience of the associates in the two collaborating organizations.

A qualitative metric to measure international communications effectiveness

In a real-life example between a producer of a fresh food product in northern Europe and a distributor of the product in the markets of a southern European country, the day-to-day interaction of the associates in each company included the negotiation and clarification of price and of product availability, which varied greatly on a week-to-week basis, as well as confirmation of order quantities, product mix, timing of deliveries, and the confirmation of deliveries and payments. Given that the associates were interacting in a fast-paced, dynamic environment, using a lingua franca, English, of which none of them was a native speaker, and each company operated its own distinct corporate culture as well as different national cultures, it was important for the sustainability of the mutual arrangements to measure how effective the inter-organizational communication was on an ongoing basis.

To do this a short questionnaire was designed that could be administered in a matter of minutes that allowed the key components of responsiveness, clarity and trust to be measured on a regular basis. In the early days of the relationship, the southern Europeans learned that if they provided the northern

Europeans with specific timings for their next actions as opposed to indicating more ambiguously 'as soon as possible', they received far fewer follow-up queries and interruptions from their northern European interlocutors. Conversely, the northern Europeans learned that the patterns of consumer shopping in southern European municipal markets and supermarkets, where the shopper prefers to buy very fresh produce in small quantities every day, as opposed to one big weekly purchase, means that order confirmations necessarily come in later and are more complex in their make-up than is the norm in northern Europe. This helped the northern Europeans to design their fulfilment system taking this reality into consideration rather than considering it some sort of laxity on the part of the southern European partner. This crucial learning helped to build trust and mutual respect between the partners, and laid the foundation for a sustainable working relationship with considerable benefits in terms of growth and profits accruing to both organizations over time.

Focus on business outcomes

When clarifying objectives and developing the metrics that will allow progress towards those objectives to be measured, it is essential that these objectives be framed in terms of outcomes that deliver real business value to the parties and that objectives are truly aligned with the overarching strategies of the businesses that the relationship is designed to underpin. For example, an over-emphasis on objectives aligned with cost control in a business aiming to deliver high-quality, highly differentiated services and products at premium rates may lead to service and quality failures that alienate customers and contradict the stated business strategy. Likewise, an over-emphasis on service-related objectives in a business whose strategy is to be the cost leader in the market may lead to an erosion of margins that endanger the survival of the business over the long term.

There needs to be a cogent and coherent connection between the strategy of the business and, the long-term inter-organizational relationship it chooses to enter with other entities and partners, and the objectives established for those relationships. Unfortunately, the reality is that this is not always what happens in practice due to the ineffective translation of business strategy into operational reality. This is most often the result of an absence of appropriate resource allocation, planning, investment, training and communication. Business strategy rarely fails in the formulation but rather more often in the execution (Weiss, 1994). Indeed, a middling quality strategy that is well executed will often deliver far greater business benefits than an excellently formulated strategy that is poorly executed. While this is an ever-present challenge within organizations, it is an even greater test of business acumen when it involves aligning strategies and objectives between two or more businesses working together to achieve mutually beneficial goals. While each organization may be pursuing a different strategy, each one needs to be fully aware and cognizant of how the relationship between them is going to underpin both their own strategy and that of their cooperating partner or partners. This requires a highly sophisticated level of understanding and communication within and between the key stakeholders in the partner companies.

Governance and control

One of the greatest challenges to the full realization of the promise of supply chain management's systemic approach to maximizing business value is the asymmetry in size and power that exists between many of the supply chain partners that interface with each other in the myriad relationships that make up the fabric of modern production networks. In effect, some players are just so much bigger and more powerful than others, and therefore the tensions associated with the governance and control of supply chains and the capturing of the value created in these supply chains is a constant feature of supply chain relationships. Indeed, some organizations hold such a dominant position in the value chain that they are in effect the de facto controllers of the supply network's value creation and this puts them in a position to set the rules of the game and appropriate the lion's share of the value created. Think of the position that companies such as Apple, Walmart, Toyota and Tesco occupy in the global production networks that they form part of and the level of control they exercise over the firms that make up the supplier bases of these networks. These very large supply chain companies, controlling suppliers in the case of Apple and Toyota and controlling producers in the case of Tesco and Walmart, hold sway over the key strategic functions of product design, logistics, sales and marketing.

It might be feared that such asymmetries could lead to abuse and exploitation of the smaller party in the relationship. This can materialize as constant pressure to reduce prices to guarantee repeat business. This will often happen where the materials, products or services supplied are very commoditized. However, where quality, innovation and compliance are at a premium the dynamics of the network relationships, that involve both a diversification of suppliers' customer bases, as well as a mutual vested interest in success, together with the growing importance of corporate social responsibility and the need to maintain stability and learning, tend to mitigate the asymmetry of the relationship. What many of the lead companies came to realize was that, although they might take steps to optimize the core processes over which they retained direct control, in the context of the overall system or production network that was only a very small proportion of the potential for improvement to unlock competitive advantage; the rest lay in the domain of their supply chain partners and suppliers.

The key for the smaller players in these relationships is to avoid being viewed as the simple vendor of a commoditized product or service and to invest continuously and proactively in the supply chain relationships with the larger supply chain partners through strategies and initiatives that include information sharing, joint development initiatives, cross training and crossover personnel deployment to ensure that quality, speed and alignment to specific requirements can be satisfied. These are actions that tend to deepen the bond, to make it more difficult to replace the supplier, and to ensure that the relationship becomes more strategic and valuable to both parties. In their book *Lean Solutions: How companies and customers can create value and wealth together*, James P Womack and Daniel T Jones describe how they discovered, while visiting companies in Japan in the early 1980s, that the Toyota Motor Company had achieved a level of excellence that they had not seen before in Japan or in the United States through a combination of a focus on the optimization of their core processes, management and control of product development and production, and excellent coordination and collaboration with their suppliers and customers. In effect, they had applied supply chain management principles successfully in such a way that the whole was greater than the sum of the parts of the production network that they had built to produce their motor cars.

Summary

In this chapter we have explored the concept of systems thinking and examined how it is the foundation of the intellectual framework that has evolved and formalized itself since the 1980s as a set of tools and techniques that can help businesses understand and manage the global production networks of which they now form part. This set of tools and techniques has come to be known as supply chain management (SCM), a term coined by Keith Oliver, a consultant with the firm Booz Allen Hamilton consultants in a 1982 interview for the *Financial Times*. In systems thinking, these complex adaptive systems possess specific attributes that define them and that provide insights into their behaviour, and how that behaviour can be shaped and adapted by proactively designing, implementing and measuring the system as a whole. These attributes include:

- **components** that may be companies, people or assets;
- a **boundary** that defines what is inside the system and what is outside the system;
- **connections** or links between the components that indicate how they influence each other and how things such as materials, information and money flow between the components of the system;
- **emergence** or properties that are only observable and measurable at the aggregate level of the whole system and not at the level of the individual components;
- **sub-optimization** or the phenomenon whereby attempted optimization of all components of the system is dysfunctional because it leads to sub-optimization of the performance of the system as a whole;
- **purpose** or the fact that the system is of interest to us because it exists to achieve some sort of outcome or goal.

We examined how supply chain management came into being as a response to a fundamental shift in the configuration of the production systems of companies driven by technological, competitive, demographic and financial pressures from around the early 1970s. Up to that point in time, companies tended to organize themselves as vertically integrated enterprises holding full ownership of many of the upstream and downstream components of their supply chain. Thereafter, in order to cope with the changing competitive environment, companies began to shift to a network model of production whereby they identified and focused on their core competences and obtained the other inputs and enabling services that they required from external suppliers and service providers.

We also looked at some examples of companies such as Ryanair, Apple, Tesco and Walmart that have successfully applied the concepts and tools of supply chain management over the last 35 years or so to create immensely strong and successful business models from small beginnings, and in doing so they realized that not only could they focus on optimizing their own core processes that lie within their direct control but also that they had to extend the system of interest to include the whole system of their suppliers and their suppliers' supplier to truly unlock the efficiencies that enabled them to create huge value and competitive advantage.

Finally, we looked at the important aspect of control and governance in these global production networks where there is a constant ebb and flow of influence and control between the lead players, the large producers and buyers, and the myriad suppliers and sub-suppliers in the network. While the dominance of the lead players may lead to the risk of abuse of that position of power, the smaller players can strengthen their position by proactively taking advantage of the requirement for the whole network to maintain stability and competitiveness for mutual benefit, This is achieved through cooperation, collaboration and joint action designed to deepen the complex interactions and relationships with other players in the network. Some of the key strategies that all companies can implement to unlock the advantages of supply chain management include focusing on core competences that they can clarify for themselves through identifying what the true driving force of their business is, while at the same time rationalizing and optimizing their own supplier base and developing value-added, inter-organizational relationships and optimizing processes across these inter-organizational boundaries. By following these guidelines and relentlessly applying the insights, tools and techniques provided by supply chain management (SCM) they can truly thrive, achieve sustainable success, and ensure that the whole is truly greater than the sum of its parts.

References

Dernbach, C (2018) Mac History: Apple I, available from www.mac-history.net/apple-history-2/apple-i/2012-07-08/apple-i (archived at https://perma.cc/V7A6-4AVD)

Ford (2018) 100 Years of the Moving Assembly Line, Ford Motor Company, available from http://ophelia.sdsu.edu:8080/ford/08-12-2018/innovation/100-years-moving-assembly-line.html (archived at https://perma.cc/4RKS-2RGX)

Heckman, P, Shorten, D and Engel, H (2003) *Supply Chain Management at 21: The hard road to adulthood*, Booz Allen Hamilton

Open University (2016) *Systems Thinking and Practice* (Kindle edn), available from www.amazon.com (archived at https://perma.cc/G76W-RZHK)

Ryanair (2018) History of Ryanair, available from corporate.ryanair.com/about-us/history-of-ryanair/ (archived at https://perma.cc/QUC5-F62T)

Statista (2017a) Tesco's revenue worldwide in 2016/2017, by region (in million GBP), available from www.statista.com/statistics/238678/tesco-plc-group-sales-by-region-2010-2011/ (archived at https://perma.cc/DG6W-B82D)

Statista (2017b) Revenue value of Indian conglomerate Tata Group from FY 1996 to FY 2017 (in billion US dollars), available from www.statista.com/statistics/754924/india-annual-revenue-tata-group/ (archived at https://perma.cc/T93H-WSHQ)

Statista (2018) Walmart's net sales worldwide from 2006 to 2018 (in billion US dollars), available from www.statista.com/statistics/183399/walmarts-net-sales-worldwide-since-2006/ (archived at https://perma.cc/AVG2-ZLX3)

von Bertalanffy, KL (1968) *General System Theory: Foundations, development, applications*, George Braziller, New York, revised edn 1976, ISBN 0-8076-0453-4

Waller, M (2013) How sharing data drives supply chain innovation, *Industry Week*, 12 August, available from www.industryweek.com/supplier-relationships/how-sharing-data-drives-supply-chain-innovation (archived at https://perma.cc/C3EZ-U4QL)

Weiss, A (2002) *Value-Based Fees: How to charge and get what you're worth*, Jossey-Bass/Pfeiffer, San Francisco, CA

Delivering sustainability through supply chain management

12

Maria Huge-Brodin and Edward Sweeney

Introduction

Over the past decade, the concept of sustainability has grown immensely in importance. Sustainability-related research has provided new insights into disciplines, and has infused societal discourse with constantly renewed challenges.

Sustainability challenges create pressure on companies to comply with societal and consumer expectations, while they also bring new business opportunities to more proactive and progressive companies. Sustainability issues also trigger entrepreneurship – the idea of turning environmental problems into business opportunities results in, for example, new products based on waste material, as well as new roles for firms in a more circular economy. However, no company is an island, and companies need to manage their businesses as actors in the wider supply chains of which they are part. In the context of sustainability, supply chain management (SCM) again manifests itself as a strategic concern, and in particular global supply chains need to be managed in a more long-term and strategic manner. As noted in earlier chapters, contemporary supply chain management is complex; addressing sustainability concerns in any meaningful way adds further to this complexity. This chapter presents some critical issues relating to sustainability in supply chains, and lays the foundations for more focused discussions in subsequent chapters.

The first section of this chapter paints a broad picture of sustainability, and how it may be interpreted from a supply chain management perspective. In the second section, some key SCM issues pertinent to sustainability are highlighted. The third section describes and discusses some key challenges for sustainable supply chains. This involves both synergies and conflicts – this is significant for both sustainability and supply chains, and hence is at the heart of this chapter. The fourth and final section summarizes the main points of the chapter, and discusses potential future challenges for delivering sustainability through supply chain management.

Sustainability as corporate performance

Sustainable development

Sustainability is not new as a concept. Although its modern use is often related to the UN report *Our Common Future* (WCED, 1987), known as the Brundtland Report, sustainability has been the basis for the survival of mankind, and is in essence related to resource scarcity. With resource scarcity comes the need to use resources in the most economical ways and never to waste anything that could be useful. Over the past decades the industrialized world has accessed an abundance of natural resources, often at a cost to both developing countries and the natural environment. A growing awareness of the problems that these imbalances cause constitutes the grounds for what we today refer to as sustainability.

A common way of defining sustainability is to take a stance in three sustainability dimensions: economic sustainability, environmental sustainability and social sustainability. Each of the domains should balance their various respective needs and issues, but overall sustainable development requires that the respective dimensions are balanced against each other. Sustainable development needs to be seen as an ongoing process and not a fixed goal – ie sustainability is not a destination to be reached per se, but rather a journey towards a more sustainable future. In this context, the ambition is to maintain reasonable living conditions overall, but without compromising the need of future generations (WCED, 1987).

Environmental sustainability refers to a wide range of issues, including pollution prevention, preservation of non-renewable resources and abatement of climate change. Social sustainability includes many basic human rights (for example: the right to education; the right to decent working conditions; and the right to healthcare). Economic sustainability is concerned with the more equal distribution of wealth across the globe, and is key to attaining sustainable development in the other dimensions.

While resources and wealth are not unlimited, it is important to acknowledge the synergies and conflicts residing in overall sustainability considerations. Saving resources and minimizing waste can in general be positive for both environmental and economic sustainability – hence a wise use of natural resources demonstrates sustainability synergies on a global level. However, many sustainability conflicts are related to the balance between holistic perspectives and narrower sectoral or company views, and to the balance between different regions of the world. While wealth, manifested through efficient manufacturing, brings increased economic strength to both companies and regions, it may be at the cost of decent working conditions for low-wage employees in distant locations. The relocation of manufacturing to lower labour cost bases, for example, may create the impression of 'environmental problems solved' as their immediate environment is less polluted – it may even contribute to profitability and increase wealth locally. However, such approaches risk the impairment of living conditions for many people elsewhere – not only in the short term but perhaps for generations ahead. These are but a few illustrations of actual synergies and conflicts for sustainable development on a global level. The complexity of the sustainability challenge is also captured in the United Nations' Global Sustainable Development Goals (UN SDG, 2020), in which sustainability is addressed through 17 challenge areas, for example No Poverty, Quality Education, Affordable Clean Energy and Industry, Innovation and Infrastructure. The challenges are complex, with each including multiple dimensions and conflicts, and to sustainably develop them requires that nations as well as societal sectors coordinate their efforts.

Corporate and supply chain sustainability

Supply chains fulfil many functions in society. Their efficient functioning is critical to societal wellbeing and development. In this context, design, planning and control of supply chain operations need to become more sustainable. In this, our stance is that supply chains are the result of coordinated action within and between companies – the remainder of this chapter mainly takes a company perspective.

Companies' sustainability efforts are described in different frameworks that aim to capture the full scope of sustainability – this is sometimes referred to as Corporate Social Responsibility or CSR (see, for example, further definitions by the European Commission, 2021). Such frameworks aim to relate companies' activities to the various sustainability dimensions. Environmental sustainability refers to preventing pollution from manufacturing and transportation, and to avoid exploitation of natural resources – in particular to minimize the use of non-renewable resources. The social sustainability dimension is practically manifested differently depending on which part of the world a company operates in, but in general includes decent working conditions for employees. In addition, many companies also see a role as societal reformers as part of their sustainability work. In this context, they may fund local educational and health efforts in the regions where they or their suppliers operate. In a corporate context, ethical considerations are sometimes seen as part of social sustainability, with the detail of this depending on cultural and geographical context. Finally, economic sustainability for companies refers to their potential for long-term survival, which can sometimes be in conflict with their shareholders' desire for more short-term profitability. Nevertheless, companies need to finance their activities, and companies that do 'too much' good outside their budget frame will not survive. There needs to be a balance, therefore, between the various sustainability dimensions in order for firms to contribute meaningfully to sustainable development.

Monitoring and demonstrating corporate sustainability

Managing a sustainable supply chain entails monitoring results and controlling activities. To be able to benchmark competitors, as well as to communicate clearly with shareholders, customers and media, standardized systems and frameworks are called for. While few if any exist at the supply chain level, some have emerged at the company level. One is the GRI (Global Reporting Initiative – see GRI, 2020), which provides a framework of standardized measurements and support for monitoring sustainability. The well-known ISO Standards (2020) support not only quality management processes (ISO 9001), but also environmental management (ISO 14001) and sustainability (ISO 26001). These standards are obtained and maintained through regular certification processes by external auditors. Another way of measuring companies' sustainability more clearly in the context of their business success is the Dow Jones Sustainability Indices (DJSI, 2020). Since 1999, this family of indices has been used to assess companies' environmental, social and economic corporate performance. A number of commercial applications claim to embrace a supply chain perspective in their evaluations of sustainable performance but no standardized framework has yet emerged.

Turning to the topic of sustainable development of supply chains, some of the aspects mentioned above are dealt with in other chapters. Chapter 10 focuses on global sourcing and supply, one of the phenomena that underlines the importance of sustainability in supply chains. In Chapter 13 the environmental issues are the focus, with a particular emphasis on green logistics. Ethical supply chains are further described and discussed in Chapter 16. A specific area of focus that captures multiple dimensions of sustainability is humanitarian supply chain management. This is explored in detail in Chapter 17.

How supply chains can foster sustainable development

The supply chain from a sustainability perspective

Sustainability has grown into a major corporate concern for many companies. That implies that sustainability is infusing strategic decisions as well as operational activities. From the perspective of supply chains and SCM, sustainable development relies not only on internal company issues, but also on inter-organizational issues and business-to-business (B2B) collaboration. A starting point in many discussions is that lack of inter-company collaboration hinders and slows down sustainable development while increased collaboration between companies in supply chains will contribute to the acceleration of sustainable development. In essence, the core characteristics of SCM – collaboration and integration – are not only desirable for increasing supply chain effectiveness and efficiency; they can strongly contribute to making supply chains more sustainable (see, for example, Touboulic and Walker, 2015).

With our backgrounds in the logistics discipline, we define the supply chain based mainly on material flows between firms and processes. A by now classical description of a supply chain is provided by Lambert and Cooper (2000). In their definition of a supply chain, it starts with a focal company and – novel at that time – acknowledges the network structure of the wider supply chain of which that firm is a part. The definition defines the core material flows to and from this company, and depicts the main supply chain actors. Those actors are the focal company, its suppliers and its customers – all actors that are in control of the goods along the defined material flow path. Complementary to this picture is the addition of logistics and transport providers (ie logistics service providers or LSPs). With few exceptions these companies actually do not own the goods, but are still responsible for their movement between the various nodes in the supply chain. The activities of LSPs, therefore, contribute significantly to the environmental performance of the supply chain, and can also offer challenges in terms of social aspects for the supply chain as a whole. These considerations are in addition to the more obvious reasons for making them supply chain members, which is often to increase efficiency by cutting costs. A supply chain structure that includes LSPs is shown in Figure 12.1. The LSP actors include various types of companies, from door-to-door transport providers (ie hauliers), forwarders who may perform transportation but also coordinate transportation activities based on customer needs, and 3PLs (third-party logistics providers) who in addition to transport services, or even without them, offer services such as warehousing, warehouse management, labelling and other value-adding services. Lately the concept of control towers has emerged, which means that a company may outsource its complete logistics management and operations to a third party that offers higher efficiency and effectiveness through expertise and economies of scale.

Sustainable development through integration and collaboration

Sustainability issues and challenges may occur anywhere in the supply chain, depending on, for example, which products the supply chain is to deliver, or in what regions it operates. Nevertheless, a supply chain perspective emphasizes many of the issues relating to inter-organizational relationships. Through inter-organizational relationships, companies in the product supply chain can influence their suppliers to become more sustainable. More successful examples can be found where customers and suppliers develop their sustainability plans together in partnerships. By supporting the development of a supplier, a buyer contributes to the more long-term development of the wider business ecosystem. Joint development means higher investments, but at the same time offers higher yields in terms of lower

Figure 12.1 A supply chain structure including the product supply chain and the transport provision chain

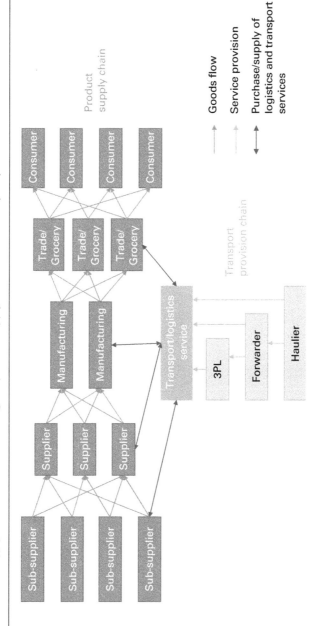

sustainability risks. It also facilitates the building of trust, thereby reducing the risk of short-term and opportunistic behaviour (for more details, see Touboulic and Walker, 2015).

While partnerships over a longer time period often require increased integration between companies, increased sustainable development can also take place in more collaborative settings. Openness and transparency vis-à-vis supply chain partners may come from the open-book principles often promoted to support both social and environmental sustainability. And these principles in turn contribute to building trust between supply chain partners, no matter if they are highly integrated or maintain a less formalized but still long-term collaboration. At the other end of the spectrum, transactional business arrangements and short-term business deals, often based on one-sided requirements and demands, tend to encourage unsustainable development.

The same arguments as above can be used for the transport provision chain. While product supply chains have been analysed both as to environmental and social sustainability, transport provision chains have received most attention relating to environmental performance. The transport provision industry at large is a low-margin industry that to a large extent responds to customer demands. This is a barrier for LSPs in driving environmental and social sustainability initiatives. One way of overcoming this barrier involves LSPs partnering with proactive customers that initiate, support and contribute to collaborative sustainable development (see, for example, Sallnäs and Huge-Brodin, 2018). In general, increased collaboration between LSPs and shippers has facilitated the generation of supply chain process innovation. In addition, both partners in such a collaboration may use their experiences to inspire their respective networks – in this way, the greening of transport and logistics can be described as a positive feedback loop. As for the product supply chain, improvements can be made without formal partnerships – for example more long-term contracts between LSPs and their customers will allow for the LSPs to make any necessary investments in equipment, vehicles and the education of staff. Such measures also contribute to the promotion of environmental and social sustainability in the transport provision part of the supply chain.

A wicked problem

As can be seen above, the challenge of developing more sustainable supply chains can be addressed in many ways. Through the various sustainability dimensions and the many nodes in the supply chain network, company types and geographical and cultural contexts, sustainable supply chain management constitutes a formidable and multi-dimensional challenge. It is not uncommon that high levels of ambition are hampered not only by resisting supply chain members, but as a result of limited resources. In such situations, what is to be prioritized? As the contexts and situations vary constantly, the usefulness of any general book of rules would be very limited, and particular problems need to be addressed from multiple angles and with the help of many different competences. As such, sustainable development in essence presents a wicked problem for society, and in particular for supply chain management. In this setting we can detect a number of conflicts that hinder or slow down sustainable development. But there are also synergies to be found, and many innovations in sustainable supply chains take advantage of these. The next section provides some examples.

Sustainable supply chains: contemporary and future challenges

This section describes and discusses some of the synergies and conflicts that are common in sustainable supply chain management. The illustrations below include sustainable supplier development, greening logistics, and the role of the supply chain as a vehicle to spread sustainability competence and passion.

From reactive to proactive and sustainable development

Sustainable supply chains consist of sustainable operations throughout, or at least as far as is possible to monitor and control. In the earlier days of the most recent sustainability era, many companies were eager to clean up their supply chains, to be able to secure they were sustainable. As global information access grew, it started to become easier for researchers, reporters and the media to follow up on which suppliers the companies used, and how well they followed basic rules of sustainability. In parallel, outsourcing also grew at this time, and the main reason for companies in developed countries to outsource was the cost savings attained due to relatively low labour costs in developing countries. The garment and fashion industry is one example of this; furniture and home decoration is another.

While lower labour costs were the goal for many companies that out-sourced, very low wages were grounds for criticism by the media, as well as by consumers. In addition, a low level of working conditions and employee safety has over the years resulted in catastrophes such as the Rana Plaza collapse in 2013 with a death toll of more than 1,100.

A spinal reflex among companies was to end all contracts with such unsustainable suppliers, in order to ensure that only socially sustainable companies took part in the manufacture of their products. In the short term, and on the companies' balance sheets, they had now more sustainable supply chains. Nevertheless, the socially less sustainable suppliers continued to supply their products to other, perhaps less conscious customers, with the result that overall sustainability did not necessarily increase. Even if the supplier firm went out of business due to loss of contracts, the employees still needed to support themselves and their families. Hence, to support a more long-term sustainable development globally, some companies work in different ways to develop their suppliers into more sustainable ones, instead of abandoning them. This includes improving the employees' working conditions, and providing educational opportunities.

The expected synergies are many. By internal education, by supporting employees through part-time education and by improving working conditions gradually, proactive companies now – to a greater extent than a few decades ago – define their sustainability through investments in their suppliers that also benefit the wider society at the suppliers' location. By investing in education, the general competence level is improved, as well as the economic situation for many families. These synergies also rely heavily on the relationship dimension of SCM. Building long-term relationships is believed to be financially beneficial, *and* it can support social sustainability in supply chains. A drawback may be in the lock-in effects, ie the perception that a supplier becomes so dependent on its customer that there is no real choice but to continue the collaboration. However, as transparency increases, this problem is likely to be exposed in the long term.

This situation illustrates the importance of long-term relationships for developing sustainable supply chains, and it illustrates possible synergies between social and economic sustainability.

Greening versus de-greening of supply chains

Developing the environmental sustainability of supply chains is often referred to as the *greening* of supply chains. As indicated in Figure 12.1, the transport provision chain and the LSPs are important when it comes to greening supply chains.

Logistics service provision as an industry can be characterized by its responsiveness to customers. If this logic is extended to the environmental dimension of sustainability, LSPs should then respond also to the environmental requirements of their customers, alongside the service requirements that are the basis of the service provided. The LSP industry is often seen as slow moving and not so innovative. As the impact of freight transportation on climate and on the natural environment at large has become more acknowledged, demands have been raised for this industry to take more initiatives and to contribute more actively to decreasing its environmental impact.

Herein lies an embedded conflict. While LSPs are in essence responding to their customers' demands, they are also expected to drive the development. In addition, the LSP industry is a low-margin industry, which means that the possibilities to take risks and to make investments are generally quite low. Nevertheless, there are examples that demonstrate how LSPs can thrive both financially and decrease their environmental impact – and this is in most cases accomplished through long-term and close collaboration with customers.

An LSP may have good intentions and present environmentally smart and viable solutions. However, if the customer shows no or low interest many initiatives will not be realized. Some initiatives create financial and environmental sustainability – typically those that involve less resource usage such as efficiency measures that reduce fuel consumption. However, some of these measures rely on the cooperation and willingness of customers to possibly adjust their demands – for example by allowing for more generous delivery windows or setting their orders more in advance – thereby creating opportunities for efficiency at the LSP. Other measures require investments at the LSP – for example, more education or new equipment – which can also be supported by more long-term contracts or even investments by customers. If the customer is not willing to make efforts on its side, green initiatives tend to fade, no matter how proactive the LSP is (for further reading, see Huge-Brodin, Sweeney and Evangelista, 2020).

On the other hand, a positive and environmentally demanding customer with long-term collaborative ambitions – or even partnership – can make green initiatives among the LSPs flourish. An example is a forwarder in Sweden, known to be environmentally proactive, that won a long-term contract with a grocery retailer. During the negotiation before the contract was signed, the forwarder offered to purchase two biofuel trucks for the purpose of this specific assignment. The suggestion was that the retailer contributed to the investment financially. After some consideration, the retailer reverted, resulting in six biofuel trucks being ordered with the same degree of co-investment. Through this contract, the LSP now has experience of using this type of vehicle, and has been able to raise its image as a green logistics provider thereby bringing in new business opportunities.

The situation in this example illustrates again the importance of joint development and long-term relationships for developing sustainable supply chains. Synergies can be found in the environmental and the economic dimensions. But the synergies can also be related to mutual investments and even higher mutual benefits, as the experiences can be utilized and exploited in the respective supply chain partners' extended networks. Even if sometimes there is an unwillingness from the shipper side to get involved in deep partnerships (outsourcing of logistics has, after all, been undertaken mainly for financial reasons and requires costs savings), longer contracts may promote investment in sustainable practices among LSPs that enable them to, for example, renew their fleet of vehicles and to maintain high educational levels among the employees.

Sustainability as an internal value: growth from within

Not only do customers care – employees also care. For example, millennials more than older generations want to be proud of their work from a sustainability perspective, and there are indications that a growing proportion of young people prefer to work for sustainable employers. This trend creates an interesting and synergetic situation. By supporting sustainable development, and being transparent and trustworthy, companies are better placed to attract conscientious employees. Next, when these employees become established in the organization, they will most probably contribute with sustainability knowledge and competency. And this passion and mindset may also spread to other employees.

This phenomenon is of particular interest for the supply chain. In integrated supply chains with collaboration and exchange between the supply chain partners, competence and passion have a potential to be spread not only to suppliers, but also to customers. In this way, sustainable initiatives have the potential to grow beyond company and supply chain boundaries.

Synergies and conflicts in sustainable supply chains

In the sections above, some potential synergies in sustainable supply chains were described. The concept of synergies is attractive at many levels, as it indicates that by doing something, you can gain even more. Synergies need to be exploited, meaning they need to be unveiled and clearly communicated. Decisions involving sustainability-related synergies tend to be easy to make – or at least propose. And from the discussion above it is obvious that a supply chain perspective reveals more synergies than a narrower corporate one. In summary, such synergies contribute to accelerating sustainable development in supply chains and in society.

Conflicts are more challenging in general, and the word 'conflict' itself suggests unwillingness and resistance. Nevertheless, conflicts occur in the sustainable supply chain, between the various sustainability dimensions, as well as between its members. As conflicts tend to hinder or slow down sustainable development they need to be identified and if possible resolved, often through trade-offs or negotiations.

Finally, the conflicts and synergies displayed above are merely examples, and can serve as inspiration for future initiatives. The really crucial success factor for accelerating sustainability in supply chains is to acquire a general mindset for handling conflicts and synergies relating to sustainability, as the challenges will inevitably change over time. This is true both in relation to the intrinsic nature of the challenges and their relative levels of importance.

Some concluding comments

In order for supply chain management to contribute to sustainable development, this chapter has pointed out some critical challenges. In support of sustainable development at large, companies are definitely part of the societies that they serve and are critical to societal development. In this context, companies that extend their sustainability ambitions to their wider supply chains can help to drive sustainable development. Through its inherent focus on relationships between companies, sustainable SCM has a potentially pivotal role to play.

We can only guess what future challenges will arise, but they will no doubt require that we maintain a high level of preparedness and a mindset that allows for higher degrees of resilience. We need to identify and make use of the synergies that are central to the sustainability concept but also need to develop strategies for handling the conflicts that sustainable supply chains inevitably entail.

An overall challenge is to decouple economic growth from consumption. A future with less consumption or very changed consumer patterns will fundamentally change the conditions for supply chains as we know them. Increased reuse and recycling of clothes, for example, will potentially decrease the environmental impact of the garment industry. But at the same time developing countries may, as a consequence, suffer from decreased corporate success, which in turn may impact the social and economic development in a negative way.

Another formidable challenge for supply chains as a result of the climate-related changes will be to handle catastrophes of various types and to configure supply chains that can support the protection against the consequences of climate change.

Delivering sustainability through the effective adoption of contemporary supply chain management thinking represents a significant opportunity. The challenges described in this chapter provide examples of the complex situation that lies ahead. Addressing the challenges is a key focus now and into the future for supply chain professionals working in practice and in research.

References

DJSI (2020) Dow Jones Sustainability Indices, www.spglobal.com/spdji/en/ (archived at https://perma.cc/2J33-SQNY)

European Commission (2021) Corporate Social Responsibility and Responsible Business Conduct, ec.europa.eu/growth/industry/sustainability/corporate-social-responsibility_en (archived at https://perma.cc/KCR8-BRQU)

GRI (2020) Global Reporting Initiative, www.globalreporting.org/ (archived at https://perma.cc/N7AV-YMVL)

Huge-Brodin, M, Sweeney, E and Evangelista, P (2020) Environmental alignment between logistics service providers and shippers – a supply chain perspective, in *International Journal of Logistics Management*, Vol. **31** (3), pp 575–605

ISO (2020) The International Organization for Standardization, www.iso.org/ (archived at https://perma.cc/M467-ZMUT)

Lambert, D and Cooper, M (2000) Issues in supply chain management, in *Industrial Marketing Management*, **29**, pp 65–83

Sallnäs, U and Huge-Brodin, M (2018) De-greening of logistics? Why environmental practices flourish and fade in provider-shipper relationships and networks, in *Industrial Marketing Management*, **74**, October, pp 276–87

Touboulic, A and Walker, H (2015) Love me, love me not: A nuanced view on collaboration in sustainable supply chains, in *Journal of Purchasing and Supply Management*, **21** (3), pp 178–91

UN SDG (2020) The UN Sustainable Development Goals Knowledge Platform, sustainabledevelopment.un.org/?menu=1300 (archived at https://perma.cc/5PD6-VVDC)

WCED (1987) *Our Common Future: The Brundtland Report*, Report of the World Commission on Environment and Development

Greening of logistics

13

Cutting pollution and greenhouse gas emissions

Alan McKinnon

Introduction

Logistics is responsible for a significant proportion of the emissions that pollute the atmosphere and warm the planet. Concern about the damaging effect of noxious emissions from trucks and ships on local air quality dates back to the 1960s and '70s. Fifty years of technological advances, government regulation and changes in business practice have now reduced these emissions of nitrogen oxide (NOx), particulate matter (PM) and sulphur dioxide (SOx) to a small fraction of their previous levels, particularly in more developed countries. In the meantime, attention shifted to the potentially more destructive impact of another gas emitted in vast quantities by logistical activity, carbon dioxide (CO_2). By far the most common of the greenhouse gases (GHGs) emitted by logistical activities, CO_2 is heating the planet at an alarming rate, presenting mankind with unquestionably its greatest environmental challenge.

The air pollution and global warming caused by logistics have a common origin in the burning of fossil fuel. Worldwide, the vast majority of freight movements, terminal operations and materials handling are powered by oil, gas or coal, either directly or indirectly via the electricity they consume. This means that reducing the heavy dependence of logistics on fossil fuel simultaneously addresses the pollution and climate change problems. In this sense, these two environmental problems, one essentially local and the other global, are intimately linked. Their solutions are also closely, but not entirely aligned. There is, for example, some mis-alignment in the 'greening' of road freight operations where efforts to reduce the amount of NOx emitted by a diesel-powered truck usually impairs engine efficiency and, as a result, increases fuel consumption and CO_2 emissions (Krishnamurthy et al, 2007). Air quality is then improved at the expense of more global warming.

Fortunately within the realms of 'green logistics' such conflicts between environmental objectives are quite rare. The vast majority of the initiatives that companies can apply to improve the environmental sustainability of their logistics both clean the air and mitigate climate change. This chapter will review these initiatives, especially those relating to freight transport, though reference will also be made to warehousing operations. First, however, it is important to get a sense of the magnitude of the logistics emission problem.

Emissions from logistics

Air pollutants

The World Health Organization (WHO) estimates that 91 per cent of the global population is exposed to levels of air pollution exceeding its recommended limit, with exposure highest in low- and middle-income countries. Polluted air inhaled outdoors 'accounts for an estimated 4.2 million deaths per year due to stroke, heart disease, lung cancer, acute and chronic respiratory diseases' (WHO, 2020). Emissions from freight vehicles are responsible for a significant, though unquantified, proportion of the pollution that causes this high level of morbidity. Four types of emission are responsible for most of the air pollution from freight movement (Piecyk *et al*, 2015):

- *Particulate matter (PM):* this is composed of tiny soot particles released by diesel engines, varying in their size and impact on human health. Much of the early research focused on the effect of particles with a diameter of less than 10 microns (PM10 – 1 micron = 1,000th of a millimetre), though today there is more concern about particles smaller than 2.5 microns in diameter (PM2.5) which, when regularly inhaled, can impair health in many more ways than previously thought. In addition to cardiovascular problems and lung damage, ultrafine PM2.5 particles have now been associated with dementia and found to travel through the placenta into unborn babies.

- *Nitrogen oxide (NOx):* another by-product of the combustion of transport fuel, also decreases lung function when regularly inhaled and in high concentrations can trigger asthma attacks.

- *Hydrocarbons (HCs), including volatile organic compounds (VOCs)*: in health terms, the most serious of the HCs is benzene, which is a carcinogen. VOCs also interact with NOx in sunlight to produce ozone which in high concentrations in urban areas causes respiratory problems, particularly for the young and old.

- *Sulphur dioxide (SOx)*: until recently the heavy fuel oil (HFO) powering most of the world's shipping has had relatively high levels of sulphur, which converts to SOx in the combustion process. It too exacerbates respiratory problems, particularly in the vicinity of major ports (Merk, 2015).

Since the early 1990s, governments in many parts of the world have imposed tightening restrictions on exhaust emissions of NOx and PMs from new trucks. This has dramatically reduced the permitted level of air pollution by these vehicles. For example, the latest emission standard imposed in the EU in 2013, so-called Euro VI, reduced emissions of the controlled pollutants to less than a twentieth of the level prevailing before emission standards were introduced. Other countries have adopted standards developed in Europe, the United States or Japan, often with a delay of several years. As many less developed countries (LDCs) import second-hand vehicles from Europe and North America they 'inherit' the higher emission standards in used vehicles, typically after 4–8 years. In many lower-income countries the upgrading of truck emission standards is constrained by the high sulphur content in local diesel fuel which is incompatible with the after-treatment systems installed by truck manufacturers to control exhaust emissions of NOx and PMs (Xie *et al*, 2020). For example, the normal requirement is for Euro VI trucks to run on diesel with sulphur content less than 10 parts per million (ppm). Oil refining capacity in LDCs will have to be upgraded to produce the ultralow sulphur diesel that has been available in developed countries for many years.

The removal of sulphur from bunker fuel has been a major issue in the maritime sector as the HFO burned by ships has traditionally had extremely high sulphur content; in 2012 it was 1,800 times higher than that allowed in US road transport (Pyper, 2012). In that year the International Maritime Organization restricted the sulphur content in marine fuel to 3.5 per cent by weight. It reduced this limit in 2020 to 0.5 per cent, a decision partly prompted by a study which estimated that retaining the previous limit 'would contribute to more than 570,000 additional premature deaths worldwide between 2020 and 2025' (International Maritime Organization, 2016). In four Emission Control Areas (ECA) designated by IMO, around the Baltic Sea, North Sea, coastal areas off the United States and Canada, and the US Caribbean Sea area, the sulphur weight limit is even lower at 0.1 per cent.

As restrictions on those freight transport emissions that impair air quality at the local level have been tightened, particularly in more developed countries, the main focus of environmental concern has shifted to logistics' contribution to global warming.

Greenhouse gases

GHGs are currently warming the planet faster than at any time in the climatic record going back three million years. According to the World Meteorological Organization (2017), in climatic terms we are in 'truly uncharted territory', and, in the words of the naturalist David Attenborough, 'facing a man-made disaster on a global scale' if we continue to allow GHG emissions to rise at their current level. The disastrous effects of climate change are already being felt in the increasing frequency and intensity of extreme weather events, melting ice-caps and glaciers and rising sea level. There is also mounting concern that increasing GHG concentrations in the atmosphere will push the planet over a series of climatic and geophysical tipping points whose impact would be catastrophic and irreversible. Climate modelling suggests that to minimize the risk of this happening, the increase in average global temperature between 1850 and 2100 should be kept within 1.5°C. As the planet has already warmed by 1.1°C since 1850, urgent action is required to cut GHG emissions to a small fraction of their current level. Research by the Intergovernmental Panel on Climate Change (2017) has indicated the required magnitude and speed of the emission reduction. It expresses this in terms of the maximum amount of GHG that we can now emit if we want to have a two-thirds chance of staying within the 1.5°C global temperature increase. At the current rate of GHG emissions we will reach this maximum within around 10 years, then exhausting the remaining 'carbon budget' for the 1.5°C limit.

The gravity of this situation is now recognized by most governments and much of the business world. The Paris Climate Agreement of 2015 was a landmark event in the development of global climate policy. Since then, however, worsening climatic trends and new scientific research has forced a reassessment of the required policy response. Since 2016, 33 national governments have declared a climate emergency while the UNFCC (2020) has launched a 'Race to Zero' initiative encouraging governments and companies to become carbon neutral as soon as possible. By December 2020, over

Figure 13.1 Proportions of CO_2 emissions from freight transport modes

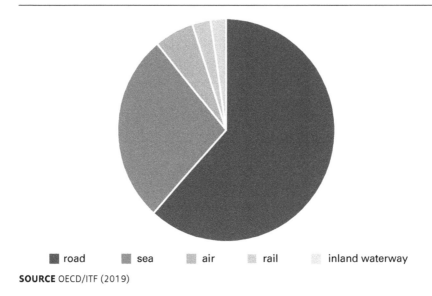

■ road   ■ sea   ■ air   ■ rail   ■ inland waterway

SOURCE OECD/ITF (2019)

110 countries and over 1,100 businesses had committed to being net-zero-carbon by 2050 or earlier.

It is against this background that pressure is now mounting to decarbonize logistics operations. This will be difficult, partly because demand for logistics activities is forecast to rise steeply over the next few decades but also, as mentioned earlier, because they are almost entirely powered by fossil fuel (McKinnon, 2018a). CO_2 emitted by this fossil fuel accounts for over 90 per cent of GHG emissions from logistical activities worldwide. This makes logistics responsible for around 10–11 per cent of total energy-related CO_2 emissions. Most of these logistics emissions, probably around 85 per cent of them, come from freight transport operations, the remainder from warehouses, terminals and related office activities. Figure 13.1 shows how freight transport emissions are divided among the main transport modes (OECD/ITF, 2019). These shares reflect differences in the amounts of freight that the various modes move (measured in tonne-kms) and their average carbon intensities (expressed as gCO_2 per tonne-km). Although three-quarters of tonne-kms are moved by sea, the average carbon intensity of shipping is around a tenth that of trucking. Once allowance is made for the wide modal variations in carbon intensity (Figure 13.2), the movement of freight by road is by far the biggest emitter, representing two-thirds of all freight transport CO_2 emissions globally.

Figure 13.2   Average carbon intensity of freight transport modes: gCO_2 per tonne-km

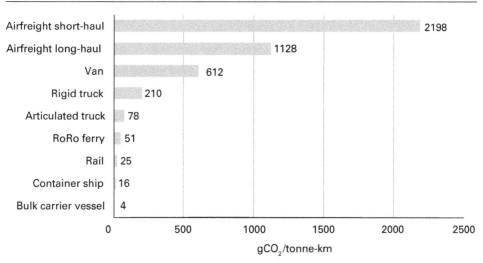

SOURCE DBEIS/DEFRA (2020)

The other GHGs associated with logistics are emitted in relatively small quantities, but have much higher global warming potentials (GWPs) than CO_2, ie they heat the planet much more per unit of weight. The measurement of GWP is time-specific as GHGs vary in the length of time they remain in the atmosphere. GWP is generally measured against a standard 100-year time period, using CO_2 as the 'yardstick' against which other GHGs are compared. On this basis, three other GHGs emitted by logistics, methane, nitrous oxide and hydrofluorocarbon (HFC 123) have, respectively, GWPs 21, 310 and 11,700 times greater than CO_2 (UNFCCC, 2017). The leakage of methane from vehicles and vessels running on natural gas (and the pipelines supplying them) and of refrigerant gases, such as HFC123, from temperature-controlled supply chains can, therefore, significantly inflate the GHG footprint of some logistics systems.

In addition to these gases, the emission of minute particles known as 'black carbon' from diesel-powered trucks and ships burning heavy fuel oil (HFO) can also exert a potent global warming effect. They are classed as 'short-lived climate pollutants' because they spend relatively little time in the atmosphere, though while there can absorb large amounts of solar radiation. Although black carbon has a GWP roughly 3,200 times that of CO_2 over a 20-year period and is released in large quantities by freight vehicles and vessels, it seldom appears in company audits of greenhouse gas emissions. Efforts are, nevertheless, being made to raise awareness of black carbon's contribution to global warming (Climate and Clean Air Coalition, 2020), and to encourage logistics businesses to calculate and report this category of emissions (Greene, 2017).

Managerial and analytical frameworks

Getting logistics onto a net-zero emission trajectory as quickly as possible presents a major challenge for the providers and users of logistics services. Applying a few ad hoc measures will not be enough. It will require a transformation of business practices and the deployment of an array of new technologies, IT innovations and alternative energy sources. To maximize their impact these changes will need to be applied systematically and in a coordinated manner. Figure 13.3 outlines a 10-stage managerial procedure that companies can use to formally develop an emission-reduction strategy for their logistics operations. As each stage has a word beginning with the letter 'C', I call it the 10C framework (McKinnon, 2018a).

It starts with the need for *corporate motivation* to incentivize management to take the radical actions that will be required. Companies must then *calculate* their emissions to determine where they are coming from and in

Figure 13.3   10C framework for developing an emission-reduction strategy for logistics

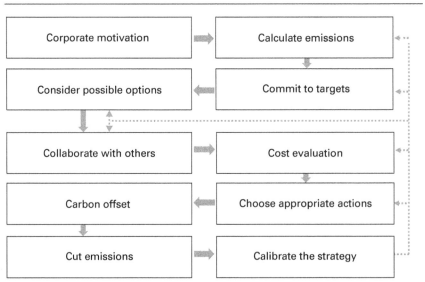

SOURCE McKinnon (2018a)

what quantities. Major advances have been made over the past decade in the carbon auditing of logistical activities, improving its accuracy and harmonizing methodologies and reporting standards. Many businesses now follow the guidance of the Global Logistics Emissions Council (2019) in measuring their emissions thereby ensuring the consistency and comparability of the data. Once the level of emissions is known, the next step is to *commit to targets* for reducing them (McKinnon and Piecyk, 2012). Many companies are today setting Science Based Targets for their GHG emissions, aligning them with the climate science and getting onto a pathway that will lead to net-zero emissions by 2050 or earlier (Science Based Target Initiative, 2019).

At Stage 4 in the procedure companies *consider the possible options* for reducing emissions by the targeted amount. Fortunately, there are many options available, most of them mutually reinforcing. They can be classified into five categories:

1 repower logistics with cleaner, lower carbon energy;

2 increase the energy efficiency of logistical activities;

3 improve the utilization of logistics assets;

4 shift freight to greener transport modes;

5 reduce demand for freight movement.

It is widely acknowledged that to achieve deep reductions in their logistics GHG emissions companies will have to work together to share their logistics assets, consolidate their loads and coordinate their planning to a much greater extent than today. At the fifth stage in the framework companies should explore new opportunities for *collaborative initiatives* likely to cut logistics emissions. The next stage involves *cost evaluation* of the emission-reducing measures, comparing their relative cost-effectiveness. A technique called Marginal Abatement Cost (MAC) analysis can be used for this purpose. This assesses, for each measure, the average mitigation cost per tonne of emission saved and the 'abatement potential', ie the weight of pollutant or GHG likely to be saved. MAC analyses generally show that many emission-reducing measures actually yield reductions in cost as well as emissions. The implementation of these so-called 'green gold' measures can therefore be justified in commercial as well as environmental terms. In a recent survey of European managers, 40 per cent indicated that more than half of carbon-reducing measures in logistics also cut costs (McKinnon and Petersen, 2021).

This suggests that many businesses are currently in what might be called the 'low hanging fruit' phase of green logistics. Harvesting all this financially and ecologically enticing 'fruit' will not, however, deliver the required scale of emission reductions. While it offers a relatively painless introduction to the emission-reduction process, in the medium to long term emission mitigation costs are likely to rise, forcing companies to make more difficult business trade-offs and possibly accept lower profits and investment returns. Over this timescale, however, it is likely that carbon pricing and/or taxation will be widely applied, effectively monetizing carbon emissions, making them an item on corporate balance sheets and giving companies a stronger financial incentive to reduce them. More general internalization of the environmental costs of logistics would also put monetary values on pollutant emissions, giving companies a commercial incentive to cut them as well.

At Stage 7 a company should be able to *choose the appropriate actions* to cut their logistics emissions. This range of options needs to be tailored to the particular logistics system, taking account of its spatial structure, the nature of the products it handles, customer service levels, upstream supply links, opportunities for collaboration etc. At this point the company may discover that within the budget and schedule set for its emission-reduction programme, the chosen package of measures may not achieve the targeted reduction in emissions. It may be necessary therefore to supplement these measures with some *carbon offsetting*. This involves paying other organizations to cut emissions on your behalf, often because they can do so more cheaply. Decisions on carbon offsetting are made at the eighth stage in the procedure and should not be seen as an 'easy option' as this risks weakening the company's own efforts to decarbonize.

The company is now ready to implement its strategy thereby *cutting emissions* and learning from this experience. By monitoring the impact of the various measures on emission levels and costs, it can assess the overall effectiveness of the strategy and decide what refinements may need to be made. The final stage in the process is to *calibrate* the strategy as illustrated by the various feedback loops in Figure 13.3. This may involve successive revisions of the targets, the cost evaluations and the choice of measures until the strategy is delivering the required level of emission reductions within budget and time frame.

In the remainder of the chapter we examine the five ways of cutting logistics emissions, focusing mainly on freight transport operations and emissions of GHGs.

Repowering logistics with cleaner, low-carbon energy

This process has been underway for many years both to reduce pollutant emissions and GHGs from freight vehicles and vessels. For example, running trucks on compressed natural gas (CNG) rather than diesel fuel can cut emissions of NOx and PM by around 85 per cent and CO_2 by 10 per cent. Fuelling a ship with liquid natural gas (LNG) instead of HFO can reduce SOx, PM, NOx and CO_2 emissions by, respectively, 98, 96, 86 and 11 per cent (Elgohary *et al*, 2015). Tightening controls on SOx emissions in recent years have significantly increased the use of LNG in the maritime sector. While switching to natural gas can dramatically reduce air pollution, the related savings in CO_2 are relatively modest. It should be noted too that quoted emission reductions apply at the vehicle exhaust (or tail-pipe) or ship funnel and usually do not take account of any leakage of the gas, which is methane, from pipelines, tanks and the refuelling process. As mentioned earlier, methane has a global warming potential 21 times higher than CO_2 and so fugitive emissions can negate much of the benefit of tail-pipe CO_2 reductions (Dominguez-Faus, 2016).

Biodiesel, produced by the conversion of plant material to fuel, was thought to offer a more effective means of decarbonizing freight transport operations. In many countries legislation was introduced requiring the blending of a certain proportion of biodiesel with diesel to reduce GHG emissions. These GHG savings were again estimated at the vehicle exhaust on a so-called 'tank to wheel' basis. This, however, gave only a partial view of the total GHGs emitted by the production and distribution of biodiesel, much of which originates from palm oil plantations created by the destruction of tropical rain forest. Life cycle analysis subsequently revealed that when emissions from these upstream processes were included in the calculation, much biodiesel actually emits more GHG than conventional diesel, respectively 18, 113 and 203 per cent more in the case of biodiesel produced from rape-seed, soya and palm oil, according to T&E (2016). On the other hand, biomethane produced by the anaerobic digestion of agricultural and food waste has been shown on a life cycle basis to release on average 75 per cent less GHG than diesel fuel (DBEIS/DEFRA, 2020). There is, however, a limited supply of this form of biogas, strong competition for it from sectors other than logistics and a need to ensure than methane leakage is minimized.

Given the constraints and concerns surrounding the use of natural gas and biofuels as a means of decarbonizing logistics, there is now wide agreement that the repowering of logistical activities with renewable electricity offers a more credible and effective route to carbon neutrality for most freight movement and warehousing/terminal operations. This allows the logistics sector to take advantage of the decarbonization of grid electricity and the potential to 'micro-generate' solar- and wind-power at logistics sites, such as ports and distribution centres. The International Energy Agency (2019a) has estimated that on the basis of 'stated policies' the average carbon intensity of electricity worldwide will drop by a third between 2018 and 2040 and possibly by as much as 80 per cent if its 'sustainable development' scenario materializes. Assuming that electricity decarbonizes at an accelerating rate and there will be enough low-/zero-carbon electricity to power logistics operations, admittedly quite bold assumptions, the main challenge will be to find cost-effective ways of getting this electricity into the logistics sector.

Logistics operations directly connected to electricity grids have already been benefiting, in environmental terms, from the declining carbon intensity of electricity. These include virtually all logistics buildings and terminals, which collectively account for around 10–12 per cent of total logistics emissions (McKinnon, 2018a). Their decarbonization is being supplemented by the erection of on-site wind turbines and installation of solar panels on warehouse roofs. Some facilities are now micro-generating more than enough renewable energy to meet the needs of the warehousing operation and supplying the surplus zero-carbon electricity to other users. This can make a distribution centre 'carbon negative' and earn carbon credits that can be used to offset emissions from the freight transport operation.

The railways are by far the most electrified freight transport mode with around half of all rail freight moved in electrically-hauled trains (IEA, 2019b). This permits the direct transmission of low-carbon electricity into much of the rail network. In some countries, such as Germany, rail freight operators purchase only green electricity, thereby providing a carbon neutral service to their clients. Worldwide the proportion of the network that is electrified has been steadily rising, except in North and South America where it is tiny and stable. In the United States, locomotives powered by batteries and hydrogen fuel cells are being trialled and may offer an alternative route to rail freight decarbonization.

Highway electrification is also being trialled, allowing trucks to be powered by overhead cables using a catenary system similar to that long established on the rail network. Pilot projects in Sweden, Germany and California have demonstrated that this is technically and operationally feasible, while several studies have found that, despite the relatively high infrastructural investment, the development of e-highway networks constitutes a relatively cost-effective way of decarbonizing long-haul road freight (Ainalis *et al*, 2020).

This is one of three methods of electrifying the road freight sector and only applicable to larger heavy goods vehicles. The electrification of vans undertaking local delivery operations is already well underway in some countries using batteries. Their limited catchment areas and stop/start duty cycles are well suited to battery electrification. The switch from petrol and diesel to battery power at the local and regional levels is currently accelerating as battery storage costs drop, recharging networks expand, distance ranges lengthen and the carbon content of grid electricity diminishes. There will soon be parity in total operating costs between diesel and electric vans.

Until recently there was a widely held view that battery electrification of long-haul trucking would not be commercially viable because the batteries would be too heavy, too expensive and require too long to recharge (Sripad and Viswanathan, 2017). Recent advances in battery technology and vehicle design have now made this a viable proposition, particularly for the distribution of lower density loads over distances of a few hundred kilometres. One US study suggests that the latest truck batteries can offer weight 'parity' between diesel and electric vehicles over a distance of 400km (Phadke *et al*, 2019), while fast charging can now power a truck for a 400km journey in only 30 minutes.

Hydrogen also offers a means of running trucks on low-carbon electricity, where the electricity is used to electrolyse water; the so-called 'green' hydrogen produced by this process is distributed in compressed form and converted back into electrical energy by a fuel cell in the vehicle. The green hydrogen is then used as the medium for storing and transferring the energy rather than batteries. It is currently being heavily promoted as a future energy source for trucks, its proponents arguing that it has a lower weight penalty than batteries and permits more rapid refuelling than the recharging of a battery. Almost all the hydrogen currently available, however, is produced by the 'steam reforming' of natural gas, making it intrinsically a fossil fuel. This so-called 'grey hydrogen' could be converted to 'blue hydrogen' if the CO_2 released by the steam reforming process were captured and stored, though this is still a very immature technology. The timing of the future transition from grey to green hydrogen is also uncertain, creating doubt as to when enough of it will be available to meet the demands of long-haul trucking. Concern has also been expressed at the high energy losses in the green hydrogen supply chain between the electricity supply and the wheel of the vehicle, which can be over 70 per cent (Oeko Institute/IFEU/Fraunhofer ISI, 2016). As renewable electricity is likely to remain a precious commodity for the foreseeable future, wasting so much of it in truck decarbonization seems highly questionable, particularly when other more energy efficient options are available.

Large-scale electrification of freight movement by inland waterway, sea and air seems a distant prospect. The capacity and performance of maritime batteries are steadily improving and their cost per kWh reducing, though their application is likely to remain limited to short-distance RoRo ferry and barge operations. Onboard wind-generated electrical power will help to reduce the carbon intensity of shipping, but only at the margins. The low-carbon energy options for shipping are, in fact, very limited. Ammonia, methanol and biofuels are currently being advocated as alternatives to the HFO and marine diesel upon which the maritime sector heavily relies, though producing them at sufficient scale would be a daunting task and create other environmental and land-use problems.

Battery weight is likely to remain a major constraint on the electrification of aviation, though some researchers and commentators suggest that it may be eased by the 2030s and '40s. Airbus plans to launch a net-zero aircraft by 2035, though powered by hydrogen, either directly or in a synthetic fuel. It is not known how long it would take such technology, being developed primarily for passenger flight, to impact on the global air cargo market.

In summary, the effort, cost and time required to wean logistics off fossil fuel will vary widely by activity and freight transport mode. It will also depend on the parallel transformation of the energy industry, particularly the decarbonization of grid electricity and the supply of batteries, fuel cells, hydrogen, ammonia and environmentally sustainable biofuel. This transformation will ultimately be required to reach net-zero logistics, but it cannot happen quickly enough to deliver the deep reductions in emissions needed in the next 10–15 years. This is well illustrated by long-haul trucking in the EU. According to their trade association ACEA (2020), 'European truck manufacturers are fully committed to carbon neutrality by 2050 at the latest. This implies that by 2040 all new commercial vehicles sold will have to be fossil-free.' The replacement of internal combustion engine (ICE) trucks with low-carbon vehicles is not expected to gather momentum until after 2025. In 2017 the average replacement cycle of trucks in the EU was

13 years (Eurostat, 2020). It is not surprising therefore that a recent study (Neuhausen *et al*, 2020) suggested that, even in 2035, 54 per cent of the trucks on European roads will still be running on diesel fuel – and that is in a continent at the vanguard of the change-over to non-fossil road freight. In other parts of the world, many of them dependent on the import of second-hand trucks from Europe, this transition will take much longer.

As the power shift to renewable energy is a longer-term decarbonization option other measures must be implemented in the meantime to meet medium-term carbon reduction targets for logistics. In addition to delivering GHG savings more rapidly, these measures will also lessen the amount of logistics energy that will need to be 'de-fossilized' at a later stage. Deployment of the next four sets of initiatives will ease reliance on the repowering options.

Raising the energy efficiency of logistics operations

The amount of energy consumed in moving freight and handling products in warehouses and terminals can be cut in many different ways. Companies have a strong financial incentive to do this as energy costs can represent a sizeable proportion of total operating costs. For example, energy use typically accounts for around a third of the cost of running a truck in Europe and up to 50–60 per cent of total ship operating costs (Stratiotis, 2018). Hence, efforts to decrease energy use are generally motivated more by a desire to save money than to cut emissions, though companies are increasingly citing CO_2 reduction as an important justification for energy-saving programmes in logistics.

Although the energy efficiency of all freight modes has greatly improved in recent decades, the potential exists for further improvement through a combination of technical and operational measures. In countries such as Japan, China, the United States and EU member states, truck manufacturers are now legally obliged to meet rising fuel economy standards. In the EU, for example, all new trucks sold after 2025 must be at least 15 per cent more fuel-efficient than the average new truck in 2019 and this figure rises to 30 per cent from 2030 onwards. This additional fuel efficiency is being achieved by, among other things, re-design of the engine and transmission (known collectively as the powertrain), lightweighting the vehicle and improving its aerodynamics. It is also possible to retrofit devices to existing vehicles to improve aerodynamic profiling, automatically inflate tyres to the most fuel-efficient pressure and control the amount of engine idling. It is estimated that such idling represents around 8 per cent of total fuel consumed by US trucks, releasing over 20 million tonnes of CO_2 annually (NACFE, 2014).

Total emissions from a truck over its working life are not simply a function of its fuel efficiency when new. They also depend on how well it is maintained and driven. Where the standard of maintenance is deficient 'a poorly tuned engine, a misaligned axle, a leaking fuel pipe and an under-inflated tyre can each increase fuel consumption, and CO_2 emissions by 1–3 per cent' (McKinnon, 2018a). Training truck drivers to drive their vehicles more fuel-efficiently, electronically monitoring their subsequent performance and providing follow-up guidance where necessary can typically cut fuel consumption by 5–10 per cent, making this one of the most cost-effective ways for decarbonizing the road freight sector. In the longer term truck platooning and vehicle automation may, respectively, offer further fuel savings of 5–10 per cent and 15–20 per cent. Technically much easier and quicker to implement is a reduction in the maximum speed of a truck. Several large trucking companies in the United States and Europe have done this, cutting fuel use and emissions with minimal loss of service quality (McKinnon, 2016).

It is in the maritime sector where deceleration has had the greatest impact on fuel consumption and emissions. Since 2008, a practice known as 'slow steaming' has been widely adopted, particularly in container shipping where speed reductions of 10 per cent and 20 per cent translate into fuel and CO_2 savings of, respectively, 15–19 per cent and 36–39 per cent (ICCT, 2011). Although this practice was introduced primarily for commercial reasons, it has yielded significant environmental benefit and proved much less disruptive of global supply chains than expected (McKinnon, 2013). The average energy efficiency of ships has also been improving in other ways. Increases in vessel size have been lowering the carbon intensity of container shipping, though savings in energy and emissions appear to taper at the upper end of the vessel size range. Just as fuel economy standards have been introduced for new trucks, so the International Maritime Organization (IMO) has, since 2013, required new ships to achieve minimum energy efficiency standards defined in terms of an Energy Efficiency Design Index (EEDI), standards which are steadily rising through time. IMO also encourages shipping lines operating vessels with gross weights in excess of 5,000 tonnes to develop and implement 'Ship Energy Efficiency Management Plans'

(SEEMPs) comprising a broad set of best practice measures. Although the SEEMP scheme is voluntary it has had a reasonably high uptake.

The energy efficiency of the other major freight transport modes has also been improving. Globally, the average energy intensity of rail freight operations has been declining (International Energy Agency and International Union of Railways, 2017) while a combination of locomotive engine upgrades, lightweighting, improved aerodynamics and more efficient train operation are expected to maintain this downward trend. It is difficult to measure the average energy efficiency of air cargo operations, partly because around half of airfreight is moved in the bellyholds of passenger aircraft. This does mean, however, that the freight sector benefits from improvements in the energy performance of passenger planes. According to the International Energy Agency (2020), this energy efficiency rose by 2.8 per cent per year between 2000 and 2020 though the rate of improvement has been declining. In its 'zero climate impact international aviation pathway', however, the International Civil Aviation Organization (2019) envisages 'fleet-wide fuel efficiency improvements of 2.5 per cent pa from 2020 to 2050'.

Increasing the utilization of logistics assets

Loading more freight onto a vehicle reduces the number of trips it must make to deliver a given quantity of freight, cutting vehicle-kms, fuel consumption and emissions. Chapter 7 discusses in detail how the under-loading of vehicles can be measured, why it happens and how it can be minimized. Here, attention will be confined to the potential emission savings that can accrue from raising vehicle load factors. These savings are difficult to calculate because macro-level data on weight utilization is very limited while on volumetric utilization it is virtually non-existent (McKinnon, 2018a). Nevertheless, attempts have been made to model the possible contribution of improved loading to the decarbonization of road freight operations. The International Energy Agency (2017), for example, saw it contributing around a fifth of the CO_{2e} savings achievable between 2015 and 2050 in its 'modern truck scenario'. The Energy Transitions Commission (2019) estimated that just over 300 million tonnes of CO_{2e} might be saved by 2040 by 'supply chain collaboration', which would be likely to impact mainly on vehicle utilization. As explained earlier, collaboration resulting in greater sharing of logistics assets could play a key role in the decarbonization of logistics operations in the short to medium term. It does not require major technical advances, high levels of capital expenditure or fundamental regulatory change. As a recent survey of European businesses revealed (McKinnon and Petersen, 2020), the main barriers to be overcome relate essentially to business practice, managerial mindsets and concerns about trust and data privacy. Mounting case study evidence shows that when these constraints are relaxed and companies work together to cut empty running and increase vehicle fill, the environmental gains can be substantial (Cruijssen, 2020). One such case study involved logistical collaboration between Nestlé and PepsiCo in the Benelux countries. Modelling suggested that by combining and collaboratively synchronizing many of their deliveries they could cut CO_2 emissions per tonne of product distributed by 54 per cent relative to each company handling its logistics separately.

The available government statistics on vehicle utilization, which relate solely to the road freight sector and are available for relatively few countries, suggest that trends in key variables such as empty running and weight-based load factors have either been stable or moving, in environmental terms, in the wrong direction. In the UK, for example, the proportion of truck-kms run empty increased from 27 per cent to 30 per cent between 2000 and 2019, while the average load factor went up only marginally from 60 to 61 per cent (Department for Transport, 2020). This contrasts sharply with the optimistic predictions of a panel of a hundred logistics specialists who participated in a Delphi survey in 2008 (Piecyk and McKinnon, 2010). The absence of clear evidence that average load factors have been improving, despite exhortation from governments, environmental organizations and trade bodies, causes some specialists to doubt that industry is likely to make the managerial changes necessary for a major improvement in vehicle utilization, at least in the short to medium term. This partly explains the bias in favour of technological approaches to road freight decarbonization. As discussed in greater detail in Chapter 7, however, there are reasons to believe that levels of asset utilization will rise over the next 5 to 10 years as a result of digitalization, new collaborative business models and regulatory reforms.

Shifting freight to greener transport modes

Emissions of pollutants and GHGs per tonne-km vary enormously between transport modes (Figure 13.2). It is understandable therefore that politicians and planners have traditionally regarded modal shift as the primary means of 'greening' the freight transport system. For example, the EU's recently published 'Sustainable and Smart Mobility Strategy' has a 'flagship' section entitled 'greening freight transport' which is almost entirely devoted to the displacement of freight from road to rail and waterborne services (European Commission, 2020). In Europe, and many other parts of the world, modal shift involves reversing a long-term erosion of freight from the 'greener' modes to road, something that has proved very hard to achieve. Over the past 20 years, despite strenuous efforts by the EU and national governments to increase the rail and inland waterway share of the freight market, road has strengthened its market dominance. This casts doubt on the credibility of the EU's new Green Deal targets to increase rail freight traffic by 50 per cent by 2030 and 100 per cent by 2050, and to increase traffic on inland waterways and short sea shipping by 25 per cent and 50 per cent by, respectively, 2030 and 2050. Their credibility can be further challenged on the grounds that, over these time periods, rail networks and inland waterways will be losing coal and oil traffic, commodities that have represented a large share of their total tonne-kms. In the UK, for example, where electricity generation has switched rapidly from coal to renewables, the tonnage of coal moved by rail dropped 88 per cent over six years (between 2013/14 and 2019/20), reducing total rail tonnage by 39 per cent over this period. In many countries, the railways will have a formidable challenge just replacing the lost fossil fuel traffic with other types of commodity.

Against this fairly sobering assessment of the prospects for modal shift can be put several more positive messages. First, in the recent survey of European businesses mentioned earlier, transferring freight to low-carbon modes was considered the most cost-effective means of decarbonizing transport operations (McKinnon and Petersen, 2021). Second, the electrification of much of the rail network and ability of freight trains to draw low-/zero-carbon electricity directly from the grid will become an increasingly important source of competitive advantage. Third, the concept of synchromodality, which facilitates modal interchange, has yet to be fully embraced by rail and waterway operators and shippers, despite offering significant cost and emission savings, especially when incorporated into supply chain management (Dong *et al*, 2018). Finally, intermodal transport is getting what the European Commission (2020, p 10) calls a 'substantial revamp', not just in Europe. After decades of logistical dependence on trucking, very few factories and warehouses are located beside railway lines or waterways and so must rely on intermodal services to access these alternative networks. In Europe, India, Mexico and other parts of the world governments are channelling investment into intermodal corridors in geographically targeted efforts to shift freight to rail and water where the potential economic and environmental benefits are greatest.

Reducing the demand for freight movement

The most environmentally-friendly freight movements are the ones which can be avoided either by reducing the amount of stuff to be transported or rationalizing the systems of production and distribution. The first option, often called 'dematerialization', can be achieved in many ways such as promoting more sustainable patterns of consumption, making economies more 'circular', minimizing waste, downsizing and lightweighting products, and digitizing more news, entertainment and educational products, essentially converting them from physical consignments to electrons. Additive manufacturing, which includes 3D printing, can also reduce the material content of products and cut wastage. It also reduces the demand for freight transport by eliminating links in the supply chain and promoting a spatial convergence of production and consumption. There is still considerable uncertainty, however, about the net effect of this technology on future levels of logistical activity and related emissions (Boon and van Wee, 2017; World Economic Forum, 2020).

There is also disagreement about the extent to which future restructuring of global value chains will affect freight traffic levels. Some studies anticipate substantial re-shoring and near-shoring of manufacturing capacity from low-labour-cost countries to Europe and North America, shortening supply chain links and cutting demand for long-haul freight services (Boston Consulting Group, 2015). Others envisage greater diversification of regional economies combined with continued reliance on intercontinental links (World Economic Forum/Kearney, 2020). Having exposed the vulnerability of their supply chains, the coronavirus pandemic is causing many companies to examine ways of minimizing their risk exposure and improving their resilience. Some of these resilience-enhancing measures are also likely to increase the environmental sustainability of logistics systems (McKinnon, 2018b).

One way of reducing freight demand, or at least containing its growth, would be to reverse a spatial process that has driven much of the growth in freight traffic over the past few decades, namely the centralization of production and distribution operations in a smaller number of larger factories and warehouses. However, returning to more decentralized logistical systems would be a radical, long-term option with a high carbon mitigation cost and no guarantee that on a life cycle basis it would yield a large GHG saving. It would reduce transport-related emissions, but inflate emissions from the dispersed production and warehousing operations and the construction of new buildings required to accommodate them.

In summary, suppressing the demand for freight transport would involve reversing several well-established, longer-term business and logistical trends. Despite national declarations of a climate emergency there is little political will at present to introduce policy measures that might induce such a reversal. Many of the other freight demand management measures outlined in the previous sections offer quicker, more realistic and less controversial means of cutting logistics emissions.

Conclusions

Progress made over the past 30 years in curbing air pollution from the movement of freight has been variable both by transport mode and geographically. It has been impressive in the road freight sectors of developed countries thanks to a combination of technology, regulation and operational efficiency. The rate of emission reduction has been much slower in the maritime sector and in lower-income countries where freight transport emissions are still responsible for high levels of illness and premature death. Although worldwide the decarbonization of logistics is now commanding much greater attention, the air quality problems of the developing world should remain high on the green logistics agendas of international organizations and corporations. Thankfully, most of the measures that companies will have to introduce to achieve net-zero logistics by 2050 will also clean the air and bring health benefits to millions of people.

The scale and urgency of the required decarbonization of logistics operations poses a major challenge for managers, scientists and public policymakers. This chapter has outlined the many levers that will need to be pulled, some of them very aggressively, to get logistics GHG emissions onto the right downward trajectory. This will entail transformational changes in logistics hardware, IT systems and business practice, giving the greening of logistics a more central role in corporate climate change strategies.

References

ACEA (2020) *Road freight transport on the way to carbon neutrality*, Policy Paper, ACEA, Brussels

Ainalis, DT, Thorne, C and Cebon, D (2020) *Decarbonising the UK's long-haul road freight at minimum economic cost*, White Paper, Centre for Sustainable Road Freight, University of Cambridge, Cambridge

Boon, W and van Wee, B (2017) Influence of 3D printing on transport: A theory and experts judgment based conceptual model, *Transport Reviews*, **38** (5), pp 556–75

Boston Consulting Group (2015) Reshoring of Manufacturing to the US Gains Momentum, *BCG Perspectives*, Boston, MA, retrieved from: www.bcgperspectives.com/content/articles/lean-manufacturing-outsourcing-bpo-reshoring-manufacturing-us-gains-momentum/ (archived at https://perma.cc/ERS7-8EL4)

Climate and Clean Air Coalition (2020) *Black carbon*, retrieved from: www.ccacoalition.org/en/slcps/black-carbon (archived at https://perma.cc/CB5Z-CHXR)

Cruijssen, F (2020) *Cross-chain Collaboration in Logistics: Looking back and ahead*, Springer, Cham

DBEIS/DEFRA (2020) *UK government GHG conversion factors for company reporting*, Department for Business, Energy and Industrial Strategy and Department of the Environment, Food and Rural Affairs, London

Department for Transport (2020) *Road Freight: Domestic and international statistics*, Department for Transport, London

Dominguez-Faus, R (2016) *The Carbon Intensity of NGV C8 Trucks*, (revised) UC Davis Institute of Transportation Studies, University of California

Dong, C, Boute, R, McKinnon, AC and Verelst, M (2018) Investigating synchromodality from a supply chain perspective, *Transportation Research Part D: Transport and Environment*, **61**, pp 42–57

Elgohary, MM, Seddiek, IS and Salem, AM (2015) Overview of alternative fuels with emphasis on the potential of liquefied natural gas as future marine fuel, *Proceedings of the Institute of Mechanical Engineers*, Pt M, **229** (4), pp 365–75

Energy Transitions Commission (2019) *Mission Possible: Sector focus – heavy road transport*, retrieved from: ETC-sectoral-focus-HeavyRoadTransport_final.pdf

European Commission (2020) *Sustainable and Smart Mobility Strategy*, retrieved from: ec.europa.eu/info/law/better-regulation/have-your-say/initiatives/12438-Sustainable-and-Smart-Mobility-Strategy (archived at https://perma.cc/9XPX-VM8R)

Eurostat (2020) *Road Freight Transport by Vehicle Characteristics*, retrieved from: https://bit.ly/3dJfmV0 (archived at https://perma.cc/UH36-FN7W)

Global Logistics Emissions Council (2019) *Framework for Logistics Emissions Accounting and Reporting*, retrieved from: www.smartfreightcentre.org/en/how-to-implement-items/what-is-glec-framework/58/ (archived at https://perma.cc/P2QT-6FJN)

Greene, S (2017) *Black Carbon: Methodology for the Logistics Sector*, Smart Freight Centre, Amsterdam

ICCT (2011) *Reducing Greenhouse Gas Emissions from Ships: Cost effectiveness of available options*, International Council for Clean Transportation, Washington, DC

Intergovernmental Panel on Climate Change (2017) *Mitigation Pathways Compatible with 1.5°C in the Context of Sustainable Development*, retrieved from: www.ipcc.ch/site/assets/uploads/sites/2/2019/05/SR15_Chapter2_Low_Res.pdf (archived at https://perma.cc/6S2T-TGSJ)

International Civil Aviation Organization (2019) *Envisioning a 'zero climate impact' international aviation pathway towards 2050*, Montreal

IEA International Energy Agency (2017) *The Future of Trucks: Implications for energy and the environment*, IEA, Paris

IEA International Energy Agency (2019a) *World Energy Outlook*, IEA, Paris

IEA International Energy Agency (2019b) *The Future of Rail: Opportunities for energy and the environment*, IEA and UIC, Paris

IEA International Energy Agency (2020) *Tracking Report: Aviation*, retrieved from: www.iea.org/reports/aviation (archived at https://perma.cc/U7ZA-LB3Q)

IEA International Energy Agency and International Union of Railways (2017) *Railway Handbook 2017: Energy consumption and CO_2 emissions*, IEA/UIC, Paris

International Maritime Organization (2016) *Air pollution and energy efficiency: Study on effects of the entry into force of the global 0.5% fuel oil sulphur content limit on human health*, IMO, London

Krishnamurthy, M, Carder, DK, Thompson, G and Gautam, M (2007) Cost of lower NOx emissions: Increased CO_2 emissions from heavy-duty diesel engines, *Atmospheric Environment*, **41**, pp 666–75

McKinnon, AC (2013) The possible influence of the shipper on carbon emissions from deep-sea container supply chains: An empirical analysis, *Maritime Economics and Logistics*, **16** (1), pp 1–19

McKinnon, AC (2016) Freight transport deceleration: Its possible contribution to the decarbonisation of logistics, *Transport Reviews*, **36** (4), pp 418–36

McKinnon, AC and Piecyk, MI (2012) Setting targets for reducing carbon emissions from logistics: Current practice and guiding principles, *Carbon Management*, **3** (6), pp 629–39

McKinnon, AC (2018a) *Decarbonizing Logistics: Distributing goods in a low carbon world*, Kogan Page, London

McKinnon, AC (2018b) Balancing efficiency and resilience in multimodal supply chains, *International Transport Forum Discussion Papers*, OECD, Paris

McKinnon, AC and Petersen, M (2021) *Measuring industry's temperature: An environmental progress report on European Logistics Center for Sustainable Logistics and Supply Chains*, Kühne Logistics University, Hamburg

Merk, O (2015) *Shipping Emissions from Ports*, OECD/International Transport Forum, Paris

NACFE (2014) *Confidence Report: Idle Reduction Solutions*, North American Council for Freight Efficiency

Neuhausen, J, Foltz, C, Rose, P and Andre, F (2020) *Making zero-emission trucking a reality: Truck Study 2020 – Routes to decarbonizing commercial vehicles*, Strategy&, PwC, retrieved from: www.strategyand.pwc.com/de/de/studien/2020/green-trucking/truck-study-2020.pdf (archived at https://perma.cc/F7RU-Y7BA)

OECD/ITF (2019) *Transport Outlook 2019*, OECD/International Transport Forum, Paris

Oeko Institute/IFEU/Fraunhofer ISI (2016) *Alternative drive trains and fuels in road freight transport: Recommendations for action in Germany*, Oeko Institute, Berlin

Phadke, A, Khandekar, A, McCall, M, Karali, N and Rajagopal, D (2019) *Long haul battery electric trucks are technically feasible and economically compelling*, Working paper 5, International Energy Analysis Department, Lawrence Berkeley National Laboratory, Berkeley, CA

Piecyk, MI and McKinnon, AC (2010) Forecasting the carbon footprint of road freight transport in 2020, *International Journal of Production Economics*, **128** (1), pp 31–42

Piecyk, MI, Cullinane, S and Edwards, J (2015) Assessing the external impacts of freight transport in *Green Logistics: Improving the Environmental Sustainability of Logistics*, eds AC McKinnon, M Browne, MI Piecyk and A Whiteing, Kogan Page, London

Pyper, J (2012) EPA bans sooty ship fuel off US coasts, *Scientific American*, retrieved from: www.scientificamerican.com/article/epa-bans-sooty-ship-fuel-off-us-coasts/ (archived at https://perma.cc/JR9W-CGNC)

Science Based Targets initiative (2019) *Transport science-based target setting guidance*, retrieved from: sciencebasedtargets.org/resources/legacy/2018/05/SBT-transport-guidance-Final.pdf (archived at https://perma.cc/D5L2-M57Y)

Sripad, S and Viswanathan, V (2017) Performance metrics required of next generation batteries to make a practical electric semi truck, *ACS Energy Letters*, **2**, pp 1669–673

Stratiotis, E (2018) *Fuel costs in ocean shipping*, retrieved from: www.morethanshipping.com/fuel-costs-ocean-shipping/ (archived at https://perma.cc/3Y4W-QKZN)

T&E (2016) *Biodiesel 80% worse for climate than fossil diesel*, Transport and Environment, retrieved from: www.transportenvironment.org/sites/te/files/bulletin_245_april.pdf (archived at https://perma.cc/KD7Y-LL25)

UNFCCC (2017) *Global Warming Potentials*, United Nations Framework Convention on Climate Change, retrieved from unfccc.int/ghg_data/items/3825.php (archived at https://perma.cc/T5LC-4TPP)

UNFCCC (2020) *2020 Race to Zero Campaign*, retrieved from: unfccc.int/climate-action/race-to-zero-campaign (archived at https://perma.cc/G8GV-L8YV)

World Economic Forum (2020) *3D printing: A guide for decision-makers*, retrieved from: www.weforum.org/whitepapers/3d-printing-a-guide-for-decision-makers (archived at https://perma.cc/UG83-Q296)

World Economic Forum/Kearney (2020) *How to rebound stronger from Covid-19: Resilience in manufacturing and supply systems*, retrieved from: www.weforum.org/whitepapers/how-to-rebound-stronger-from-covid-19-resilience-in-manufacturing-and-supply-systems (archived at https://perma.cc/GF6Z-8WBV)

WHO (2020) *Ambient Air Pollution: A major threat to health and climate*, World Health Organization, retrieved from: www.who.int/airpollution/ambient/en/ (archived at https://perma.cc/U7SC-93QK)

World Meteorological Organization (2017) *Climate breaks multiple records in 2016 with global impacts*, retrieved from: public.wmo.int/en/media/press-release/climate-breaks-multiple-records-2016-global-impacts (archived at https://perma.cc/VA68-2SC4)

Xie, Y, Posada, F and Minjares, R (2020) *Diesel sulfur content impacts on Euro VI soot-free vehicles: Considerations for emerging markets*, Working paper 2020-11, International Council for Clean Transportation, Washington, DC

People powering contemporary supply chains 14

John Gattorna

Introduction

Since the last edition, much has happened in the world at large. Rapid advances in technology have underpinned great strides forward in supply chain designs, but we have also been given a rude wake-up call by the extreme disruption caused by the Covid-19 virus, which has brought entire economies to their knees, and seriously interfered with global trade.

Perhaps it is possible that something good can come out of this otherwise destructive crisis. Indeed, we have the opportunity to make generational change in the way we design work and do business, and supply chains will be at the forefront of this shift. If we get it right, we will learn to cope with the greater volatility that will surely come from both supply- and demand-side markets in the future. And looking even further afield, we should begin to think how we might better prepare for the unexpected and very severe disruptions that come along from time to time, like Covid-19, which is a once in a hundred years event!

As such, this chapter is about blending human and technological forces to create supply chains with the resilience bandwidth to operate under all operating conditions, from stable through to extreme. In effect, we are talking about contemporary supply chains as full-blooded *socio-technical ecosystems*, living systems that are pervasive in our lives. Indeed, if supply chains stop for some reason, we are doomed as humans to regress back to 'local' living, devoid of the luxuries that we have previously enjoyed as a result of global trade flows.

Tensegrity: balancing external and internal forces acting on the enterprise

More than ever before, we have to think in terms of designing our future business enterprises to counter the forces emanating from the external operating environment, forces which act on, and influence, customers' buying behaviours. This concept is called 'tensegrity',[1] and it is a dynamic condition as depicted in Figure 14.1.

Our proprietary Dynamic Alignment™ business model[2] helps us to achieve the much sought-after *dynamic* equilibrium, by ensuring that the internally generated capabilities and operating strategies are fully aligned with customers' expectations in the external target market. In this way we are able to eliminate the over- and under-servicing associated with a 'one-size-fits-all' design, and use the resources saved to embed greater resilience in our supply chain network, at no incremental cost. The Dynamic Alignment™ business model is described conceptually in Figure 14.2.

Based on this model, our understanding of the external operating environment in general, and customers' expectations in particular, informs us how to precisely configure our enterprise supply chains and associated

Figure 14.1 Tensegrity

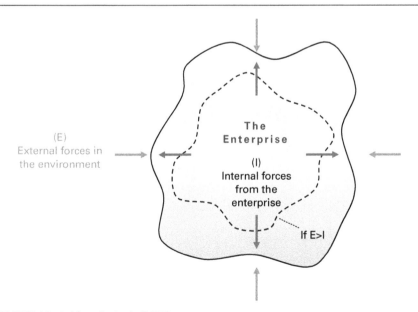

SOURCE Adapted from Benjamin (2013)

Figure 14.2 The Dynamic Alignment™ business model

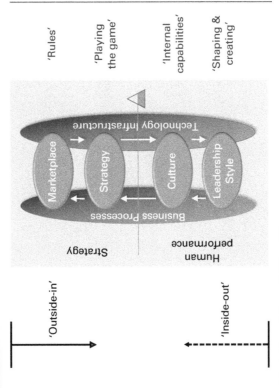

'Rules'

'Playing the game'

'Internal capabilities'

'Shaping & creating'

Underlying Logic
An organization must be aligned with its operating environment.

Usefulness
Shows the interaction between customers' needs, the formulation of appropriate strategic responses, and the successful execution of these strategies by shaping the necessary internal capabilities and corresponding leadership styles.

Prerequisite
Understanding of the customers' fundamental needs and buying behaviours that ultimately drive sales, revenues and profit.

SOURCE Adapted from Gattorna (2015, p 25)

underpinning capabilities. This is what we mean by 'outside-in' thinking, which starts by segmenting customers' expectations in the target market.

Segmenting customers versus segmenting supply chains

Confusion reigns when it comes to customer segmentation and the associated methodology. Often, we hear industry commentators speaking in terms of 'supply chain segmentation', which is wrong and quite misleading. What we should be focusing on is segmenting our customers along behavioural lines, period, and using the insights gained to reverse engineer the design of *differentiated* supply chain configurations internally to deliver a portfolio of *value propositions* to match the customer behavioural segments identified in the target market. This ideal situation is depicted in Figure 14.3.

Unfortunately, any other type of segmentation (such as institutional, industry sector, size, and profitability to name a few) does nothing to inform supply chain design, and at worst can be quite misleading.

To illustrate this point, refer to Figure 14.4, which describes a series of institutional segments in the building industry, eg Customer Types A to G. Inside each institutional segment, depicted by the different shading, there are four different buying behaviours, present, in different combinations. If you ignore this reality, and choose to configure only one supply chain type (say Lean, to address the Transactional buyer), you will by definition be misaligned with the other three customer sub-segments in that institutional segment! Herein lies the problem with existing design methodologies: they are not taking into account the presence of several different buying behaviours within the same institutional segment!

We must achieve a *direct link* with our customer base, and use this experience to inform supply chain design. Anything short of this is tantamount to guessing, which sadly has been the norm for several decades, albeit hidden from view by sustained growth. But we can do better than that with what we now know, and we must do, because the future is going to be much more volatile than the past. There will simply be no place to hide.

From our fieldwork across numerous industries and geographies over the last three decades, we found that up to 16 behavioural segments exist, but the most common combination are as depicted in Figure 14.5, ie Collaborative, Transactional, Project Accumulation, Dynamic and Innovative

Figure 14.3 Different supply chains with corresponding value propositions focused on particular customer segments

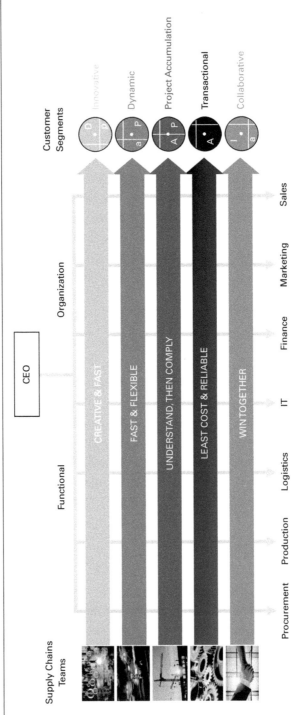

SOURCE Gattorna Alignment Research (2021)

Figure 14.4   Mix of behavioural segments in each institutional segment

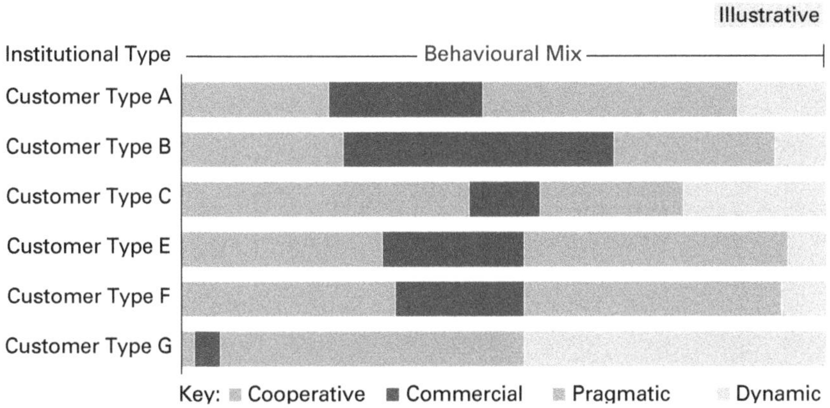

SOURCE Adapted from Figure 2.13, Gattorna (2015, p 76)

Solutions. The corresponding supply chain types for each segment are also depicted at the bottom of Figure 14.5.

The task for management everywhere is to mix and match all the elements that go into the formation of enterprise supply chains in such a way that they can each deliver products and services *precisely* according to the expectations of the target customer, and do this on a reliable and competitive basis, with minimal exceptions. It is the exceptions that drive the cost-to-serve up as evidenced in the one-size-fits-all paradigm. We know what all these elements are; we just need to get the formula right for each supply chain type. This is what differentiates one supply chain configuration from another.

Managing in a parallel universe

Building on the above thinking, we have the possibility of four supply chain configurations which taken together can manage demand (and supply) patterns which range from stable (nil variability) through to, say, reasonable volatility (±60–80 per cent variability), ie from Collaborative through to Agile. We collectively think of the four corresponding supply chain types as Business-as-Usual (BAU).

And the fifth type of supply chain configuration has now become self-evident in times of extreme and unexpected disruption, ie the Fully Flexible supply chain. Pre-Covid we were suggesting this was mostly a part-time supply chain type, but given the experience of many companies during the

Figure 14.5 The five most common behavioural segments and the requisite supply chain response

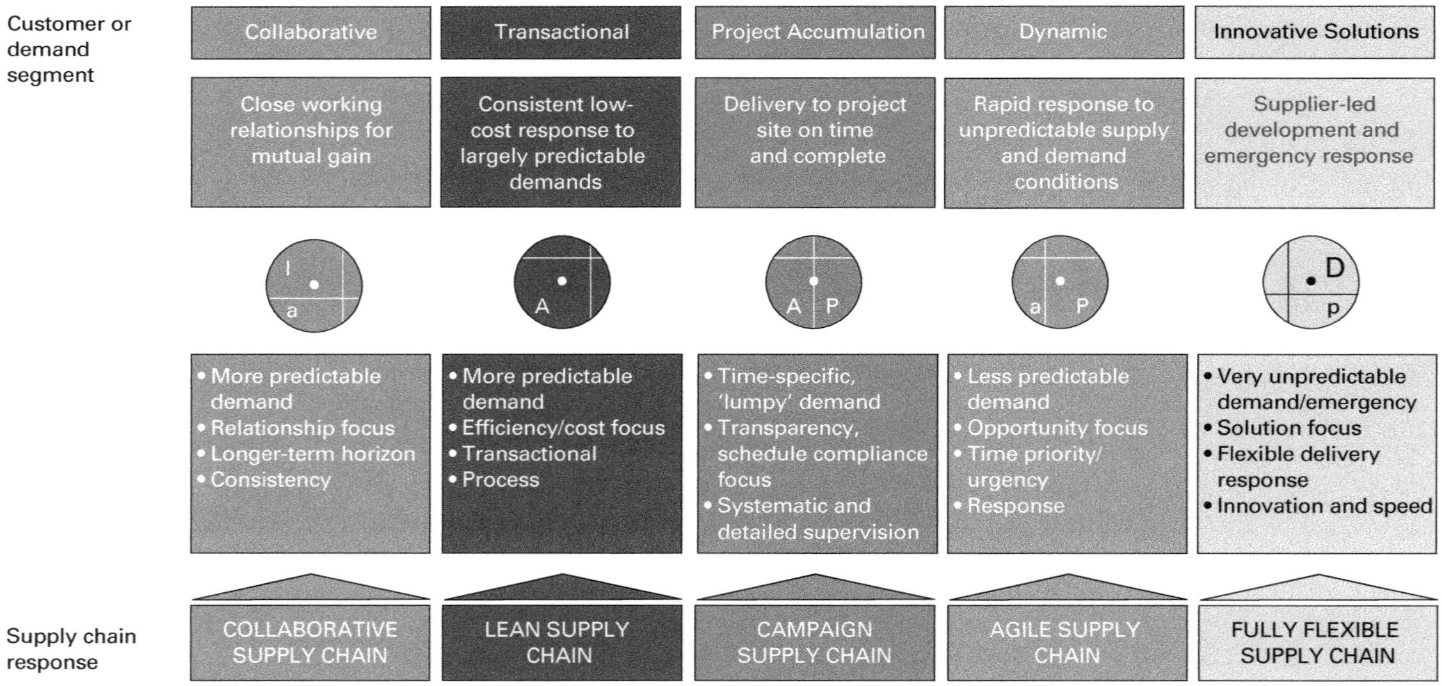

Customer or demand segment	Collaborative	Transactional	Project Accumulation	Dynamic	Innovative Solutions
	Close working relationships for mutual gain	Consistent low-cost response to largely predictable demands	Delivery to project site on time and complete	Rapid response to unpredictable supply and demand conditions	Supplier-led development and emergency response
	• More predictable demand • Relationship focus • Longer-term horizon • Consistency	• More predictable demand • Efficiency/cost focus • Transactional • Process	• Time-specific, 'lumpy' demand • Transparency, schedule compliance focus • Systematic and detailed supervision	• Less predictable demand • Opportunity focus • Time priority/ urgency • Response	• Very unpredictable demand/emergency • Solution focus • Flexible delivery response • Innovation and speed
Supply chain response	COLLABORATIVE SUPPLY CHAIN	LEAN SUPPLY CHAIN	CAMPAIGN SUPPLY CHAIN	AGILE SUPPLY CHAIN	FULLY FLEXIBLE SUPPLY CHAIN

SOURCES Adapted from Table 1.3.1 in Gattorna (2003, p 32); see also Gattorna (2006, p 41)

Covid-19 crisis, which is ongoing, we now believe that this supply chain should be designed and manned full-time by a small, dedicated team of experienced managers. Yes, it seems a costly approach, but the alternative is even more costly, bordering on the unthinkable.

The full portfolio of supply chain types as described above is depicted in Figure 14.6.

As will be seen from Figure 14.6, significant differences exist between each supply chain type, in terms of focus, technology and socio-cultural conditions. The trick is to embed the appropriate mix of different elements under these three headings, and if successful, *cost-to-serve* and service satisfaction will both improve significantly. This is part of the formula for creating greater *resilience*.

The overall result looks something like that depicted in Figure 14.7. The supply side is the mirror image of the demand side.

Digitalization is mandatory

In order to derive full benefit from the conceptual design outlined above, it is necessary to achieve end-to-end (E2E) digitalization of all the critical processes and associated data involved. This is the essential *joining of the dots* that allows operators to see, in real time, what is happening along the myriad supply chains that connect the enterprise with its customers and supply base. In effect, you are creating a *digital twin* of the physical activities on the ground.

And the essential perquisite to this desired condition is a clean set of Master Data files, something which major corporations are struggling with as we speak. It is a relentless task, but one that is so critical that we advocate a small, dedicated team inside the business be allocated as an ongoing project. How actively you pursue this task will determine how long it takes to achieve E2E digitalization, and beyond that, the much-desired faster decision making so important to achieving increased resilience.

We are aware of companies that have been on the digitalization journey for eight years, and only now are achieving genuine E2E visibility. For those companies which haven't even started yet, there is a world of hurt coming as you become increasingly uncompetitive. And your customers will be the judge in this respect by way of their responses to any customer satisfaction surveys that you may engage them in.

Figure 14.6 Managing in a parallel universe

SC Configuration	Focus	Technology/IT Systems	Socio-Cultural Conditions
EXTREME DISRUPTION			
Fully Flex™ SC	Risk/Reward	• Event management • E2E digitalization • Network optimization modelling to drive scenarios • MTO in short lead times • Prototyping	• Individual decision making • Extreme risk taking • OD: part- or full-time emergency team • Team members selected on basis of creativity + speed • Analytics • Project management
BUSINESS-AS-USUAL			
Agile SC	Response Time	• SCP • COV • APS • Network optimization modelling	• Individual decision making • Risk taking • Individual KPIs + incentives • Formal/regular comms • Action orientation • Problem solving
Campaign™ SC	Compliance	• Absolute reliability/DIFOT • Inventory visibility • Stock security • Track + trace • Expedite	• Teaming: cost/time management • Detail conscious • Results driven • Incentives: cash + in-kind • Individual KPIs
Lean SC	Reliability/ Efficiency	• ERP • Network optimization modelling • WMS • TMS	• Central decision making • KPIs: DIFOT; forecast accuracy • Conformance to policy • Emphasis on analytics • Regular/structured comms
Collaborative™ SC	Relationship/ Stability	• ERP • CRM • VMI • CPFR • S + OP	• Consensus decision making • Shared KPIs: customer retention • Team building • Consultative/face-to-face • Focus on loyal customers

SOURCE Gattorna Alignment Research (2020)

Figure 14.7 Fundamental re-design of enterprise supply chains

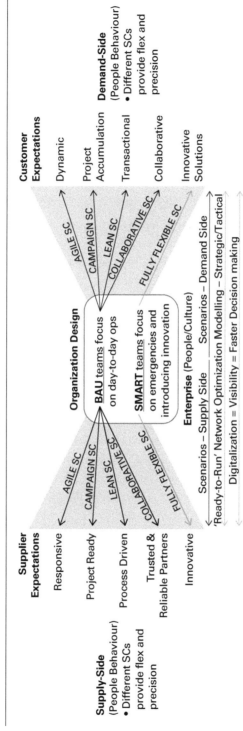

SOURCE Gattorna Alignment Research (2020)

Developing a digital supply chain strategy looks something like that outlined in Figure 14.8.

The data from transaction files within the business will most likely have to be supplemented by selected inputs from Internet of Things (IoT)-powered sensors, placed at critical points along the enterprise's supply chains.

The live data should be monitored and analysed as it happens, preferably in a Control Tower environment. When deviations to planned commitments made to customers are detected, 'alerts' should immediately be sent to customers to inform them accordingly.

At a more aggregate level, the same data can be used to test potential tactical scenarios, especially in times of significant disruption when normal forecasting methods are not viable, and to make changes to the overall network infrastructure if required. In any case, a company with revenue of, say, USD 1 billion revenue needs to establish two specialized groups inside the enterprise, ie Analytics and Modelling. Without these capabilities you will not be able to survive extreme disruptions of the kind experienced during the Covid-19 pandemic.

From 'static' to 'dynamic' organization designs

In today's volatile world, the real elephant in the room is organization design, ie the way we structure how people work. Unfortunately, we are still using the vertical functional structure that was first introduced in the Industrial Revolution, over two centuries ago. It worked well then, because the operating environment was relatively stable, and production ruled the world. Customers took what they were given, and had no further say. They were effectively disempowered. This structure is depicted in Figure 14.9.

In this structure, the vertical silos or functions dominated, but they were also tasked with managing the horizontal flow of materials, products and services horizontally, from the supply side, through the enterprise, and out to customers on the demand side. At best, it was, and still is to a large extent, a haphazard, poorly coordinated process.

Fast forward to the world we now live in, where, aided by social media, customers and consumers are increasingly flexing their buying muscle, and becoming ever more demanding. This effect is flowing over from the consumer world to the industrial world of business too. Lead times are being

Figure 14.8 Elements of a digital supply chain strategy

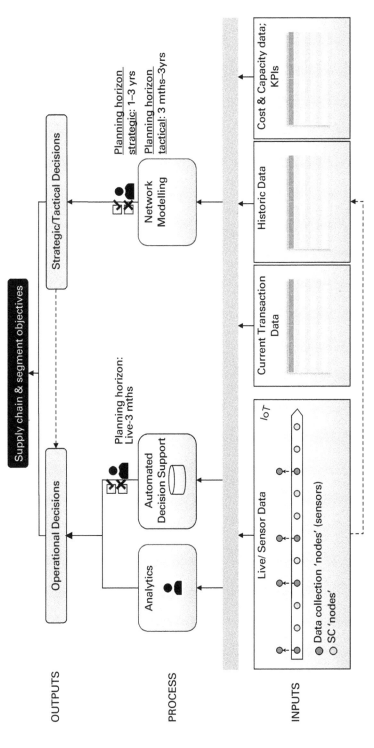

Supply chain & segment objectives

OUTPUTS

Operational Decisions

Strategic/Tactical Decisions

PROCESS

Analytics

Automated Decision Support

Planning horizon: Live-3 mths

Network Modelling

Planning horizon strategic: 1–3 yrs

Planning horizon tactical: 3 mths–3yrs

INPUTS

Live/ Sensor Data

IoT

● Data collection 'nodes' (sensors)

○ SC 'nodes'

Current Transaction Data

Historic Data

Cost & Capacity data; KPIs

SOURCE Adapted from Figure 8.10, Gattorna and Ellis (2020, p 155)

Figure 14.9 Conventional organization design

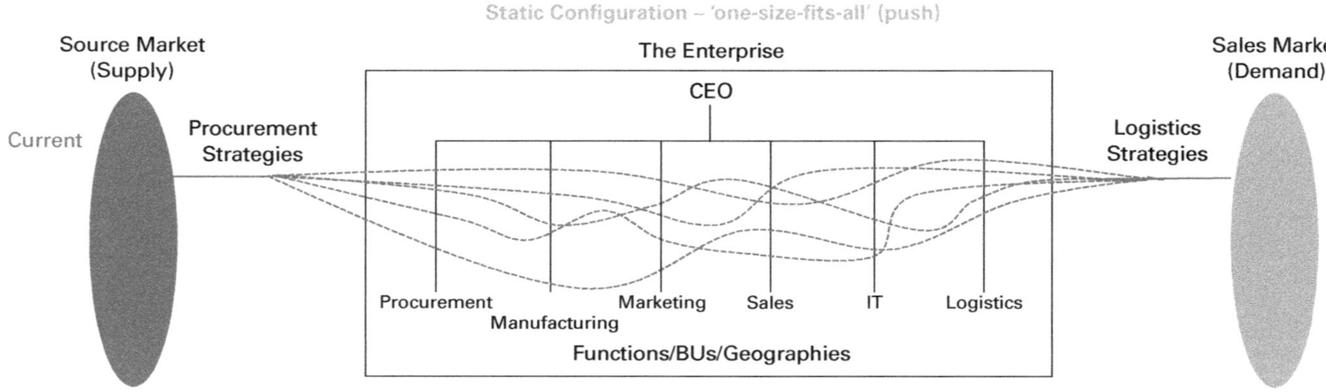

Static Configuration – 'one-size-fits-all' (push)

Source Market (Supply)

Sales Market (Demand)

Current

Procurement Strategies

Logistics Strategies

The Enterprise

CEO

Procurement
Manufacturing   Marketing   Sales   IT   Logistics

Functions/BUs/Geographies

SOURCE Adapted from Gattorna and Ellis (2020, p 173)

squeezed, and customers are mostly taking an unforgiving view of service failures.

Over time, and certainly by the turn of the new century in 2000, it became obvious that the pace had quickened to such an extent that the old structure could no longer manage both the vertical and horizontal flows, simultaneously. Something had to give.

In my 2015 book, *Dynamic Supply Chains* (3rd edition) I undertook a comprehensive review of all the organization designs that had been tried to date, and concluded that the way forward involved two separate organization designs overlaid on each other, working in synch, ie retain the functional, vertical specialisms, because these are indispensable but over this conventional structure superimpose a new organization structure, specifically tasked with managing the cross-functional horizontal flows through to the customer.

This organization would comprise a number of teams or clusters of executives, seconded for fixed periods from the traditional functions, to form a number of multidisciplinary units that reflected in size, importance and culture the external customer segments that they were tasked to serve, generally as depicted in Figure 14.10. This entire dual structure would then be underpinned by a shared services organization to bring Finance, HR and IT to both the vertical specialisms and horizontal customer supply chain teams.

Some organizations have already adopted this format, with success, but few if any have addressed the micro detail of selecting each team based on the appropriate array of technical skills and mindsets to reflect the particular subculture that is a best fit with the particular target segment faced in the market. This is important, because our research found that one of the major reasons otherwise good operational strategies were poorly implemented, was because of a misalignment between the internal subcultures, the intended strategies and external customer segments.

Suffice to say, a lot of work remains to be done in this area of replicating inside the enterprise the structure and subcultures present in the external customer–market. Finally, we feel that managing the horizontal teams driving supply chains is so important that a new, dedicated position should be introduced to the newly recommended format as depicted, ie the Chief Customer Supply Chain Officer (CCSCO), who would manage the selection and daily operation of these teams to achieve a high level of precision alignment with the full array of customers' expectations. And if customers move between the different segments because of the situation they find themselves in, then one of the other supply chain configurations can take over the service task.

Figure 14.10 From 'static' to 'dynamic' organization design

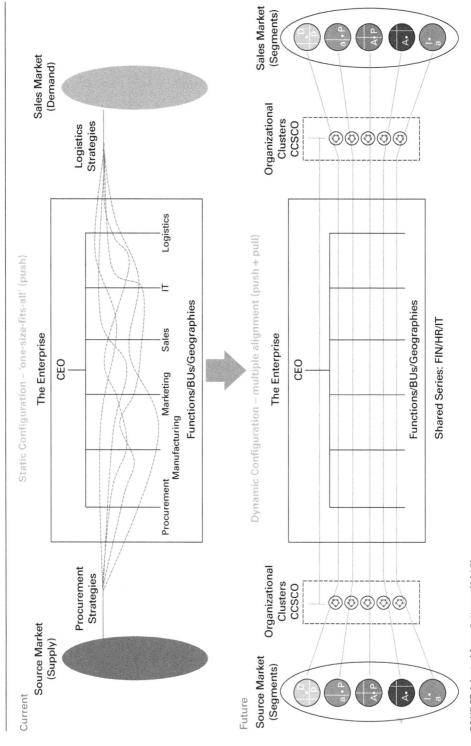

SOURCE Adapted from Gattorna (2015)

So, by hard-wiring a select number of supply chains inside the enterprise, *dynamic* coverage is possible without creating myriad exceptions that would drive up the cost-to-serve. It's this lack of a *dynamic* capability in previous designs that have so constrained their effectiveness.

New focus on the supply side

It is also timely to revisit the role and positioning of the Procurement function in the enterprise. The *guiding principle* must be that any actions taken by Procurement on the supply side, must be fully aligned with customer-focused strategies on the demand side. Unfortunately, this is rarely the case in enterprises these days because of the functional organization design discussed above. The Covid-19 virus has highlighted that things have to change.

This is because even in some of the best run companies, the biggest impacts of Covid-19 has been felt on the supply side. Globalization, coupled with the conventional KPIs that drive the behaviour of Procurement personnel, have led inevitably towards many instances of dependence on single, remote sources. This can work for stable businesses in stable times, but is a material hindrance if the market is dynamic – and is disastrous in times of severe disruption such as that which we are experiencing in 2020.

For example, we know of a company that is attempting to return its production facilities to full capacity in order to supply the Chinese market as demand returns, but is running short of specialty chemicals sourced solely from Italy, one of the countries worst hit by the virus in the early stages.

Another company which makes bleach and disinfectant is seeing a huge increase in consumer demand for its products during the crisis, but can't get beyond two production shifts because the childproof caps used to seal the product containers are also sourced exclusively from – you guessed it – Italy! And there are numerous other examples we could cite.

Undoubtedly, we have gone too far in the relentless pursuit of cost efficiencies, and in the process made our supply chains brittle, unable to withstand sudden unexpected disruptions – or surges in demand! Now we must move back along the efficiency spectrum and accept that we may need some level of in-built redundancy, in the cause of achieving increased resilience.

We also need to think about where Procurement personnel sit in the organization and the degree to which their decision making is integrated with the rest of the supply chain. We know theoretically that strategic decision making in silos is not optimal, but this crisis has highlighted just how dangerous it can be – whether it be sourcing strategy, cost optimization, risk management or inventory policy – only an end-to-end view of the trade-offs gives us a chance of weathering significant disruptions.

Here are some specific factors to consider:

1 Change your organization design and bring the Procurement function under the Chief Supply Chain Officer (CSCO); this will increase internal coordination. Some of the best run companies have already made this key adjustment.

2 If you are a global manufacturer, divide your world up into regions, and review sourcing lines within each region. Are they/can they, be self-supporting? And can you engineer a greater overall *diversity* of your supply base by having options across several regions?

3 In each region, segment your supplier base along *behavioural and capability lines*, eg which suppliers do I wish to develop strong collaborative relationships with, that will be sustainable even through difficult times? Which suppliers can provide lowest cost for large quantities of product or components, albeit with long lead times? Which suppliers have excess capacity and could supply our requirements at short notice, albeit at a higher cost? Which suppliers are noticeably more innovative and will always find creative ways to meet our inbound supply requirements? A portfolio of capabilities increases flexibility in the supply base. In short, we need to segment our supply base along behavioural lines, something that very few enterprises have done to date.

4 For some manufacturers, the solution will be to become more vertically integrated, by taking control of critical inbound materials and components, sourcing them from another division. If the business has found itself competing for scarce supply during this crisis, the balance of *insource versus outsource* might need to be reviewed, and a new balance struck.

5 In some exceptional cases, where the danger of being starved of key supplies has become apparent, it may be worthwhile to buy out or joint-venture with selected suppliers of critical inputs to your manufacturing process. In this way your control is increased, and risk reduced.

But none of this can happen without strong, overt leadership from the top. Leaders will need to be fearless in adopting new modes of operation in the future, and the climate for making major change will never be better than in the next few years. At the individual, business and government levels we have found that the paradigm can be changed overnight – so we need to apply the lessons learned, quickly, and not let them get lost in the depths of the *long-term strategy* stockpile.

Resilience, delivered

After years of focusing on efficiency and taking cost out in our supply chains, the tide has inexorably turned. The increasing incidence of natural disasters and cyber threats, reinforced by the Covid-19 pandemic, has forced us to move back along the continuum towards greater resilience.

But resilience is not an easy state to reach, nor is it a static condition that can be set and forgotten.

Leaving aside the short-term initiatives that have to be taken when a major disruption occurs, we need to look ahead further to futureproof our supply chains, and there are many moving parts that have to be engaged for this purpose, some of which we have already covered earlier in the chapter. In summary:

On the supply side:

1 Seek to diversify your supply base, in terms of supplier capability and geographic location.

2 Segment suppliers to better understand their respective selling expectations so that more aligned procurement strategies can be devised.

3 Seek to go back upstream in the supply chain to better understand the role of tier 1, 2 and 3 suppliers in the channel.

4 Investigate which products are suitable for local production (re-shoring) in order to reduce the length of your supply chains.

5 In the case of critical suppliers, consider buying or acquiring equity to reduce the risk of collapse of vital sources.

6 Revisit the potential for vertical integration in the make or buy decision.

7 Bring the Chief Procurement Officer (CPO) under the CSCO.

On the demand side:

1 Segment customers along buying behaviour lines and design and implement a matching portfolio of supply chain types.

2 Revisit existing channel arrangements for relevance and possible overhaul.

3 Put a dedicated team in charge of cleaning up and maintaining the master data files, and undertaking ongoing analytics.

4 Fast track digital projects to achieve end-to-end (e2e) digitalization.

5 Set up an internal modelling group to model strategic network infrastructure, and undertake tactical scenario testing as required.

6 Set up a control tower to monitor, in real time, all product movements from time of order through to final delivery, and take immediate actions if/when delays occur.

7 Re-engineer all internal processes so that the enterprise runs at an overall higher clock-speed, thus speeding up decision making across the board.

A final word

Going forward, the secret sauce will be in how enterprises manage their available *capacity*, and how they overcome the effects of short- and longer-term disruptions of various intensity that emanate from the operating environment. There is no single solution to this problem – just a patchwork quilt of components that have to be stitched together at the time. Technology will be a great enabler in this endeavour, but in the end the result will rest on how good the leadership of the enterprise really is. It's time to stand up and lead from the front.

Notes

1 Adapted from Colin Benjamin, Tensegrity as a framework for strategic thinking, unpublished paper, Melbourne, 2013.
2 The Dynamic Alignment™ model is a global trademark of Gattorna Alignment, Sydney, Australia.

References

Gattorna, J (2003) *Handbook of Supply Chain Management*, 5th edn, Gower Publishing, Aldershot
Gattorna, J (2006) *Living Supply Chains: How to mobilize the enterprise around delivering what your customers want*, FT Prentice Hall, Harlow
Gattorna, J (2009) *Dynamic Supply Chain Alignment*, Gower Publishing, Farnham, UK
Gattorna, J (2015) *Dynamic Supply Chains*, 3rd edn, FT Publishing, Harlow, UK
Gattorna, J and Ellis, D (2020) *Transforming Supply Chains*, FT Publishing, Harlow, UK

Leadership in logistics   15

Richard J Atkinson CBE

What is leadership, and why should we develop leadership skills?

Good leadership can be the only difference between mediocre or failing organizations, and those that flourish and succeed. The author has served as a senior commander of combat forces in the Royal Air Force (RAF), a director of x-government strategic planning in London, a director of operations for NATO, and as a global director of media and communications. Throughout, he has seen first-hand the dependencies and dedication that must be afforded to leadership and logistics, if operations are to be successful. Through more than three decades in leadership roles, he has fermented some, hopefully, useful views on leadership in logistics.

So, what is good leadership, and what should we do to achieve it? First, we must be clear why we are leading, and where we are leading to. We are leading people and so we must also engage with colleagues – to share our vision and to inspire their very best contributions. Meanwhile, we certainly should not do junior colleagues' work, simply from an elevated position. Nor should we glorify 'busy-ness' – ie forever espousing how busy we are, whilst failing to actually lead, or simply finding 'problems for every suggested solution'. Fundamentally, pessimists cannot lead, so an optimistic approach is necessary. As Winston Churchill famously said '...a pessimist sees the difficulty in every opportunity; an optimist sees the opportunity in every difficulty.'

This chapter brings together leadership ideas for logistics professionals. 'Professionalizing the logistics profession' is vital, and this starts with leadership. The chapter looks at: helpful legislation; best practice; some of the issues the profession faces; and, how one of the world's most important professions might 'step up' to professional status and thereby achieve greater effectiveness.

Better practice, and the law

Corporate Governance Code

Much that has gone before regarding good leadership has been captured in the UK Corporate Governance Code (UK FRC, 2018). Although 'captured' in the UK, this code enshrines lessons from globalized businesses over several decades. The 'Code' sets our guiding principles for board leadership. The principles are compelling and widely applicable. Key words from the first five (of 16) principles are emboldened, as an *aide memoire* for consideration of leadership factors.

Principle A: A successful company is led by an effective and entrepreneurial board, whose role is to promote the **long-term sustainable success** of the company, **generating** value for shareholders and **contributing to wider society.**

Principle B: The board should **establish the company's purpose, values and strategy,** and satisfy itself that **these and its culture are aligned.** All directors must **act with integrity, lead by example** and **promote the desired culture.**

Principle C: The board should **ensure that the necessary resources** are in place for the company to meet its objectives and measure performance against them. The board should also establish **a framework of prudent and effective controls,** which **enable risk to be assessed and managed.**

Principle D: In order for the company to meet its responsibilities to shareholders and stakeholders, the board should ensure **effective engagement** with, and encourage participation from, these parties.

Principle E: The board should ensure that **workforce policies and practices are consistent with the company's values** and support its long-term sustainable success. The workforce should be able to raise any matters of concern.

Companies Act 2006

Meanwhile, the UK Companies Act 2006, sets out the seven legal duties of directors. These are not dissimilar to other legal provisions around the globe. In any case, of the UK directors' seven legal obligations, the following one makes universal sense:

- **Provision 172(1):** A director of a company must act in the way s/he considers, in good faith, would be most likely to promote the success of the company for the benefit of its members as a whole, and in doing so have regard (amongst other matters) to:

  a the likely consequences of any decision in the long term;

  b the interests of the company's employees;

  c the need to foster the company's business relationships with suppliers, customers and others;

  d the impact of the company's operations on the community and the environment;

  e the desirability of the company maintaining a reputation for high standards of business conduct; and

  f the need to act fairly as between members of the company.

Together with the highlights from the Corporate Governance Code, these legal requirements are already painting a picture of a desirable leader, who should:

- be entrepreneurial;
- promote success for the longer term;
- generate value, and contribute to society;
- establish purpose, value and strategy;
- be honest and establish the company's culture, by example;
- acquire necessary resources, establish controls and manage risks;
- engage stakeholders;
- decide for the longer term;
- have regard for employees' interests;
- build good relationships;
- be mindful of surrounding communities and environments;
- have high standards; and
- be fair.

The leader that comes to mind to achieve all of this is:

- an entrepreneur;
- well versed/schooled in strategy, vision and value propositions;
- able to set organizational culture by demonstrating integrity, fairness and high standards;

- a capable resource/risk manager, self-aware and skilled at building relationships with stakeholders; and,
- a deft negotiator/decision maker, making choices for the longer term, mindful of the community and environment.

There are undoubtedly exceptional leaders already within the logistics profession. Together, we can increase this pool of talent. Notwithstanding the law and good practice, leadership is also about the many great attributes that can simply be expressed in single words: **energy, passion, courage, justice, duty and inspiration** – ie having the tireless determination and optimism to inspire people to perform superbly well on a journey. A journey from one place in the market to another where greater success can be enjoyed. Good leadership could not be more necessary for the logistics profession. With lean margins, intense competition and high customer expectations, we should become really good at leadership. We owe it to customers, employees and shareholders alike to develop this key competitive advantage.

The problem (opportunity)

Where are we, as a profession?

The logistics profession is not yet renowned for its leadership culture; the language of leadership is not yet common parlance at industry conferences and seminars. Perhaps as a consequence, logistics roles are yet to become preferred professions of choice. It is probably safe to presume that there is rarely a rampant rush to the logistics tables at careers fairs. However fast-paced, action-packed, problem-solving, innovative and well-rewarded careers in logistics may be, they are not yet widely perceived this way. Where does the responsibility for this lie? Leaders in these professions certainly have a key role to play in communicating the reality of these rewarding roles – and communication is a key element of leadership.

Attracting talent is another crucial need for leaders to consider. We should actively engage with the stakeholder group: 'future colleagues'. By doing this we might secure a brighter future for the profession, ie one where logistics is seen less as a necessary evil that adds cost, but rather as a prized ingredient that adds value. As parents engage with their offspring regarding hopes and dreams for their professional futures, the popular preferred professions reoccur: doctor, lawyer, engineer, financial manager, footballer, soldier, etc. Interestingly, they all end with an 'er' sound. But how should professionals in supply chain roles be referred to – 'supply chain-ers'? It is likely going to be difficult to attract top talent if we do not yet know what to call ourselves. We lack the maturity of a professional collective noun. Doctors are not just doctors – they are paediatricians, gynaecologists, anaesthetists and so on. Soldiers are not just soldiers – they are infantry, artillery, cavalry, engineers, etc. But, collectively, these professionals are prepared, and pleased to be known as doctors or soldiers. Collective nouns have the benefit of being simple, unambiguous, universal and easy to use. Without accessible, memorable language we should not be surprised if we are too easily forgotten. Moreover, we do not help ourselves with our disparate 'brand descriptors' – Smiths Haulage, Johnson Freight-forwarding, Stevens' Transport, Langley Logistics, etc. It seems that other professions might have an advantage when trying to attract top talent.

We also seem to promote from within the business or the profession, courting the risk of the 'blind leading the blind' where professional leadership is concerned. Moreover, many say they 'just fell into' logistics roles and have since 'ended up' in leadership positions. This may well be so, but it does not make for inspiring back-stories. With no common language, no promotional activity, 'the blind leading the blind' and those that just 'fell in', is this really a breeding ground for excellent leadership? No, not yet, but it needs to be if we are to really lead sustainable solutions for the customer needs of the future. So, whose issue is this? Leaders have a fundamental role in this regard to portray and promote their profession fairly, and well. For now, it may be that our leaders of today fell into logistics roles, but it is not always necessary to let that be known. Perhaps it is better to skip that bit and instead eulogize the fun, as well as the fulfilling and fabulous successes that have been enjoyed. It is probably also better to share how fundamental these roles are to a country's national interests: security, freedom, wellbeing and prosperity are all powered by logistics.

Meanwhile, customers' insatiable demands keep on increasing, and the profession keeps on responding – brilliantly – giving the customer almost everything they ask for. But, is it what they need? Is it what the profession needs? Concurrently, the characterization of a group uncertain of its identity is further dogged by the unwelcome attention 'supply chain-ers' attract for the perceived contributions they make to the twin perils of congestion and pollution.

Could magnificent leadership be more widespread in our professions – thereby improving performance and profit, and benefiting our people and the planet? I think so.

What leadership is not

Tactics without strategy is the noise before defeat.

SUN TZU

Meet 'Roger'

We all know 'Roger'. Roger is not a particular leader, he's a type of leader found in all walks of life. Roger has 'seen it, done it, bought the T-shirt'; he knows lots of practical detail and he's not a bad person – he's just not a leader. He's never studied leadership and never wondered, or worried about it. Roger reacts to problems, rather than leading around them. Roger likes to be liked, and so busies himself with trivia, alongside tactical activity and other peoples' work, to try to 'support'. The result is a lack of empowerment for colleagues to make important decisions, whilst no one actually leads. Roger doesn't like strategy or setting a vision, yet without a vision and a strategy to fulfil it, the destination for Roger's team is literally unknown to them (or to Roger). As a result, the 'ship' is cumbersome and unresponsive to the helm. We all know a Roger; they have a problem for every solution.

Meet 'Sally'

We all also know 'Sally'. Sally is not a particular leader, she's a type of leader found in all walks of life. Sally smiles, and is smart, sharp, and 'superior'. But Sally is toxic. It can be difficult to measure toxicity but there are clues. Sally doesn't like sharing, doesn't like inclusivity, doesn't like strategy, and everyone knows what she is really, but are too scared to say so. Sally's driving interests are Sally's driving interests; the business, and her role within it, are merely the means to 'Sally's success'. Sally has the ear of the CEO and says what bosses like to hear. She has little time for junior colleagues and no time for complaints. We all know a Sally.

What should we do?

Motivation

Leadership is not a rank or a role, it is a behaviour – you do not need to have many, or any, direct reports to be a good leader. Without motivation, it is difficult to build sustainable improvement. So, what motivates leaders? Is it intrinsic or extrinsic, somewhere in between, a sliding scale, or something more?

Intrinsic motivation involves doing something because it is personally rewarding to you. Extrinsic motivation involves doing something because you want to earn a reward or avoid a penalty. It might be that we are not compellingly drawn on an insatiable quest towards a logistics career and that we just needed a job – ie a reward. Should we continue to reward good productivity with promotion? Do we consider the transition to intrinsic motivation when we have more than a job, when we have responsibility for others? Surely leadership must be more than doing those junior things in a 'senior way'. Why employ good people and then spend time telling them what to do? How crushing this must be for eager junior employees. Good leaders should be able to move from deploying motivational skills to inspirational ones. Where motivation might be more tangibly transactional, inspiration lays out the exciting vision ahead and how our endeavours will benefit others. Our engagement with colleagues is to inspire them, empower them and guide them in fulfilling their potential – to be all they can be. General Bernard Law Montgomery reflected on the need for leaders to find '…the capacity and the will to rally men and women to a common purpose and the character which inspires confidence.' We too, must determine how best to inspire and unite colleagues to their common purpose.

Investment

Leadership is not just a responsibility for the 'boss' (whoever they may be), or the board. Leadership is required at all levels. Individuals at any level, suitably empowered, can lead by example and should be rewarded for doing so. The traditional divide of leaders and followers should, by now, have all but evaporated. If it is still evident in your environment then something needs to be done about it.

Investment does not just mean spending cash on courses or top talent. We can also: invest our personal energy; take an interest in the 'shopfloor'; form 'shadow boards' of junior colleagues to challenge the board's thinking; introduce reverse-mentoring and 360-degree reporting; invite thought-leaders from other sectors to look at our business; and listen intently, however uncomfortable it might make us feel. We can show we care and we can act on new ideas. Furthermore, if we work really hard to describe where we want the business to be in the future (and articulate it well), we can inspire others with our vision.

The advent of professional qualifications for supply chain managers and leaders is a great step forward. Moreover, leaders can take a personal interest in how learners are progressing to become qualified managers and leaders in supply chain and logistics. Think of 10, 50 and 100 years ahead – good managers can *ensure* today, tomorrow and likely this year; good leaders *assure* us of everything else. Regarding investing in people, Sir Richard Branson commented '...train people well enough so they can leave, treat them well enough so they don't want to.' We too can reflect on the wisdom of investing in our people and the positive effects upon retention that can ensue.

Leading innovation

Historically, the UK – for example – revelled in truly world-leading innovation. This led to untold levels of wealth, development and progress for the world. How did this happen? The world's first mass-manufacture mills were in Manchester (though processing slave-picked cotton). The world's first power station was in Newcastle. The first commercial railroad, moving cotton, was from Liverpool to Manchester. The Manchester Ship Canal was arguably the greatest engineering feat of Victorian times. The first million square feet of the Singer sewing machine factory was in Glasgow – American aspiration combined with British ingenuity and innovation to make it a reality. These innovations helped make Britain the world's most successful country of the day. Not all was good of course. Working life in the mills was dire and often short, and so came the first free public park – Peel Park in 1846 – paid for by the mill owners to help employee wellbeing and productivity. The first public library was in Salford in 1851. Some 82,000 children sang for Queen Victoria's opening of these innovations!

The 1833 UK Factory Act led the world in introducing innovations to protect workers – and to increase productivity. Someone was leading well, and not just those in London – Bullough, Peel, Addison, Bevan are all stories of leadership worthy of study. UK Northern cities, and the sons of Wales and Scotland, were helping make the UK the richest Empire the world had ever known. Knowing some history of leadership is valuable too.

These are only examples, and innovation was certainly not a UK invention. How can global innovation in logistics be consistently led well today? Certainly, it is not for leaders to come up with all the great ideas; rather, leaders need to know how to bring the greatness out in others. My experience points to a number of important guidelines in this regard:

- be inclusive – even if you have heard most of the ideas before, there will be a 'nugget' at some point;
- welcome challenge, however much it hurts;
- promote diversity of thought;
- have different people from different spaces and places look at your issues and opportunities (your board might actually have pretty narrow experience and thinking – either by demographic or industry characteristics it may be less well suited to leadership than is perceived).

Overall, in harnessing the very best elements of our resources, we can draw on the wisdom of John Buchan, Lord Tweedsmuir, who said '...the task of leadership is not to put greatness into humanity, but to elicit it, for the greatness is already there.' This being so, we have a grand responsibility to bring out the greatness in all colleagues.

Organizational context

All organizations comprise three components: the physical component (infrastructure, assets and people); the moral component (leadership, motivation and cohesion); and the conceptual component (principles of professional practice, professional body of knowledge, and conceptual innovation). This thinking is rooted in British Defence Doctrine (DCDC, 2014). 'Conceptual innovation' can be further divided into three parts: imagination, creativity and implementation, ie our ability respectively to: imagine an alternative future; conceive how we might deliver our services in that future; and implement the (objectively assessed) best ideas of how to do so. It is for leaders to unlock the potential and capability of all colleagues by creating the space and conditions for these vital elements: ie imagination, creativity and implementation. The leader's part is to provide the vision (ie the focus for their attention) and the right environment.

An environment for innovation

Our capacity to innovate depends upon culture and culture is inspired by leadership. To create the conditions for innovation, leaders should create a cultural environment that is inclusive, promotes diversity of thought and welcomes challenge. Having created the conditions for innovation, it should then be harnessed. Innovations should be integrated into policies, practices, processes and procedures, which, in turn, become enshrined in professional bodies of knowledge – otherwise known as 'doctrine'.

Innovation is often misperceived as being concerned only with technology applications. More properly, innovation comes from culture – ie the culture that leaders create – and can be new ideas for all aspects of how we work. An innovation is simply something that is new to us and that adds value to our business. Answering a number of important questions is instructive in this context:

- Do your people feel enabled to innovate and are your managers at ease with risk management?
- Do line managers and heads of department support creativity?
- Do we eradicate gender gaps?
- Is 'innovation' a standing topic in departmental meetings?
- Is it built into the culture?
- Would your people say that you are inclusive; that diversity of thought is encouraged, and that challenge is welcomed?
- Are they afforded latitude in their work to be imaginative and creative to inform future choices? and,
- Does the strategic vision inspire and focus the collective thinking?

Such questions might be included in a company attitude survey. If the answers are not a resounding 'yes', there is a tremendous opportunity for development – development that could increase employee engagement, productivity, further innovation and profit. Such opportunities cannot afford to be ignored.

Barriers to innovation

Barriers to innovation need to be overcome. The following might be considered barriers to innovation: criticism of new ideas; internal competition; risk avoidance; preservation of the status quo; time pressures; expectations for productivity; distractions from creative work; steep hierarchy; lack of diversity, and lack of framework. Active examples, policies and practices are required to overcome these barriers. This is a rewarding role for leaders – to engage with colleagues; to break down barriers; to establish the creative conditions, and to promote diversity of thought. If leaders do not do this then nobody will and the barriers are likely to entrench.

Enablers of innovation

Innovation enablers are likely to include: recognition of opportunities; being comfortable living with chaos; engaging in market lessons; developing new business models; acquiring essential resources; managing transformation; and valuing individual initiatives and ideas.

In making a start, leaders would likely not go far wrong by addressing the barrier of time management. This can be augmented by exploring the opportunities to demonstrate how much leaders value the thoughts and ideas of colleagues. Again, leaders can leave others to routine management whilst they actively enable innovation by, for example: rewarding those who contribute ideas; welcoming disruption and challenge; and taking junior colleagues on 'explorations of the market' to see what others are doing. Being a leader is both a humbling duty and fabulous fun! Creation of the enabling conditions for innovation requires active scheduling as a high priority. This might not seem as important as a pressing board report or a health and safety incident, but it is. Jack Welch said '…before you are a leader, success is all about growing yourself. When you become a leader, success is all about growing others.' As leaders, dedicating energy to the growth of others is crucial, and would likely boost business performance as well.

Making way for improvement

Time should not be squandered on repeatable, mundane, machine-programable activity. Furthermore, conditions that waste time – eg confusion, conflict and clutter – should be corrected. Wherever possible, necessary bureaucracy and management systems should be streamlined, simplified and standardized. Such developments in corporate maturity release more time for innovations that add value for our beneficiaries.

Flatter structures, reverse-mentoring, peer review, external scrutiny, think-tanks and other initiatives should also enable the innovations required to sustain claims to be market leaders. It is too late to start innovating when crises emerge. Alternatively, you can innovate now to assure your unique selling propositions (USPs) and to differentiate yourself from myriad organizations or new entrants with similar offerings. You could also manage time to imagine new approaches to engagement, and to create ideas that better stimulate and reward colleagues – the package is not just money. This would enable leaders to engage in continual development and so enhance the quality of the offer, thereby adding greater value to customers, and helping to retain valuable, talented colleagues. Ultimately, as a profession, we can switch so that innovation becomes a natural habit.

Strategy

Warren Buffett once commented that '...an idiot with a plan can beat a genius without a plan.' Also, the UK Code of Corporate Governance, makes clear that leaders should lead the development of strategy. This does not mean they have to do it all by themselves; nor should they – this is a great opportunity for inclusivity and diversity to enrich the necessary strategy and plans that emerges.

Atkinson's strategic planning

There are myriad guides available for strategic planning. After years of leading strategic planning and transformation, the author has developed a four-step approach to strategic planning.

First, **where are we?** Be inclusive and hear from all quarters about what the real condition of the business is – state of the infrastructure, wellbeing of colleagues, condition of the fleets, the numbers, etc.

Then, similarly with the help of others, work out (second) **where do you want to be?** This is not simply in terms of monetary targets, but in terms of market profile, position, leverage, unique characteristics, culture – ie your agility, your productivity and your resilience.

Third, imagine the environment where your business will operate in the future, and the various ways you might best operate in that environment. By objectively comparing and contrasting the options, you can answer (third) **how shall you get there?** (ie to where you want to be).

Lastly, good leaders know to measure success, ie to answer (fourth) **how do we know we have arrived?**

Engagement

All countries have codes and laws. For example, the UK Corporate Governance Code and the Companies Act imply that leaders should be adept at engagement with all stakeholders. This key talent requires study, practice and expertise.

Leaders can start their engagement practice with stakeholder mapping – who are the stakeholders, what are their relative priorities and what influence do we wish to have upon them? Then, it can be determined which key messages would best achieve those influence effects. From this basic stakeholder map, entire engagement plans can be created, prioritized and resourced. Moreover, good leaders should wish their 'army of champions' to feel empowered to do just that – ie to speak out and eulogize for an organization that they believe in. The 'engagement team' might have communications professionals at the centre but they should also ideally include every employee, customer, supplier, neighbour and their families.

Notwithstanding the leader's personal talent as an engaging and inspiring speaker, and their deftness at negotiating with stakeholders, leaders will also need to be skilled at crisis communications. However massive the corporate damage might be, there might also be human victims involved, for whom the world has just turned upside down. To be first with the truth, mindful of any victims involved, is not a bad starting premise. Those that put denial of wrong-doing and/or shareholder wealth ahead of any victims would likely be doing the organization a disservice.

'How' not 'who'

However great they are, leaders can benefit from the help of a framework, structure and business rhythm for the leadership of their business.

Perhaps frameworks might be based on a five-year strategy cycle. From that, an annual review of strategic objectives can be aligned to annual reporting. Regular brainstorming and inclusive think-tanks help to provide the innovations for increased performance and retention. Routine meetings should be more forecasting than reporting. If things went as they were previously forecast to do, valuable leadership time should not be needed in regaling it. Much time can be lost remarking on the unremarkable that has gone as planned.

Functional leadership

Functional leadership is not about who leads, but how the good behaviours necessary for optimal leadership are achieved to enable organizational effectiveness. John Adair inspired this line of thinking from interpreting group behaviours and balancing the needs of the team, the individual and the task (Adair, 2019). Taking account of these needs and group perspectives in a structured way is the basis of functional, or action-centred, leadership. A particular portion of functional leadership is about how decisions are made, and how this can be consistently repeated. Without a process for decision making, we run the risk of just guessing.

Decision making

Decision making can be thought of as: the cognitive process resulting in the selection of a belief or a course of action among several possible alternative options, being either rational or irrational; or a reasoning process based on assumptions of values, preferences and beliefs of the decision maker (Herbert, 1977). Just as important as how we make decisions is how we communicate them in line with our engagement strategy (see above). In our interconnected world, all stakeholders may have formed their own perceptions on the situation and what decisions should be made. Peter Drucker, in saying '…wherever you see a successful business, someone once made a courageous decision…', was reiterating the importance of decision making, and the importance of making decisions well.

There are a number of types of decision making (Jakoby, 2017), each suited to one circumstance or another:

Type A: The leader alone decides – This is used in situations when immediate action is required, without hesitation. This could relate to an immediate and/or existential threat when the leader is best positioned – because of clarity, scale and responsibility – to make the decision.

Type B: The leader makes the decision with input from selected stakeholders – Input from others assists by providing additional information so the leader may better understand the issue to be decided upon. Deciding without key insights could be very unwise. The leader, nevertheless, reserves the right – and has the duty – to decide independently, once apprised.

Type C: The leader builds agreement with input from a specific team, but has the final say – In this type of decision making, the leader calls on an expert group or subcommittee that can work on behalf of the entire business or organization to provide recommendations. The leader decides once recommendations are reviewed.

Type D: A vote – There are appropriate times when the entire team must weigh in on a decision, such as when the commitment involved goes 'above and beyond' what is routinely required. Debate clarifies the issues so that a vote can be taken and the decision implemented.

Type E: Consensus – The leader fully delegates the decision to a group and becomes an equal single voice. The group discusses, discerns and decides on behalf of the organization. Compromise is commonly a feature of consensus decision making.

Strong leaders are savvy about all levels of the decision-making process. To be most effective at all levels, leaders must be fully transparent about what type of process is being used and why.

Following our gut (or not)?

In making decisions, good leaders are also well versed in the downside of instinct and intuition, where rigour, examination and due diligence are more properly required.

Our instincts serve us very well, especially when we are in danger. Information taken in and processed in our adaptive subconscious activates our warning systems. This superb human override mechanism is what enables us to prepare for fight or flight – eg ready to leap out of the way of a speeding car's path with barely a split second to spare. Unfortunately, many of the same feelings kick in for ill-equipped leaders at all the wrong times. They feel the pressure of the unknown, the fear of the new, and their internal alarm bell ringing, reminding them that they are not equipped to make decisions. As the 'temperature rises', without a 'handrail' (see below) very similar physiological 'fight or flight' reactions occur. The ill-equipped leader, feeling lonely and on a pedestal, with all eyes upon them for a decision is now fully in fight or flight mode just when sophisticated analysis and reasoning are required. Almost invariably, the decision will be poorly founded and the 'leader' will likely be unable to justify it with more than bullish rhetoric, bluff or bluster.

This author likes to believe that intuition can be little more than recognition of the known, even when we cannot recall relevant previous experience into our conscious minds. The subconscious brain attempts to recognize, process and use patterns of thinking based on prior experience and a best guess – that is to say, we use unconscious information to guide our behaviour. In 'intuition mode', our minds might conduct a pair-wise correlation of the current challenge with all the individual previous experience and knowledge, looking for a 'match'. If unable to find a match, the mental process allows the search to expand until a 'match' is found. This may well be a memory quite distant from the actual circumstances that currently prevail and so the actions taken might be wholly unsuitable.

Having a 'handrail' to get you underway, to engage others and to start due diligence, markedly reduces the chances of error from just using gut instinct.

Empowerment

To build resilience and agility in our leadership capability, we should give direction that empowers others. These empowered colleagues should be responsible for making decisions for which the leader will be held accountable. To achieve this, leaders can most usefully describe the desired outcome and sustainable condition, rather than views on the process or steps required. We can start with *why* we think something should happen, set only the conditions and constraints – such as available resources and timeline – and then stand well back from all the decisions about how the task shall be achieved. Empowered colleagues are far more able to make these determinations, and will feel all the more engaged to be allowed to do so. The trust that has been extended can be reinforced by giving credit when things go well, and by owning the responsibility when things do not. Failure is not the opposite to success; it is part of the journey to it.

Summary

This chapter offers but a few pointers and a framework for the foundations of developing logistics leaders. There is a priceless, irresistible, opportunity to fully seize upon our responsibilities towards leadership expertise and to create the culture to match. By doing so, our organizations, and the logistics profession, can accelerate and gain whole new levels of recognition, professional standing, performance and productivity. By embracing better practice, developing leadership talent and through better understanding of the purpose of leadership, the next era for logistics shall emerge before us.

And so, finally, who might we get to lead?

Succession planning, talent spotting, developing and investing for the successful continuity of leadership is vital. In this context, an active programme of personal development and talent spotting is at the heart of the business. After all, we lead people not buildings. Could this advert attract your new CEO?

Logistics business seeks new leader

Candidates should be entrepreneurs, well versed/schooled in strategy, vision and value propositions. They can readily influence organizational culture by demonstrating integrity, fairness and high standards. S/he is a capable resource/risk manager, skilled at building relationships with stakeholders and is a deft decision maker, making choices for the longer term, mindful of the community and environment. The successful candidate will be amply equipped with energy, passion, courage and inspiration, wrapped in humility from knowing that leadership is a service to others. An individual whose level of confidence is balanced with levels of demonstrable competence.

Could this be you?

References

Adair, J (2019) *Action-Centred Leadership*, Kogan Page, London

DCDC (2014) *Joint Doctrine Publication 0-01 (JDP 0-01)*, 5th edn, The Development, Concepts and Doctrine Centre, Ministry of Defence, Shrivenham, November

Herbert, AS (1977) *The New Science of Management Decision*, Prentice-Hall

Jacoby, B (2017) Strong leaders use the five levels of decision making, *HR Daily Advisor*, hrdailyadvisor.blr.com/2017/12/20/strong-leaders-use-five-levels-decision-making (archived at https://perma.cc/YUA6-EELV)

UK FRC (2018) *The UK Code of Corporate Governance*, UK Financial Reporting Council

Ethics in supply chains 16

An illustrated survey

Steve New

I have concluded that in truth Boohoo has not felt any real sense of responsibility for the factory workers in Leicester and the reason is a very human one: it is because they are largely invisible to them. It is hard for people to empathize with the plight of those of whom they know little.[1]

Introduction

In this chapter I provide a brief introduction to the field of supply chain ethics and use the case of Boohoo – a UK-based online fast fashion retailer – to reflect on two key issues: what drives ethical change in the supply chain, and what is the nature of supply chain responsibility? The term 'supply chain ethics' is open to several interpretations, but here I concentrate on how firms handle those issues (for example, worker exploitation, environmental harm) that arise in a firm's extended supply base.

Boohoo is a UK-based fast fashion retailer. On 5 July 2020, the UK's *Sunday Times* ran a front-page story about the firm's suppliers in Leicester. In particular, the article made claims that suppliers were paying less than the minimum wage. The accusations followed several years of claims of exploitative sweatshop labour in the city, and concerns that workers were being forced to labour in unsafe conditions during the Covid-19 pandemic. The story had an astonishing short-term impact: within the next two weeks the company's share price dropped by over 45 per cent, taking over £2 billion off the value of the firm. The firm responded by commissioning an independent review by the eminent lawyer Alison Levitt QC (Levitt, 2020), and in the following months the firm's leaders were grilled by two parliamentary committees.[2] The case provides an insight into the operations and culture of the firm that would normally be inaccessible to conventional academic inquiry. Although there are obvious dangers in tying an analysis to the details of a single firm in a single industry, the Boohoo story is rich and complex enough to give substance to arguments that could otherwise appear abstract and merely theoretical.

The chapter is organized as follows. I first provide an overview of the field, making comments on both supply chain ethics as handled in practice and research. Next I pick out two key issues (the drivers for supply chain ethics and the nature of the ethical connection between buyer and supplier) to develop a simple framework for understanding different types of responsibility. I then deploy these ideas to help illuminate the Boohoo case, before offering some concluding thoughts.

Characterizing the field of supply chain ethics

Alternative narratives

It is possible to choose different embarkation points for a discussion of supply chain ethics. One starting point is to point to the horrors of modern slavery, child labour, exploited and unsafe workers and environmental damage that persist across the globe. In this view, the industrial system that has worked so brilliantly to bring unimaginable wealth and comfort to the privileged comes at the cost of cruelty and injustice for others. If *my* cheap goods come at the cost of *your* suffering, the response needs to be outrage. It is easy to juxtapose the mental images from 'different ends of the chain': plenty versus starvation, freedom versus bondage, instant gratification versus environmental catastrophe. These vignettes bring immediate moral clarity: a global economy that rests on oppression and harm is just *wrong*. We (the consumer, the global firms) are culpable as the beneficiaries of institutionalized injustice, because the system of trade and exchange – which the textbooks tell us should lead to mutual benefit – is broken. The problem is that in every exchange, at every opportunity, the powerful seem to wring advantage at the expense of the weak. Prices are driven down; corners are cut. Multinational companies seek out the supplies from the places with the weakest standards and lowest wages. The supply chain is a story of moral failure. In the words of Martijn Boersma (2014), 'Global supply chains link us all to [the] shame of child and forced labour.' The supply chains of major firms are thought to be responsible for nearly a fifth of all carbon dioxide emissions (Zhang *et al*, 2020).

But, alternatively, we might see the supply chain as a story of hope. The world economy – and thus, ultimately, all of human society – rests on trade. That trade is dominated by firms buying from one another. What if we could inject ethicality into firms' procurement practices? Perhaps there is space for a 'market-embedded morality' (Shamir, 2008)? What if we could change the supply chain from one that generates harms into one that raises standards (Girling, 2020)? Perhaps even those workers working in countries with feeble legal protection from their own state might find shelter and help in the munificent influence of the Walmart or the Nestlé supply chain? The great corporations can exercise extraordinary influence on their suppliers and in turn their suppliers and so on. Perhaps, as best practice cascades down the supply chain, corporate procurement can be the vehicle for delivering, *inter alia*, economic development, the empowerment of women, the safeguarding of minority rights and the protection of the environment (Hartmann and Moeller 2014; Wilhem *et al*, 2016; Aßländer *et al*, 2016; Zhang *et al*, 2017)?

Over the last 30 years or so, many organizations, activists and academics have launched out on a journey into supply chain ethics from these contrasting points of departure. What is not clear is where we've landed. If one reads the websites and reports of major corporations, it is possible to dizzy oneself with high claims of ethical commitment, virtue and progress. Expensive (and glossily photographed) corporate initiatives give an impression of huge effort and serious moral purpose. If you attend the corporate practitioner conferences associated with the various incarnations of supply chain ethics (environmental or social), it is impossible to ignore the exciting buzz: people really feel they are making a difference. But go to different conferences – for example, those of non-governmental organizations (NGOs) and activists groups – and the energy is all about the continuing struggle against the hypocrisy of those same powerful firms. It's not difficult to find media stories of exploitation and environmental damage in supply chains. Frankly, it would be difficult to argue that 30 years of firms' interest in supply chain ethics has made significant improvements. The much predicted 'cascade effect' doesn't seem to be a reality yet (Villena and Gioia, 2020). But it is clear that the field continues to generate substantial interest and activity in both management practice and academia.

Supply chain ethics as practice

There is no doubt that over recent years supply chain ethics – broadly defined – has become a major element of corporate 'best practice'. Leading firms produce extensive reports detailing considerable levels of activity. Comparing, say, the corporate responsibility reports of Intel Corporation from 2010 and 2020, one can see that, although the format and structure of activities remain broadly the same (and the layout of and structure of the reports are eerily similar), the more recent report shows an increasing level of sophistication. In 2010, Intel reported very few onsite labour and environmental audits of suppliers (just eight per year); by 2019 this had risen to 207 per year.[3] In the 2020 report, the firm claims that they audit all high-risk supplier sites over a two-year cycle. Major consulting firms offer supply chain ethics services (eg KPMG, Deloitte[4]) and large numbers of firms have emerged offering technology solutions targeted at managing ethics and sustainability in the supply chain (for example, Ulula provides systems to enable vulnerable workers in the supply chain to report issues;[5] Provenance uses blockchain technology to enable product traceability[6]).

Despite these developments, it is fair to say that progress has been slower than predicted (including by me, New, 2010). A recent survey of 710 mostly US-based supply chain professionals reported only 62 per cent of respondents reporting that their firms monitored or evaluated their supply chains for ethical practices, even though 94 per cent reported that they felt that their organization should practise or have a plan to 'operate an ethical supply chain'.[7] In some organizations, this work is framed as part of 'compliance' (Picot, 2019) and tends to span across many functional groups in an organization (eg procurement, logistics, accounting); what is clear is that the apparatus of supply chain ethics can become highly bureaucratic (Neef, 2004; Cranmer and New, 2012).

Supply chain ethics in research

The academic literature related to this field is vast, and this chapter will not attempt a systematic review. However, it is worth making some observations about the range of academic lenses which can be applied to the domain, each bringing different disciplinary and philosophical perspectives. These are illustrated in Table 16.1.

Table 16.1   A rough characterization of the relevant literature

Perspective	Commodity Chains/ Global Production Networks	Sustainable Supply Chains	Law	Ethical Theory
Conceptual Anchors	Industrial relations, development economics, politics, human geography	Supply chain management; procurement; marketing; reputation management; corporate social responsibility	Human Rights, corporate regulation	Responsibility
Focus	Policy	Business processes	Legislation/ regulation	Moral philosophy
Explicit discussion of ethics	Rare. Often based on implicit assumption of ethical priority of, for example, better working standards, collective bargaining	Occasional. Although individual companies are often discussed, direct criticism is very rare	Common, but complicated	Central, but under-developed

Although the extensive body of work on global commodity chains and global production networks – which very loosely might be associated with the work of Gary Gereffi and others (eg Gereffi and Lee, 2016; Gereffi, 2019; Coe and Yeung, 2015) – rarely addresses ethical issues head on, it is undeniably connected with the broad idea of supply chain ethics. The work typically rests on implied ethical assumptions about the merits of economic development and the desirability of improved working conditions. Several threads of this work construct the question of supply chain ethicality in terms of private regulation (eg companies and corporate groups applying standards, certification and inspection regimes) versus state regulation (Vogel, 2010). This body of work often draws on disciplinary perspectives such as politics, geography and economics, frequently dealing with macro-level data. It is largely targeted towards the discourse of national and international policy. This is an academic tradition which is often concerned with supply chain ethics, even though the terms 'supply chain' or 'ethics' may not be deployed.

In contrast, another substantial body of work is more commonly based within business schools and tends to be more interested in the actions and programmes of companies; in recent years this has typically been characterized by framing questions of supply chain ethics within a broader context of sustainability, where the 'social' becomes a subset of a wider set of issues associated with the environment. 'Sustainability' becomes a coverall term for a generalized sense of virtue (Montiel, 2008). This fusion makes some sense as the machinery of what organizations actually do (eg audits, supplier prequalification, codes of practice) applies in similar ways to both domains. This body of work is very diverse but is perhaps best exemplified by the prolific contributions of Stefan Seuring at University of Kassel in Germany (Seuring and Müller, 2008; Yawar and Seuring, 2017) and Rob Klassen at the Ivey Business School at Western University in Canada (Linton *et al*, 2007; Klassen and Vereecke, 2012). In recent years there has been a spate of slightly repetitive review articles which attempt to summarize this burgeoning field: these include Gimenez and Tachizawa (2012); Tachizawa and Wong (2014); Köksal *et al* (2017), Nakamba *et al* (2017); Sodhi and Tang (2018); Koberg and Longoni (2019); and Govindan *et al* (2020).

It is interesting to note that while much of the work discussed in these reviews is empirical, there tends to be more discussion of companies' practices than of actual ethical outcomes. For example, work on modern slavery in this framing often considers data about companies' policies more than the actual experiences of exploited workers. Most of this work also tends to skip quite lightly over the core ethical questions, and in some cases is conceptually located in the field of reputation management. This reflects an assumption that an important – if not the major – reason why firms should be interested in supply chain harms is that it could damage corporate reputations and thus diminish profits or the share price. This – perhaps curiously – permits a discourse where ethical concerns conveniently align with a financial logic: supply chain ethics can be then seen as unthreatening to business even from a Friedman-esque view of the primacy of shareholder value, and so arguably stops being about ethics at all and becomes a branch of marketing. In other words, it means that the question of supply chain ethics becomes less about the question 'what is right?', and becomes 'what will important stakeholders perceive as serving their interests?' This may even lead to a perverse position where what is 'ethical' is that which you can get away with.[8] This is illustrated in many firms' approach to the 'risks of modern slavery in the supply chain' – the risks in question are not the risks of actual people being actually exploited, but the risks of a reputational scandal. In this perspective, due diligence activities are driven by a desire primarily to protect the firm, rather than eliminating the harm. Protecting people becomes a means to an end, not an end in itself.

Supply chain ethics are also considered by many legal researchers; the work is typically framed in the context of human rights and company law. Although the relationship between law and ethics is complex (for example, see Starr, 1983), there has been an explosion of research from this perspective, particularly with the emergence of legal instruments which seek to either directly regulate or encourage good behaviour in supply chains, such as the California Transparency in Supply Chains Act of 2010, and the UK's Modern Slavery Act of 2015. Recent contributions in this vein include Cullen (2016); Nolan and Bott (2018); Landau (2019); and Hess (2019).

Relatively little research concerns itself directly with the detailed ethical theory of supply chain ethics, and that which has emerged has made little impression on the debates in the other academic silos. The recent thesis by Kingston (2019) makes a detailed argument that the fundamental premise underlying most work in the field is flawed. Buyers (consumers or firms), in his view, do not have obligations for the behaviours for their trading partners other than in very narrow circumstances. Kingston makes important arguments about the limitations of ethical shopping in terms of the extent to which consumers/buyers can fully understand the 'harms' in the chain, and the extent to which applying remedies can have unintended consequences.

This brings to the surface the distinction between deontic and consequentialist reasoning. In the former, ethical arguments start from the idea of non-negotiable principles that guide action whatever the context: for example, don't murder people. These principles might be disputed between people and subject to definitional complexity, but when someone holds a deontic principle, the value of action is not subject to the balancing of pros and cons – something is wrong (or right) and that's it. In contrast, a consequentialist view is one in which an action is evaluated by considering all of the effects of the action, and calculation of the net ethical effect: the overall ends might justify controversial or problematic means. In supply chains, nearly all discussions of ethics are framed in consequentialist terms. For example, applying the principle that 'child labour in supply chains is a bad thing' seems sensible at first glance, and seems like an important ethical idea that should be rigorously applied. But as Berlan (2013) shows, once the lived experience of children is understood, in some circumstances, some kinds of child labour might be preferable to the available alternatives. In Berlan's study, she illustrated how some Ghanaian children were stopped from working on family cocoa plantations as a result of the producers needing to receive Fairtrade certification. However, the schooling that was available as an alternative was in many senses more dangerous. This doesn't mean, of course, that, overall, education is not to be preferred to child labour, but it points out that in any given circumstance there may be complex trade-offs. A firm may drop a supplier for unsafe working practices – but where does that leave the workers and their families if no alternative employment is available? This level of complexity means that the application of supply chain ethics requires deep understanding of the situation in question, and a need to avoid approaches in which rules and codes are applied in a ham-fisted or short-sighted way. For Kingston, this risk – together with some less convincing arguments about compromising 'liberal democratic values' – means that the exercise of supply chain ethics is intrinsically misguided.

An alternative critique by Amaeshi *et al* (2008) focuses on the logic of transferring ethical responsibility from, say, a firm providing poor working conditions to its employees (for example, Foxconn in 2012) to the firm's customer (Apple; see Garside, 2012). This makes sense, they argue, only in situations in which the buying firm has particular kinds of power over the supplier. This resonates with an argument I made in an earlier contribution (New, 2004). In normal discourse, some types of responsibility seem obvious: 'of course big food companies have obligations to the poor farmers that provide the crops'. But although it is easy to jump to the conclusion, for example, that Mars Inc might be culpable for the use of child and forced labour in the West African cocoa production involved in its products, on what basis should that culpability be allocated to Mars? Why not ascribe the responsibility to the (several) intermediary stages in the supply chain – or why not to the cocoa farmers themselves? Or – going in the other direction along the chain – why not to Walmart, or the tiny corner shops who sell the products? In practice, people generally allocate responsibility to those perceived to have some kind of controlling influence. This seems to be fairly obvious in some cases, but not in others: in the car industry, for example, it is fairly easy to generate an approximate map in which the major assemblers are seen as the 'kings' of the supply network, with successive tiers representing often smaller and smaller firms. This matches a logic in which the buyer has more power over the suppliers, although of course the degree of influence will depend on the detailed structure of the network: some suppliers may have many customers, so the influence of a single customer might be very small. As one goes down the network towards raw materials, it is likely that firms in the supply network are supplied by firms much larger and more powerful than they are: in this case, the idea of projecting upstream ethical responsibility becomes problematic. The implications of this for supply chain ethics are significant, as it calls into question the idea that buyers can necessarily have influence on their suppliers, either by Voice (ie exercising power within a relationship) or by Exit (ie using the threatened or actual end of a relationship to exert power – Hirschman, 1970; Pedersen and Andersen, 2006). The extent of possible influence depends on not only the relative size of the firms, but also their relative interdependency, the availability of alternative trading partners, the switching costs involved and the level of asset specificity reflected in the relationship (Williamson, 2008). In ethical terms, a lack of power must have some relevance to the degree of responsibility: Tesco and Walmart have great power over many of their supplying firms, whereas an independent corner shop selling the same goods does not. This does not mean that the corner shop has no ethical issues to consider in its supply – it could still, in some cases, choose to simply not sell products originating from particular suppliers or geographies. But its ability to exercise influence over, say, Kraft or Unilever is minimal. In terms of supply chain ethics, it seems a reasonable position that those actors with significant power carry a heavier ethical responsibility than those who don't. Hoejmose *et al* (2013) find some evidence that collaboration between buyers and suppliers is more successful in conditions where the power is balanced between them.

Another perspective on supply chain ethics is provided by the work of Ha-Brookshire (2017). In a clutch of interesting papers, she draws on Kantian ideas for considering supply chain obligations (in the context of sustainability) as either 'perfect' or 'imperfect' obligations (terms which are well established in ethical theory, but uninformative and potentially misleading to the casual reader). The former category relates to universal and absolute duties that are universally applicable (such as telling the truth, not murdering people); the second relates to things that are good to do, but not ethically necessary (such as giving to charity). Imperfect duties, in this sense, are acts of choice which allow flexible interpretation. In Ha-Brookshire's view, sustainability in corporate operations (including supply chain operations) is often perceived as falling into the imperfect category, because it is understood to play a secondary role to the organization's core goal of financial success. In this case, the best that can be hoped for is for a supply chain that is 'consistently sustainable' or 'occasionally sustainable' in only selective areas of operations. She also points to the problem of corporate hypocrisy in undermining efforts to achieve sustainability, concluding that '...corporations must work on having clear and convergent goals, and a well-defined corporate structure toward sustainability.'

For firms working in the supply chains, there are interesting choices to be made regarding this distinction. For several years many major companies (Unilever and Sainsbury's are good examples) have adopted a public stance whereby their work in the supply chain is targeted at going well beyond simply 'not being bad'. For example, they have engaged with educational and gender equality issues in the communities in which their suppliers operate. Other firms – often those without direct contact with consumers – tend to settle for more limited ambitions. However, an important question that follows from Ha-Brookshire's distinction is the extent to which the 'imperfect' agenda might serve as a kind of 'greenwash' or smokescreen to steer attention away from a firm's limited success with perfect obligations. There is also a possibility that concern with ambitious imperfect obligations might act as a distraction mechanism for managers within a company – in Sendlhofer's (2020) evocative phrase, 'visionary procrastination' – which pulls them away from more prosaic and less glamorous perfect obligations.

Two key issues in supply chain ethics

Drivers

A key element in much work in supply chain ethics is the idea of transmission of 'pressure' in trading relationships, and much attention has been given to the 'ethical shopping' element of consumers bringing ethical concerns into their purchasing behaviour. Ethical pressure is assumed to make virtue ripple down the chain. However, after many years of predictions of the growth of this phenomenon, much of the literature is nowadays concerned with why there is so little ethical shopping, and why, to the extent that it does happen, ethical shoppers are so fickle and inconsistent. Many writers (eg Nicholls and Lee, 2006; Chatzidakis *et al*, 2007; Eckhardt *et al*, 2010) observe that there seems to be a persistent divergence between consumers' espoused values and their actual purchasing behaviour: the so-called 'attitude–behaviour gap' (also sometimes reported as the 'value–action gap' or the 'intention–behaviour gap'). This might be driven by a range of factors: Bray *et al* (2011) enumerate them as price sensitivity (ie ethical products too expensive, or non-ethical products very cheap); personal experience (ie not recognizing the ethical consequences of purchasing choices); ethical obligations (ie prioritizing different agendas, feeling that actions would have no impact); lack of information; assumptions that ethicality implied lower quality; inertia; cynicism; the limited availability of ethical goods; and effort. On this last point, Reimers *et al* (2016) discuss the complexities faced by consumers who might be presented with environmental and ethical credentials across a range of issues: if someone is seeking to buy ethical meat, they not only, say, have to appraise performance on animal welfare, the labour standards in production, or the energy used in production, or the use of additives and preservatives, and the recyclability of the packaging, but also have to operate some mechanism for rolling together these evaluations into an overall preference. In decision theoretic terms, not only are they faced with a large number of variables, but also the mathematical function with which to combine these variables into a composite score. Furthermore, they have to account for the credibility of the information provided. To this could be added that consumers may be interested in the supplier's overall *corporate* performance, not just the attributes of a particular *product*. For products with complex, multi-stage supply chains, the cognitive burden of 'ethical shopping' is vastly more than consumers might be reasonably expected to process.

Jacobs *et al* (2018) also point out that it is not always the case that 'green' or 'ethical' consumption – even when it happens – is necessarily driven by ethical principles. Although it is possible that preferences for ethical products might be driven by ethics of benevolence and universalism (Schwartz, 1994) it is also the case that they might be driven by the desire for self-affirmation and display (ie showing off to oneself or others).

In the context of business-to-business markets, it appears that the obstacles to ethical procurement are not dissimilar, although in previous studies (New *et al*, 2000a; 2000b) it was observed that 'customer pressure' for ethicality is sometimes reified by those within firms as a justification mechanism for (in the cases studied, environmental) initiatives which are in fact driven by more institutional reasons. These might include pressures from leaders within the organization (either expressing their own ethical agenda, or using ethical issues as a political device). The recent paper by Soderstrom and Weber (2020) illustrates the complex organizational processes that can lead to organizations adopting environmental initiatives, including the example of a supply chain manager's 'self-image as a sustainability professional'.

Ethical supply chain management practices may also be driven by the owners and investors in a firm, and there is increasing interest in the strengths and weaknesses of the so-called ESG approach, which entails the aggregated ranking of firms according to Environmental, Social and Governance indicators (Bassen and Kovács, 2008; Buchanan and Rogers, 2020). However, there are widespread criticisms – mirroring the challenges facing putative ethical shoppers – that the complexity of firms' operations is at odds with the desire to simplify things down to simple ratings and rankings (Thamotheram, 2012; Poh, 2019). The key test is the extent to which firms with poor performance on supply chain ethics are punished with low share prices.

Two other sets of actors that need to be discussed in relation to supply chain ethics are civil society and governments. Civil society relates to the disparate web of activists, campaign groups and non-governmental organizations who attempt to hold firms to account; also included in this heading are investigative journalists and (occasionally) academics. The extent to which civil society groups can be effective in providing some regulatory force depends heavily on the extent to which firms reveal information – an issue discussed in depth in New (2021). One of the key problems here is the extent to which a firm's approach to transparency enables outsiders to challenge and test corporate claims. In recent years, governments in several jurisdictions have passed laws relating to modern slavery which require firms to make declarations about their actions towards the elimination of modern slavery in their supply chains. The legislation is crafted in the hope that consumers and civil society then act on the published information to provide a kind of outsourced regulation that relieves the government from the need to explicitly monitor or regulate itself. The effectiveness of this approach has been widely debated, and it is fair to say that there is an emerging consensus that it has serious limitations (LeBaron 2020; Hsin *et al*, 2021; New and Hsin, 2021). Civil society's ability to participate in the regulation of firms is fundamentally hamstrung if neither consumers nor investors are able to interrogate and test the firm's claims (New, 2021).

Power and culpability

If a supplier does some kind of harm – how much and what kind of ethical responsibility is carried by the customer? To support the discussion that follows, consider the model presented in Table 16.2. This takes into account the different types of responsibility, and focuses on what the buyer knows and doesn't know about the harm in question.

Table 16.2 Types of responsibility

	Suspicion of harm	Knowledge of harm
Active Responsibility	Example: a buyer demands price reductions paid in the knowledge that this will likely result in corners being cut in the safety of workforce	Example: A firm directs its supplier to use cheap raw materials known to be produced by forced labour
Structural Culpability	Example: a firm's buying processes mean that it is likely but not certain that a supplier's workers will need to work excessive unplanned overtime	Example: a firm knowingly deals with its suppliers in a way that it knows will result in exploitative practices
Passive Complicity	Example: a firm suspects its supplier of applying racist and discriminatory employment practices, but does not seek to check this	Example: A firm knowingly buys from a supplier that pollutes its local water supply

The three levels of the model refer to increasingly significant levels of connection between the buyer and the supplier; the two columns refer to the degree of knowledge and certainty the buyer has about the harm in question. In the bottom right of the diagram, the situation is one where the supplier knows about the problem and 'passive complicity'. Here, the buyer is not to blame for the harm, but finds itself implicitly condoning the supplier's conduct by continuing to trade. At one level it is easy to imagine a situation where the buyer says, 'The problem is nothing to do with me; my actions probably won't make a difference, so I have no ethical issue to address.' At a trivial level, this is the position taken by many consumers who have significant reservations about, for example, the tax arrangements of Amazon and Starbucks; I might rationalize my continuing custom and shrug off a feeling of moral contamination or ethical repugnance. However, it is important to note that it seems that this kind of position is always contingent on the degree of the harm involved. It is always possible to imagine some level of harm that would make the ongoing connection untenable. For example, many people and organizations would draw the line at knowingly buying products produced by forced labour or modern slavery (New, 2015). Even if their actions (ie to boycott or to continue to trade) might have no significant consequence one way or another on the situation, there is an ethical urgency in not wanting to have anything to do with the harm.

Otherwise, the buyer becomes complicit in the harm. An example of this kind of situation is provided by the way in which western clothes retailers have responded to the claims regarding the human rights situation in Xinjiang, China (Kelly, 2020).

The next level in the table – structural culpability – is the situation in which the harm *does* have something to do with the buyer, even if the buyer did not directly cause the harm. This can be where, for example, the buyer's business model is such that it encourages or necessitates the supplying organization towards the harm in question. The seminal work of Richard Locke (Locke, 2013; Distelhorst *et al*, 2017) and his colleagues illustrates this idea well: following a series of high-profile scandals, Nike committed to extensive programmes of supplier factory inspection and audit. Locke and his team discovered that years of effort ended up having little effect on actual working conditions – but that problems were in part generated by Nike themselves in their ordering patterns (resulting in excessive unplanned overtime). One rather simplified takeaway from this and subsequent studies is that Nike might better direct its efforts at being a better customer (smoother schedules, sharing expertise) than by seeking to police its suppliers.

This speculation is important because the thrust of much work (including my own, eg New, 2015; 2021) is that suppliers' bad behaviour is driven by the (bad) fundamental business approach applied by powerful buyers. For example, supermarkets might adopt extensive policies and procedures for ethical procurement but *simultaneously* use the exercise of brute commercial force to drive down costs to the point at which exploitation becomes inevitable. In other words, the exploitation of the workers (or the suppliers' environmental corner-cutting) is fundamentally driven by the exploitation of the suppliers. From this perspective, the key issue is the imbalance of power within the organization-to-organization relationship. Indeed, it could be argued that some of the ethical sourcing initiatives of large companies are merely distracting window-dressing if the question of the concentration of corporate power is not addressed.

The top level of Table 16.2 represents the most egregious case where the buyer has explicitly caused or specified the harm. This does not absolve the supplier, of course, but means that the harm ultimately originates from the intention of the buyer.

The model in Table 16.2 seeks to capture more of the reality of supply chains by including the left-hand column. In many – perhaps most – cases in real supply chains, there is a degree of opacity in the relationship between the buyer and supplier. The buyer may have grounds for suspecting the harm in question, but does not know for certain. If challenged, the buyer might be able to say that they were ignorant of the harm, and it might be difficult for anyone to prove that they did. The crucial issue here is that firms may choose to ensure that this comforting veil of ignorance is in place. How can you be responsible for things you did not know? However, there is not only an ethical principle at play in respect of acting on what you know; there is also – in some circumstances – an ethical obligation to know things, and to acquire the knowledge in order to be able to act ethically (Ginet, 2000; New, 2004; Zimmerman, 2008).

These puzzles – how pressure is exerted on organizations, what type of ethical connection is drawn between supplier and buyer, what is known and unknown – turn out to be central to understanding the Boohoo case, to which I now turn.

The Boohoo case

The tale of Boohoo's public shaming in 2020 is rich and complex: a full exposition will not be attempted here (the Levitt report is itself 234 pages long, and the press coverage extensive). Instead, the bare bones of the story will be presented, with enough detail provided only to sustain the analysis.

The background

The global fashion industry has undergone very substantial changes in recent years, and is probably the sector in which the ethical concerns about sweatshops and environmental damage have been most sharply in the public focus. This is not new: the textile industry was central to the Industrial Revolution, and was central in the emergence of slavery in antebellum USA.[9] For many, clothing plays an important role in defining personal identity: vast sums are spent on advertising and marketing. The global industry was transformed with the abolition of the Multi-Fibre Arrangement in 2005, which hastened the shift towards increasingly globalized production.[10] As production has become global – and distant from many of the consumers – there has been a rise in interest in studies that address 'where do our clothes come from?'[11] and an increasing interest in the possibilities of 'ethical' fashion. Many NGOs have been founded specifically to monitor safety, labour standards and environmental impact in the fashion sector,[12] with concern particularly rising after the Rana Plaza disaster in 2013.

In the UK, the British textile industry – once the driving force of the economy – entered steep decline in the 1920s, following a long period of limited investment, insufficient scale and a reluctance to invest in new technology. By the 1990s, with some specialist exceptions, the UK garment sector was heavily dependent on one retailer, Marks and Spencer; this firm operated in a widely reported 'partnership' mode with highly dependent suppliers. Driven by cost-cutting initiatives, the firm proceeded to shift its sourcing offshore, causing the collapse of several of its major suppliers (Toms and Zhang, 2016). Meanwhile, the new global sourcing (and then the arrival of the internet) led to an extraordinary drop in the costs for consumers: in the UK the prices of clothes dropped in real terms by approximately over two-thirds in the period 1991 to 2020.[13]

This is the context of the rise of Boohoo – an extraordinarily successful Manchester-based (UK) online fashion retailer. Founded by 2006 by Mahmud Kamani and Carol Kane, the firm has achieved astonishing growth by targeting young (16–30) consumers; it listed on the London (AIM) stock market in 2014, since when its annual turnover has grown from £110 million to £1.2 billion and 2,700 direct employees.[14] The firm has expanded organically, and also by buying other brands: the business trades under the boohoo, boohooMAN, Prettylittlething, Nasty Gal, Misspap, Karen Millen and Coast labels. The firm has been one of the main UK exponents of the so-called 'fast fashion' approach, pioneered by Zara (Inditex) (Ferdows *et al*, 2005; MacCarthy and Jayarathne, 2010). This approach enables the firm to go from design to initial sale of an item very quickly, enabling it to be highly responsive to rapid developments in fashion; the firm's marketing makes extensive use of social media, producing clothes at very low prices. The business model is one which relies on high levels of consumption, and there has been extensive debate about the very high environmental cost of clothes that move within days or weeks 'from influencer to landfill' (EAC, 2019; Davis, 2020). Laville (2019) reports an estimate that a typical dress would be discarded by consumers after a mere five weeks.

As Boohoo has grown, it has become increasingly reliant on clothes production in Leicester, a city of 552,000 that has a large ethnic minority population that is just over two hours' drive from Manchester and two and half hours from the firm's main distribution centre in Burnley. Once one of Europe's most prosperous cities, Leicester has experienced substantial economic decline, but many of the large and decrepit factory buildings have become the home of many small garment manufacturers (often with fewer than 50 workers). For several years, the city had come under scrutiny for exploitative and unsafe working practices: in addition to academic reports (eg Hammer *et al*, 2015), the Channel 4 investigative series *Dispatches* made television documentaries in 2010 ('Fashion's Dirty Secret') and 2017; the latter mentioning Boohoo as a customer to the firm in question.[15,16] A major *Financial Times* article gave a similar account in the following year (O'Connor, 2018), as did a BBC report the year after (Heighton-Ginns and Prescott, 2019): both reports also mentioned Boohoo, but scrupulously avoiding making direct accusations. In the BBC story, Boohoo was given space to explain the measures it was taking to ensure good working practices, including making 'unannounced site visits monthly to every manufacturer' and setting up an office to maintain close ties with local suppliers. Also in 2019, a review by HM Revenue & Customs across the whole UK textile sector found it to be rife with exploitation and underpayment. One of the problems identified by Adam Mansell, chief executive of the UK Fashion and Textile Association (UKFTA) was the 'phoenix system' where factories 'close one day, and then open up under a different name the next day' (BBC, 2019).

By August 2019, approximately 40 per cent of Boohoo's clothing was made in the UK, mostly in Leicester. In June 2020, the activist group Labour Behind the Label published a report claiming the workers at Boohoo's Leicester suppliers were being forced to work in unsafe conditions during the first UK Covid-19 lockdown, and that some workers were forced to attend work even when sick with the virus (Labour Behind the Label, 2020). On 4 July, the *Daily Mail* ran with similar stories, again name-checking Boohoo (Bracchi, 2020). So when the *Sunday Times* ran its front-page story the next day, the ground was already laid for widespread media interest. The key additional evidence was obtained by an undercover journalist, who was offered work at a supplier at less than the minimum wage. The killer blow was the photographic evidence of Nasty Gal products being made in the factory.

Boohoo's immediate response was to issue a Regulatory News Service posting (a press release system for listed companies) which declared:

> We are grateful to the *Sunday Times* for highlighting the conditions at Jaswal Fashions, which, if as observed and reported by the undercover reporter, are totally unacceptable and fall woefully short of any standards acceptable in any workplace.[17]

It later transpired that the factory was misidentified – the sign on the wall of the factory referred to a company that had ceased to trade. However, it was clear that the work was being done for Morefray Limited – a Boohoo supplier with some complex family and corporate connections to Boohoo (Davies, 2020). Boohoo then went on to appoint Alison Levitt QC to produce an independent report into its sourcing from Leicester, promising to publish the report in full. The report was completed at speed and was published on 24 September.

It is difficult to overstate just how remarkable a document the Levitt report is. The *Financial Times* commented: 'Ohhh boy, does it contain some pretty eye-opening details' (Powell, 2020). The report was described as 'damning' in the *Guardian* (Bland and Makortoff, 2020). A piece in the *Evening Standard* called for the resignation of the firm's chairman (Armitage, 2020b). Although some groups complained the report did not go far enough, it came to some strident specific conclusions; perhaps more importantly, it painted a vivid picture of supplier relations that was chaotic, under-resourced and poorly managed. The report makes it clear that senior managers – although not necessarily aware of the specific detail of the malpractice in the supplier firms – would have had a very clear idea of the type of conduct present in the Leicester suppliers. It is also clear that Boohoo had such poor records of their supply base that they were unable to know definitively how many suppliers they had in Leicester, and certainly very poor visibility of the complex system of subcontracting used between suppliers. The report also shows that Boohoo's previous claims about its factory monitoring processes were simply untrue – claims that Boohoo had made repeatedly in, for example, its Modern Slavery Statements, to the press, and to parliamentary select committees.[18] They had a very small and poorly organized process of factory inspections, and although they had begun to establish a more formal system by the time of the *Sunday Times* story, they were still in the early days of establishing appropriate systems and procedures.

Following the report, Boohoo have made a number of commitments to transform their approach, including more extensive training for buyers, and the establishment of their own 'model' factory in Leicester, at which Boohoo staff (including buyers) can become more familiar with manufacturing and costing processes. The firm has also committed to improve its internal technology so it can more easily track what is being made where. It has also promised to publish supplier lists in early 2021, although it is perhaps instructive that the firm remained unable to reveal the information (or even numbers of suppliers) when grilled by a parliamentary select committee on 16 December 2020. The firm recruited a 'Responsible Sourcing and Product Operations Director' in mid-September 2020, and this may have some impact in the future approach taken by the firm.

Analysing the Boohoo case: drivers

The Boohoo story provides a discouraging story about the prospects of supply chain ethics being driven by consumers, investors or managers.

Boohoo's customers appear to be completely unaffected by the scandal. Just six days after the publication of the Levitt report, the company was able to report a 'profits surge' (Nazir, 2020); although there was a very brief burst of the hashtag #boycottboohoo on social media, this subsided as the firm was able to ensure its products were endorsed by key fast fashion influencers on Instagram and YouTube, notably Chandra and Sydney Crouch (Armitage, 2020a). The firm was actually able to raise forecasts of sales and profits from that predicted in early 2020.

Equally, despite the rapid sell-off of the firms' stock, the share price rapidly rose to nearly completely recover the losses by the time the Levitt report was released. The publication triggered another fall, but by the end of 2020 the firm's share price had still risen by over 6 per cent over the year (compared to a drop of about 12.5 per cent for the FTSE100 Index). Some analysts were predicting that the stock would rise strongly in the following year, on the basis that the publication of the report would enable the firm to put the reputational issues behind them (Oscroft, 2020).

The Levitt report makes it clear that many senior managers in the organization did not consider the working conditions in the supply base to be of much interest – Levitt is clear that she is shocked by the attitude taken by some. She concludes that commercial concerns 'were prioritized in a way which made substantial areas of risk all but invisible at the most senior level'.

In terms of civil society, the Boohoo story suggests some important conclusions. Firstly, the persistent coverage of the Leicester supply base by journalists over a 10-year period eventually allowed the *Sunday Times* story to have substantial impact; it is unlikely that the paper would have run with the story were it not building on the previous investigations by the *Financial Times* and Channel 4 in the years before. However, it is interesting to note that other fast fashion chains also operate from Leicester, and the focus on Boohoo may give those other firms a degree of 'cover'. It may be the exhaustive coverage of Boohoo will have now 'exhausted' the media's appetite for similar stories, making it more difficult for NGOs to gain traction with further campaigns on the same issues. It is also salutary to note that the chairman of the firm, when repeatedly challenged by MPs at the December select committee meeting, refused to engage in any way with trade unions to discuss the situation in Leicester.[19]

But perhaps the most telling conclusion about the role of civil society that emerges from the Boohoo story is unequivocal proof that the glossy statements made by the firm (for example in the Modern Slavery Statements for 2018 and 2019) about their scrutiny of the supply base were unreliable. Many cynical readers of these statements might suspect that the truth is often stretched by companies in these declarations; the literature refers to the idea of what is euphemistically called 'decoupling' between firms' statements and actions (Boxenbaum and Jonsson, 2008; Bromley and Powell, 2012), and the use of 'aspirational' language (Christensen *et al*, 2013). The Levitt report is interesting because it does not shy away from pointing out this dishonesty; it is difficult to imagine an academic research project which would either have sufficient access to a company's operations to come to the conclusion, or a mandate which allowed publication without censorship from the organization. This finding casts significant doubt on the value of civil society activity which focuses on merely summarizing or comparing the statements and policies generated by firms. The case shows that these cannot be taken at face value. It also shows that a firm's dishonesty can be broadcast widely – and even posted on its own website (as Boohoo have done with the Levitt report) and not face serious long-term commercial harm.

Analysing the Boohoo case: power and culpability?

The Levitt report provides a vivid explanation of how Boohoo's buying practices led the firm to be ruthless in reducing the prices paid to supplying firms. The pattern of operation intrinsic to the firm's fast fashion model was driven by three elements which contributed to the abuses in Leicester.

The first of these is that the fast fashion model used by the firm relied on small quantities of clothes under a system known in the firm as 'Test and Repeat' (Sullivan, 2017; MacDonald, 2018) in which small quantities (fewer than 300 items) would be designed, manufactured and available for sale in as fast as two weeks (with an average of between four to six weeks); this compared with approximately five weeks for fast fashion pioneer Zara. If successful, more repeat orders could follow. These small, urgent batches were suitable for small production facilities – so-called CMT units ('cut, make and trim') – with as few as 10 employees. The lack of continuity for these second-tier suppliers meant they were kept eager for new work.

The second element of the model was that the allocation of work to suppliers was done largely by buyers who were not equipped to make judgements about the actual costs of manufacturing, but who were socialized to relentlessly drive down prices. Suppliers would be forced to underbid one another in what one supplier described as 'a cattle market': 'It's ruthless' (O'Connor, 2018). Levitt (2020, p 98) notes that:

> There seemed to be little or no recognition at board level of the danger that Boohoo's predominant place in the Leicester clothing industry meant that this may not be a free negotiation.

The final element in the model arose from the chaotic processes for administration in the firm in terms of keeping track of subcontracting between suppliers; although formally a system of approval was needed before work was allocated, the speed of the business meant that this could not work properly, and standards of record keeping were too low to enable a systematic approach.

Levitt's report is fascinating not just for its rigour, but also the vivid picture it paints of the attitudes of senior managers in the firm. She states (p 210):

> ...the fundamental allegations made in the articles are plainly true, that is to say, that much of the time, Boohoo has simply no idea where its clothes are being made and thus has no chance of monitoring the conditions of the workers who make them.

She adds that, in relation to where the clothes that featured in the *Sunday Times* article were made (p 212): 'They did not know and did not really care.' Also striking is the report's account of the defensiveness and air of denial of some senior people in the organization; this tone is strongly echoed in Mahmud Kamani's performance at the meeting of the parliamentary Environmental Audit Committee on 16 December 2020.[20] In both cases, it is easy to see the main features of the 'neutralization techniques' (Ball, 1966) that are used by criminals to explain or justify their actions: 1) the denial of responsibility; 2) the denial of injury; 3) the denial of the victim; 4) the condemnation of the condemners; and 5) the appeal to higher loyalties (in this case, the support for 'British manufacturing').

It is interesting to note a slight disjuncture between the wording in Levitt's summary and the grisly detail of the full report. Despite the information given in the report, Levitt (p 224) concludes that:

> I am satisfied that Boohoo did not deliberately allow poor conditions and low pay to exist within its supply chain, nor did it intentionally profit from them. I do not accept that Boohoo's business model is founded on exploiting workers in Leicester.

Figure 16.1   Subjectively locating Levitt's (2020) conclusions (A) and content of report (B)

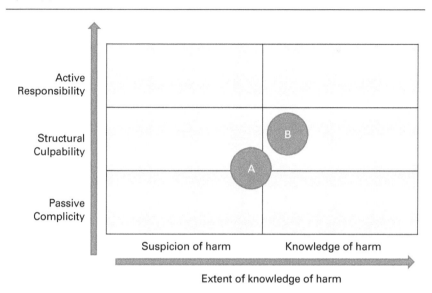

In terms of the model presented in Figure 16.1, how should we classify the Boohoo case? Although the initial diagram was presented as a categorical table, if it is reinterpreted as a crude interval scale, then this places Levitt's conclusion (in the current author's judgement) somewhere around the zone marked A on Figure 16.1. However, if the full meat of the report is taken into account, it could be argued that the region marked B would be more appropriate. In either case, it is clear that there are elements of structural culpability in this story. Furthermore, it seems likely that the lack of visibility that Boohoo had over its supply chain was a design feature and not an accidental flaw.

It is interesting to note that subsequent to the report, at the end of 2020, further allegations were made about Boohoo's sourcing in Pakistan (Bland *et al*, 2020; Chua, 2020). In this case the media coverage was slight, and there appears to be no prospect of anything similar to the Levitt report to address the international supply base.

Concluding comments

This chapter has presented a brief overview of a number of key issues in the field of supply chain ethics. It is instructive that even a discussion of this length can do little more than scratch the surface of the subject. Particular attention has been given to the drivers for supply chain ethics and the nature of responsibility of buyers, and these issues illustrated with reference to the Boohoo case.

There are three final observations that are worth pulling out of the current discussion that serve as recommendations for future research. Firstly, it is worth noting that the extensive body of research relevant to supply chain would benefit from more work which sought to span the disciplinary silos sketched out earlier (Table 16.1).

Secondly, the current discussion makes clear that there is a need for explicitly addressing the ethical/philosophical issues that underpin the idea of supply chain ethics. In moral philosophy, it is common to use little paradigmatic devices or illustrations to try to guide reasoning (for example, Butt, 2007); however, supply chain relations have distinctive features that are not easy to capture in this way, and so ethical reasoning needs to be more grounded in specific examples.

Finally, this chapter has highlighted the extraordinary value of an independent review of the detail of a firm's operations that is produced without the need for either clearance by the firm concerned or without the need for retaining the firm's favour. Perhaps a crucial element in the progress of research in supply chain ethics is finding a way for academics to speak and write with greater candour about specific organizations.

Notes

1 Levitt (2020:9)
2 House of Commons Environmental Audit Committee (2020). *Oral evidence: Fixing Fashion: follow-up, HC 874*, 16 December, committees.parliament.uk/oralevidence/1442/pdf/ (archived at https://perma.cc/7T6X-GYAB); House of Commons Business, Energy and Industrial Strategy Committee (2020). *Oral evidence: Forced labour in UK value chains, HC 890*, 5 November, committees.parliament.uk/oralevidence/1161/pdf/ (archived at https://perma.cc/EBA9-ZJ7E)
3 Intel Corporation (2010) *2010 Corporate Responsibility Report*, www.compromisorse.com/upload/estudios/000/143/CSR2010.pdf; (archived at https://perma.cc/RY4N-A5GZ) Intel Corporation (2020) *2019–2020 Report: Corporate Responsibility at Intel*, csrreportbuilder.intel.com/pdfbuilder/pdfs/CSR-2019-20-Full-Report.pdf (archived at https://perma.cc/VHQ4-DT5S)
4 home.kpmg/uk/en/home/insights/2020/08/ethical-supply-chain.html; www2.deloitte.com/uk/en/pages/risk/solutions/ethical-value-chain.html (archived at https://perma.cc/735V-5VRL)

5 ulula.com/home/ (archived at https://perma.cc/49KY-3GJX)

6 www.provenance.org/ (archived at https://perma.cc/QLK9-RDB3)

7 scg-scmr.s3.amazonaws.com/pdfs/SCMR1811_Ethical%20Supply%20 Chain_SCMR_APICS%202018.pdf (archived at https://perma.cc/G6SR-EEM4)

8 Kitson and Campbell (1996) comment that '…maintaining a strict ethical stance can be important in projecting the right image of the company.'

9 Beckert, S (2014) *Empire of Cotton: A Global History*, Vintage, New York, NY

10 Lopez-Acevedo, G and Robertson, R (2012) (eds) *Sewing Success? Employment, Wages, and Poverty following the End of the Multi-fibre Arrangement*, World Bank, Washington, DC

11 Rivoli, P (2005) *The Travels of T-Shirt in the Global Economy*, Wiley, New York; Bennett, J (2008) *Where Underpants Come From*, Pocket Books, London; Brooks, A (2015) *Clothing Poverty: The hidden world of fast fashion and second-hand clothes*, Zed Books, London; Thomas, D (2019) *Fashionopolis: The price of fast fashion and the future of clothes*, Head of Zeus, London.

12 RCGD (2020) *Seven organisations working to improve labour conditions in fashion amid the covid-19 crisis*, 17 April, www.rcgdglobal.com/2020/04/17/7-ngos-working-to-improve-labour-conditions-in-fashion-amid-the-covid-19-crisis/ (archived at https://perma.cc/6GAJ-P3F3); Doyle, M (2018) *Five sustainability groups reshaping fashion*, 15 August, www.ordre.com/en/news/sustainable-fashion-textiles-ngos-589 (archived at https://perma.cc/34AS-QJPD)

13 Adjusting for general inflation (using the consumer price index), the UK cost of clothing in 2020 dropped to just over 30% the 1991 level, although this number is very difficult to estimate as the clothing bought shifts with demography, consumer taste and clothing technology, www.statista.com/statistics/285120/clothing-and-footwear-cpi-uk (archived at https://perma.cc/E37P-4U7Y)

14 Boohoo Group plc 2020 annual report, www.boohooplc.com/investors/results-centre/year/2020 (archived at https://perma.cc/2UFZ-V8GE)

15 www.channel4.com/press/news/dispatches-fashions-dirty-secret (archived at https://perma.cc/986F-5L8B)

16 www.channel4.com/press/news/undercover-britains-cheap-clothes-channel-4-dispatches-mon-30th-jan (archived at https://perma.cc/RSN2-QPL4)

17 www.investegate.co.uk/boohoo-group-plc--boo-/rns/response-to-media-commentary/202007060700060571S/ (archived at https://perma.cc/8HJA-S3M9)

18 House of Commons Environmental Audit Committee (2018), Environmental Audit Committee, *Oral evidence: Sustainability of the fashion industry*, *HC 1148*, 27th November, data.parliament.uk/writtenevidence/committeeevidence.svc/evidencedocument/environmental-audit-committee/sustainability-of-the-fashion-industry/oral/93123.html

19 House of Commons Environmental Audit Committee (2020, *Oral evidence: Fixing Fashion: follow-up, HC 874*, 16 December 2020, committees. parliament.uk/oralevidence/1442/pdf/

20 House of Commons Environmental Audit Committee (2020). *Oral evidence: Fixing Fashion: follow-up, HC 874,*16 December 2020, committees.parliament. uk/oralevidence/1442/pdf/

References

Amaeshi, KM, Osuji, OK and Nnodim, P (2008) Corporate social responsibility in supply chains of global brands: A boundaryless responsibility? Clarifications, exceptions and implications, *Journal of Business Ethics*, **81** (1), pp 223–34

Armitage, J (2020a) Boohoo bounces back from scandal as cash-strapped influencers keep plugging its brands, *Evening Standard*, 5 August, www.standard.co.uk/business/boohoo-prettylittlething-nasty-gal-influencers-scandal-a4517411.html (archived at https://perma.cc/MM4W-JFAQ)

Armitage, J (2020b) Boohoo's founder-chairman Mahmud Kamani has to quit after scathing report on Leicester scandal, *Evening Standard*, 25 September, www.standard.co.uk/business/boohoo-prettylittlething-khamani-leicester-slavery-a4556306.html (archived at https://perma.cc/62CM-8B2W)

Aßländer, MS, Roloff, J and Nayır, DZ (2016) Suppliers as stewards? Managing social standards in first-and second-tier suppliers, *Journal of Business Ethics*, **139** (4), pp 661–83

Ball, RA (1966) An empirical exploration of neutralization theory, *Criminologica*, **4** (2), pp 22–32

Bassen, A and Kovács, AM (2008) Environmental, social and governance key performance indicators from a capital market perspective, *Zeitschrift für Wirtschafts und Unternehmensethik*, **9** (2), pp 182–92

BBC (2019) Textile sector 'rife' with exploitation and underpayment, 25 January, www.bbc.co.uk/news/business-46992499 (archived at https://perma.cc/MB7G-LXUU)

Berlan, A (2013) Social sustainability in agriculture: An anthropological perspective on child labour in cocoa production in Ghana, *The Journal of Development Studies*, **49** (8), pp 1088–100

Bland, A and Makortoff, K (2020) Boohoo knew of Leicester factory failings, says report, *The Guardian*, 25 September, www.theguardian.com/business/2020/sep/25/boohoo-report-reveals-factory-fire-risk-among-supply-chain-failings (archived at https://perma.cc/G3TN-Y234)

Bland, A, Baloch, SM and Kelly, A (2020) Boohoo selling clothes made by Pakistani workers 'who earned 29p an hour', *The Guardian*, 22 December, www.theguardian.com/business/2020/dec/22/boohoo-selling-clothes-made-by-pakistani-workers-who-earned-29p-an-hour (archived at https://perma.cc/8CVP-TPTC)

Boersma, M (2014) Global supply chains link us all to shame of child and forced labour, *The Conversation*, 30 October, theconversation.com/global-supply-chains-link-us-all-to-shame-of-child-and-forced-labour-33593 (archived at https://perma.cc/3G2F-QUL7)

Boxenbaum, E and Jonsson, S (2008) Isomorphism, diffusion, and decoupling, in *The Sage Handbook of Organizational Institutionalism*, eds R Greenwood, C Oliver, K Sahlin and R Suddaby, pp 299–323, Sage, London

Bracchi, P (2020) Leicester's fast fashion to die for: Cramped ragtrade workshops in the pariah city where staff on as little as £4 an hour reveal they dare not go home if they have Covid symptoms... is this the REAL reason it's been quarantined? *Daily Mail*, 4 July, www.dailymail.co.uk/news/article-8488859/Leicesters-fast-fashion-die-Cramped-ragtrade-workshops-pariah-city.html (archived at https://perma.cc/9VN8-3JK7)

Bray, J, Johns, N and Kilburn, D (2011) An exploratory study into the factors impeding ethical consumption, *Journal of Business Ethics*, **98** (4), pp 597–608

Bromley, P and Powell, WW (2012) From smoke and mirrors to walking the talk: Decoupling in the contemporary world, *Academy of Management Annals*, **6**, pp 483–530

Buchanan, A and Rogers, C (2020) ESG-related supply chain issues, Linklaters, 5 August, www.linklaters.com/en/insights/blogs/linkingesg/2020/august/esg-related-supply-chain-issues (archived at https://perma.cc/6PAZ-ECGN)

Butt, D (2007) On benefiting from injustice, *Canadian Journal of Philosophy*, **37** (1), pp 129–52

Chatzidakis, A, Hibbert, S and Smith, AP (2007) Why people don't take their concerns about fair trade to the supermarket: The role of neutralisation, *Journal of Business Ethics*, **74** (1), pp 89–100

Christensen, LT, Morsing, M and Thyssen, O (2013) CSR as aspirational talk, *Organization*, **20** (3), pp 372–93

Chua, JM (2020) 'I would run out of the factory if I saw this,' auditor says of Boohoo investigation, *Sourcing Journal*, 22 December, sourcingjournal.com/topics/labor/boohoo-pakistan-garment-factory-minimum-wage-fire-safety-auditor-252297/ (archived at https://perma.cc/UP23-LJJW)

Coe, NM and Yeung, HW-C (2015) *Global Production Networks: Theorizing economic development in an interconnected world*, Oxford University Press, Oxford

Cranmer, L and New, SJ (2012) Managing Supply Chain Risk: Reputational–Ethical–Environmental–Legal, Saïd Business School, Working Paper, RP 2018-04

Cullen, H (2016) The irresistible rise of human rights due diligence: Conflict minerals and beyond, *George Washington International Law Review*, **48** (4), pp 743–80

Davies, R (2020) Boohoo co-founder Jalal Kamani linked to Leicester garment factory, *The Guardian*, 10 June, www.theguardian.com/business/2020/

jul/10/boohoo-co-founder-jalal-kamani-linked-to-leicester-garment-factory (archived at https://perma.cc/GZ6B-BZ4G)

Davis, N (2020) Fast fashion speeding toward environmental disaster, report warns, *The Guardian*, 7 April, www.theguardian.com/fashion/2020/apr/07/fast-fashion-speeding-toward-environmental-disaster-report-warns (archived at https://perma.cc/MHU7-KRBV)

Distelhorst, G, Hainmueller, J and Locke, RM (2017) Does lean improve labor standards? Management and social performance in the Nike supply chain, *Management Science*, **63** (3), pp 707–28

EAC (2019) *Fixing Fashion: Clothing consumption and sustainability*, House of Commons Environmental Audit Committee, London, publications.parliament.uk/pa/cm201719/cmselect/cmenvaud/1952/1952.pdf (archived at https://perma.cc/PV9K-JUXL)

Eckhardt, GM, Belk, R and Devinney, TM (2010) Why don't consumers consume ethically?, *Journal of Consumer Behaviour*, **9** (6), pp 426–36

Ferdows, K, Lewis, MA and Machuca, JA (2005) Zara's secret for fast fashion, *Harvard Business Review*, **82** (11), pp 98–111

Garside, J (2012) Apple's efforts fail to end gruelling conditions at Foxconn factories, *The Guardian*, 30 May, www.theguardian.com/technology/2012/may/30/foxconn-abuses-despite-apple-reforms (archived at https://perma.cc/3LWV-395E)

Gereffi, G (2019) *Global Value Chains and Development: Redefining the contours of 21st century capitalism*, Cambridge University Press, Cambridge

Gereffi, G and Lee, J (2016) Economic and social upgrading in global value chains and industrial clusters: Why governance matters, *Journal of Business Ethics*, **133** (1), pp 25–38

Gimenez, C and Tachizawa, EM (2012) Extending sustainability to suppliers: A systematic literature review, *Supply Chain Management*, **17** (5), pp 531–43

Ginet, C (2000) The epistemic requirements for moral responsibility, *Philosophical Perspectives*, **14**, pp 267–277

Girling, W (2020) Responsibly sourced supply chains can benefit everyone, *Supply Chain Digital*, 30 June, www.supplychaindigital.com/procurement/responsibly-sourced-supply-chains-can-benefit-everyone (archived at https://perma.cc/6CNP-5QNR)

Govindan, K, Shaw, M and Majumdar, A (2020) Social sustainability tensions in multi-tier supply chain: A systematic literature review towards conceptual framework development, *Journal of Cleaner Production*, in press, doi.org/10.1016/j.jclepro.2020.123075 (archived at https://perma.cc/P6GJ-94WH)

Ha-Brookshire, J (2017) Toward moral responsibility theories of corporate sustainability and sustainable supply chain, *Journal of Business Ethics*, **145** (2), pp 227–37

Hammer, N, Plugor, R, Nolan, P and Clark, I (2015) *New Industry on a Skewed Playing Field: Supply chain relations and working conditions in UK garment*

manufacturing focus area – Leicester and the East Midlands, Centre for
Sustainable Work and Employment Futures, University of Leicester, Leicester

Hartmann, J and Moeller, S (2014) Chain liability in multitier supply chains?
Responsibility attributions for unsustainable supplier behavior, *Journal of
Operations Management*, 32 (5), pp 281–94

Heighton-Ginns, L and Prescott, K (2019) Leicester: A city fighting fast-fashion
sweatshops, BBC News, 10 May, www.bbc.co.uk/news/business-48226187
(archived at https://perma.cc/M5P6-7RWM)

Hess, D (2019) The transparency trap: Non-financial disclosure and the
responsibility of business to respect human rights, *American Business Law
Journal*, 56 (1), pp 5–53

Hirschman, AO (1970) *Exit, Voice, and Loyalty: Responses to decline in firms,
organizations, and states*, Harvard University Press, Cambridge, MA

Hoejmose, SU, Grosvold, J and Millington, A (2013) Socially responsible supply
chains: Power asymmetries and joint dependence, *Supply Chain Management:
An International Journal*, 18 (3), pp 277–91

Hsin, L, New, SJ, Pietropaoli, I and Smit, L (2021) Accountability, monitoring
and the effectiveness of section 54 of the Modern Slavery Act: Evidence and
comparative analysis, Modern Slavery Policy and Evidence Centre, London

Jacobs, K, Petersen, L, Hörisch, J and Battenfeld, D (2018) Green thinking but
thoughtless buying? An empirical extension of the value-attitude-behaviour
hierarchy in sustainable clothing, *Journal of Cleaner Production*, 203,
pp 1155–169

Kelly, A (2020) 'Virtually entire' fashion industry complicit in Uighur forced
labour, say rights groups, *The Guardian*, 23 July, www.theguardian.com/
global-development/2020/jul/23/virtually-entire-fashion-industry-complicit-
in-uighur-forced-labour-say-rights-groups-china (archived at https://perma.cc/
SZ3P-KDW6)

Kingston, ED (2019) Bad Goods: On the political morality of production and
consumption in global supply chains, Doctoral dissertation, Duke University,
Durham, NC

Kitson, A and Campbell, R (1996) *The Ethical Organisation*, pp 185–94, Palgrave,
London

Klassen, R and Vereecke, A (2012) Social issues in supply chains: Capabilities link
responsibility, risk (opportunity), and performance, *International Journal of
Production Economics*, 140 (1), pp 103–15

Koberg, E and Longoni, A (2019) A systematic review of sustainable supply chain
management in global supply chains, *Journal of Cleaner Production*, 207,
pp 1084–98

Köksal, D, Strähle, J, Müller, M and Freise, M (2017) Social sustainable supply
chain management in the textile and apparel industry: A literature review,
Sustainability, 9 (1), doi:10.3390/su9010100

Labour Behind the Label (2020) Boohoo & Covid-19, Labour Behind the Label, Bristol, labourbehindthelabel.net/wp-content/uploads/2020/06/LBL-Boohoo-WEB.pdf

Landau, I (2019) Human rights due diligence and the risk of cosmetic compliance, *Melbourne Journal of International Law*, **20**, pp 221–47

Laville, S (2019) The story of a £4 Boohoo dress: Cheap clothes at a high cost, *The Guardian*, 22 June, www.theguardian.com/business/2019/jun/22/cost-cheap-fast-fashion-workers-planet (archived at https://perma.cc/3X4Z-JZ68)

LeBaron, G (2020) *Combatting Modern Slavery: Why labour governance is failing and what we can do about it*, Polity, London

Levitt, A (2020) Independent Review into the Boohoo Group PLC's Leicester Supply Chain, 24 September, www.boohooplc.com/sites/boohoo-corp/files/final-report-open-version-24.9.2020.pdf (archived at https://perma.cc/7PLN-VUED)

Linton, JD, Klassen, R and Jayaraman, V (2007) Sustainable supply chains: An introduction, *Journal of Operations Management*, **25** (6), pp 1075–082

Locke, RM (2013) *The Promise and Limits of Private Power: Promoting labor standards in a global economy (Cambridge Studies in Comparative Politics)*, Cambridge University Press, Cambridge

MacCarthy, B and Jayarathne, P (2010) Fast fashion: Achieving global quick response (GQR) in the internationally dispersed clothing industry, in *Innovative Quick Response Programs in Logistics and Supply Chain Management*, pp 37–60, eds TCE Cheng and T Choi, Springer-Verlag, Heidelberg

MacDonald, N (2018) 'Test and repeat' a supply chain success story for Boohoo.com, LinkedIn News, 27 April, www.linkedin.com/pulse/test-repeat-supply-chain-success-story-boohoocom-natalie-macdonald (archived at https://perma.cc/VD5Y-ZDYD)

Montiel, I (2008) Corporate social responsibility and corporate sustainability: Separate pasts, common futures, *Organization & Environment*, **21** (3), pp 245–69

Nakamba, CC, Chan, PW and Sharmina, M (2017) How does social sustainability feature in studies of supply chain management? A review and research agenda, *Supply Chain Management*, **22** (6), pp 522–41

Nazir, S (2020) Boohoo Group profits surge despite 'most challenging time', *Retail Gazette*, 30 September, www.retailgazette.co.uk/blog/2020/09/boohoo-group-profits-surge-despite-most-challenging-time/ (archived at https://perma.cc/2RZU-8Y3Z)

Neef, D (2004) *The Supply Chain Imperative: How to ensure ethical behavior in your global suppliers*, Amacom, New York

New, SJ (2004) The ethical supply chain, in *Understanding Supply Chains: Concepts, critiques and futures*, eds SJ New and R Westbrook, pp 253–80, Oxford University Press, Oxford

New, SJ (2010) The transparent supply chain, *Harvard Business Review*, **88**, pp 1–5

New, SJ (2015) Modern slavery and the supply chain: The limits of corporate social responsibility, *Supply Chain Management: An International Journal*, 20 (6), pp 697–707

New, SJ (2021) Modern slavery and supply chain transparency, in *The Oxford Handbook of Supply Chain Management*, eds TY Choi, JJ Li, DS Rogers, T Schoenherr and SM Wagner, in press, Oxford University Press, Oxford

New, SJ and Hsin, L (2021) *Deconstructing Modern Slavery Statements: A detailed analysis of Arcadia Group and Babcock International*, Working Paper

New, SJ, Green, K and Morton, B (2000a) Deconstructing green supply and demand: PVC, healthcare and the environment, *Risk, Decision and Policy*, 4 (3), pp 221–54

New, SJ, Green, K and Morton, B (2000b) Buying the environment: The multiple meanings of green supply, in *The Business of Greening*, ed S Fineman, pp 35–53, Routledge, London

Nicholls, A and Lee, N (2006) Purchase decision-making in fair trade and the ethical purchase 'gap': Is there a fair trade 'Twix'? *Journal of Strategic Marketing*, 14 (4), pp 369–86

Nolan, J and Bott, G (2018) Global supply chains and human rights: Spotlight on forced labour and modern slavery practices, *Australian Journal of Human Rights*, 24 (1), pp 44–69

O'Connor, S (2018) Dark factories: Labour exploitation in Britain's garment industry, *Financial Times*, 17 May, www.ft.com/content/e427327e-5892-11e8-b8b2-d6ceb45fa9d0 (archived at https://perma.cc/ZQT8-Q2SC)

Oscroft, A (2020) Why I think the Boohoo share price could double in 2021, The Motley Fool, 18 December, www.fool.co.uk/investing/2020/12/18/why-i-think-the-boohoo-share-price-could-double-in-2021/ (archived at https://perma.cc/HT52-EL3Y)

Pedersen, ER and Andersen, M (2006) Safeguarding corporate social responsibility (CSR) in global supply chains: How codes of conduct are managed in buyer–supplier relationships, *Journal of Public Affairs: An International Journal*, 6 (3–4), pp 228–40

Picot, N (2019) *The State of Compliance 2019*, Assent Compliance USA Ltd, Columbus, OH, www.assentcompliance.com/stateofcompliance/ (archived at https://perma.cc/2MYN-D2BH)

Poh, J (2019) Conflicting ESG ratings are confusing sustainable investors, *Bloomberg*, 11 December, www.bloomberg.com/news/articles/2019-12-11/conflicting-esg-ratings-are-confusing-sustainable-investors (archived at https://perma.cc/Q4D9-TWMK)

Powell, J (2020) Boohoo's Levitt report: The highlights, *Financial Times*, 28 October, www.ft.com/content/a450acb0-7c8b-4b98-b77e-a1df4d52574b (archived at https://perma.cc/758Q-9SCT)

Reimers, V, Magnuson, B and Chao, F (2016) The academic conceptualisation of ethical clothing: Could it account for the attitude behaviour gap?, *Journal of Fashion Marketing and Management*, 20, pp 383–99

Schwartz, SH (1994) Are there universal aspects in the structure and contents of human values?, *Journal of Social Issues*, **50**, pp 19–45

Sendlhofer, T (2019) Decoupling from moral responsibility for CSR: Employees' visionary procrastination at a SME, *Journal of Business Ethics*, **167** (2), pp 361–78

Seuring, S, and Müller, M (2008) From a literature review to a conceptual framework for sustainable supply chain management, *Journal of Cleaner Production*, **16** (15), pp 1699–710

Shamir, R (2008) The age of responsibilization: On market-embedded morality, *Economy and Society*, **37** (1), pp 1–19

Soderstrom, S and Weber, K (2020) Organizational structure from interaction: Evidence from corporate sustainability efforts, *Administrative Science Quarterly*, **65** (1), pp 226–71

Sodhi, MS and Tang, CS (2018) Corporate social sustainability in supply chains: A thematic analysis of the literature, *International Journal of Production Research*, **56** (1–2), pp 882–901

Starr, WC (1983) Law and morality in HLA Hart's legal philosophy, *Marquette Law Review*, **67**, pp 673–90

Sullivan, C (2017) Boohoo business model pushes fast fashion to step up a gear, *Financial Times*, 22 May, www.ft.com/content/f1a24648-3a19-11e7-ac89-b01cc67cfeec (archived at https://perma.cc/7YQG-JKN6)

Tachizawa, ME and Wong, CY (2014) Towards a theory of multi-tier sustainable supply chains: A systematic literature review, *Supply Chain Management*, **19** (5–6), pp 643–63

Thamotheram, R (2012) Finance failure and the weakness in the system: The inside view, *The Guardian*, 26 November, www.theguardian.com/sustainable-business/blog/inside-finance-system-failure-sustainable-investment (archived at https://perma.cc/AAR4-YTZ4)

Toms, S and Zhang, Q (2016) Marks & Spencer and the decline of the British textile industry 1950–2000, *Business History Review*, **90** (1), pp 3–30

Villena, VH and Gioia, DA (2020) A more sustainable supply chain, *Harvard Business Review*, March–April, **98** (2), pp 84–93

Vogel, D (2010) The private regulation of global corporate conduct: Achievements and limitations, *Business & Society*, **49** (1), pp 68–87

Wilhelm, MM, Blome, C, Bhakoo, V and Paulraj, A (2016) Sustainability in multi-tier supply chains: Understanding the double agency role of the first-tier supplier, *Journal of Operations Management*, **41**, pp 42–60

Williamson, OE (2008) Outsourcing: Transaction cost economics and supply chain management, *Journal of Supply Chain Management*, **44** (2), pp 5–16

Yawar, SA and Seuring, S (2017) Management of social issues in supply chains: A literature review exploring social issues, actions and performance outcomes, *Journal of Business Ethics*, **141** (3), pp 621–43

Zhang, M, Pawar, KS and Bhardwaj, S (2017) Improving supply chain social responsibility through supplier development, *Production Planning & Control*, **28** (6–8), pp 500–11

Zhang, Z, Guan, D, Wang, R, Meng, J, Zheng, H, Zhu, K and Du, H (2020) Embodied carbon emissions in the supply chains of multinational enterprises, *Nature Climate Change*, **10** (12), pp 1096–101

Zimmerman, M (2008) Ignorance and responsibility, in *Living with Uncertainty: The moral significance of ignorance (Cambridge Studies in Philosophy)*, pp 169–205, Cambridge University Press, Cambridge

Humanitarian logistics and supply chain management

17

Yasmine Sabri

Introduction

The world is experiencing extraordinary developments in relation to the coronavirus global health emergency which has affected nearly 80 million worldwide.[1] It has disrupted supply flows and demand patterns,[2] and was preceded by a decade[3] of armed conflicts that led to soaring numbers of displaced populations – to an unprecedented level of 79.5 million uprooted people – with critical humanitarian needs.[4] The world is also dealing with an increasing number of man-made and natural disasters, and a global hunger epidemic that affected nearly 821 million in 2018 (one in every nine people).[5] These developments have uncovered an acute need for coordinating the efforts of all stakeholders in the humanitarian arena – to come together and face these global challenges united. Humanitarian logistics and supply chain management, as a relatively nascent field of study, was developed to respond to humanitarian needs and to help alleviate human suffering. As such, it deals with uncertainty on both the supply and demand sides of the supply chain. The central idea behind humanitarian logistics and supply chain management is to avoid taking desperate measures in desperate times. It is rather the contrary, ie in times of crisis supply chains need to be well prepared and positioned for immediate response. Hence, the management of humanitarian supply chains should enhance prevention, improve response and recovery, and use mitigation as a strategy for better preparedness. In this chapter, I discuss the importance of humanitarian logistics and supply chains, strategies for managing humanitarian logistics and the need for resilience. In the same context, I discuss the design and management of the Covid-19 supply chain system as this has become the most pertinent humanitarian crisis at the present time.

The significance of humanitarian logistics and supply chain management

The multilateral efforts in managing supply chains in humanitarian situations were crowned by the award of the Noble Peace Prize for 2020 to the United Nations World Food Programme (WFP), which is the lead agency for the UN Logistics Cluster and considered by many as the key humanitarian supply chain actor (Logistics Cluster, 2019). Though humanitarian logistics and supply chain management account for 60 to 80 per cent of the total expenditure of humanitarian aid agencies worldwide (Lacourt and Radosta, 2019), the important role of supply chains in the humanitarian context has only attracted attention quite recently as a result of the aftermath of Asian tsunamis in 2004, followed by Hurricane Katrina in the United States in 2005 (Altay and Green, 2006; Kovács and Spens, 2007). In the past two decades, many researchers have warned about the increasing trend of disasters (see, for example: Altay and Green, 2006; Kovács and Spens, 2007; Pettit and Beresford, 2009; Christopher and Tatham, 2011). This was recently echoed by the United Nations High Commissioner for Refugees (UNHCR), which warned that the magnitude and frequency of disasters, particularly those that are man-made, are increasing to unprecedented levels (Grandi, 2016). The implications of catastrophes and disasters underline the significance of humanitarian logistics and supply chain management in delivering aid to beneficiaries in affected locations. According to the Nobel Prize website, the Prize motivation was 'for its [WFP] efforts to combat hunger, for its contribution to bettering conditions for peace in conflict-affected areas and for acting as a driving force in efforts to prevent the use of hunger as a weapon of war and conflict' (Nobel Prize, 2020). Humanitarian supply chains help alleviate human suffering (Wagner, 2020) through the provision of water and energy supply, food, shelter and medicines to affected communities once a disaster strikes (Christopher and Tatham, 2011).

Contrary to corporate for-profit supply chains, humanitarian supply chains are organized in such a way as to: satisfy the demand of beneficiaries in locations affected by man-made or natural disasters (Blanco and Goentzel 2006), with an objective to respond immediately after a disaster strikes; and, to save human life and help people survive the massive impact of disasters (Behl and Dutta, 2018; Wagner, 2020). These supply chains comprise a network of actors and involved parties, and extend to include local and central governments, military, media, aid agencies, supply chain personnel, international humanitarian organizations, international and local non-governmental organizations, as well as the donors, affected communities and the individual beneficiaries (Van Wassenhove, 2006; Kovács and Spens, 2007). Collectively, these actors are responsible for managing the humanitarian supply chain efficiently and effectively to ensure rapid delivery of supplies from point of origin (or donors) to affected locations (Kunz and Riner, 2012).

The idiosyncrasy of humanitarian supply chains is the high uncertainty of both supply and demand. A closer look at the design and operations of humanitarian logistics and supply chains will result in finding a number of similarities with corporate operations (Christopher and Tatham, 2011). For example, the concept of managing physical, information and financial supply chain flows is common between these supply chains (Kovács and Spens, 2007). The differences can be internal and external to the supply chain. Internal differences are related to objectives and strategy: whilst humanitarian supply chains seek to help maintain human life and alleviate the suffering of affected communities who are not involved in economic transactions, corporate ones seek to add value to a customer after a financial transaction has been made by the customer. As such, humanitarian supply chains do not have the luxury of losing the effectiveness focus because, in these contexts, time and service levels usually mean saving lives. Other internal differences relate to the uneven contribution of all the actors to the value creation process in humanitarian supply chains, where many actors are not directly involved in satisfying demand and others may have different motivations to continue in the supply chain (Kovács and Spens, 2007). Further internal differences relate to supply and demand management processes. In humanitarian supply chains, the end-user (beneficiary) is not usually the entity who places the purchase order or its specifications; in many instances the actual beneficiaries of the aid have no choice in specifying the demand (Kovács and Spens, 2007). Furthermore, the demand specifications and volumes vary significantly depending on the various disaster characteristics, as well as those of the affected location. Hence the supply network needs continuous updating, including management of the addition of new suppliers when needed, which may have adverse effects on supply chain inter-organizational relationships. Whilst there are multiple differences between corporate and humanitarian supply chains, the striking difference is in fact an external one, in which the operations of humanitarian supply chains oftentimes take place in locations with destabilized infrastructure where there is lack of proper communication or road networks, and in armed conflict zones where there are serious safety and security concerns (Jahre *et al*, 2012; ICRC, 2016 and 2020).

Humanitarian logistics and supply chains phases

The USA Federal Emergency Management Agency (FEMA, 2006) conceptualizes disaster management as a group of interrelated and partly overlapping activities including prevention, preparedness, response, recovery and mitigation. As a type of supply chain that is usually triggered in response to man-made and natural disasters, humanitarian supply chains usually comprise all the efforts in disaster relief operations (Altay, 2008). Figure 17.1 demonstrates the four phases of a humanitarian supply chain based on Altay and Green (2006), Kovács and Spens (2007) and Behl and Dutta (2018). This four-phase approach is rooted in the concepts of emergency management, risk management and the disaster management life cycle (Altay and Green, 2006) and roughly corresponds to pre-disaster phase (preparedness), operations phase (response), and post-disaster phase (recovery and mitigation) (Behl and Dutta, 2018).

Preparedness

The preparedness phase is vital for preparing communities and personnel for rapid response, and is particularly important in disaster-prone locations.[6] It is concerned with training and recruitment of personnel, prepositioning of critical supplies, developing proper communication and information sharing strategies, enhancing public awareness, preparing volunteer groups, conducting hypothetical disaster drills (Van Wassenhove, 2006; Altay and Green, 2006; Oloruntoba and Kovács, 2015), developing evacuation plans and training personnel and individuals on evacuation (Kovács and Spens, 2007), decentralization of inventory and focusing on regional warehouses (Thomas, 2003; Salvadò *et al*, 2016), postponement of relief supplies, budgeting and preparation of financial resources, pooling resources among the

Figure 17.1   Four phases of a humanitarian supply chain

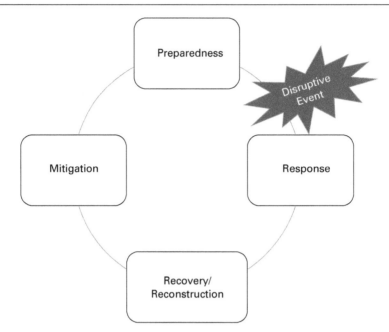

SOURCES Based on: Altay and Green (2006); Kovács and Spens (2007); Behl and Dutta (2018)

humanitarian actors (Maghsoudi *et al*, 2018), establishing early warning systems (Behl and Dutta, 2018), needs assessment evaluation and network planning for effective response (Tomasini and Van Wassenhove, 2009; Sabri *et al*, 2019) and vetting suppliers in advance (Kovács and Falagara Sigala, 2020). As such, the preparedness phase extends to include all the efforts to predict and analyse potential risks and hazards, and to build local capacities so as to reduce uncertainty and improve the supply chain response when a disaster strikes. Hence, it is tightly linked to the concept of supply chain resilience.

The preparedness phase is centred on capacity building and emergency planning through the adoption of a structured approach and risk-informed decision making (Baird, 2010). Many donor agencies are reluctant to invest in developing local skills or infrastructure in the long term, as they prefer the donations to go directly to affected communities. This could become the main obstacle in enhancing preparedness through strategic planning (Kovács and Spens, 2007), resulting in less resource sharing among the humanitarian actors leading to challenges in coordination (Balcik *et al*, 2010; Maghsoudi *et al*, 2018).

Response

Response is the phase that is triggered immediately after a disaster takes place and is considered the central phase in humanitarian supply chains. The speed of response and proper delivery is the ultimate performance indicator of humanitarian supply chains where the time window available for response is usually limited (Pettit and Beresford, 2009; Maghsoudi *et al*, 2018). Not surprisingly, it became the centre of researchers' attention with the majority of research focused on the response phase (Leiras *et al*, 2014).

In this phase, supply chain and logistics officers need to decide on deployment and allocation of resources, sharing information and coordinating the efforts of involved actors. This is the phase in which all the plans set out in the preparedness phase should be implemented (for example: search and rescue, plans pertaining to evacuation, resource mobilization, customs clearance to ensure delivery of critical supplies, firefighting, provision of water, energy, nutrition and shelter). Response benefits from a meticulously performed needs assessment to determine the volumes and timing of supplies, prepositioning and postponement of inventory in strategic locations and improving of infrastructure (eg warehouse networks, road and airport networks, and communication platforms), as well as sending appeals for donations. As such, its operations can be quite complex and daunting depending on the situation and context of the humanitarian supply chain (Thomas, 2003). Hence, cross-sector collaboration and coordination of multilateral efforts is key in establishing successful emergency response systems (Maghsoudi *et al*, 2018; Sabri *et al*, 2019). Furthermore, technology applications, in particular innovative digital technologies can be used to facilitate rapid and effective response (Rodríguez-Espíndola *et al*, 2020). These include: using drones in blood and medicine supply chains; artificial intelligence techniques in needs assessment to inform resources allocation; block chain and big data analytics; and 3D printing for on-site production (Dubey *et al*, 2018; Rodríguez-Espíndola *et al*, 2020). Poor response can be a result of lack of coping capacity and resilience, poor information sharing and communication that results in duplication of efforts and poor coordination, and misalignment of objectives, strategies, and/or resources (such as focusing on timeliness, shortening response time while ignoring quality, service level and cost-efficiency). Poor response can also be a result of inadequate preparedness, yet there should be the flexibility to update plans as the situation evolves.

Recovery

Recovery (also termed reconstruction) is the phase subsequent to immediate response. This phase is crucial to avoid short-term response and insufficient inflow of supplies. Hence, a longer-term perspective is adopted in the recovery and reconstruction phase to ensure continuity of response plan implementation (Kovács and Spens, 2007; Wagner, 2020). This phase includes: rebuilding of roads, transport and communication networks; building of shelters, refugee camps and housing reconstruction; ensuring sustainable energy and clean water supply; and removal of unwanted waste and cleaning of debris (Altay and Green, 2006; Matopoulos *et al*, 2014; Behl and Dutta, 2018).

Mitigation

The mitigation phase is concerned with the learned lessons from the overall disaster relief experience and the management of the humanitarian supply chains specifically. In this phase, action plans are developed and implemented that are necessary to prevent the disaster from recurring or to reduce the severity of its repercussions had it reoccurred (Altay and Green, 2006). This includes, for example, seeking insurance to reduce the financial impact of disasters and development of solid building codes to mitigate the impact of earthquakes (Matopoulos *et al*, 2014). Mitigation tools can also be supported by the use of disruptive technology such as big data analytics in supply and demand planning (Behl and Dutta, 2018; Dubey *et al*, 2018).

A framework for managing humanitarian logistics and supply chains

The management of supply chains in humanitarian contexts is becoming increasingly challenging due to the complexity of logistics, procurement and operations, in addition to the interconnectedness and interdependence between the multiple stakeholders in the humanitarian context. In this section, I draw on earlier research to propose a framework for managing humanitarian logistics and supply chain management (Figure 17.2). The framework comprises three core supply chain activities: supply and demand planning, procurement, and fulfilment management; and four elements pertaining to the wider humanitarian context, which I find necessary to successfully manage supply chains in these contexts.

Figure 17.2   A framework for managing humanitarian supply chains

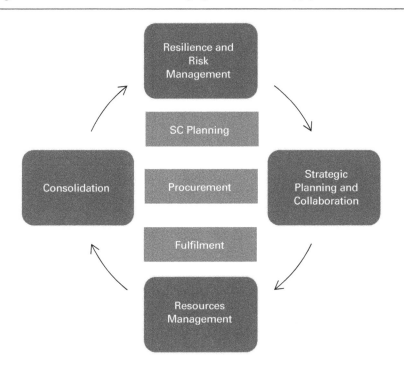

Strategic supply chain planning and collaboration

Strategic planning is concerned with decision making using a long-term approach. By doing so, the strengths and weaknesses of any given situation are analysed to enhance supply chain preparedness. As multiple actors exist, strategic planning is key in defining the role of these humanitarian actors based on the phase that they will be involved in. It includes: understanding the corporate strategy and capacity of each organization; establishing communication and collaboration strategies; deciding on the supply chain design (including warehouse location decisions); prepositioning, inventory management, a strategic approach for supply management; and long-term supplier relationship management, as well as related performance management (Falagara Sigala *et al*, 2020a). Modgil *et al* (2020) synthesized the focus of humanitarian supply chain strategic planning in six interrelated dimensions, as follows: 1) develop supply chain resilience; 2) multi-channel demand fulfilment; 3) disaster risk reduction; 4) fleet and routing decisions; 5) long-term planning to advance affected communities; and 6) establishing robust and flexible infrastructure (soft and hard) for effective recovery in the future.

Research in this field is challenged by the need to respond to the rapid changes in the real-life situation, as well as to contribute to closing the gap between theoretical studies and real-life events. To address such complex tasks, humanitarian supply chain research is expected to generate knowledge that contributes to development of the collaborative approaches that are needed to integrate the multilateral efforts of the different humanitarian actors (Sabri *et al*, 2019). Lessons learned from disasters around the globe encourage a continuous evolution towards a more integrated and collaborative approach to disaster management (Birkmann *et al*, 2013). This steers the efforts to focus not only on day-to-day disaster relief practices, but also to develop collaboration strategies so as to strengthen inter-organizational relationships among the humanitarian stakeholders. Hence, establishing effective communication, coordination and collaboration is key to improving supply chain performance (Altay 2008; Balcik *et al*, 2010).

Resources management

Resources management is needed for effective and efficient management of humanitarian supply chains (Behl and Dutta, 2018; Wagner, 2020). As a context that often faces resources scarcity, the pooling of resources among the actors involved is encouraged in humanitarian supply chains, with resource scarcity often found to be linked to poor responsiveness (Maghsoudi *et al*, 2018). Matopoulos *et al* (2014) categorized humanitarian supply chain resources into physical, human and organizational. Resources can also be tangible (eg physical resources) or intangible (eg knowledge) (Maghsoudi *et al*, 2018). Physical resources relate to material flow and inventory management of supplies where decisions on, for example, push–pull systems should be taken. The management of physical resources is, therefore, concerned with the planning and control of volume and the timing of materials flow in logistics supply chains (Pettit and Beresford, 2009). Human resource management is key in managing humanitarian supply chains, particularly in training and education of volunteer groups, personnel recruitment and skills enhancement, culture and human factor management, and volunteer development (Matopoulos *et al*, 2014; Pettit and Beresford, 2009).

Consolidation

Consolidation refers to the grouping of efforts, assets, materials and activities so as to improve the performance of humanitarian supply chains (Vaillancourt, 2016). It can be based either on time, quantities or a hybrid approach of time-quantity (Mutlu *et al*, 2010). For example, collaborative procurement can be used in international humanitarian organizations (eg the United Nations) for more efficient supply management, consolidation of purchase orders to benefit from quantity discount, and consolidation of shipments and transportation services to reach economies of scale and reduce transportation costs. Furthermore, standardization at the design and manufacturing stages helps in establishing effective consolidation of material storage in warehouses. As such, consolidation oftentimes results in cost reduction, reducing unnecessary movements or time waste, and improved asset utilization.

Resilience and risk management

Humanitarian supply chains operate in a volatile context tied not only to the uncertainty of demand and supply but also to the irregularity of demand and high time pressure (Pettit and Beresford, 2009; Kunz and Gold, 2017). Overcoming uncertainty and enhancing the resilience of humanitarian supply chains can be through effective planning that will facilitate supply and demand integration (Wagner, 2020). This involves enhancing trusting relationships (Schiffling *et al*, 2020), information sharing, developing collaborative strategies, and establishing supply chain agility – ie 'the ability to respond rapidly to unexpected changes in demand or supply conditions' (Christopher and Tatham, 2011, p 4). Adopting technology such as advanced analytics and artificial intelligence can lead to more accurate demand measurement which in turn will decrease uncertainty (Behl and Dutta, 2018). The development of resilience practices is done across the various phases of humanitarian supply chains, through investing in planning and preparedness, building local and institutional capacities, collaboration and involving local communities in recovery plans, and integrating disaster risk reduction into national emergency response systems (UNDP, 2012).

SC planning, procurement and fulfilment management

At the heart of this framework are the main supply chain activities of planning, procurement and fulfilment management. Supply chain planning is concerned with integrating demand and supply, or what is termed in corporate supply chains as sales and operations planning. This activity represents all the efforts to efficiently and effectively match supply with demand. It extends to include shaping, measuring and managing demand signals based on accurate needs assessment and historical data. Supply management is needed to ensure that only critical supplies are received and flawless

Figure 17.3 Disasters and resilience

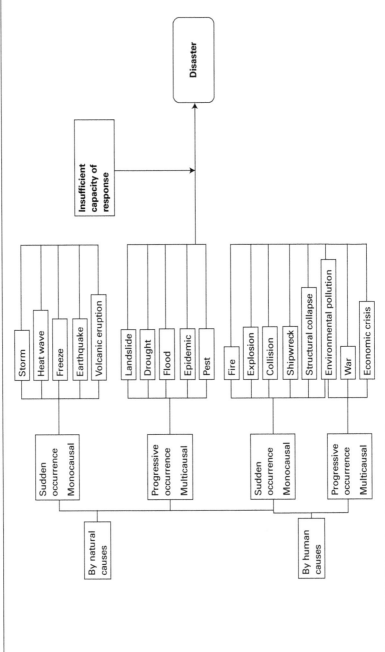

SOURCE WHO (2002) Hazards and disasters classification

material flow from suppliers/donors to affected locations. Fulfilment management is the group of activities needed to ensure effective delivery of the ordered items to the beneficiary. This includes transport, warehouse and inventory management, as well as last mile distribution (often a challenging supply chain activity in humanitarian contexts as a result of damaged infrastructure and security concerns).

In light of the above discussion, a humanitarian supply chain's level of preparedness and response will vary according to the magnitude and nature of the disaster (Thomas, 2003). Myriad disaster profiling taxonomies and typologies have been developed (see, for example: Van Wassenhove, 2006; Yadav and Barve, 2015; Mackay *et al*, 2019) to classify disasters based on complexity, speed of occurrence, and the scale and impact of the disruptive event. Figure 17.3 demonstrates what makes a disruptive event disastrous or – even worse – catastrophic, ie insufficient coping and responding capacity. If governments have the capability to ramp up their response capacity and have implemented resilience in their supply chain systems, then sudden events do not necessarily trigger grave implications and transform into disasters.

Against this background, in the following section I reflect on the case of Covid-19 supply chain systems.

Pandemic supply chain: Covid-19 supply chain systems

Covid-19 supply chains are vital for the delivery of critical medical supplies (eg blood, syringes, swabs and disposable gloves), personal protective equipment (PPE), medical devices (eg ventilators) and the vaccine, under extreme supply uncertainty conditions (Falagara Sigala *et al*, 2020a) and significant distribution challenges (Mancini and Miller, 2021). The repercussions of the novel coronavirus have shocked global supply chains in that it has disrupted supply flows and shaken established demand patterns (World Bank, 2020a; Sarkis, 2020). We have witnessed first-hand scenes of panic buying and the stockpiling of functional products and food commodities. This introduced unprecedented levels of the bullwhip effect in the manufacturing sector (Handfield *et al*, 2020) as it became obvious that current supply chain strategies were unable to respond rapidly to changing customer demand. As a result, there have been direct effects on supply chain management due to forced lockdowns, as well as indirect effects where the Covid-19-related recession has seen the fastest and steepest downgrades of global economic growth since 1990 (World Bank, 2020b).

To advance the international response effort, a global initiative, the Pandemic Supply Chain Network, was set up between private-sector organizations and the WHO (WEF, 2020) and a UN supply chain task force has been convened to establish the Covid-19 Supply Chain System (WHO, 2020c). The task force takes a strategic approach to planning and coordination. A major challenge for the coronavirus pandemic supply chain system is finding ways to ensure equitable distribution of critical medical items, treatments and vaccines across the globe, particularly to ensure low- and lower-middle-income countries will receive a fair share of critical tests and vaccines in a timely manner. The management of Covid-19 supply chains depends on a number of factors, in particular strategic planning to ensure supply chain visibility and international collaboration. In response to this global health emergency, the World Health Organization (WHO) has set out guidance on Covid-19 supply chain preparedness and response which is centred on collaboration at country, regional and global levels (WHO, 2020b).

As outlined in the earlier section on humanitarian actors and shown in Figure 17.4, the Covid-19 medical humanitarian supply chain is a multi-stakeholder one that involves donors, local governments, the UN and WHO, private-sector pharmaceutical manufacturers, logistics providers, warehousing and wholesalers, non-governmental organizations, hospitals and healthcare providers (Falagara Sigala *et al*, 2020a).

Covid-19 supply chain management depends on accurate needs assessment – where it has been reported that countries most affected by the coronavirus will be prioritized to receive vaccination supply – that is performed based on reported positive cases, the number of patients admitted to hospitals and emergency care units, and the size of the population to be protected. These data will feed into forecasting algorithms to be shared with the WHO, international humanitarian organizations and pharmaceutical manufacturers to ensure supply continuity of the vaccine in the future (WHO, 2020b). Demand management, planning and forecasting during a health pandemic are crucial in enhancing humanitarian supply chain preparedness and in informing decision making (Nikolopoulos *et al*, 2020). Taking into account the epidemiological analysis, as well as factors such as community and localized transmission and imported cases, will help not only to decide on vaccine supply volumes but also in making operational decisions (in relation to, for example, lockdowns or curfews, production planning, shipping and

Figure 17.4 Medical humanitarian supply chains

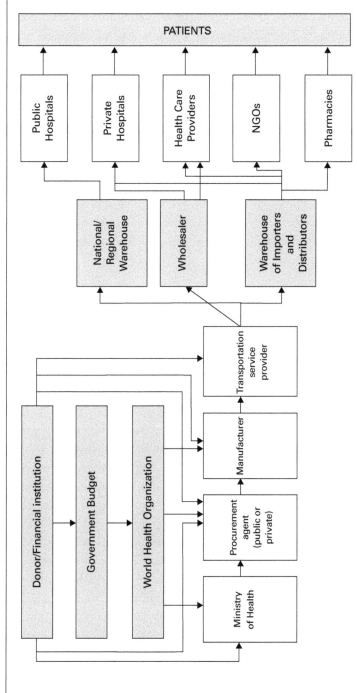

SOURCE Falagara Sigala et al (2020a)

inventory management), which will eventually affect the performance of the supply chain (WHO, 2020b; Nikolopoulos *et al*, 2020). In this case, demand consolidation can help in better informing supply requirements and in the streamlining of demand fulfilment processes with its shipments, storage and inventory management dimensions (WHO, 2020c).

Collaborative procurement is another key dimension that will help to satisfy the objectives of the pandemic humanitarian supply chain system and to ensure continuous flow of critical medical supplies – particularly the vaccine – to low- and lower-middle-income countries. After agreeing on the technical specifications that meet local government requirements, the coordinated approach for demand and procurement will also help establish strong negotiating positions for buyers. Distribution and storage is key in Covid-19 vaccination programmes, particularly for certain types of vaccines which need ultra-cold chain facilities (Falagara Sigala *et al*, 2020b). International consolidation hubs strategically located around the world will be used for regional storage to ensure seamless global distribution (WHO, 2020c).

Concluding remarks

In this chapter I introduced humanitarian logistics and supply chain management based on a four-phase approach, and I have put forward a framework for managing humanitarian logistics and supply chains that incorporates the three core supply chain activities of planning, procurement and fulfilment management (along with resilience, strategic planning, collaboration and resources management). This chapter offers many transferrable lessons from the humanitarian context to corporate supply chains, in particular when dealing with dual supply and demand uncertainty in the context of the global Covid-19 pandemic.

Humanitarian logistics and supply chain management is an exciting and dynamic field with the noble objectives of saving lives and alleviating human suffering. However, it is worth noting that the field of humanitarian supply chain can be a challenging one where practitioners and academics face significant security and safety challenges (Jahre *et al*, 2012; Sohn, 2018; ICRC, 2016 and 2020). There exists a lack of information and an inconsistency of data (Altay, 2008; Jahre *et al*, 2012), linguistic and cultural barriers (Pedraza-Martinez *et al*, 2013; Kunz and Gold, 2017), and damaged infrastructure (Kovács and Spens, 2007; Jahre *et al*, 2012) which accentuates the remoteness of affected locations (Pedraza-Martinez *et al*, 2013; Prasad *et al*, 2017). That is in addition to centralized decision making and high personnel turnover (Thomas, 2003; Altay, 2008). Finally, lack of funding can be a key hurdle in managing these supply chains. For example, in 2018 it has been estimated that almost 40 per cent of humanitarian needs were not met due to a funding gap (Lacourt and Radosta, 2019).

Notes

1 WHO Situational Report (2020) Weekly Epidemiological and Operational updates, as of 27 December 2020
2 The World Bank (2020) *A shock like no other: Coronavirus rattles commodity markets*
3 2010–2019
4 UNHCR Global Trends, *Forced Displacement in 2019*
5 UN, FAO (2020) *The State of Food Security and Nutrition in the World 2020*
6 It can be hard to predict natural disasters but it is not impossible. Some disasters have predictable patterns, for example, hurricanes that hit the Caribbean and Central America are cyclical and have known seasons. Countries where the earthquake belt passes through are usually better prepared to respond.

References

Altay, N (2008) Issues in disaster relief logistics, in *Large-Scale Disasters: Prediction, control and mitigation*, ed M Gad-el-Hak, pp 120–146, Cambridge University Press, New York, NY

Altay, N and Green, WG (2006) OR/MS research in disaster operations management, *European Journal of Operational Research*, **175** (1), pp 475–93

Baird, ME (2010) *The Phases of Emergency Management: Background Paper*, Intermodal Freight Transportation Institute (ITFI), University of Memphis

Balcik, B, Beamon, BM, Krejci, C, Muramatsu, KM and Ramirez, M (2010) Coordination in humanitarian relief chains: Practices, challenges and opportunities, *International Journal of Production Economics*, **126** (1), pp 22–34

Behl, A and Dutta, P (2018) Humanitarian supply chain management: a thematic literature review and future directions of research, *Annals of Operations Research*, 283 (1), pp 1001–44

Birkmann, J, Cardona, OD, Carreno, ML, Barbat, AH, Pelling, M, Schneiderbauer, S, Kienberger, S, Keiler, M, Alexander, D, Zeil, P and Welle, T (2013) Framing vulnerability, risk and societal responses: the MOVE framework, *Natural Hazards*, **67**, pp 193–211

Blanco, E and Goentzel, J (2006) Humanitarian supply chains: A review, Presentation given at *The 17th Annual Conference of the Production and Operations Management Society*, MIT Centre of Transportation & Logistics

Christopher, M and Tatham, P (eds) (2011) *Humanitarian logistics: Meeting the challenge of preparing for and responding to disasters*, 2nd edn, Kogan Page, London

Dubey, R, Bryde, DJ, Foropon, C, Graham, G, Giannakis, M and Mishra, DB (2020) Agility in humanitarian supply chain: An organizational information processing perspective and relational view, *Annals of Operations Research*, pp 1–21

Falagara Sigala, I, Kovács, G, Alani, H, Smith, B, Xu, J, Wu, G, Rollo, A, Cicchetta, G, Boersma, K, Grant, D, Riipi, T and Wan, K (2020a) *D31 – Gap analysis and recommendations for securing medical supplies for the Covid-19 response*, Health Emergency Response in Interconnected Systems, www.heros-project.eu/output/deliverables (archived at https://perma.cc/8GKX-EPZE)

Falagara Sigala, I, Kovács, G, Maghsoudi, A, Piotrowicz, P, Storsjö, I and Vega, D (2020b) *Fact sheet to prepare for Covid-19 vaccination programmes*, Humanitarian Logistics Institute, Hanken School of Economics

FEMA (2006) Principles of Emergency Management, Independent Study, IS230, Federal Emergency Management Agency, Washington, DC

Grandi, F (2016) World Humanitarian Summit: Addressing forced displacement, www.un.org/en/chronicle/article/world-humanitarian-summit-addressing-forced-displacement (archived at https://perma.cc/PX97-RVNM)

Handfield, RB, Graham, G and Burns, L (2020) Coronavirus, tariffs, trade wars and supply chain evolutionary design, *International Journal of Operations & Production Management*, **40** (10), pp 1649–660

ICRC (2016) Syria: Attack on humanitarian convoy is an attack on humanity, International Committee of the Red Cross, www.icrc.org/en/document/syria-attack-humanitarian-convoy-attack-humanity (archived at https://perma.cc/RA8K-TLVX)

ICRC (2020) Yemen: 3 ICRC staff members killed in airport blast, www.icrc.org/en/document/yemen-2-icrc-staff-members-killed-1-unaccounted-after-airport-blast (archived at https://perma.cc/A8XT-7B9E)

Jahre, M, Dumoulin, L, Greenhalgh, LB, Hudspeth, C, Limlim, P and Spindler, A (2012) Improving health in developing countries: Reducing complexity of drug supply chains, *Journal of Humanitarian Logistics and Supply Chain Management*, **2** (1), pp 54–84

Kovács, G and Falagara Sigala, I (2020) Lessons learned from humanitarian logistics to manage supply chain disruptions, *Journal of Supply Chain Management*, doi.org/10.1111/jscm.12253 (archived at https://perma.cc/5J6F-THBQ)

Kovács, G and Spens, KM (2007) Humanitarian Logistics in Disaster Relief Operations, *International Journal of Physical Distribution & Logistics Management*, **37** (2), pp 99–114

Kunz, N and Gold, S (2017) Sustainable humanitarian supply chain management: Exploring new theory, *International Journal of Logistics Research and Applications*, **20** (2), pp 85–104

Kunz, N and Reiner, G (2012) A meta-analysis of humanitarian logistics research, *Journal of Humanitarian Logistics and Supply Chain Management*, **2** (2), pp 116–47

Lacourt, M and Radosta, M (2019) *Strength in Numbers: Towards a more efficient humanitarian aid – pooling logistics resources*, ©Réseau Logistique Humanitaire

Leiras, A, de Brito Jr, I, Queiroz Peres, E, Rejane Bertazzo, T and Tsugunobu Yoshida Yoshizaki, H (2014) Literature review of humanitarian logistics research: Trends and challenges, *Journal of Humanitarian Logistics and Supply Chain Management*, **4** (1), pp 95–130

Logistics Cluster (2019) *A Year in Review, 2019 Annual Report*, Logistics Cluster, World Food Programme, Rome, Italy

Mackay, J, Munoz, A and Pepper, M (2019) A disaster typology towards informing humanitarian relief supply chain design, *Journal of Humanitarian Logistics and Supply Chain Management*, **9** (1), pp 22–46

Maghsoudi, A, Zailani, A, Ramayah, T and Pazirandeh, A (2018) Coordination of efforts in disaster relief supply chains: The moderating role of resource scarcity and redundancy, *International Journal of Logistics Research and Applications*, **21** (4), pp 407–30

Mancini, DP and Miller, J (2021) Vaccine makers race to secure supply chains, *Financial Times*, on.ft.com/3hJbTIa

Matopoulos, A, Kovács, G and Hayes, O (2014) Local resources and procurement practices in humanitarian supply chains: An empirical examination of large-scale house reconstruction projects, *Decision Sciences*, **45** (4), pp 621–46

Modgil, S, Singh, RK and Foropon, C (2020) Quality management in humanitarian operations and disaster relief management: a review and future research directions, *Annals of Operations Research*, pp 1–54

Mutlu, F, Çetinkaya, S and Bookbinder, JH (2010) An analytical model for computing the optimal time-and-quantity-based policy for consolidated shipments, *IEEE Transactions on Engineering Management*, **42** (15), pp 367–77

Nikolopoulos, K, Punia, S, Schäfers, A, Tsinopoulos, C and Vasilakis, C (2020) Forecasting and planning during a pandemic: Covid-19 growth rates, supply chain disruptions, and governmental decisions, *European Journal of Operational Research*, **290** (1), pp 99–115

Nobel Prize (2020) The Nobel Peace Prize for 2020, press release, www.nobelprize.org/prizes/peace/2020/press-release/ (archived at https://perma.cc/RY3F-TYKL)

Oloruntoba, R and Kovács, G (2015) A commentary on agility in humanitarian aid supply chains, *Supply Chain Management: An International Journal*, 20 (6), pp 708–16

Pedraza-Martinez, AJ, Stapleton, O and Van Wassenhove, LN (2013) On the use of evidence in humanitarian logistics research, *Disasters*, 37 (S1), pp S51–S67

Pettit, S and Beresford, A (2009) Critical success factors in the context of humanitarian aid supply chains, *International Journal of Physical Distribution & Logistics Management*, 39 (6), pp 450–68

Prasad, S, Sundarraj, RP, Tata, J and Altay, N (2017) Action-research-based optimisation model for health care behaviour change in rural India, *International Journal of Production Research*, 56 (21), pp 6774–792

Rodríguez-Espíndola, O, Chowdhury, S, Beltagui, A and Albores, P (2020) The potential of emergent disruptive technologies for humanitarian supply chains: The integration of blockchain, artificial intelligence and 3d printing, *International Journal of Production Research*, 58 (15), pp 4610–630

Sabri, Y, Zarei, MH and Harland, C (2019) Using collaborative research methodologies in humanitarian supply chains, *Journal of Humanitarian Logistics and Supply Chain Management*, 9 (3), pp 371–409

Salvadò, LL, Comes, T, Lauras, M, Grenade, M (2016) A study on the sub-regionalization of Humanitarian Supply Chain: the IFRC case, *Proceedings of the ISCRAM 2016 Conference*, Rio de Janeiro, Brazil

Sarkis, J (2020) Supply chain sustainability: Learning from the Covid-19 pandemic, *International Journal of Operations & Production Management*, 41 (1), pp 63–73

Schiffling, S, Hannibal, C, Fan, Y and Tickle, M (2020) Coopetition in Temporary Contexts: Examining swift trust and swift distrust in humanitarian operations, *International Journal of Operations & Production Management*, 40 (9), pp 1449–473

Sohn, M (2018) So much of research is context: Fieldwork experience in humanitarian logistics, in *The Palgrave Handbook of Humanitarian Logistics and Supply Chain Management*, eds G Kovács, KM Spens and M Moshtari, Palgrave Macmillan, London, pp 149–77

Thomas, A (2003) *Humanitarian Logistics: Enabling disaster response*, Fritz Institute

Tomasini, RM and Van Wassenhove, LN (2009) From preparedness to partnerships: Case study research on humanitarian logistics, *International Transactions in Operational Research*, 16 (5), pp 549–59

UNDP (2012) *Putting Resilience at the Heart of Development: Investing in prevention and resilient recovery*, United Nations Development Programme, Representative Office in Japan

Vaillancourt, A (2016) A theoretical framework for consolidation in humanitarian logistics, *Journal of Humanitarian Logistics and Supply Chain Management*, 6 (1), pp 2–23

Van Wassenhove, LN (2006) Humanitarian aid logistics: Supply chain management in high gear, *Journal of Operational Research Society*, **57** (5), pp 475–89

Wagner, SM (2020) Humanitarian Operations and Supply Chain Management, in *The Oxford Handbook of Supply Chain Management*, 1st edn, eds TY Choi, JJ Li, DS Rogers, T Schoenherr and SM Wagner, Oxford University Press, UK

WEF (2020) World Economic Forum, Pandemic supply chain network, www.weforum.org/projects/pandemic-supply-chain-network-pscn (archived at https://perma.cc/V8RR-3TS2)

WHO (2002) *Disasters & Emergencies*, Pan-African Emergency Training Centre, Addis Ababa

WHO (2020a) *Covid-19 Supply Chain System*, www.who.int/emergencies/diseases/novel-coronavirus-2019/covid-19-operations (archived at https://perma.cc/6DXT-V4SJ)

WHO (2020b) *Novel Coronavirus (2019-nCoV): Strategic Preparedness and Response Plan*, World Health Organization, Geneva, Switzerland

WHO (2020c) *Covid-19 Supply Chain System: Requesting and receiving supplies – Health Emergencies Programme*, World Health Organization, Geneva, Switzerland

World Bank (2020a) *A Shock Like No Other: Coronavirus rattles commodity markets*, World Bank, bit.ly/3b4WkcA (archived at https://perma.cc/6LYU-588D)

World Bank (2020b) *The Global Economic Outlook during the COVID-19 Pandemic: A changed world*, World Bank, bit.ly/3b4WkcA (archived at https://perma.cc/6LYU-588D)

Yadav, DK and Barve, A (2015) Analysis of critical success factors of humanitarian supply chain: An application of interpretive structural modeling, *International Journal of Disaster Risk Reduction*, **12**, pp 213–25

Digitalization in global supply chain operations 18

Andreas Taschner and Hazel Gruenewald

Introduction

Logistics has undergone tremendous changes over the past few decades. Above all with the advent of the digital age, we have witnessed the significant impact of new technologies on supply chains in terms of business transformation, increased agility and performance. However, many businesses have chosen to harness the full potential of these technologies to create further value (Bughin *et al*, 2017). High investment costs, fears for cyber security, a lack of expertise in the workforce and insufficient awareness of the concrete benefits of these technologies are just some factors hampering the decision to adopt digital technologies.

The following chapter draws on the findings of both recent quantitative and qualitative research conducted by practitioners and academics. Since the focus of much current scholarship is on MNCs (multinational corporations), this prompted the authors' decision to carry out a two-part empirical study with a special focus on SMEs (small and medium-sized enterprises). In Phase One, responses were collected from more than 140 supply chain and logistics experts in a worldwide online survey (Sweeney *et al*, 2020). In Phase Two, 13 semi-structured interviews were conducted with selected experts from Europe, the United States and Asia to elicit the drivers, motives and barriers behind adoption and usage of digital technologies in supply chains. Based on this empirical research, this chapter aims to present an overview of where such companies stand today in their quest to digitalize global supply chains.

We will begin by outlining today's digital technology landscape with respect to supply chain management, highlighting the relevance and possible benefits of new technologies for global supply chains. We will go on to look at current rates of adoption, exploring reasons why some companies are quick to embrace the potential of digitalization[1] while others rather adopt the role of followers, even at the risk of becoming laggards. We will conclude by investigating in detail the challenges that digitalization seems to pose to global supply chains.

Digital technologies and their relevance for global supply chains

Logistics is commonly understood as managing the procurement, movement and storage of materials, parts or finished goods through the organization and its adjacent channels (Christopher, 2016). Transportation and storage tasks are core to the logistics discipline. While transport deals with the bridging of physical or geographical distances, storage bridges temporal distances, ie the time between supply or creation of an object and its subsequent use or consumption. Without a related exchange of information, the movement of physical objects would not be possible. Modern logistics, therefore, integrates the information flows that relate to physical flows based on the premise that communication between the points of origin and consumption of assets and objects is vital (Zijm et al, 2019; Christopher, 2016). The inevitable corollary is increased functional integration within organizations. In other words, for modern logistics to work efficiently, different business functions (eg purchasing, production planning and scheduling, warehousing) have to work together.

Functional integration in today's complex global environment often goes beyond given organizational boundaries to include value-adding tasks and activities that are performed by external partners (suppliers, distributors, logistics service providers, etc). The sequence – or rather, network – of value-adding tasks and activities across various firms is at the heart of the supply chain concept. Chopra and Meindl simply define supply chains as '...all functions involved in receiving and filling a customer request' (Chopra and Meindl, 2016, p 13). Mentzer et al describe supply chains as 'a set of three or more entities (organizations or individuals) directly involved in the upstream and downstream flows of products, services, finances, and/or information from a source to a customer' (Mentzer et al, 2001, p 4). In short, the supply chain concept involves inter-organizational collaboration ranging from physical flows to information and financial flows.

Managing these complex upstream and downstream relationships with suppliers and customers is the task of supply chain management (SCM). SCM aims at delivering superior customer value at less cost to the supply chain as a whole (Christopher, 2016, p 3). Unsurprisingly, modern SCM is heavily reliant on digital technologies. Modern supply chains are increasingly evolving into 'digital supply chains'. So-called digital supply chains comprise all systems (eg software, hardware, communication networks) that support interactions between distributed organizations and orchestrate the activities of the supply chain partners (Bhargava *et al*, 2013). It is irrespective as to whether the products and services being exchanged between supply chain layers are 'traditional' (ie non-digitized) or not. It is the digitalization of processes and transactions that makes a supply chain a 'digital supply chain' (Xue *et al*, 2013).

Digitalization of business processes – be they intra- or intercompany – is not a new phenomenon. Digital technologies have long had an impact on how companies implement their processes. Nonetheless, some digital technologies and applications are already in the late phase of their life cycles and are increasingly substituted by other solutions, while others are in the earlier stages and await widespread adoption (see Figure 18.1).

Digitalization of processes is typically not feasible with one single technology only; rather, it is based on a combination of multiple information, computing, communication and connectivity technologies. This also involves physical elements (eg delivery vans, forklift trucks, transportation containers) that are equipped with new, digital, components and sensors (Cichosz *et al*, 2020). The usage of barcodes and – more recently – RFID tags or near-field communication (NFC), for instance, has become fairly common in many supply chains today. Modern enterprise resource planning (ERP) systems allow integration of such data into a firm's standard operating processes. Such technologies are used to track the location of shipments, derive real-time productivity data from devices and machines, or log process-related data and time stamps (Scholz *et al*, 2018).

A whole new range of emerging digital technologies linked to the concept of Industry 4.0 have opened the path to a higher level of interoperability and integration across all supply chain layers and elements (Bär *et al*, 2018; Ardito *et al*, 2019):

Cloud computing: The sharing of hardware and software resources over the internet, so that information can be easily stored and accessed remotely by different users.

Figure 18.1 Example digital technologies and their life cycle stage

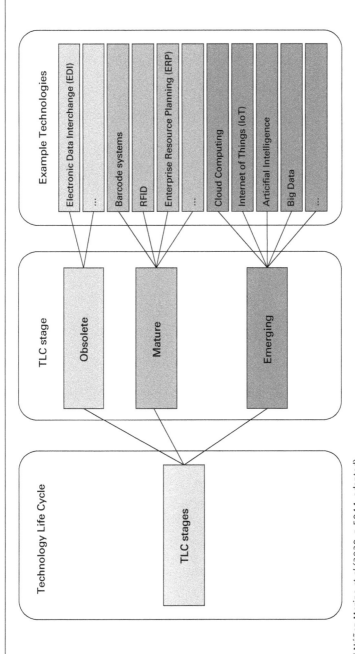

SOURCE Núñez-Merino et al (2020, p 5044, adapted)

Industrial IoT:	The use of IoT (Internet of Things) technologies to ensure interoperability between devices and machines, thus allowing real-time data exchange across value chain layers. IoT devices are 'smart' in the sense that they generate real-time data through integrated sensors and exchange this data with other devices and machines over the internet.
Artificial intelligence:	Intelligent systems that make decisions autonomously and execute tasks accordingly. The need for human intervention and interaction is reduced or entirely eliminated.
Big data:	Technological solutions that allow storing and analysing extremely large data-sets and support real-time decision making.

These new, still emerging, digital technologies have a profound impact on global supply chains in at least two respects:

1 They greatly facilitate the exchange and integration of data across organizational boundaries. What used to be restricted to operational processes within a single firm can now be extended much more easily across different supply chain players.

2 They make way for storage, retrieval, analysis, sharing and distribution of data that is no longer purely transaction-oriented (as is standard in ERP systems), but pertain to the entire supply chain environment. This also includes internet data, camera and surveillance footage, imagery, and environmental data (eg weather) (Sanders and Ganeshan, 2018).

By adopting these emerging digital technologies and integrating them into SCM, businesses change the way they perform supply chain planning and execution tasks and interact with their supply chain partners. In fact, integration of digital technologies in supply chains can even lead to the creation of entirely new business models (Farahani *et al*, 2017; Vendrell-Herrero *et al*, 2018) that were not possible before. Moreover, digital technologies constitute an important resource for creating, delivering and capturing value.

Digital technologies clearly have the potential to impact all facets of supply chain management. Digital supply chains are expected to increase efficiency in operative tasks such as warehousing, picking and packing, and order handling. They provide improved analytical capabilities for demand forecasting, inventory management and screening of the supply chain's environment. Digitalization takes collaboration between supply chain partners to a higher level by facilitating interoperability of previously separated systems and devices, automating data exchange and processing, and providing real-time access to shared data. Finally, digital supply chains allow the development of new business models, such as geographically distributed on-demand manufacturing of customized objects (additive manufacturing), or new value propositions to the final customer (eg remote servicing, predictive maintenance).

It is probably fair to say that digitalization of supply chains is primarily about generating, structuring, analysing and acting on large amounts of structured and unstructured data along all stages of the supply chain. As already outlined above, this is not limited to the treatment of operating data to support current supply chain processes. Data can even replace physical goods as the main supply chain object and turn into the main artefact that is moving between business partners. Such a set-up turns the 'digital supply chain' into a 'data supply chain' (Spanaki *et al*, 2018).

Even if physical objects remain the main artefacts traded between partners, the supply chain's business success will increasingly depend on its digital capabilities. Calatayud *et al* predict that in the future 'self-thinking supply chains' will be decisive for competitiveness:

> Driven by new digital technologies, the supply chain of the future will increasingly be self-aware, think by itself and require minimum, if any, human intervention to manage risks. The self-thinking supply chain will continuously monitor supply chain performance by analysing quintillion bytes of data generated by objects; forecast and identify risks; and automatically take actions to prevent risks before they materialize. The supply chain will autonomously learn from these activities and use such knowledge in future decisions. Importantly, large amounts of data and the use of powerful analytical and simulation models will allow the supply chain to predict the future with minimum error and take actions to, for example, address constant shifts in demand. The self-thinking supply chain will, thus, push supply chain flexibility and agility to limits yet to be discovered.
>
> **SOURCE** Calatayud *et al* (2019, p 22f)

For the vast majority of organizations and their networks, the concept of smart, self-thinking supply chains, however, still remains a vision rather than an empirical finding. The following section looks, for example, at discrepancies between the current rate of adoption of digital technologies in global supply chains compared to the potential that many businesses see with respect to the implementation of these technologies.

Current adoption of digital technologies

Given the significant potential of digitalization, as outlined above, one might expect that companies readily embrace new digital technologies and adapt their supply chain operations accordingly. This claim, however, must be further substantiated. This section summarizes what we know today about the adoption of digital technologies in the given supply chains under investigation. It not only presents empirical findings about current adoption rates and implementation levels, but also discusses potential drivers and inhibitors of adoption (see Figure 18.2).

Figure 18.2   Conceptual model of digital technology adoption in supply chains

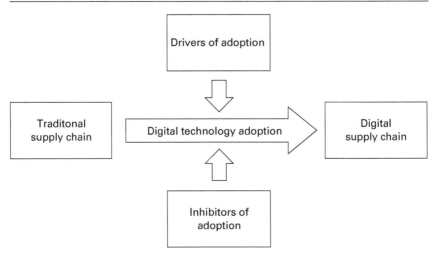

This discussion includes both the results of qualitative interviews conducted by the researchers with supply chain practitioners mainly coming from SMEs, as well as the findings of other recent studies in the field carried out by practitioners and academics (see Table 18.1).

Technology adoption

Given the variety of digital technologies available, it is not surprising to see very different adoption levels among firms. Our own research revealed

Table 18.1 Overview of empirical surveys

	Author	Year	Method	Respondents	Sample Size	Companies	Industries	Focus
1	AT Kearney	2015	online survey + in-depth interviews	SC managers	60	companies from 16 countries, more than 1/3 from Germany	various	Ways that digitization[1] in all of its formats impacts SCM
2	Stegkemper GmbH	2016	anonymous online survey	Decision makers from the fields of SCM and logistics	60	mostly SMEs (80% with <1,000 employees), 90% from Germany	aerospace	Current status + future challenges in digitalization of the supply chain
3	Korn Ferry	2017	survey	Senior SC executives + academics and consultants	100	not disclosed	not disclosed	Implications of digitization of SCs on talent, capabilities and culture
4	Tarofder et al	2017	online survey	Screened and recruited sample of senior managers	236	Malaysia only, many small companies	tourism, IT industry, partly manufacturing	Internet adoption in SC activities
5	Deloitte	2018	survey + executive interviews	Executives	>200	manufacturing companies	manufacturing	Opportunities and challenges involved in implementing a digital supply network

Table 18.1 *continued*

	Author	Year	Method	Respondents	Sample Size	Companies	Industries	Focus
6	CapGemini	2018	survey	Decision makers in SCM at various hierarchical levels	1,001	only large companies (>US$ 500m)	retail, manufacturing, consumer products	Adoption of digital initiatives in SCs and derived benefits
7	Bienhaus/ Haddud	2018	online survey	Employees to middle management in procurement and SCM	414	worldwide	manufacturing, finance, services	Impact of digitization on procurement and SCM, potential barriers
8	Brinch et al	2018	Delphi study + panel	Experts from larger Danish organizations + supply chain executives	23 (Delphi) + 49 (panel)	larger Danish companies	various	Identify and rank applications of big data in SCM, assess practical use
9	jda + KPMG	2019	survey	Executives	93	only large companies (>US$ 500m)	retail, manufacturing, 3PL	Drivers and inhibitors of investment in digital SC
10	Deloitte	2019	survey	Decision makers and influencers from various functional areas	156	mostly big companies	broad mix	Digital investment and adoption trends in SCs

11	Makris et al	2019	interviews + online survey	purchasing, operations, procurement	7 (interview) + 24 (survey)	international, mostly MNCs	chemicals, pharma, food, high-tech, retail	How multinational companies from five industries can adapt to SC 4.0
12	PWC	2020	survey	Supply chain executives and decision makers	1,601	worldwide, size distribution not disclosed	manufacturing, process, retail, consumer good	SC capabilities and supporting technologies, plans for next 5 years
13	EY	2020	survey	Supply chain leaders	212	not disclosed	varying	Digital skills and talent requirements of digital SC
14	MHI	2020	survey	Executives and middle managers	1001	wide range of company sizes, all continents	wide range of company types and industries	Adoption of SC technologies, Supply Chain Digital Consciousness Index (DCI)
15	Authors	2019 + 2020	online survey	Decision makers in SCM	142 (survey) + 13 (expert interviews)	mix of SMEs and big corporations	mostly manufacturing	Adoption of digital technologies, perceived benefits + challenges, link with performance

NOTE 1. As mentioned in chapter endnote 1, the terms 'digitalization' and 'digitization' are used interchangeably in scholarship and practice. The authors have used those terms that occurred in the original texts.

SOURCE Authors' compilation

relatively high adoption rates for big data, cloud computing and mobile computing applications, respectively. Other technologies, such as 3D printing, robotics and virtual reality, have not yet found widespread acceptance (see Figure 18.3). These findings are very much in line with other empirical surveys:

- Respondents to the AT Kearney 2015 survey planned their highest investments in technologies for IT integration across their own company functions and with supply chain partners, together with big data analysis applications. Robotics and 3D printing, in turn, ranked last.

- The Deloitte 2018 survey identified advanced analytics, cloud computing and IoT platforms as the technologies in which manufacturers invested most. 3D printing and augmented reality devices ranked in the middle, while robotics and blockchain came out at the low end of manufacturers' priority list.

- The EY 2020 survey showed highest adoption rates for cloud computing and mobile computing. IoT applications ranked third. Companies were much more reluctant to adopt 3D printing technologies, artificial intelligence or big data applications.

These findings give rise to a number of possible explanations and conclusions. Firstly, the technologies surveyed are at different stages in their respective life cycles. Mobile computing or cloud computing applications, for instance, have been available for many years already and one can consequently expect higher adoption rates for them. Secondly, firms seem to prioritize technologies that provide immediate benefits for integration, collaboration, communication and planning tasks. The key motive can be termed 'Help me understand my supply chain!' One of the interviewees claimed: 'Digital = cloud + connectivity + big data!' In this sense, digitalization revolves around making full use of IT solutions that are perhaps not entirely new, but provide significant business benefits when combined and implemented at full scale. This quest for deeper integration originates within one's own organization and is subsequently rolled out to supply chain partners. Many of the interviewed experts mentioned the roll-out of new ERP systems and the integration of subsidiaries and locations into a single ERP system as the most important initial step towards a digital supply chain. A quote from a UK expert underlines this:

> The biggest change on the supply chain side relates to the implementation of an ERP platform. This now gives us a single system to plan all parts of the supply

Figure 18.3 Current adoption rates of digital technologies

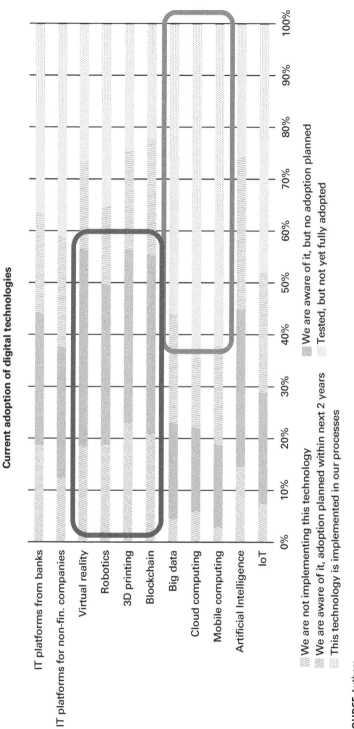

Current adoption of digital technologies

IT platforms from banks
IT platforms for non-fin. companies
Virtual reality
Robotics
3D printing
Blockchain
Big data
Cloud computing
Mobile computing
Artificial Intelligence
IoT

0% 10% 20% 30% 40% 50% 60% 70% 80% 90% 100%

We are not implementing this technology
We are aware of it, adoption planned within next 2 years
This technology is implemented in our processes
We are aware of it, but no adoption planned
Tested, but not yet fully adopted

SOURCE Authors

chain and replaces several legacy systems almost completely… our supply chain simply could not function now without the system.

Digitalization of the supply chain certainly does not end with ERP systems. The majority of respondents in our survey perceived their own company as 'moderately digitalized' today and expected a growing importance of digital solutions in the future (Sweeney *et al*, 2020). On the one hand, companies aim for an even deeper integration level of different software systems and corporate functions. In the PWC 2020 survey, for instance, approximately 50 per cent of all companies that had already started integration projects also included CRM systems, warehouse management, or transport management systems, respectively. Such a fully integrated digital environment opens the path towards 'smart' logistics and supply chains. On the other hand, firms also look into new technologies that affect the 'physical' elements of their supply chains, such as automated warehousing equipment, robotics-based automation, drones or autonomous vehicles. Current adoption rates are still significantly lower for these technologies than for integrated software solutions. However, they are earlier in their technology life cycle and one could expect rising adoption rates in the future.

Despite their comparatively low adoption levels today, some emerging technologies have significant disruptive potential. In fact, the jda + KPMG 2019 survey identified artificial intelligence and cognitive analytics as the technologies with the biggest impact, but autonomous vehicles and robotics also showed significant increases in perceived impact between 2018 and 2019. In the MHI 2020 survey, respondents identified robotics and automation, as well as sensors and automatic identification (eg RFID), as the technologies with the biggest potential to disrupt business or create new competitive advantage – followed by predictive analytics and artificial intelligence. As of today, firms seem to prioritize 'software-based' innovations in their investment plans and only gradually recognize the potential of 'hardware-based' technologies.

Strictly speaking, simple adoption rates of the kind 'x per cent of firms have adopted technology y' are not very informative. Technology adoption is not a binary yes/no decision. Firms typically test technologies in small-scale pilots and roll them out only after successful piloting (see again Figure 18.3). In the CapGemini 2018 survey, the percentage of firms experimenting with new digital technologies (eg through proof of concept studies or pilots) was approximately five times higher than the percentage of firms that had fully implemented them – this is across all technologies surveyed. A somewhat more differentiated picture was found in the EY 2020 survey, where large-scale deployment was significantly higher than pilot testing for cloud computing and mobile computing and about equal in percentage for robotics, 3D printing and machine learning. Some digital technologies have clearly established themselves already in global supply chains both in terms of breadth (percentage of firms adopting) and in depth (scale of implementation), while other technologies still need to prove their benefits to businesses in a multitude of small-scale pilots and test scenarios. As one German expert put it:

> We use it [ie pilot test] to gain experience, whether it could support us in one process or another. But here we do very clear pilot projects and then use it and gain experience and ask ourselves if it helps us and where?

It is, therefore, safe to say that the adoption of digital technologies in global supply chains shows a complex pattern not only across different technologies, but also as regards the speed of adoption: digitalization forerunners (full implementation) surpass digitalization laggards (pilots or no adoption at all). This pattern was also observable in our 2019 survey (Sweeney *et al*, 2020), which identified a particular relationship between digitalization and perceived importance of digitalization. Perceived importance grows with a firm's current level of digitalization (as could be expected), but there is also a positive correlation between perceived current importance and expected future importance, ie companies that already take digitalization seriously today are preparing for an even more important role in the future. This points to a widening gap (or a 'digital divide') between leaders and laggards in terms of technology adoption (Sweeney *et al*, 2020).

One digital innovation that (as of today) is, for the most part, still in its pilot phase is blockchain technology. In the Deloitte 2018 survey, only 17 per cent of firms were investing in blockchain technology (compared to 26 per cent for artificial intelligence and 40 per cent in advanced analytics). The CapGemini 2018 survey found that 12 per cent of companies had already implemented blockchain, but 64 per cent were experimenting with it. In the PWC 2020 survey, the share of blockchain users was down to a mere 5 per cent, while 49 per cent were piloting or at least expressing interest in it. Leaving aside sampling differences and random errors between the different surveys, the overall pattern is fairly consistent: among all digital technologies investigated, blockchain is probably the one that is still in its infancy and most companies have not yet identified a clear business case for it.

Demographic differences

Industry differences

Digitalization is a seemingly ubiquitous phenomenon that affects all businesses independent of the specific industry they are operating in. It is not surprising to see that firms across all industries consider supply chain digitalization a key area of management attention. In the CapGemini 2018 survey, approximately half of the surveyed organizations described supply chain digitalization as one of their top three priorities. This share did not differ significantly between manufacturers, consumer goods companies and retailers.

The situation changes, however, when individual technologies are considered. As one respondent to our expert interviews put it: 'The adoption of technology is based on solving a business need and so yes it is industry dependent.' Several other experts confirmed this view, highlighting that processes depend on the product and its specific industry characteristics, and that benefits derived from digital solutions will, therefore, vary across industries. In the jda + KPMG 2019 survey, for instance, retail firms showed a significantly higher interest in cloud solutions for forecasting and replenishment than manufacturers or logistics service providers (LSPs). While LSPs considered predictive load balancing a key use case for artificial intelligence (AI) in the same survey, manufacturers were highlighting demand forecasting, with retailers emphasizing inventory optimization.

The example of AI at the same time points to a possible explanation for different adoption levels across digital technologies. Some of these technologies provide benefits in a wide variety of potential use cases, while others are more limited in scope and possible application areas. Cloud solutions or mobile computing constitute clusters of individual use cases. This flexibility makes them potentially attractive to companies in many different industries. Regarding some other innovative technologies, fewer beneficial use cases are perceived or the usage scenarios tend only to apply to firms in specific industries. 3D printing or autonomous vehicles are cases in point. The different adoption rates of digital technologies, therefore, do not only reflect their current life cycle stage, but also their flexibility and adaptability to different industry requirements.

Logistics service providers have an important role to play as well. Since many logistics activities are outsourced, '...a significant proportion of the digital transformation (DT) of logistics rests on LSPs' shoulders. LSPs can serve as architects of the further development...' (Cichosz *et al*, 2020, p 210). Given the specific range of activities and services under LSPs' responsibility, their technology adoption pattern will differ from manufacturing companies, for instance. As one IT director put it: 'DT [digital transformation] in the logistics service industry is different from DT in, for example, the telecoms. It isn't taking place only in virtual reality, but the flow of goods must be organized in the analogue world' (Cichosz *et al*, 2020, p 219).

MNCs versus SMEs

The speed and scope of adopting digital technologies does not only depend on a firm's main field of business, but is potentially also affected by its size. Several respondents in our expert interviews agreed that larger companies are typically forerunners in technology adoption due to higher budgets available and the higher synergy potential of digital solutions in large firms. The key challenges in technology adoption (see next section) are often more pronounced in smaller companies: lack of financial and human resources, expertise shortages and consequently a limited capability to handle the potential complexity of a new technology all work against them. The Deloitte 2018 survey indeed identified higher shares of technology adopters among large firms across almost all technologies surveyed. The survey used non-standard size clusters, however, and categorized all companies with less than $1 billion revenues as 'small'. In our own 2019 survey, SMEs tended to show lower degrees of digitalization, but these differences were not statistically significant. In general, empirical evidence for a systematic gap between small and large companies is limited.

We have also found the contrary statement that SMEs are more entrepreneurial than their larger peers. A CEO in our expert interviews explained: 'Digitalization is an experiment. As such, it is not size-dependent.' SMEs in our survey showed slightly different adoption motives than their larger peers. While large companies frequently cited productivity increases and cost reduction as key motives, SMEs put a significantly larger emphasis on new market opportunities created by technology adoption. Rather than postulating slow adoption among SMEs in general, it is probably more appropriate to focus on technologies' specific use cases again and to investigate their applicability for companies of different sizes.

Challenges

Even when a clear use case is given, companies might still not adopt a particular technology, because the problems and challenges are too big to overcome. In a recent literature review, Agrawal *et al* identified 12 different barriers to digital transformation of supply chains: no sense of urgency, lack of digital skills and talent, lack of strategic orientation, inappropriate organizational structure, misaligned business objectives, inflexible business processes, fear of losing confidential information, risk of taking initiative, inability to keep pace with digital business dynamism, lack of industry-specific guidelines, lack of top management support, and high implementation and running cost (Agrawal *et al*, 2020).

A lot of empirical research has been done on the key factors that can hamper or block technology adoption. In our own 2019 survey, respondents rated a lack of financial and human resources, high complexity and cyber security risks as the key challenges for their adoption plans (see Figure 18.4). Expert interviews mostly confirmed the survey findings: cost, lack of expertise, company inertia, resistance to change among management and staff, and the potentially overwhelming implementation complexity were most frequently mentioned.

These findings are largely consistent with results in other surveys. In the Stegkemper 2016 survey respondents showed consensus with the statements that data protection must be safeguarded and investment cost should be manageable. Standardization and coordination across entire industries, for instance, received lower support. Respondents in the Korn Ferry 2017 survey rated a lack of strategy, availability of 'digital talent' and missing management support as the main barriers of company digitalization. The Deloitte 2018 survey identified budget constraints, data fragmentation (ie lack of standards and interoperability) as key barriers. The top ranked challenge was difficulty in finding and training staff with the right skills. This view was confirmed by the findings by Bienhaus and Haddud. In their survey, the statements 'Employees have enough resources and capacities for digital transformation' and 'Employees have the appropriate capabilities' received least support – these items were identified as the key barriers among respondents (Bienhaus and Haddud, 2018). Hiring and retaining qualified staff was also identified as the key challenge in the EY 2020 and the MHI 2020 surveys.

A fairly consistent pattern of challenges can be seen across empirical surveys and it is fair to say that digitalization of supply chains is far from being perceived as an easy task by companies. A few points merit additional consideration.

Figure 18.4 Key challenges in digital technology adoption

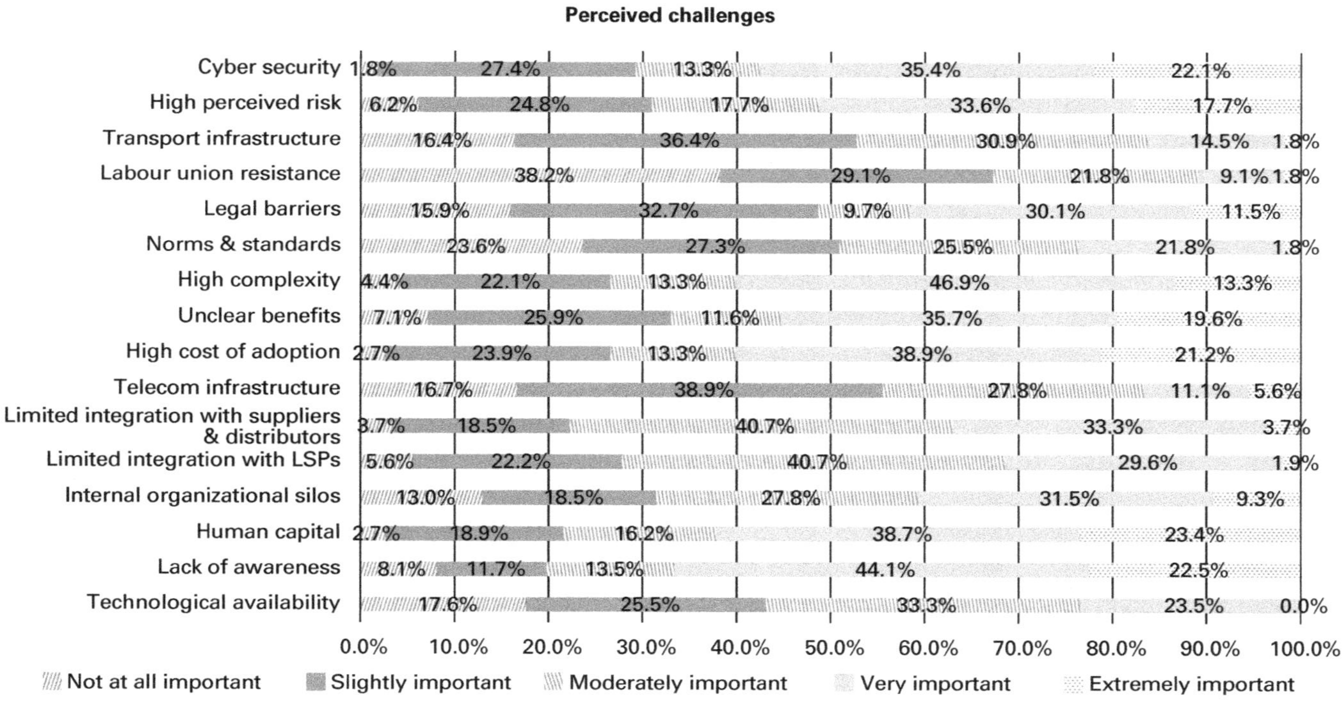
Perceived challenges
Cyber security 1.8% 27.4% 13.3% 35.4% 22.1%
High perceived risk 6.2% 24.8% 17.7% 33.6% 17.7%
Transport infrastructure 16.4% 36.4% 30.9% 14.5% 1.8%
Labour union resistance 38.2% 29.1% 21.8% 9.1% 1.8%
Legal barriers 15.9% 32.7% 9.7% 30.1% 11.5%
Norms & standards 23.6% 27.3% 25.5% 21.8% 1.8%
High complexity 4.4% 22.1% 13.3% 46.9% 13.3%
Unclear benefits 7.1% 25.9% 11.6% 35.7% 19.6%
High cost of adoption 2.7% 23.9% 13.3% 38.9% 21.2%
Telecom infrastructure 16.7% 38.9% 27.8% 11.1% 5.6%
Limited integration with suppliers & distributors 3.7% 18.5% 40.7% 33.3% 3.7%
Limited integration with LSPs 5.6% 22.2% 40.7% 29.6% 1.9%
Internal organizational silos 13.0% 18.5% 27.8% 31.5% 9.3%
Human capital 2.7% 18.9% 16.2% 38.7% 23.4%
Lack of awareness 8.1% 11.7% 13.5% 44.1% 22.5%
Technological availability 17.6% 25.5% 33.3% 23.5% 0.0%
0.0% 10.0% 20.0% 30.0% 40.0% 50.0% 60.0% 70.0% 80.0% 90.0% 100.0%
Not at all important
Slightly important
Moderately important
Very important
Extremely important

SOURCE Authors

Cyber security and data protection

Digital supply chains are marked by the interconnection of previously separate IT systems, the growing use of cloud-based solutions and the increasing trend to equip logistical devices with 'smart' components to facilitate communication with each other. Cyber security and data protection concerns, therefore, should also rise on managers' agendas. The empirical evidence is mixed, however. In some surveys, data protection is clearly perceived as a key challenge for digital supply chain initiatives. More than 50 per cent of respondents in the Stegkemper 2016 survey agreed to the statement that digitalization of the supply chain is possible only if elementary data is protected (the highest number of all statements). In the MHI 2020 survey, however, less than one-third of respondents considered cyber risks to be extremely or very challenging for their digitalization initiatives. In other surveys, cyber security does not make it into the top rank of digitalization challenges at all (eg Deloitte, 2018, jda + KPMG, 2019).

These seemingly contradictory results might be due to a sampling effect: the importance of cyber security and data protection is perceived differently by staff in operating functions and in IT functions. In our expert interviews, cyber security was often mentioned as an 'IT issue'. Staff with operational functions are not fully aware of what it entails and what needs to be done and, hence, tend to pass the issue on to their IT colleagues. As one interviewee expressed:

> I honestly believe it depends on who you're asking. If you ask a department head now, he usually says it's no big deal. But if you ask an IT guy now, they're extremely worried. I don't think we as business people know enough about it, I don't know how easy it is to get my data or spy on it. I just don't know enough about that.

This view is confirmed by another expert: 'I am, first and foremost, a logistics specialist. The topic of cyber security is one that is driven elsewhere in the organization.' Such a disconnect between corporate functions can pose a major threat to supply chain digitalization – not only in the implementation phase, but even more so in the operating phase, when sensitive data is collected and automatically exchanged between different systems and devices. If staff lack awareness of the potential cyber risks involved in a digitalized supply chain, malevolent parties can exploit negligent behaviour of individual employees, unidentified data leaks or inadequate data protection mechanisms.

Standardization

Standardization presents itself as a double-edged sword. Digitalization requires a certain standardization of processes, which in turn helps reduce costs and improve process quality. At the same time, many experts who were interviewed expressed concerns that IT solutions might impose unwanted standardization to customer-specific solutions. Overall, a certain ambivalence towards standards could be detected: on the one hand, standard solutions were seen as hampering flexibility; on the other hand, a lack of standards was believed to increase the complexity of adoption.

In a supply chain context, standardization plays an even bigger role, since interconnection of partners' systems and smooth data interchange depends on shared data formats and standardized interfaces. Standards can be industry-specific only. The Stegkemper 2016 survey focused on the aerospace industry only. Roughly half of all respondents agreed to the statement that digitalization of their supply chain was possible only if there were industry-wide initiatives. Standardization in this sense is not limited only to technical standards and interconnectivity, but also encompasses process standards – which can be more industry-specific than technical standards.

A special case in point is the perspective of logistics companies and third-party logistics. One of the experts from a third-party logistics company summarized the dilemma as follows:

> Most trading partners are still using systems that are 5 to 10 years old which makes the movement of digital information across multiple trading partners platforms complex. It requires supporting multiple file formats, some of which are not supported, proprietary or emerging but not yet supported as a standard.

With specialized logistics service companies playing an ever bigger role in many supply chains, their problems are symptomatic of the difficulties that can arise along the wider supply chain.

Missing standards can have different effects on small and big companies. While MNCs often have the resources to develop and implement company-specific solutions (and subsequently urge their smaller supply chain partners to adopt these), SMEs often depend on standardized solutions that are easier and less costly to implement. By reducing both costs and risks, standardization also opens the path towards adoption of digital technologies for smaller companies.

The role of digital talent and leadership

According to the McKinsey 2017 report 'Digital supply chains: Do you have the skills to run them?', capability constraints are a key reason for the slow adoption of digital technologies in global supply chains. Moreover, as part of the McKinsey 2015 Global Survey, over 900 C-level executives listed talent shortages as a major challenge holding businesses back from achieving their strategic digital aspirations. As the survey goes on to point out, many organizations are confronted with a gap for talent and leadership that combines analytical and new technical skills with supply chain expertise. Our own empirical study strongly reaffirmed the issue of skills deficits. One expert, for example, stated: 'The need to continuously upskill and retrain staff in the context of rapidly developing technology is an ever present challenge.'

Besides a general lack of know-how and awareness of new technologies in organizations, another issue raised in our research was a deficit with respect to forward thinking and adaptability. One of the experts interviewed in our study highlighted how vital it is for leaders and supply chain professionals to think ahead and demonstrate flexibility to keep digitalization projects on track even when they hit hurdles. This ties in closely to another recurrent theme emerging in the study, which is a shortage of appropriate leadership capabilities. Future leaders need to be able not only to understand what digital innovations are, but also whether and how they create value for the organizations they are intended to support (McKinsey, 2017).

It is critical that leaders proactively keep up with technological and industry trends, since the business environment is changing at a rapid pace. At the same time, they need to think and act strategically, adapting processes or trajectories accordingly to ensure that business goals are met. A big issue that many leaders encounter, however, is resistance to change, when it comes to implementing new or emerging technologies. Not only can it be a struggle to challenge the current status quo, to allay fears that technologies will replace jobs, but as already mentioned, there is a great deal of uncertainty about the benefits digitalization brings and what the right path forward is with respect to the implementation of new technologies. A number of experts interviewed in our empirical study mentioned the need to shift the mindset of employees. Effective change management is, therefore, vital. Top-down commitment is a 'must'. Key stakeholders from across the organization have to be guided along the transformational journey. It is crucial, too, that leaders communicate the value of the changes for the workforce and the business as a whole, whilst addressing concerns and fears.

As many studies have already pointed out, a further critical success factor in the digital transformation process is an end-to-end strategy encompassing all areas of the supply chain and integrating all the key players. The digital tools made available to employees need to be intuitive and the data they receive must be presented in a simple and easy-to-absorb format. The introduction of supply chain visibility tools can improve collaboration between professionals from different departments as well as increase productivity, if significant thought is given to creating compatible processes, so that individuals can work at the same pace and base their decisions on the same data (LaBombard *et al*, 2019).

Conclusions

What the research described in this chapter confirms is that digital technologies, although seemingly ubiquitous, have not yet become mainstream. Adoption rates depend on a variety of factors, including company size and sector, although little difference is seen when considering the different tiers of the supply chain. Once we take a closer look at the individual technologies in question, however, significant patterns emerge. Big data, cloud computing and mobile computing applications, respectively are among the technologies to be most frequently adopted, whereas other technologies, such as 3D printing, robotics and virtual reality, still await widespread acceptance.

Despite the perceived benefits of digitalization and its envisioned strategic importance, many companies still struggle with the implementation. According to *Forbes*, 84 per cent of companies fail at digital transformation. A 2017 survey demonstrated that a key issue is that many organizations view digitalization as a technology-driven endeavour involving simply IT transformation (Solis and Littleton, 2017). These findings align closely with the results of our own empirical study, even though many interviewed experts recognized the need for their companies to undergo significant cultural and organizational changes in order to achieve the desired business transformation through the implementation of digital technologies.

As this chapter demonstrates, a wider array of challenges faces companies that seek to harness the potential of modern technologies to digitalize their supply chains. These range from a lack of standardization both on an intra- and intercompany level, different regional legal requirements, fears for cyber security, insufficient awareness of the clear added-value, talent shortages, and deficits in leadership and governance.

Note

1 The terms 'digitization' and 'digitalization' are sometimes used interchangeably in scholarship and practice. The authors use the term 'digitalization' in accordance with Gartner's definition of the concept as 'the use of digital technologies to change a business model and provide new revenue and value-producing opportunities; it is the process of moving to a digital business'. In other words, digitalization is a transformation as opposed to 'digitization', which is a conversion of data and processes.

References

Agrawal P, Narain R, Ullah I (2020) Analysis of barriers in implementation of digital transformation of supply chain using interpretive structural modelling approach, *Journal of Modelling in Management*, **15** (1), pp 297–317

Ardito, L, Messeni, P A, Panniello, U and Garavelli, AC (2019) Towards Industry 4.0: Mapping digital technologies for supply chain management-marketing integration, *Business Process Management Journal*, **25** (2), pp 323–46

Arenkov, I, Tsenzharik, M and Vetrova, M (2019) Digital technologies in supply chain management, doi: 10.2991/icdtli-19.2019.78

Bär, K, Lee Herbert-Hansen, ZN and Khalid, W (2018) Considering Industry 4.0 aspects in the supply chain for an SME, *Production Engineering*, **12**, pp 747–58

Bhargava, B, Ranchal, R, ben Othmane, L (2013) Secure information sharing in digital supply chains, 3rd IEEE International Advanced Computing Conference, pp 1636–640

Bienhaus, F and Haddud, A (2018) Procurement 4.0: factors influencing the digitisation of procurement and supply chains, *Business Process Management Journal*, **24** (4), pp 965–84

Bughin, J, LaBerge, L and Mellbye, A (2017) The case for digital reinvention, *McKinsey Quarterly*, February, available at www.mckinsey.com/business-functions/digital-mckinsey/our-insights/the-case-for-digital-reinvention (archived at https://perma.cc/J748-GWUD)

Calatayud, A, Mangan, J and Christopher, M (2019) The self-thinking supply chain, *Supply Chain Management: An International Journal*, **24**(1), pp 22–38

Chopra, S and Meindl, P (2016) *Supply Chain Management: Strategy, planning, and operation*, 6th edn, Pearson, Harlow

Christopher, M (2016) *Logistics and Supply Chain Management*, 5th edn, Pearson, Harlow

Cichosz, M, Wallenburg, CM and Knemeyer, AM (2020) Digital transformation at logistics service providers: Barriers, success factors and leading practices, *The International Journal of Logistics Management*, **31** (2), pp 209–38

Farahani, P, Meier, C and Wilke, J (2017) Digital supply chain management agenda for the automotive supplier industry, in *Shaping the Digital Enterprise: Trends and use cases in digital innovation and transformation*, eds G Oswald and M Kleinemeier, pp 157–72, Springer

LaBombard, M, McArthur, A, Sankur, A and Shah, K (2019) The human side of digital supply chains, available at www.mckinsey.com/business-functions/operations/our-insights/the-human-side-of-digital-supply-chains (archived at https://perma.cc/H5LL-7SDF)

McKinsey & Company (2015) *Cracking The Digital Code*, available at www.mckinsey.com/business-functions/mckinsey-digital/our-insights/cracking-the-digital-code (archived at https://perma.cc/FRQ4-V3FR)

McKinsey & Company (2017) *Digital Supply Chains: Do you have the skills to run them?*, available at www.mckinsey.de/business-functions/operations/our-insights/digital-supply-chains-do-you-have-the-skills-to-run-them# (archived at https://perma.cc/G5UJ-EYP9)

Mentzer, JT, DeWitt, W, Keebler, JS, Min, S, Nix, NW, Smith, CD and Zacharia, ZG (2001) Defining Supply Chain Management, *Journal of Business Logistics*, **22** (2), pp 1–25

Núñez-Merino, M, Maqueira-Marín, JM, Moyano-Fuentes, J and Martínez-Jurado, PJ (2020) Information and digital technologies of Industry 4.0 and Lean supply chain management: A systematic literature review, *International Journal of Production Research*, **58**, (16), pp 5034–61

Sanders, NR and Ganeshan, R (2018) Big data in supply chain management, *Production and Operations Management*, **27**, (10), pp 1745–748

Scholz, J, De Meyer, A, Marques, AS, Pinho, TM, Boaventura-Cunha, J, Van Orshoven, J, Rosset, C, Künz, J, Kaarle, J and Nummila, K (2018) Digital technologies for forest supply chain optimization: Existing solutions and future trends, *Environmental Management*, **62**, pp 1108–133

Solis, B and Littleton, A (2017) The 2017 State of Digital Transformation, Altimeter, a Prophet Company, available at sites.prophet.com/altimeter/2017-state-digital-transformation/?fbclid=IwAR13Dm8d7FBkWaNY_6YCoygynnfWrRJRqXCmjALyeAkjNRytYeHGDXKLa8A#.YD9b3-co93h (archived at https://perma.cc/5NDR-BKRX)

Spanaki, K, Gürgüç, Z, Adams, R and Mulligan, C (2018) Data supply chain (DSC): Research synthesis and future directions, *International Journal of Production Research*, **56**, (13), pp 4447–466

Sweeney, E, Taschner, A and Gruenewald, H (2020) Disruptive digital technology adoption in global supply chains, *Journal of Supply Chain Management, Logistics & Procurement*, **3** (1), pp 77–90

Vendrell-Herrero, F, Parry, G, Bustinza, OF and Gomes, E (2018) Digital business models: Taxonomy and future research avenues, *Strategic Change*, **27** (2), pp 87–90

Xue, L, Zhang, C, Ling, H and Zhao, X (2013) Risk mitigation in supply chain digitization: System modularity and information technology governance, *Journal of Management Information Systems*, **30**, pp 325–52

Zijm, H, Klumpp, M, Heragu, S and Regattieri, A (2019) Operations, logistics and supply chain management: Definitions and objectives, in *Operations, Logistics and Supply Chain Management, Lecture Notes in Logistics*, eds H Zijm, M Klumpp and A Regattieri, pp 27–42, Springer, Berlin

Digitalization and Industry 4.0 in logistics

Pietro Evangelista and Witold Bahr

19

Introduction

In recent years, rapid advances in industrialization, technology and globalization have radically changed the competitive scenario in which companies operate, giving rise to more volatile markets, more intense competition and rising demand for customized products and services with shorter life cycles. These changes also complicated the management of logistics presenting many challenges for companies operating in the supply chain. Industry 4.0 is viewed as a promising approach to face this new scenario with its key objective of collecting and using real-time information to achieve vertical and horizontal integration. Its focus is on integrating value chain networks and product life cycles through the adoption of digital technologies.

Logistics is an important component of Industry 4.0 and it is an enabler of this innovative approach. In this context, the use of emerging digital technologies in this field is labelled as Logistics 4.0. Logistics 4.0 involves the networking and integration of logistics processes through a high degree of digitalization and automation, right up to decentralized real-time control of logistics networks. The adoption of this concept has significant consequences for the logistics sector especially in terms of the speed, flexibility and controllability of its processes.

Against this background, Logistics 4.0 is becoming particularly important for logistics service providers (LSPs). As a result of the outsourcing processes, LSPs play a more critical role as supply chain orchestrators. However, despite the benefits associated with the application of the Logistics 4.0 concept, there are a number of challenges that need to be addressed if the digital profile necessary to fully exploit the opportunities is to be achieved.

The objective of this chapter is to analyse the concepts of Industry 4.0 and Logistics 4.0 in order to identify the main challenges that LSPs need to face to successfully implement this approach. It is organized into four sections. Following this introduction, the next section discusses the application of Industry 4.0 and the adoption of digital technologies in logistics. The subsequent section provides an overview of the application of the Logistics 4.0 approach in the logistics service industry and the related obstacles that LSPs need to overcome for its full implementation. The final section provides some concluding comments.

The uneasy road to digitalization in logistics: from Industry 4.0 to Logistics 4.0

In any sector, the long-term success of companies depends on the capacity to generate innovation. Digital innovation is unanimously considered one of the most critical areas of innovation not only for the company's expansion but also for its long-term capacity to stay in the market. In recent years, the diffusion of digital innovation has affected all areas of logistics management to the extent that innovative digital technologies are fast becoming necessary tools for the transformation of the supply chain. These new technologies are instrumental in optimizing capacities, reinforcing performance, and improving quality to ensure the efficiency of the supply chain. In addition, new digital technologies are able to change the way shipments and cargo flows are organized and managed, improve cooperation between supply chain actors, increase supply chain visibility and real-time management of cargo flows, reduce the complexity of administrative issues, and enable better use of infrastructure. Consequently, the implementation of innovative solutions capable of deploying the potential offered by digital technologies is expected to increase over the coming years. The World Economic Forum forecasted in 2016 that digitalization in logistics could grow up to $1.5 trillion in value by 2025 and an additional $2.4 trillion in terms of benefits for the company following the digital transformation of the industry (WEF, 2016).

Digital transformation of processes and the implementation of new technologies are collectively referred to as Industry 4.0. Since the German government in 2011 first coined the term Industry 4.0, it has steadily gathered interest from companies across all industries. According to

Rüßmann *et al* (2015), nine technological innovations power Industry 4.0 leading to interconnected sensors, machines, workpieces and IT systems within a cyber-physical system (CPS). The internet and supporting technologies serve as a backbone to integrate physical objects, human actors, intelligent machines, production lines and processes across organizational boundaries to form an intelligent, networked and agile value chain (Ganzarain and Errasti, 2016). Tjahjono *et al* (2017) identified the following four main characteristics of the Industry 4.0: a) vertical networking of smart production systems; b) horizontal integration; c) through-life engineering support across the entire value chain; and d) acceleration through exponential technologies.

Application of Industry 4.0 in logistics requires radical changes in systems, processes and activities. Considering that the complexity of logistics has increased substantially as a result of globalization and vertical disintegration of the supply chain, it may be expected that the Industry 4.0 approach will facilitate the management of logistics and supply chain activities. A recent review of the literature carried out by Neumann and Evangelista (2019) on the relationship between Industry 4.0 and logistics has identified two main approaches to research into this phenomenon.

The first approach comprises studies focused on the impact of Industry 4.0 on logistics and its possible consequences for the management of logistics. For example, Hofmann and Rüsch (2017) argued that the application of the Industry 4.0 concept would cause a decoupling of the strategic level (eg supplier and site selection) and the operational level (eg picking, loading and stocktaking) in logistics management. Nevertheless, the impact of Industry 4.0 will primarily be at the operational logistics level where human interaction will become limited largely to control and monitoring activities. Skapinyecz *et al* (2018) argued that Industry 4.0 would increase the application of digital technology in logistics as a result of trends such as the diversity of products handled, the new technologies introduced in production and services, the operation of various networks, and the need for globalization. Only automated and optimized complex structures and processes might allow the necessary increase in the transparency of logistics systems to be achieved. Tjahjono *et al* (2017) arrived at a similar conclusion. They argued that effects of Industry 4.0 on logistics (such as increased flexibility, quality standards, efficiency and productivity) will better allow companies to meet customers' demands, creating value through introducing new products and services to the market. In this context, collaboration between suppliers, manufacturers and customers is crucial; it may be achieved through information exchange on a real-time basis to increase the transparency of all supply chain steps.

The second approach involves a group of papers that discuss how changes in logistics may facilitate the adoption of Industry 4.0. The common base of these studies is that the success of Industry 4.0 directly depends on the ability of logistics to support the progress of Industry 4.0 giving rise to the emergence of the 'Smart Logistics' or 'Logistics 4.0' concept. In other words, the papers belonging to this approach consider logistics as an enabler of Industry 4.0. Barreto *et al* (2017) defined 'Smart Logistics' as a new paradigm based on the increased use of the internet to enable communication between machines and humans in real time. Maslarić *et al* (2016) share this view to the extent that they consider the (digital) transformation of logistics as a prerequisite for adopting the Industry 4.0 approach. To achieve this, the required transformation of logistics should reflect the new way to move, store and supply freight known as the Physical Internet (Montreuil, 2011).

Most of the above literature is based on the assumption that the adoption of new digital technologies included in the Industry 4.0 paradigm significantly increases the efficiency of logistics systems. It emphasizes the implications for the transformation of manufacturing, logistics and supply chain management (SCM) processes. Nevertheless, in the extant literature, as well as business practice, there is limited evidence concerning the implementation of the Industry 4.0 approach and related digital technologies in the logistics service industry. On the other hand, most logistics activities are outsourced nowadays. The last annual study on the state of logistics outsourcing reports that 52 per cent of shippers' total logistics expenditure is related to outsourcing (Langley, 2020). This means that logistics service providers (LSPs) are directly involved in the development of the digital transformation of logistics (the so-called Logistics 4.0) and act as orchestrators in the implementation of Industry 4.0 approach (Delfmann *et al*, 2018).

The next section analyses the state of development of Logistics 4.0 and digitalization in the logistics service industry.

Digitalization in the logistics service industry: challenges towards Logistics 4.0

From the analysis above, it can be clearly seen that logistics is one of the most important elements for the successful implementation of any Industry 4.0 projects and that the main objectives of the fourth Industrial Revolution can only be achieved through the adaptation of logistics. This adaptation should concern the main features of Industry 4.0 such as networking, decentralization, real-time capability and service orientation. On the other hand, considering the high rate of logistics outsourcing, any changes in logistics must necessarily involve logistics service providers. For this reason, LSPs play a critical role in this context but this requires that their business models shift from a physical to a digital approach. In this way, LSPs may pave the way for the establishment of the Logistics 4.0 concept. For example, paperless processing of transport orders with digital waybills or pallet exchanges in the digital age are important basic requirements for Logistics 4.0 to function properly.

The term Logistics 4.0 refers to a 'logistical system that enables the sustainable satisfaction of individualized customer demands without an increase in cost and supports the development in industry and trade using digital technologies' (Winkelhaus and Grosse, 2020, p 21). A very critical role in Logistics 4.0 is played by data that are turned into actionable intelligence and (autonomous, semi-autonomous, human) actions (Roblek *et al*, 2016). A data source is a network of different kinds of interlinked sensors. The sensors' networks transmit data in real time to IT systems that have the task to put data into context and provide them with particular meaning. As a result, a huge amount of data (the so-called Big Data) might be available instantly and through effective data analytics valuable information may be retrieved. The World Economic Forum (2016) has estimated the benefits of digital transformation for the logistics industry at around $3.9 trillion.

However, there are a number of challenges that LSPs have to address if the potential benefits of digitalization and Logistics 4.0 are to be realized.

From an innovation point of view, logistics companies have introduced innovation at a slower pace than other industries. This was documented by Wagner (2008) who investigated the adoption of innovation in different industries in Germany and found that the logistics service industry ranked last in innovativeness. The share of innovators in the transportation and logistics industry was only 30 per cent. This is in comparison with 60 per cent in manufacturing industry and 52 per cent in the knowledge-intensive services industry (which includes software firms and consultancies). The study defined 'innovative firms' or 'innovators' as those companies that had successfully completed at least one innovation project and had brought new products and/or services to market or introduced new processes to the firm during the observation period.

The low rate of innovation in the sector is reflected in the capacity of logistics companies to invest in new digital technologies. While other industries with close ties to logistics, such as retailing, have been completely transformed by digital technology, this has not occurred to nearly the same extent in the logistics services industry. In fact, the rise of e-commerce has led to big new digital players who have assumed control of the 'last mile' of the delivery market. To achieve the benefits of digitalization, LSPs need to innovate their processes to connect different entities in the supply chain, and to react more quickly to changing customer demands through service customization. This is challenging for any logistics service provider as connecting different entities in the supply chain is not easy and requires substantial investment in sophisticated digital infrastructures and applications. This is confirmed by the amount of the digital transformation spending in the logistics market that is estimated to be around $95 million by 2026 (Transparency Market Research, 2018). Unfortunately, ICT investment (including digital technologies) in the logistics sector has generally been low entailing potentially dangerous risks even for the largest players in the sector (Evangelista and Sweeney, 2006).

The reluctance to invest in information and digitalization technology by LSPs has been investigated by several researchers. For example, the research conducted by Langley (2020) studied the 'IT gap' that is the difference between shippers' opinions as to whether they view information technologies as necessary elements of LSP expertise and whether they are satisfied with their LSPs' IT capabilities. This gap has been estimated from 2010 until 2019 and, even though the gap has been progressively narrowing over this period, it remains high (ie at around 38 per cent in 2019). This means that while shippers' expectations of providers' digital capabilities continue to grow, LSPs' adoption of these technologies and competencies remains low, even though they are becoming increasingly important.

The evidence collected by Evangelista et al (2013) showed that there was a low level of ICT expenditure by small and medium-sized LSPs with few companies adopting formal technology investment strategies. Unclear time of return on investment and difficulties in selecting the most appropriate applications were identified as the most important reasons.

More recently, Cichosz et al (2020) identified a number of success factors and barriers to digital transformation in the LSP industry. Among the barriers, shortages of financial and human resources were the main obstacles and the impact of these depends on the size of the LSP. In relation to the financial factor, the challenge is that generally financial institutions are not willing to lend their money for risky projects involving technological solutions to small companies operating in a low-margin industry. From the human resources point of view, LSPs suffer from a shortage of staff with digital capabilities. Again, the magnitude of the impact of this factor varies according to the size of the LSP. Larger LSPs are able to invest in training programmes, while in smaller companies this problem is more acute.

Conclusions

This chapter highlights the fact that digital transformation of the logistics business is rich in opportunities but there are several challenges that LSPs have to face in order to achieve a fully digitalized status. Logistics is a key component in the context of the overall Industry 4.0 concept. Its successful implementation requires adaptation of the logistics sector and changes to the business models of LSPs.

Despite the large number of benefits associated with the digitalization of logistics, there are a number of challenges and obstacles to overcome in order to achieve the status of digital logistics providers. The logistics industry suffers from a traditionally slower rate of innovation in comparison with other manufacturing and service sectors. Without innovation, LSPs will see their service offerings become commodities and long-term profitability will reduce. Any lack of innovation in LSPs should also be of concern to shippers and it may detrimentally affect the overall value chain. This phenomenon is rooted in the fact that business practices related to the management of physical assets have always prevailed in the sector. Little consideration has generally been given to less tangible assets such as information. This reflects the supply chain role that LSPs have in different evolving phases of their business. It also reinforces the need for a shift towards an approach oriented more towards information and knowledge. This in turn requires investment in digital technology and knowledge (Durst and Evangelista, 2018).

Furthermore, there is not only a difference between the IT expectations of customers (ie shippers) and their level of satisfaction with their LSPs' IT capabilities (ie the IT gap), but shippers are increasingly using data to optimize their networks and to drive supply chain decisions. In this area, there is also an 'Analytics Gap' in LSPs, ie a lack of specific applications aimed at obtaining valuable information from large amounts of data. On this point, the research conducted by PwC (2016) indicated that '...only 10 per cent of transportation and logistics companies rate the maturity of their data analytics capabilities as advanced. This is less than in other sectors.'

The technology gap affects predominantly small and medium-sized LSPs that are the backbone of the sector. This presents an implicit limitation to the wide adoption of Logistics 4.0 in the sector. Considering that shippers have become more expert purchasers of IT systems and applications, further research is needed to identify factors that have an impact on relationships between shippers and LSPs when developing collaborative IT-based services and the types of applications that are most relevant to these relationships. Finally, another important point relates to the lack of people equipped with digital capabilities. This problem is particularly evident in smaller logistics companies where investment in digital skills development is virtually absent.

References

Barreto, L, Amarala, A and Pereira, T (2017) Industry 4.0 implications in logistics: an overview, Engineering Society International Conference (MESIC), *Procedia Manufacturing*, **13**, pp 1245–252

Cichosz, M, Wallenburg, CM and Knemeyer, AM (2020) Digital transformation at logistics service providers: Barriers, success factors and leading practices, *The International Journal of Logistics Management*, **31** (2), pp 209–38

Delfmann, W, ten Hompel, M, Kersten, W, Schmidt, T and Stolzle, W (2018) Logistics as a science: Central research questions in the era of the fourth industrial revolution, *Logistics Research*, **11**, (9), pp 1–13

Durst, S and Evangelista, P (2018) Exploring knowledge management practices in third-party logistics service providers, *VINE: The journal of information and knowledge management systems*, Special Issue: Knowledge management evaluation: Research and practice perspectives, **48**, Issue 2, pp 162–77

Evangelista, P and Sweeney, E (2006) Technology usage in the supply chain: The case of small 3PLs, *The International Journal of Logistics Management*, **17** (1), pp 55–74

Evangelista, P, McKinnon, A and Sweeney, E (2013) Technology adoption in small and medium-sized logistics providers, *Industrial Management and Data Systems*, **113** (7), pp 967–89

Ganzarain, J and Errasti, N (2016) Three Stage Maturity Model in SME's towards Industry 4.0, *Journal of Industrial Engineering and Management*, **9** (5), pp 1119–128

Hofmann, E and Rüsch, M (2017) Industry 4.0 and the current status as well as future prospects on logistics, *Computers in Industry*, **89**, pp 23–34

Langley, C. John Jr and Infosys (2020) 24th Annual Third-Party Logistics Study: The State of Logistics Outsourcing, available at: www.3plstudy.com/ic3pl/ic3pl. ic3pl.ic3pl_2020downloads (archived at https://perma.cc/V375-6RM6)

Maslarić, M, Nikoličić, S and Mirčetić, D (2016) Logistics response to the Industry 4.0: The physical internet, *Open Engineering*, **6** (1), doi: 10.1515/eng-2016-0073

Montreuil, B (2011) Towards a physical internet: Meeting the global logistics sustainability grand challenge, *Logistics Research*, **3** (2–3), pp 71–87

Neumann, G and Evangelista, P (2019) The role of knowledge management in driving the application of Industry 4.0 in logistics, *Proceedings of the 20th European Conference on Knowledge Management*, 5–6 September, Universidade Europeia de Lisboa, Lisbon, Portugal

PwC (2016) Industry 4.0: Building the Digital Enterprise – Transportation and logistics key findings, available at www.pwc.com/gx/en/industries/industries-4.0/landing-page/industry-4.0-building-your-digital-enterprise-april-2016.pdf (archived at https://perma.cc/4NJF-T8KX)

Roblek, V, Mesko, M and Krapez, A (2016) A Complex View of Industry 4.0, *SAGE Open*, April–June 2016, pp 1–11

Rüßmann, M, Lorenz, M, Gerbert, P, Waldner, M, Justus, J, Engel, P and Harnisch, M (2015) *Industry 4.0: The future of productivity and growth in manufacturing industries*, The Boston Consulting Group

Skapinyecz, R, Illés, B and Bányai, A (2018) Logistic aspects of Industry 4.0, Proceedings of the XXIII International Conference on Manufacturing (Manufacturing 2018), *IOP Conference Series: Materials Science and Engineering*, **448** 012014

Tjahjono, B, Esplugues, C, Aresc, E and Pelaezc, G (2017) What does Industry 4.0 mean to Supply Chain?, Engineering Society International Conference (MESIC 2017), 28–30 June, *Procedia Manufacturing*, **13**, pp 1175–182

Transparency Market Research (2018) *Digital Transformation Spending in Logistics Market*, available at www.transparencymarketresearch.com/digital-transformation-spending-logistics-market.html (archived at https://perma.cc/E38J-VA22)

Wagner, SM (2008) Innovation management in the German transportation industry, *Journal of Business Logistics*, **29** (2), pp 215–31

WEF (2016) *Digital Transformation of Industries: Logistics*, World Economic Forum, White Paper in collaboration with Accenture, available at reports. weforum.org/digital-transformation/wp-content/blogs.dir/94/mp/files/pages/files/wef-dti-logisticswhitepaper-final-january-2016.pdf (archived at https://perma.cc/2UEN-5R2C)

Winkelhaus, S and Grosse, EH (2020) Logistics 4.0: A systematic review towards a new logistics system. *International Journal of Production Research*, 58 (1), pp 18–43

Performance measurement and management in the supply chain

20

Alan Braithwaite

Measure to manage

Lord Kelvin (1824–1907), the famed physicist and mathematician, is quoted as saying, 'If you cannot measure it, you cannot improve it.' More prosaic is the current jargon that says 'what gets measured gets fixed'.

With the aid of computing and communications, we now live in a world that measures, targets and analyses almost everything across business, politics and sport. The 2020 Covid pandemic has brought the importance of measurement into the sharpest of focus. There can scarcely be anyone who has not taken in the key measures of infections per 100,000 people by area and the 'reproduction rate'. These measures of the progress of the virus carry through into the rate of hospital admissions and, sadly, patient mortality. Reducing or containing the number of infections reduces the hospital admissions and ultimately the deaths. Over the duration of the pandemic, the absolute numbers of the infection, its rate of spread and how that has driven the experience in the hospitals have been observed to change. That has required further analysis which has shown causes such as increased testing finding asymptomatic cases, increased infectivity of mutant virus variants and improved treatments. Covid-19 has proved to be a frightening example of the sort of complex interdependencies that are encountered in measuring any supply chain.

The political implications of measuring and publishing were in full view in 2020; they provided a direct and visible measure of how well the system was responding to the sequence of events – a daily judgement call. It hardly needs to be said that no elected official wants to hear, on their watch, stories of hospitals overwhelmed, and turning dying patients away.

The temptation to be not entirely truthful with the data when things are going badly cannot be ignored. In December 2020, the BBC reported that President Erdoğan of Turkey had failed to manage the pandemic and had turned to managing the statistics.

Indeed, the academic literature and the press are full of analysis and reports both of measurements being falsified and behaviours being modified to secure target outcomes with unpalatable side effects. Performance measurement and management is a fertile ground for driving less than desired behaviours; in short, targeting on outcomes invokes the law of unintended consequences.[1]

This chapter will unpack the landscape of performance measurement and management in business and across supply chains.

Financial reporting measures

Measurement and reporting of KPIs (key performance indicators) is a core discipline in business for governance and accountability. It has been grounded historically in the backward-looking accounting disciplines of recording profit and solvency. These are also statutory obligations for company directors.

Company accounting is not a real-time process of measurement and monitoring. The accounting periods are annual, with some companies issuing quarterly statements. The preparation of results can incur further time. When released, their publication is the subject of analysts' detailed scrutiny and comment. The requirement for compilation of performance measures in terms of financial health and its disclosure is vital for all stakeholders: shareholders, creditors, bankers and employees. For quoted companies there is an 'industry' of financial analysis that picks over the reported results and statements and attempts to forecast the prospects. Accounting standards bodies such as the Securities and Exchange Commission in the United States and the Accounting Standards Authority in the UK regulate the preparation of such company information. The trend has been to require increasing disclosure

Figure 20.1   The five levers that the CEO cares about (after Ram Charan)

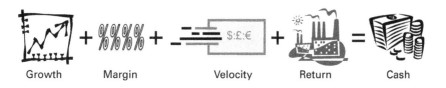

Growth   Margin   Velocity   Return   Cash

not just financially but also in respect of subjects such as corporate social responsibility (CSR).

Ram Charan is his book *What the CEO wants you to know* identifies the five levers available to CEOs which determine their success, or not, and form the basis of the judgements made by the markets.[2] This may enhance the value of their businesses which is usually a primary personal goal. Figure 20.1 shows Charan's five levers in diagram form.

The impact of these on company performance and how they interact becomes clear from looking at each in turn. First, growth is important for most CEOs as the top-line revenue drives earnings and shareholder value, with a significant but not dominant correlation coefficient. Stock market expectations of sales growth tend to drive elevated price–earnings ratios in anticipation of increased earnings. The argument is that profit and cash will always follow. CEOs are highly motivated by growth because it is a measure of the market acceptance of the customer proposition and the company's operational effectiveness in delivering it. A business is unlikely to grow if it is not providing compelling value to its customers, or if there are problems with its service.

Margin is about operating profitability and is a more crucial measure; analysis of the FT Global 500 for revenue and profit correlation with market valuations shows that company value is more closely linked to profit than to revenues.[3] For a business to survive and thrive it must earn the margin to give a return on the investment in the business. CEOs are seriously interested in benchmarks against the competition for both gross margin and operating expenses; together these combine to give net margins, or earnings.

The third lever is 'velocity' and this term is used to convey the idea of the speed with which the cash, stock and capital in the business is turned. The easiest way to represent velocity is by measuring the cash-to-cash cycle; this is the days of sale in cash terms that are locked up in the business from the day it pays for supplies to when it gets paid by its customers, including the stock that sits in the business. The shorter the cash-to-cash cycle the more agile and adaptable the business will be to changes in its market, and the lower the risk of having to write off stock or debtors. Short cash-to-cash cycle businesses also require less funding for sales growth; consequently they are perceived better by the markets in terms of value.

Return on investment is the fourth lever and this is a measure of both fixed and working capital efficiency. Measures such as return on capital employed (ROCE) and return on shareholders' funds (ROSF) show how the company is returning against its invested base of buildings, equipment, vehicles, stock and net debtors, together with any know-how or goodwill that it has capitalized. It is not uncommon for a company to grow in both revenue and earnings while diluting its return on investment.

Finally, 'cash is king'. A business that is cash generating will be generating good margins, will have excellent velocity in terms of cash-to-cash and be delivering good returns on investment. Cash is the ultimate outcome and a business that generates cash will have the capacity to invest and grow; it will be able to borrow prudently and make acquisitions. In addition it will be able to pay substantial performance-related benefits to its executives and reward shareholders with increased dividends.

With extended financial reporting timetables and the potential to window-dress the presentation, the process of creating reports and accounts has been likened to 'driving down the motorway steering through the rear view mirror with a telescope'. And the integrity of such reporting is frequently drawn into question through major corporate scandals such as Enron and, most recently, Carillion. These two episodes, among many, show that it is possible to sustain false positions for long periods through the 'managed' reporting of high-level measures, notwithstanding certified audits. In response to these cases there has been progressive hardening of regulations and legislation on corporate governance as well as eye-watering fines for auditors.

Measuring outcomes versus inputs

Published accounts report results – outcomes. As well as not being very timely, they provide few insights into how the business is going to grow, return and generate cash. That requires that companies identify and measure (faster and more frequently) the inputs that will determine their ultimate performance. The measures on which the stakeholders judge the business are not open to direct action. So, as examples of many cause-and-effect constructs, we cannot act directly on:

- sales revenue, and the economies that go with scale, without dealing with the levels of customer satisfaction that are achieved in terms of value for money, inventory availability and service turnaround;

- inventory levels in the chain without dealing with processes such as forecasting accuracy, frequency and horizon, and inventory record accuracy;

- cost-to-serve by product and customer without having designed the network for optimum sourcing and fulfilment.

Table 20.1 illustrates a simple example of input and output measures in a manufacturing case study (the figures are illustrative only). The input measures reflect the major changes that were made in this company and the output measures were the consequences of these actions, and illustrate the shareholder value that was created.

The story was that the company moved to a cell system of manufacturing based on a major reduction in set-up times. This enabled inventory reductions of 80 per cent, which enabled distribution rationalization and major cost savings in logistics. The cell system was also cheaper in manufacturing as waiting times were reduced along with waste. Sales grew because the company was more responsive to customer demand. Overall profits increased by 75 per cent.

All of these improvements were achieved through a long-term commitment to performance measurement, process standard adherence, and supply chain governance leading to the rebalancing of the company's supply chain. Supply chain governance is an idea that is developed later in this chapter.

The balanced scorecard: the strategic standard for goal setting and measurement

The Balanced Scorecard was originally proposed by Kaplan and Norton to address this challenge of linking business strategy and direction to the setting of organizational performance objectives: Inputs versus Outputs.[4] The scorecard offers a contained and comprehensive approach to addressing the strategic direction for the company and unpacking it into management specifics and control actions; it is a reference for many Fortune 500 corporations, and it fits especially well with supply chain thinking. This chapter will adopt it as the strategic reference point for performance measurement.

Table 20.1 Input and output measures in a performance improvement case

Measure	Start	Finish
INPUT MEASURES		
Forecast accuracy	Poor	Improved but less important
Manufacturing change time	8 hours	15 minutes
New product introduction	Months	Weeks
Logistics structure	3 depots	Single national site
OUTPUT MEASURES		
Sales		+10%
Customer service (OTIF)	96%	99%
Stock	12 weeks	2 weeks
Obsolescence	High	Minimal
Distribution costs	14% of turnover	9% of turnover
Manufacturing unit cost		Reduced by 20%

A balanced scorecard provides a picture of a business's direction by making the linkage between financial measures and specific operational targets for customer satisfaction, key internal processes, costs and organizational learning and growth. The conceptual framework is captured in Kaplan and Norton's diagram in Figure 20.2.[5]

The balanced scorecard strategy map calls for specific goals for customer satisfaction in terms of price, time, quality, performance, service and cost as well as relationship, brand and product leadership. The key is to understand how these measures need to change to meet the strategic goals of the business. From that, the internal perspective builds from those goals to realize the results: the outputs. It focuses on core competencies, processes, decisions and actions that have the greatest impact on attaining customer satisfaction. In modern terms, these are the 'killer apps' that make the customer value proposition truly compelling.

At its foundation, the balanced scorecard has a learning and growth perspective; this sets the measures for continual improvements with people, systems and processes. This is about embedding the strategic changes in operational programmes. Ultimately it is what drives the attainment of the desired financial measures, connecting 'output' measures (financial and customer satisfaction) with performance drivers input measures, such as value proposition, internal processes, learning and growth. Every measure selected for a scorecard should be part of a chain of cause-and-effect relationships, leading to the financial objectives that represent the strategic themes for the business.

Kaplan and Norton outline four key processes that the balanced scorecard relies on to connect short-term activities to long-term objectives:[6,7,8]

1 Translating the vision: managers are required to translate their vision into actual measurements linked directly to the people who will realize the vision.

2 Communicating and linking: the scorecard indicates what the organization is trying to achieve for both shareholders and customers. The high-level strategy map is translated into 'business unit' scorecards and eventually 'personal scorecards' so that the individual understands how their personal goals and performance supports the overall strategy.

3 Business planning: once the performance measures for the four perspectives have been agreed the company identifies the key drivers of the desired outcomes and defines the milestones that mark progress towards achieving their strategic goal.

Figure 20.2 Kaplan and Norton's balanced scorecard framework

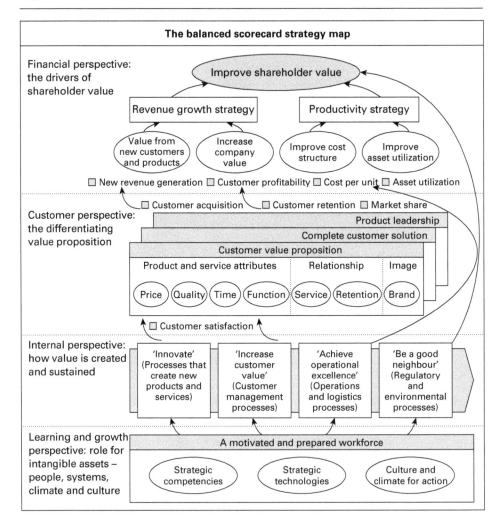

4 Feedback and learning: this allows for regular performance reviews to enable continuous improvement of the strategy and its execution.

In summary the scorecard puts strategy and vision, not control, at the centre. The measures are designed to pull people toward the overall vision. This methodology is consistent with the approach of supply chain management by helping managers overcome traditional functional silos and ultimately leads to improved decision making and problem solving.

The fundamentals of supply chain performance measurement

There are many definitions of logistics and supply chain management in circulation which try to capture the essence of the concept. A detailed academic examination of the meaning, usage and distinctions between the terms 'supply chain management' and 'logistics' found that they are used somewhat interchangeably.[9]

This analysis observed that recent writing suggests the supply chain management (SCM) concept goes further than some standard definitions and that it transcends firms, functions and business processes. This makes SCM more than just logistics, positioning it as a complete business operations framework covering all functions and operating over extended networks with suppliers and customers.

In this context, this author provides a description of the supply chain concept as:

> A process orientation to managing business in an integrated way that transcends the boundaries of firms and functions; leading to cooperation, through-chain business process synchronization, effective ranging and new product introduction, as well as managing the entire physical logistics agenda.

The mechanism by which the network of entities, that together comprise a company's supply chain(s), works is through shared information and closely aligned processes. The vision for these networks is that they are characterized by high levels of communication and transparency, supported by synchronous operations and performance measurement and management.

Experience of applying supply chain management (even partially) within a business is that improved visibility and synchronization leads to some or all of:

- improved customer service experience;
- reduced inventories;
- lower operating costs and reduced waste;
- improved use of fixed assets.

The ultimate benefit can be taken through improvements in a mix of profitability, shareholder value and growth or market share depending on the strategic priorities of the firm. The potential is for supply chain management

Figure 20.3 Balancing the supply chain

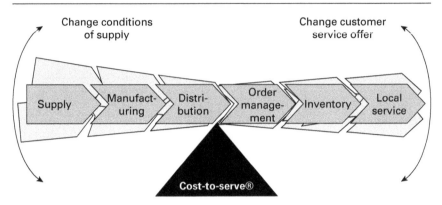

Change conditions of supply

Change customer service offer

Supply — Manufacturing — Distribution — Order management — Inventory — Local service

Cost-to-serve®

SOURCE Braithwaite and Samakh[10]

thinking and practice to transform a company in terms of its overall performance. The leverage through the combination of many small (albeit radical in their conception) improvements in the operating and process architecture of a company can be remarkable.

The big idea that sits behind the supply chain concept is a move from functional management to the management of cross business processes; the principle is that business effectiveness is enhanced by optimizing across the whole chain compared with optimizing individual functions. Experience shows that the aggregation of individually optimized functions drives inefficiencies and waste at their interfaces and does not give the best overall performance.

As a result, striking the right balance between optimized functional goals and those modified to reflect business optimization is the core concept of SCM. It is important to note that breaking down the barriers between functions to improve supply chain integration is not a substitute for functional excellence. Companies need to secure both dimensions – retaining and improving their competence in all the functions in the supply chain as well as integrating processes to eliminate waste.

The laws of supply chain management capture the key concepts through seven maxims for excellence.[11] Among these, the laws of lowest total cost and organizational difficulty point to the waste that is driven by interfunctional sub-optimization. The laws point to the need for a systematic functional rebalancing based on the end-to-end cost-to-serve – at least internally but preferably looking additionally inside both its customers' and suppliers' operations. This holistic approach delivers the required service at the lowest total cost. The idea is illustrated in Figure 20.3.

Performance measurement and management is a critical component of this rebalancing initiative; appropriate functions and cost components should be measured and targeted against integrated goals. Supply chain performance measurement and management is the operational microclimate of the balanced scorecard that Kaplan and Norton have given us.

Mastering the complexity of supply chain and logistics performance management

Supply chain and logistics at this detailed level is complex in its detail. The biggest challenge in setting up measurement and management programmes is mastering that complexity to create an internally consistent framework of goals that reflect the true relationships of cause and effect: inputs and outputs.

The conditions for each company, even within the same sector, will be different. The drivers of cost and service performance will be a combination of both its structural determinants and management determinants respectively.

The idea of 'structural' and 'management' determinants and the distinction between them is important. Structural determinants relate to the 'business we are in': our products and customers. Here the choices for management are limited; if you are in the fertilizer or seeds business you have farmers and merchants as customers and deliver to farms. The characteristics of the product are well defined, and the nature of demand is local or national. In contrast, microchip manufacturers operate on an international scale using airfreight and with billions of dollars invested in plant. The fundamental difference in the products is driven home by the cost per tonne of microchips being more than \$1,000,000 whereas the cost per tonne for fertilizer is typically less than \$200. There is no escape from these realities.

Management determinants reflect the areas where management has choices to make within the constraints of the nature of the business, ie the structural determinants discussed above. There are big decisions to be made here on the operating model in relation to sourcing, capacity investment and characteristics, marketing positioning and service levels, business process design and operational effectiveness.

These choices interact with each other and the structural determinants to drive the end-to-end performance and cost. Figure 20.4 makes the point that the scale and degree of interaction across the various areas of cost and performance is multivariate and complex. The challenge that emerges for

Figure 20.4   The complexity of supply chain and logistics, viewed through determinants

Supply Chain Performance Determinants

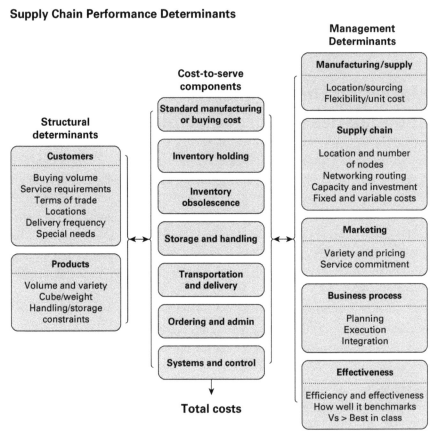

performance measurement and management in the supply chain is to correctly define the driving relationships in the context of the choices that the company has made in its markets. From the definition of these relationships arises the precise specification of the measures to be used and the values to be set as goals for the individual functional managers.

Setting goals across the chain through service level agreements

The case in Table 20.1 illustrates the complex interaction of supply chain variables between functions; for example, improvements in manufacturing can reduce stock and enable lower cost structures in distribution and logistics as well as reducing waste in manufacturing. It emphasizes the fundamental principle of securing rebalancing for business performance improvement. The common question on performance measurement is 'How should functional goals be set in the chain to secure the business potential?'

And there are a further series of sub-questions, which arise from this major question:

- How does a function see its role and contribution to improving the whole supply chain?
- What levels of visibility should be given, between functions, of the goals and attainment by others?
- How does a function influence the performance of other members in the chain, which can impact its own performance but are out of its direct control?
- Who sets the measures of performance across the chain?

The idea of cross-functional service level agreements (SLAs) is a means to resolve the first three of these questions. SLAs can provide a framework in which the various functions within a company and between organizations (both customers and suppliers) are measured. Each SLA defines meaningful objectives that will generate overall supply chain performance improvement.

The first big idea embedded in such SLAs is that they are not just sequential between players in the physical chain but also recognize the obligations of every member of the team to the others, whether or not they are next in line. The SLAs will often not be mutual: equal and opposite. Rather they will be asymmetric: 'I do this for you and you do that for me.' The second big idea is that SLAs create a team environment; rather like any sport, each player knows his place in the side, the contribution that he or she makes and the dependencies with other positions. So, to use a Rugby Union example, the half-backs and three-quarters know their respective positions and the moves that they will be making; the output measures are tries scored and the percentage of tackles made on the opposition, while the input measures are adherence to plan and position, quality of individual execution of ball control and tackling, and the speed of response to moves by either team. Each member of the back line has commitments to all the others in his line and to the forwards – and not just to the player next to him. Inter-functional SLAs in the supply chain are the same in their conception.

Figure 20.5 shows the standard concept of a sequential chain at the top. Below that it also shows an example matrix of the cross-organizational

SLAs that need to exist. Each box in this SLA framework should be populated with input measures as they reflect the performance obligations that the functions have to each other. As noted, the entries are not symmetrical as the commitments of the functions in the context of the overall goals are not mutual. So, for example, the relationship between Sales & Marketing and Production Planning is that Sales & Marketing must produce a forecast on time and to an agreed level of accuracy, while Production Planning's commitment to Sales & Marketing is to turn that forecast into available product (plus/minus a tolerance) through the creation of timely and economic schedules. Equally, Manufacturing will have commitments to the business, including Sales & Marketing, that relate to adherence to schedule, yield and quality performance; but in return they are entitled to expect levels of demand volatility and schedule stability within agreed tolerances from Sales & Marketing and Demand Planning. If anything steps outside of the tolerance, this is not a failure of one party; it is an issue for the business.

It is important to note that the SLAs are entirely about input measures such as adherence to schedule, quality and lead time. It is changes to these measures and improvements in performance that drive value through the company's supply chain and into its output measures of profit and value.

Integrating the chain through SLAs

The creation of this matrix, even in the most rudimentary form, and making it available to the entire business together with published current performance and future targets, answers the first two of the sub-questions. From this platform each function can see where it fits and how it can help to play the game.

The process of setting up the SLA matrix, populating the targets and recording the performance achieved is the way that the functions can start to resolve the tensions relating to the impact they may have on each other. This is an important organizational process and is a key role of supply chain management at the board level. It is this person (or small team) that sets the matrix in conjunction with the functional heads, and then monitors attainment and initiates corrective action where necessary. This is the idea of supply chain governance; the supply chain manager (director) holds the total vision for supply chain improvement for the firm in the context of the business objectives and the individual functional performances that will deliver the result. In sporting terms, he is the team coach.

Figure 20.5 The conventional sequential supply chain relationship and the SLA matrix

Integrating the chain through SLAs

From ↓ To →	Supply	Distribution	Head office	Outlets
Supply		• Bar code compliance • Product 99+% available on time to quality within forecast tolerance and reduced order lead time • Load collection or deliver in specified time window	• Reduced lead times for supply • 99% accuracy on supply within tolerances • Faster promos and new product intros	
Distribution 	• Forecast accuracy – orders inside tolerances • Clear supply contracts with lead times specified • Collect/receive to schedule with no delays		Subject to the linked dependencies, HO must invest and deliver to Outlets >95% OTIFNIE at a declining cost/case And work with Distn. on network changes to reduce cost	Subject to the linked dependencies, Distn. must invest and deliver to HO and Outlets > 95% OTIFNIE at a declining cost/case
Head office 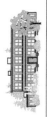	• Contract framework with accurate demand forecasts and tolerances • Visibility and collaboration on promotions and new products • Bar code specifications	• Plus 1 to max plus 2 day outlet order lead time • Actively sponsor delivery schedule changes • Actively collaborate on forecasting and replenishment through GW implant		• Stream of promotions and new products – launched without failures • Auditable performance management of Distn. with visible action on issues
Outlets 		• Receive deliveries in a prompt manner • Operate to cut off time on order changes • Support in developing efficient and sustainable schedules	• Stock on hand accuracy • Order schedule compliance • Agree cut off on order changes and delivery schedules	

SOURCE Author

For cross-chain balancing, it is necessary to introduce measures of cost as well as the input measures into the SLA matrix. The SLA matrix needs to be maintained as a living framework that responds to external forces, actual performance and continuous learning.

This is a full-time organizational role. If the supply chain director also has direct functional responsibility for some or all of planning, inventory, distribution and procurement, then they and the whole team will need to isolate the governance role within their own organization to ensure that balance and impartiality are achieved.

The delivery, recovery and governance model

Putting the SLA matrix into action is the process and activity of measuring and tracking performance against targets and identifying opportunities for improvement, not just looking back at past performance. The focus for performance management should be the future, asking 'What do you need to be able to do and how can you do things better?'

The Delivery, Recovery and Governance (DRG) model is a way of institutionalizing measurement across the business and is consistent with Kaplan and Norton's Balanced Scorecard and its requirement for learning.

Figure 20.6 is a simple representation of the DRG model designed to illustrate the working cycle in which each function measures its delivery against its SLAs in the matrix and including the cost performance goals. Reports including the identification of failures and the impact of recovery actions are produced at the functional level and then consolidated by the supply chain organization in its governance role. Recovery is an important activity with the learning that comes from it. It is unrealistic to expect supply chains to run perfectly smoothly, so it is wise to have contingencies and processes that deal with such events. The governance role is to feed back to the functions the impact on overall performance and propose changes to the SLAs, delivery performance and the means of recovery.

The model is consistent with the so-called Shewhart or PDCA cycle (Plan–Do–Check–Act, known in Japan as the Deming cycle) based on the theory of continuous improvement:[12]

1 Business understanding and strategic directions; **plan** the process.

2 Run the operation to try to deliver in line with the plan; **do** the operation and record the results.

3 Performance reporting against plan and interpretation of results; **check** by analysis and reporting of performance according to key business drivers.

4 Tactical and strategic realignment; **act** to initiate improvement efforts based on the lessons learned from experience. These experiences feed into the new plan, since PDCA is a cyclical process.

In summary, the DRG model is a way to capture the supply chain improvement vision for the firm and to record and manage progress to its attainment. It may seem daunting and potentially complex and, if this is the case, the key is to start with the simplest possible framework and build from it as the organization learns. In other words, adopt the same principles of plan–do–check–act to the process of planning and measurement across the chain as are being applied to the chain itself.

Figure 20.6   The Delivery, Recovery and Governance model

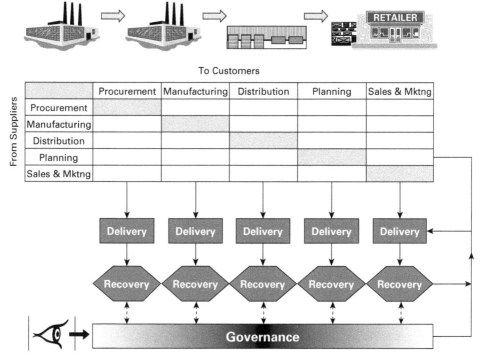

SOURCE Author

The governance role as a functionally independent 'trustee' in the organization is crucial to the DRG model and this is a difficult position to define and maintain in the organization. The person who holds the role will require vision, interpersonal skills and tenacity. The role needs the highest level of board sponsorship and the results of DRG need to be a standard part of the board agenda. It is at this point that supply chain management and corporate strategy meet and can be integrated into the balanced scorecard.

Defining the specific metrics across the chain

The input and output measures described earlier are the high-level cause-and-effect metrics for the supply chain. The input measures in the SLAs are, as has been observed, primarily about quality, compliance and time. The governance role requires these measures and the performance against them be transparent. Cost measures also need to be added to the portfolio as functional productivity measures. In this section, the specifics of the measures that can be applied across the supply chain are unpacked and described. The specification of measures is complex and detailed, so this description should be treated as an overview rather than a complete reference.

The supply chain and logistics professional and the corporate governance of the chain will want to develop an overview of the chain; a useful way to think about this is as a 'dashboard' or control tower for the business. This idea is illustrated in Figure 20.7 and many executives find the preparation of such diagrams valuable in identifying their performance issues and describing them to their colleagues. Measures may need to reflect both changes over time and also performance across the range of products, customers and suppliers.

A further important point in relation to this overview is that, while supply chain rebalancing via SLAs will be one of the key drivers for competitive advantage, firms must also recognize that an equal and parallel emphasis should remain on attaining functional excellence. The goals of functional excellence however will be tempered at the margin through an understanding that such aims can lead to overall supply chain sub-optimization. An example would be maximizing plant utilization with long runs in a way that creates inventory and leaves customers short of some product variants. The SLAs are developed over time to eliminate such potential conflicts.

Figure 20.7 Viewing supply chain metrics across the chain

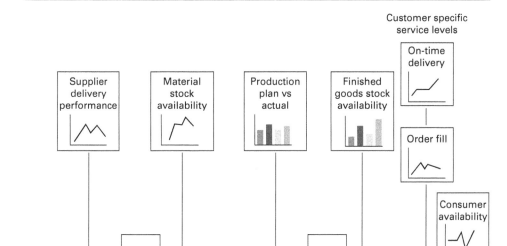

SOURCE Christopher and Braithwaite

Although the measures themselves are generic for most businesses, the precise situation and issues for each firm will vary based on its competitive situation, technology and product–market characteristics. It is helpful to think of a hierarchy of measures across the chain in terms of both input and output measures:

- Level 1 measures should provide headline metrics for the supply chain, eg orders on time in full with no invoice errors (OTIFNIE) and stock cover, all set in a balanced way that supports the vision for change.

- Level 2 measures should be used to provide further insight into the results of Level 1, eg quantity fill percentage, line fill percentage, invoice accuracy.

- Finally, Level 3 measures should provide diagnostics for use in problem resolution and improvement processes. For example, requests for credit, clear-up rate, number of days out of stock by stock-keeping unit (SKU).

Figure 20.8 provides examples of Levels 1 and 2 performance metrics across a typical retail supply chain.

Figure 20.8   Sample Level 1/2 metrics containing both input and output measures

Suppliers	Manufacturing	Forecasting	Inbound freight
• Unit cost • OTIFNIE % • Spread of failure • Lead time of supply • Fixed and firm schedule horizon • Flexibility inside fixed horizon	• Plant utilization • Output vs standard • Cost/unit of manufacturing • Overhead recovery to plan % time used in change overs • Conformance to plan • Fixed and firm schedule horizons	• Forecast accuracy at +1 week, +2 weeks, +1 month, +2 months, +3 months • By SKU and family • Demand volatility coefficient of variation • With and without promotions	• Truck utilization % tonnes or cube carried vs capacity % working time used • Cost/delivery • Cost/cu m or tonne • Dispatch to delivery time

Suppliers   Manufacturer   ?

Distribution centre	Stock	Freight	Service
• Full cost per case • Full cost per pallet • Fixed cost/sq m • Full cost/man hr • Picks/man hr • Labour utilization % • Space utilization % • Throughput utilization % • Order-to-despatch time	• Weeks of cover • Days of sale • Stock turns • OOS lines & % • Stock > 26 wks • Obsolescence/write-offs % • Stock accuracy (sku, qty and location)	• Truck utilization % tonnes or cube carried vs capacity • Deliveries per day • % working time used • Cost/delivery • Cost/cu m or tonne	• OTIFNIE % • Order-to-delivery TAT days • Line fill % • Qty fill % • Order fill accuracy % • Invoice errors/credit notes % • % to schedule/commitment

RETAILER

Manufacturer   Distribution   Retail distribution   Retailers

SOURCE Author

Figure 20.8 repays detailed study since it starts to provide insight into the levels of detail that are involved and can be used to challenge the organization as to the connections between functions and the real drivers. For example, the figure shows both 'on time in full' (OTIF) and 'order to delivery

Figure 20.9 A sample logistical balanced scorecard

Manufacture	Inbound	Stock	Service and accuracy
• 95% to plan • < 2 weeks schedule horizon	• 100% on time • 85% utilization	• 2 weeks or 25 turns for whole chain	• 99.9%+ against perfect order

Supply	Forecast	Distribution	Freight
• 99.9% reliable • substantial flexibility vs forecast	• 80% at SKU • 95% at range • At 1 month	• 99.9% accuracy • 85% utilization	• 75% to 85% utilization • Externalize fixed costs

SOURCE Author

turnaround time' (TAT). It is immediately obvious that the longer the TAT, the higher should be the OTIF – since there is more time to get it right. But at the same time the longer the TAT, the lower should be the inventory, as the more time manufacturing has to respond to actual demand. TAT is therefore an input measure, and it is also one that management may want to change, as faster service is likely to be more competitive and create increased demand.

In the same vein, measures of plant, distribution centre and transportation efficiency will be influenced by customer order turnaround time, forecast accuracy and plant changeover time – all of which are input measures.

This brief introduction to the interaction of measures should be sufficient to demonstrate that Figure 20.8 is not a complete guide; rather it should be used as a prompt for thinking through the measures that are exactly relevant to the company.

Having decided on the appropriate metrics to be used in the performance management framework, it is then necessary to ensure that these individual measures are set in a balanced way to provide an overall picture of supply chain performance and support the business in moving to its goals. A sample of a balanced set of objective measures for a fast-moving consumer goods company is included here in Figure 20.9.

The case behind this set of measures is that high service performance with low levels of stock (output measures) is secured by high levels of forecast accuracy, very short manufacturing schedule horizons, high schedule adherence and exceptional supplier performance. High levels of accuracy are also essential. The area that has been deliberately sacrificed is that of distribution and freight utilization. Setting these measures consistently, having understood the relationships, is the key to avoiding functional conflicts that can cause sub-optimal performance. Examples of this are:

- stock-holding targets that are set too low will disable customer service attainment and reduce the number of orders fulfilled on time in full (OTIF);
- freight utilization and cost targets may delay shipments leading to increased stock and a negative impact on customer service;
- manufacturing unit cost goals may drive up stocks and downstream distribution costs due to long production runs and infrequent line changes.

With performance metrics and the consequent balanced scorecard established, greater focus can be achieved on supply chain issues and opportunities. This also helps with benchmarking by identifying current and best practice in companies and their supply chains before using some of the Level 3 diagnostic metrics to develop an improvement programme.

Control towers: collecting, managing and using data

The biggest barriers to a successful performance measurement and management programme have historically been the compilation of data and its analysis and interpretation. Typically, the base data involves hundreds of thousands of transactions, many hundreds of general ledger codes, some thousands of stock-keeping units and many hundreds of customers and suppliers. All these can span a number of plants and distribution centres. Collecting and managing this data is a significant task and an area of expertise in its own right.

Measurement and reporting used to be a labour-intensive and hard-won achievement with limited potential for supplementary diagnosis and interpretation. But recent developments in mass data storage, cloud computing, artificial intelligence and sophisticated analytics now provide a platform for achieving detailed information on status against plan and root causes of any issues. Advanced software can be quickly configured to provide both standard reports and to drill down to understand specific issues. The global nature of the internet makes this possible across the widest possible span of

Figure 20.10   Creating a supply chain information backbone

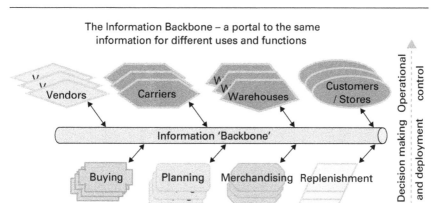

SOURCE Braithwaite (2021)

the supply chain: reporting and analytics on shorter time frames. In less than 10 years, the preparation of performance management reports and analysis has moved from being a struggle to get the data to being a struggle to cope with all the data.

The terminology 'control towers' has become the norm and that fits with the supply chain governance role described earlier. ICT technology all along the chain, both within the business and outside, is now ubiquitous, extending to feeding event management systems, drawing on GPS tracker data to follow movements and build huge data 'cubes' that can be interrogated at will.

The concept is illustrated in Figure 20.10 which shows the different elements of the chain informing and being informed by the information backbone.

This is an example from globally sourced retailing. Across the top are the physical activities and the planning and deployment functions are along the bottom. All the physical activities and decision points need to be available to all the actors across the chain, although some pairings will be more intensively used than others.

The skills and experience required to set up and run such 'big' data environments is now critical to commercial success. It is an important career path that did not exist 10 years ago.

Future directions in performance measurement

The major challenge for performance measurement in the supply chain rests in integrating performance management into the fabric of the organization to drive supply chain strategy development and implementation. In that context this section is just a short summary of the author's developing recent work and thinking.

The word integration is overused in supply chain management without great clarity as to its meaning and implications. The Strategic Crystal has been used successfully to address this question by describing the elements of an integrated supply chain strategy and showing how they interact to deliver business value in terms of customer satisfaction and economic value added.[3] Figure 20.11 shows the crystal with the key elements of:

- Business processes: the processes of generating planning and execution instructions through the chain that, if correctly designed, will increase customer service and reduce inventories and capital applied. Business process re-design in supply chain management is focused on the principles of time compression and simplification. Business processes are crucially dependent on systems, organization and KPIs, three other points in the crystal. Business processes are key input measures and a major part of the SLAs.

- Supply chain systems: the computer information systems that are applied must serve the business processes and the organization, support the network and inform the performance measurement environment.

- The supply chain network (suppliers, plants and distribution centres) is the key to the cost performance in the chain and is enabled by the processes and systems. The organization design must align to the network to enable the lowest cost operation.

- Performance management through consistent and appropriate key performance indicators is central to an effective supply chain strategy, as we have seen in this chapter. The process of performance management enables the organization to function and develop and is dependent on the systems and the processes.

- Organization design is a most under-represented area of supply chain strategy. An organization that is aligned to the strategy and is served by the systems, processes and KPIs is central to realizing supply chain value.

Figure 20.11   The strategic supply chain crystal

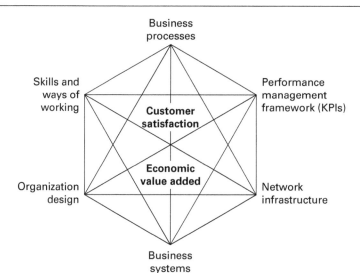

SOURCE Braithwaite and Christopher (2015)

As businesses move from a functional to a process orientation, the boundaries of traditional functional power are challenged and tensions are exposed. The SLA approach can help resolve these tensions since functional control is not required under that model. However the stewardship role is mandatory and, as discussed earlier, it must be positioned in the organization with both power and independence.

● Skills and behaviours are the final facet of the crystal and like organization design are under-represented. The skills and behaviours to move to a supply chain ethic, from function to process, are profoundly different from those that have been trained into management over many years. Skills and behaviours are connected strongly to all points in the crystal.

The picture of true supply chain integration to generate business value that emerges from the crystal is a strong one; actions on one facet will distort the crystal and generate unwanted results. Performance measurement and management is core to the overall strategic vision and the agenda for change.

As an example, a global brewer adopted a performance management framework with KPIs as its starting point in the crystal for supply chain transformation. Over a period of months, it put supply chain potential on the agenda by establishing nine KPIs that it required all of its subsidiaries to report, from Asia through Europe and Africa to the Americas. It took some months for these measures to be consistently reported, but when that was achieved the company started placing the measures in the monthly main board packs. This caused everyone to sit up and take note and benchmark their performance with their peers. Immediate improvements were seen without any perceptible corporate effort and the initiative gained credibility. The next step was expanding the measures to 14 core corporate measures and to provide help with goal setting for the subsidiaries. This goal setting for performance improvement was important because, for example, a brewer in East Africa cannot expect to target the same measures as one in Western Europe; each subsidiary would need to focus on what would give it the most immediate and greatest returns.

From this measurement exercise, that took place over about three years, each subsidiary could embark on its own blend of change around the crystal.

Conclusion

This simple case study shows the potential for improvement through the development of performance management metrics across the supply chain; it is a key differentiator of change capability and organizational agility. Firms that develop supply chain measurement, as a core business competence associated with strategic objectives, will have a strong foundation for defining realignment internally and with both customers and suppliers.

The combined use of supply chain performance metrics, balanced scorecards, and the delivery, recovery and governance framework provide the capability to report on improvement, understand the factors that are driven by the change and identify supply chain management best practice.

In conclusion, there are six key points to hold in focus when developing a supply chain performance management framework:

1 No single measure defines supply chain performance – there are many dimensions to measure.

2 Measures can be in conflict – accentuating rather than breaking functional silo issues.

3 It is important to aim for balance throughout the supply chain and be prepared to adapt and develop.

4 Measuring the overall performance at input and output levels is a key first step to making improvements.

5 This requires considerable investment of time and commitment.

6 Measurement and its interpretation is a valuable and difficult skill that organizations should develop and nurture.

Organizations that have persevered with supply chain measurement and management have experienced sustained improvements in business performance.

References

1 Merton, RK (1936) The unanticipated consequences of purposive social action, *American Sociological Review*, **1** (6), p 895

2 Charan, R (2001) *What the CEO Wants You to Know*, Crown Business

3 Braithwaite, A and Christopher, M (2015) *Business Operations Models: Becoming a disruptive competitor*, Kogan Page, London

4 Kaplan, RS and Norton, DP (1996) *Translating Strategy into Action: The balanced scorecard*, Harvard Business School Press, Boston, MA

5 Kaplan, RS and Norton, DP (1996) *Translating Strategy into Action: The balanced scorecard*, Harvard Business School Press, Boston, MA

6 Kaplan, RS (2002) *Building strategy focused organisations with the balanced scorecard*, presentation, Performance Management Association, Boston, MA

7 Kaplan, RS and Norton, DP (1992) The balanced scorecard: Measures that drive performance, *Harvard Business Review*, Jan–Feb

8 Kaplan, RS and Norton, DP (1996) Using the balanced scorecard as a strategic management system, *Harvard Business Review*, Jan–Feb

9 Cooper, MC, Lambert, DM and Pagh, JD (1997) Supply chain management: More than a new name for logistics, *International Journal of Logistics Management*, **8** (1)

10 Braithwaite, A and Samakh, E (1998) The cost-to-serve method, *International Journal of Logistics Management*, **9** (1), pp 69–84

11 Braithwaite, A and Wilding, R (2004) The Laws of Logistics and Supply Chain Management, *Financial Times Handbook of Management*, 3rd edn, Prentice Hall

12 Deming, WE (1967) Walter A Shewhart, 1891–1967, *American Statistician*, **21**, pp 39–40

Aligning technology, manufacturing and supply chain

21

Why it matters and how to do it

Aristides Matopoulos, Brian Price and Yuchun Xu

The goal of this chapter is to introduce the concepts of Technology, Manufacturing and Supply Chain and to discuss how to align these three fundamental considerations. At a more practical level the chapter proposes a toolkit for engineers, design and production managers as well as logisticians. The toolkit offers a quick way to conduct an initial assessment of the technology, manufacturing and supply chain levels of maturity which can be useful to business when embarking on a new product development project.

Introduction

In new technology development scholars often refer to the so-called 'Valley of Death', to describe the difficulties in transitioning a new technology from the stage where it is technically proven in a laboratory environment to having a successful implementation in real life. The distance between the two could be huge and companies come to the realization, sometimes rather late, that inventing a solution and developing a technology are not the hardest parts. There could be many factors threatening the possibility of developed technologies being 'ready'. We argue that in many cases one of the main problems is the lack of alignment among technology, manufacturing and supply chain capabilities. In industrial practice, businesses often overemphasize the importance of having the technology or the solution ready, but they are paying less attention in looking at the feasibility and affordability of producing the technology at the required scale and rate and having the right supply chain design in place to meet their goals – a particularly myopic oversight in an era of significant technology outsourcing. Research in manufacturing and operations management has emphasized the importance of product design for manufacture, particularly as a large determinant of the total cost of producing and delivering products. However, improvements to product design efforts have largely ignored supply chain design, which is a key component for success, particularly from a cost/margin perspective. There has been mixed success at adopting Design for Manufacturing (DfM) or Design for Assembly (DfA) principles. In this chapter we discuss this interrelationship between technology, manufacturing and supply chain and we provide a practical set of tools which can be used by businesses to address the challenges.

The evolution of concurrent engineering

Serial product development: traditional engineering

Traditional product development process takes place sequentially. It starts with the development of a product specification and aims at meeting the functional requirements to satisfy a customer need. Once this design is completed, it goes to the manufacturing phase to assess the manufacturability etc. When manufacturing difficulties for the designed product are encountered, the product will be re-designed to accommodate the manufacturing requirements. This product development is a sequential process and it normally needs a number of iterations, taking considerable time, before the product design is finalized.

Design for manufacturing: concurrent engineering

To overcome the problems with traditional product development processes, DfM tasks are developing the product's manufacturing and assembly

methods simultaneously with the design for the product's functional requirements – this is the start of concurrent engineering (CE). In CE, issues
associated with product manufacturing are considered in the product design
process, so by the end of the design process, the product is ready not only to
meet product functional requirements but also manufacturing process
requirements. This concurrent process reduces the need for multiple design
iterations and reduces overall time-to-market, as well as optimizing manufacturing costs through the use of more efficient manufacturing processes.

Adding the supply chain dimension to the mix

Unlike traditional new product development literature, which focuses
specifically on the product, CE focuses on both product and process design
using cross-functional teams (Koufteros *et al*, 2001). Starting in the 1980s,
CE gradually became more widespread, being picked up by many organizations – most enthusiastically in the automotive industry – to achieve competitive advantage in the marketplace. However, that advantage quickly
diminished when companies realized that it was important to incorporate
supply chain issues along with product and process design (Ellram *et al*,
2007). Indeed, the concurrent development of design and in-house manufacturing became more routine, but integration of the supply chain was limited
(Kauffeld *et al*, 2013).

This led to the 3-Dimensional Concurrent Engineering (3DCE) concept
that moved organizations forward in seeking competitive advantage.
Proposed by Fine (1998), 3DCE asks for a better alignment between the
product, its production processes and the supporting supply chain. The
3DCE mindset has been linked to numerous issues where there is potential
conflict among objectives – for example, environmental and resource (eg
cost, time) issues across a product life cycle (Fine *et al*, 2005; Ellram *et al*,
2008). Companies are finding that, even though product and process design
are well developed, the incorporation of the supply chain dimension is often
done in a very unsystematic way. According to Ellram *et al* (2008) supply
chain design issues to consider include make versus buy, sourcing and
location decisions, contracting decisions and relationships with other supply
chain members. Prior research has shown that concurrent engineering can
have significant implications for procurement in driving design for procurement resulting in improved procurement processes and product performance (Arnette and Brewer, 2017).

How to align technology, manufacturing and supply chain

In the following sections we propose a quick and practical set of three tools which can be used by businesses to address the challenge of aligning technology, manufacturing and the supply chain.

Quick diagnostic on technology readiness

Technology Readiness Levels (TRL) were first developed by NASA in the 1970s to ensure that mission critical technologies were mature enough to be applied with low risk. Technology maturity can be assessed by categorizing the level of proven development of a component, system or technology in order to establish a clear definition of the remaining uncertainty and therefore the risk associated with the technology (Mankins, 1995). The scalability of TRL categorization, from single components or features, up to the most complex systems and supporting technology ecosystems, provides a practical tool for managing risk and technology growth. One of the major benefits of TRL categorization is the use of a shared language around technology readiness, enabling stakeholders from different disciplines to be able to have a consistent interpretation of what might otherwise be an obscure understanding of risk requiring high levels of engineering or technical knowledge. Based on the principles of TRL assessments for the individual technologies themselves, a complementary technology maturity audit process has been designed to assess technology maturity at the organizational level. This establishes the readiness of the organization to be able to successfully develop technologies and bring products to market at low risk. The application of a technology audit assessment tool allows the stakeholders to:

- establish the technology bench strength of the organization;
- understand the current level of technology maturity;
- identify gaps in technology knowledge or confidence; and
- act as a tool to plan the next stages of technology development.

The technology readiness process starts by asking a series of yes/no questions to establish the overall state of technology maturity of an organization:

1 Do you have a good understanding of technology drivers in your sector/industry? (Horizon scanning)

2 Do you have a comprehensive understanding of the latest relevant technology developments? (Current state of the art)

3 Have you assessed technology maturity levels for relevant technologies you may wish to exploit?

4 Do you have a technology roadmap in place for your products and services? (Roll-out plan)

5 Are your technology roll-out plans aligned with your new product development strategy? (Product introduction roadmap)

6 Has proof of concept been established for planned technologies?

7 Are qualified suppliers/manufacturing capability in place for new technologies? (Scale and ramp-up)

8 Is a supporting infrastructure/ecosystem established for your planned technologies? (eg service, training, supply, etc)

9 Have you established a planned obsolescence strategy for your old technologies? (Ramp-down and legacy planning)

10 Do you have a fall-back plan for new technologies in the event of implementation issues arising? (Plan B)

Quick diagnostic on manufacturing readiness

Manufacturing readiness can be assessed by utilizing the Manufacturing Readiness Level (MRL) criteria, which are designed to manage manufacturing risk associated with new technology and product development. MRL criteria create a measurement matrix and scale for assessing and evaluating manufacturing maturity and risk (Ward *et al*, 2011). Using the MRL criteria to assess manufacturing readiness is a structured evaluation process. It is performed to understand:

- the current level of manufacturing maturity;
- the maturity shortfalls; and
- the opportunities of upscaling manufacturing maturation.

The following yes/no questions can help to do an early diagnosis of the state of manufacturing readiness:

1 Have you got your manufacturing concept and technology solution?

2 Have you assessed the producibility of your product design?

3 Have you got sufficient funding in place to carry out production?

4 Have you got all materials needed for production?

5 Have you got the manufacturing process capability and control?

6 Have you got the quality assurance and quality management strategy?

7 Have you got a competent workforce for engineering and production?

8 Have you got the facilities needed for production?

9 Have you got the tooling needed for production?

10 Have you got your production plans and schedules?

Quick diagnostic on supply chain readiness

Supply chains are not the result of a meticulous 'best for the business' design and have often evolved over time through mergers and acquisitions or organic growth. Before being involved in any meaningful supply chain (re-) design activity, you need to start with a good view of your supply chain. The following yes/no questions can help to do an early diagnosis of the state of your supply chain understanding:

1 Do you have a good view of how your supply chain is structured?

2 Can you analyse its complexity (eg who, what, when, how)?

3 Do all your functions (eg procurement, manufacturing, logistics) have the same understanding of your supply chain?

4 Do you understand the influence of your suppliers' supply chain (eg of other required components, material, tooling) on your own business?

5 Do you routinely evaluate your supply chain for warning signs of distress (eg supplier requests for accelerated payment terms or customer financing support)?

6 Can you identify risk in reaction to an incident (eg fire) at a supplier's or customer's site?

7 Do you have a plan when there is a problem within your supply chain?

8 Do you know how a change in your supply chain would impact the business?

9 Can you identify the critical paths in your supply chain?

10 Can you model and compare different supply chains (eg evaluate trade-offs and identify best alternatives if problems occur)?

Scoring and analysis

The maximum total score for each of the three questionnaires above is 10 (ie a total of 30 for all three questionnaires). Companies with technology, manufacturing and supply chain maturity scores above 7 in each of the three questionnaires present a very positive sign that there is a very good overview of the challenges. In our experience most organizations are running with a score of 2 or 3 which posits a significant threat to a company's medium- to long-term future. We argue that simultaneously understanding your technology, manufacturing and supply chain state of readiness is the first step before making any interventions and is, therefore, a critical factor in the achievement of companies' goals. It is important that organizations under- taking the readiness audits adopt an honest, almost self-critical, assessment of their capabilities. Using a wide range of stakeholder inputs helps to get a more rounded view of capabilities, providing a more complete picture of not only the organization's self-assessment, but the perceptions of partner organizations or stakeholders, each of whom may have a different perspec- tive. It is better to have a critical assessment that drives improvement, than to have an overly optimistic view that engenders complacency. This can be a challenge for any organization in holding its practices up to the mirror.

Conclusion and future research

Aligning technology, manufacturing and supply chain is essentially about compatibility. For a technology (or product) to be developed the relevant supply chain design (eg appropriate suppliers) is needed. For the supply chain the aim is to influence decisions about product and manufacturing configurations that address infrastructure or other limitations and use supply chain capabilities as they evolve throughout the life of the product. Potentially fruitful research in this area will focus on the following topics:

- *Product, process, supply chain trade-off implications* (both qualitative and quantitative): This area will help to build a more expanded body of knowledge in this field by providing empirical evidence, ideally from a range of sectors, of the product, process, supply chain trade-offs.

- *Aligning product, process and supply chain life cycles*: This topic builds on the trade-off implications theme proposed above, but takes a longitudinal perspective looking at the behaviour of a product, process and supply chain during the entire time of production life cycle (ie going beyond the development/launch phase of a product).

- *Interactions between product architecture, firm and supply chain boundaries*: This area could look into the product design decisions in relation to involving cross-functional teams as well as lower-tier suppliers (eg by exploring the factors and facilitators affecting early supplier involvement in design).

- *Adoption of the 'Design for Supply Chain'*: This topic should focus on unpacking the obstacles and drivers for adopting 'Design for Supply Chain' at the company level, but also the manager level (eg perceptions of middle or senior managers).

- *Tools for effective 'Design for Supply Chain'* (eg supply chain mapping, simulation): This topic will explore the practical implications of how to schedule and run 'Design for Supply Chain' projects.

Supply chains evolve over the years and the outcome of this 'natural evolution' process is that there is untapped potential in the existing supply chain configurations. The effective adoption of the practices outlined in this chapter offers the opportunity to remove some of the existing inefficiencies and to significantly enhance supply chain capability leading to improved competitive advantage.

References

Arnette, A and Brewer, B (2017) The influence of strategy and concurrent engineering on design for procurement, *The International Journal of Logistics Management*, **28** (2), pp 531–54

Ellram, LM, Tate, WL and Carter, CR (2007) Product-process-supply chain: An integrative approach to three-dimensional concurrent engineering, *International Journal of Physical Distribution and Logistics Management*, **37** (4), pp 305–30

Ellram, LM, Tate, WL and Carter, CR (2008) Applying 3DCE to environmentally responsible manufacturing practices, *Journal of Cleaner Production*, **16** (15), pp 1620–631

Fine, CH (1998) *Clockspeed: Winning industry control in the age of temporary advantage*, Basic Books

Fine, CH, Golany, B and Naseraldin, H (2005) Modeling tradeoffs in three-dimensional concurrent engineering: A goal programming approach, *Journal of Operations Management*, **23** (3), pp 389–403

Kauffeld, R, Mueller, C and Michaels, A (2013) Designing the right supply chain companies that align their operations to their strategy unleash superior performance, *Strategy + Business*, **70**

Koufteros, X, Vonderembse, M and Doll, W (2001) Concurrent engineering and its consequences, *Journal of Operations Management*, **19** (1), pp 97–115

Mankins, JC (1995) Technology readiness levels: A White Paper, Advanced Concepts Office, Office of Space Access and Technology, NASA, available at aiaa.kavi.com/apps/group_public/download.php/2212/TRLs_MankinsPaper_1995.pdf (archived at https://perma.cc/5KVQ-FCCC)

Ward, MJ, Halliday, ST and Foden, J (2011) A readiness level approach to manufacturing technology development in the aerospace sector: An industrial approach, Proceedings of the Institution of Mechanical Engineers, *Part B: Journal of Engineering Manufacture*, p 0954405411418753

The 'deglobalization' of logistics and supply chains

22

Operating in an increasingly nationalistic and risky world

David B Grant, David A Menachof and Christopher Bovis

Introduction

This chapter discusses issues related to 'deglobalization', an antithesis to globalization. Readers may wonder why this chapter appears in a book about global logistics; however, changing circumstances in this 21st century have fostered discussions about whether globalization is past its 'sell-by date' and what should be done about it. Hence, this book would be remiss if it did not bring this discussion into the logistics and supply chain management (SCM) domain, which is heavily embedded into globalization principles and practices.

We argue herein that a holistic or systemic approach to this topic is lacking, as is relevant academic literature due to the recency of this topic. Therefore, in this chapter we present an appreciation of logistics and supply chain deglobalization with the purpose of bringing together disparate thoughts on the effects of this phenomenon on logistics and SCM. This includes considerations of risk, synthesizing what we do know and possibly do not know, and suggesting a direction for practitioners and academics to

take a lead in expertly informing firms and governments – despite an assertion by the Rt Hon Michael Gove MP after the Brexit referendum vote in
2016 that people in the UK have had enough of experts (*Guardian*, 2016).
The following is a background discussion of deglobalization.

Background

Economic nationalism is the product of a neoliberal influence on international trade regulation (Bovis, 2015a, b, c). Such international trade regulation has promulgated a price-only and price-related decision-making
capacity in all aspects of government and corporate interfaces and investment and production, thus paving the way to a global customs union. This
has had an eroding influence on the relative strength of individual countries
and their governments to plan for systems of trade which could embrace
both free trade and domestic considerations. Globalization was founded
on the assumption that free trade is beneficial for national and regional
systems. Hence, an integration agenda has been sought by international
institutions and governments across the world with the objective of trade
liberalization and the elimination of protections and preferences by governments to national industries.

A phenomenon which could be seen depressurizing the imperative of
globalized trade regulation is the recognition of special treatment of trade
partners in need of such treatment. This leads to relaxation of the most
favoured nation (MFN) principle of international trade which underpins
globalization. Departing from the MFN principle, economic nationalism
emerges as a legitimate driver of trade relations.

The World Trade Organization (WTO), the mother of globalization, has
paradoxically introduced a potential escape route for international trade
patterns. It contains provisions which provide developing countries with
special rights and which in turn give developed countries the possibility to
treat developing countries more favourably than other WTO members.
These special provisions include, for example, longer time periods for
implementing agreements and commitments or measures to increase trading
opportunities for developing countries, handle disputes, implement technical standards, and finally special provisions related to least developed countries (LDC). These provisions are referred to as 'special and differential
treatment' (S&D) provisions and represent a prelude to the deglobalization
agenda.

However, globalization and a fully-fledged neoliberal approach to market integration in international trade have revealed significant side effects which were not previously contemplated. Political developments in the European Union (EU), particularly UK, and the United States during the second decade of this century falsified the assumption that free trade does not always serve national interests and have opened up fundamental debates related to globalization and the ensuing principle of market access and its implications on international trade. These debates are significant for logistics and supply chain activities, including sourcing, production and transportation.

We accept that globalization and free trade partially serve national interest; however we also believe that international trade functions in an increasingly nationalistic and risky world that, combined with a greater appreciation of total supply chain costs, may trend towards deglobalization of supply chains and related activities. Deglobalization suggests there would be major changes to supply chain design and implementation from several perspectives. But first, what is deglobalization?

The Economist attributed the term to the sociologist Walden Bello, who coined it in his book *Deglobalization: Ideas for a new world economy*. Bello's (2002) thesis is that market fundamentalism driving neoliberal globalization, starting in 1989 with the fall of the Berlin Wall, provided economic benefits but also had social costs that rendered it unsustainable and prompting the world economy into retreat. The economic crisis of 2008–09 exacerbated this retreat when world trade fell by about 20 per cent, and Escaith (2009) blamed global value chains and 'trade in tasks' through outsourcing and global production for deepening that crisis, arguing that global supply chains influenced the depth of such trade elasticity and the speed of trade volatility.

Almost 10 years later the UK's 'Brexit' referendum vote and the election of President Trump in the United States signalled a trend towards more nationalistic and less global outlooks in both nations, while following a populist trend that has shaped policy elsewhere, eg Hungary and Poland, and influenced elections and governments, sparked resistance to global trade agreements such as the Trans-Pacific Partnership (TPP), and affected that global climate change considerations. Indeed, Sutherland (2020) asked whether global supply chains were a good idea given the current situation.

In the UK, Delis (2017) argued that in the year after the Brexit referendum gross domestic product (GDP) growth slowed, the British pound depreciated 15 per cent internationally, inflation increased from 0.5 per cent in June 2016 to 2.9 per cent in May 2017, real weekly earnings in the UK fell

1 per cent resulting in household savings of around 5 per cent – the lowest since records began in 1963 – and the UK's trade deficit had worsened to £35 billion by the end of March 2017.

From a social perspective Wee (2017), when discussing sock manufacturing in the United States, noted the broad appeal of working in the manufacturing sector has not changed but after the 2008–09 economic crisis job gains have been concentrated in lower-wage industries and occupations, employing 2.3 million more US workers than at the start of the crisis. As a result, such jobs erode upward mobility and lead to frustration with entrenched governments noted by Bello (2002). Wee cites the *Equality of Opportunity Project*, which projects that children's prospects of earning more than their parents have dropped to 50 per cent from 90 per cent over the past 50 years.

Examining global consumer culture and global brands, Steenkamp (2019) illustrated the benefits of globalization in improving living standards; for example, rural poverty in China was reduced by 94 per cent from 1980 to 2015. He noted, however, that '…due to a host of political and economic factors, globalization appears to have stalled and could even go into reverse' (Steenkamp, 2019, p 532).

And yet, there is some scepticism to the deglobalization concept. Postelnicu *et al* (2015) noted that economists were of two minds regarding the term deglobalization. Some were quick to adopt it unhesitatingly, but others labelled it as 'absurd', 'superficial', 'simple', 'anachronistic' and even 'counterproductive'. From the logistics and SCM domain, Mangan and McKinnon, while citing Bello (2002), Grant *et al* (2017) and Mangan (2017) as examples of a move towards deglobalization, argue that the 'reality is that countries still need to trade with each other given their relative comparative advantages and thus the influence of deglobalization should not be over-estimated' (Mangan and McKinnon, 2019, p 12). They conclude that while 'there are …fundamental …shifts in international trade flows' involving '…changes in demand and structural changes to international manufacturing networks …globalization will continue' but that the volume of 'trade flows will not continue to grow …at the same fast pace as seen in recent decades' as '…it is difficult to predict …what they will look like beyond the short term given …that many analyses of medium-term and long-term trends are qualitative in nature and are at times conflicting' (Mangan and McKinnon, 2019, pp 3–5).

Mandják *et al* (2017) argued that an economic crisis may moderate a firm's relational behaviour, described by their supply chain focal firm's network behaviour model which uses constructs of valuable customer and supplier relationship, relationship strategy, delivery and innovation. They tested this model with 300 Hungarian firms with general managers answering questions related to 'customer' issues and manufacturing/operations managers answering questions related to 'supplier' issues. They found that strength of crisis perception affects firm network behaviour; the stronger the perception, the more a firm focuses on customer relationships.

Further, Balsa-Barreiro *et al* (2020) suggest that relationships and networks are important as the complexity of a networked system, ranging from the social to the economic to the political, is associated with its structural topology. Since relational interdependencies are critical for understanding trade-offs between efficiency and robustness in such systems, but are often overlooked, a poor network design can lead to the collapse of the whole system. In a logistics and SCM context, this suggests establishing and maintaining both strong relationships and networks and a comprehensive risk management intelligence and management system.

Returning to Mandják *et al* (2017), the nature of SCM enumerated by the US Council of Supply Chain Management Professionals (CSCMP) in its definition is built around relationships. Much work has been undertaken in logistics service, satisfaction and relationships and collaboration including discrete areas such as key supplier management and relationship management, and 'co-opetition' where competitors collaborate (see, for example, Grant, 2005; Hingley *et al*, 2015; Teller *et al*, 2016; Eber *et al*, 2019; and Rafi-Ul-Shan *et al*, 2020).

Altomonte and Ottaviano (2009) argued that the rise of global supply chains was not the main cause of the severe, sudden and synchronized fall in global trade flows during the 2008–9 recession, but they also noted there was insufficient data to corroborate that claim. Thus, are modern, global supply chains influencing deglobalization activities and thought? Further, whether they are or not, how should managers approach these uncertain and turbulent times and how could academics help inform their decisions?

Notwithstanding these issues, many firms began reviewing their global supply chains over the past decade due to total cost, risk and sustainability issues, which have led to some localized deglobalization through 'nearshoring' production to their home country or economic trading union and 'near-porting' distribution as well (Menachof and Grant, 2016). If deglobalization is indeed an important trend, whether it is growing or not, it is timely and relevant to examine the various effects it may have on business and firms, economic systems, trade, governments and policy, and society in general, and on logistics and SCM structures and operations, in particular. We now turn to our research approach.

Research approach

We adopted a qualitative and inductive research approach to the deglobalization issue using two stages for data collection. In the first stage we critically reviewed disparate literature that has surfaced over the last two decades by conducting academic and non-academic literature searches from 2000 using Web of Science and search engines such as Google. Our second stage included hosting seminars on these topics at logistics and SCM industry events, two UK forums (Grant, 2017; Menachof, 2017a) and one US forum (Menachof, 2017b), to gather participant feedback.

Our keywords for the first stage were Brexit, populism, nationalism, deglobalization and US President Trump which we searched in various combinations along with logistics and supply chains as second level or sub-filters to determine what literature exists. Few articles were found using these sub-filters and our lack of success with our search suggests this topic is indeed quite nascent, particularly as regards logistics and SCM and thus practitioners and academics operate in a partial vacuum on these matters.

Feedback from the second stage forums indicated most people attended because they were not aware of these issues as threats to their business operations. Most could identify downside risks to their operations and concurred that the issues increased business turbulence to some degree, although each participating firm considered they will be survivors, which may occur by shifting resources and operations to elsewhere in the world.

For example, a firm at one UK forum (Menachof, 2017a) has a Turkish parent and believed its UK domestic operations would continue as normal after Brexit and enjoy an advantage as overseas competition might face higher tariffs to enter a post-Brexit UK market. However, any expansion they planned to undertake might have to occur outside the UK when they considered trade-offs between higher export costs of their UK products against standard, ie higher, WTO tariffs being levied on imports.

Following these two stages we used extant literature and models on logistics and SCM relationships and risk management to develop a conceptual framework for firms to use for managing risks related to deglobalization, and for academics to follow for further research to determine the efficacy of our conceptual thoughts and fine-tune the framework, its features and its operations.

Proposed risk framework to address deglobalization

To begin the development of our framework we first looked at Peck's (2005) various risk management factors in what she referred to as 'levels in a landscape', as shown in Figure 22.1. The first level considers value stream/ processes that includes internal operations management and business process engineering while the second level considers assets and infrastructure dependencies such as logistics, utilities, information technology (IT) and human resources (HR). The third level considers relationships and associated dependencies with external organizations and inter-organizational networks such as business strategies, production networks and strategic purchasing while the last level considers the wider external environment, ie the natural and social environment. We argue that the first two levels contain primarily endogenous factors within the firm's control while the last two levels contain primarily exogenous factors outside of the firm's control. The elegance of Peck's model is that it classifies or categorizes types and

Figure 22.1 Risk levels in a landscape

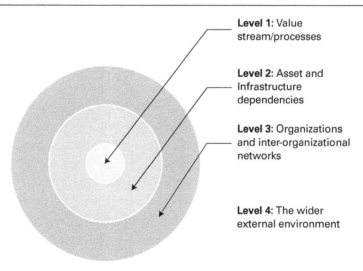

Level 1: Value stream/processes

Level 2: Asset and Infrastructure dependencies

Level 3: Organizations and inter-organizational networks

Level 4: The wider external environment

SOURCE Adapted from Peck (2005)

Table 22.1   Bello's key tenets for a deglobalized paradigm

1	Production for domestic market must again become centre of economic gravity rather than production for export markets.
2	Subsidiarity should be enshrined in economic life by encouraging production of goods at the community level and at the national level if this can be done at reasonable cost in order to preserve community.
3	Trade policy – ie quotas and tariffs – should be used to protect the local economy from destruction by corporate-subsidized commodities with artificially low prices.
4	Industrial policy, including subsidies, tariffs and trade, should revitalize and strengthen the manufacturing sector.
5	Development and diffusion of environmentally congenial technology in both agriculture and industry should be encouraged.
6	Strategic economic decisions cannot be left to the market or technocrats; the scope of democratic economic decision making should be expanded so that all vital questions, eg which industries to develop or phase out, what proportion of a government's budget is devoted to agriculture, become subject to democratic discussion and choice.

SOURCE Adapted from Bello (2002)

levels of risk for firms to easily recognize and deal with as they go deeper into our framework.

We next looked at Bello's (2002) 11 key tenets driving a deglobalization paradigm that are geared for smaller economic and governance units such as local communities, and which contain several socialist notions. However, six of his tenets are appropriate for smaller units of analysis and activity and useful to derive elements for our framework and are listed in Table 22.1.

Based on the foregoing, we concur with Witt (2019) that effects of deglobalization depend upon whether a firm only operates domestically or conducts business in international markets. Witt discusses the resulting opportunities in three areas of IB research: political strategies and roles of multinational enterprises (MNEs); global value chains; and the role of the national context. We go further by suggesting, in a neoliberal context in contrast to Bello, that for the most part firms operating domestically are likely to be small to medium-sized enterprises (SMEs) while those that operate internationally are likely to be MNEs. Figure 22.2 presents proportionate levels of business and risk which SMEs and MNEs face in either domestic or international markets.

Figure 22.2   Deglobalization impact relative to firm type and size

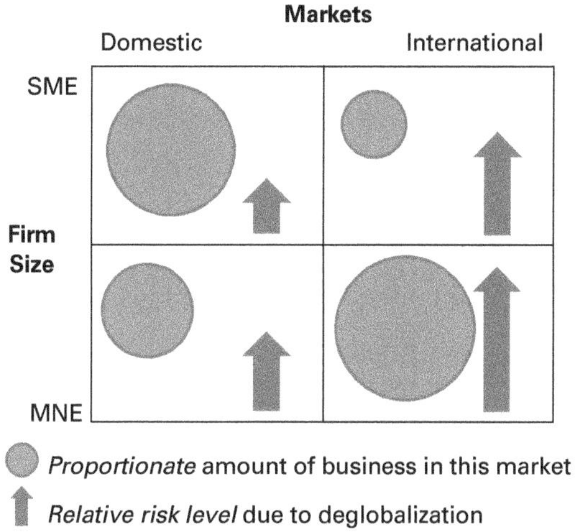

SOURCE Grant, Menachof and Bovis (2017)

The proportionate amount of business 'bubbles' and level of risk 'arrows' are not data based but are our intuitive considerations, which we consider representative. That is, an MNE will derive most of its business in international markets and face higher levels of risk (lower right quadrant) whereas an SME will derive most of its business domestically and have much lower levels of risk (upper left quadrant).

Lastly, we examined three rigorous consultancy/association reports for measures which may be useful. The first two discussed are not aimed specifically at deglobalization but feature many factors that we intuitively generated from our reading and seminars discussed above, while the third specifically considers Brexit. Sutherland (2020) noted supply chains have evolved into 'grids', as opposed to linear chains or a network, and as a result firms have five important criteria to consider: *procurement, rules and regulations, manufacturing, logistics, and marketing and sales*. FrontierStrategyGroup (2016) used six measures to build a manufacturing attractiveness index for countries in the Association of Southeast Asian Nations (ASEAN):

- *labour conditions*: average wages, minimum wages, engineers' salaries, redundancy costs, literacy rate;
- *transport infrastructure*: quality of roads, quality of ports, quality of railroads, provision of infrastructure, ownership of infrastructure networks, quality of air transport, logistics competence;

- *utilities (support infrastructure):* quality of electricity supply, electricity production, energy production, market access, broadband penetrations, mobile penetration;
- *regulatory environment:* investment freedom, tax rate, openness to foreign investment, prevalence of trade barriers, intellectual property rights; price control, quality control;
- *international trade conditions:* efficiency of import–export, number of days to import and to export, cost to import and export;
- *risk factors:* Gini coefficient of wealth distribution, ie income inequality, corruption, equity risk premium, banking sector risk, natural disaster risk, critical infrastructure risk.

Recently, China, along with other 14 Asia-Pacific countries, signed the Regional Comprehensive Economic Partnership (RCEP), which by some measures is the largest free trade agreement in the history of international trade. The deal is known to cover a third of the world population and just under 30 per cent of global GDP. The importance of the conclusion of RCEP is that multilateralism appears as the driver of deglobalization (Lewis, 2013; Rahman and Ara, 2015). RCEP and the concurrent 2018 Comprehensive and Progressive Agreement for Trans-Pacific Partnership (CPTPP), have the potential of creating a single market in Southeast Asia.

The skeleton of RCEP is ASEAN, without which RCEP would not have been concluded. ASEAN is a rules-based trade system which attempts to improve on WTO principles of free trade. The potential of RCEP in affecting international trade is enormous. The regulatory thrust of RCEP is comprehensive in a manner that it cares for supply chains across the region. However, integration of rules relating to intellectual property, state-owned enterprises, labour and environmental standards is sparing. In comparison to CPTPP, RCEP is a condensed version of an ASEAN-centred trade agreement, but it has the room to improve over time and embrace a complete spectrum of trade interfaces, including services, investment and capital movement. A sizeable positive effect of RCEP is its rules of origin regulation which will attract inward foreign investment.

The signatories in the RCEP include the 10 members of ASEAN, along with five neighbouring countries – Japan, Korea, Australia, New Zealand and China. This was Japan's first signing of a free trade agreement that includes two of its biggest trading partners – China and South Korea. The prominent role of China in the conclusion of RCEP is undisputed. The fact that the United States and India decided against joining RCEP reflects on protectionism and their respective deglobalization agendas.

However, RCEP will help China strengthen its relations with neighbouring economies and will accelerate Northeast Asian economic integration. It will have a spill-over effect in helping the conclusion of pending free trade agreements (FTA), such as the trilateral FTA between China, Japan and South Korea. Both Southeast and Northeast Asia will see benefits from free trade under RCEP. RCEP has the enormous potential to improve access to Chinese Belt and Road Initiative (BRI) funds, enhancing gains from market access by strengthening transport, energy and communications markets.

The United States must come to terms with the fact that multilateralism is an accomplished driver in international trade and President Biden's first administration is keen to restore diplomacy to assist trade rather than engage in trade wars. The EU has been the largest source of foreign direct investment (FDI) flows into ASEAN and is one of its largest trading partners. There is a plethora of EU FTAs with Singapore, Vietnam, Japan and South Korea, while Indonesia, Australia and New Zealand are close to completing comprehensive FTAs with the EU. RECP will put trade relations between the EU and China into a different perspective. Any EU-Sino treaty must reflect on the full potential of economic integration from production factors and services provision to connectivity and digital transformation and the promotion of regional and global security.

One can reasonably argue that the direct economic effects of the RCEP on globalized trade are likely to be small, but will be felt only gradually, adding the greatest worry for international partners such as the EU which is displacement of its exports to RCEP members due to the treatment accorded to the other signatories, known as trade diversion. RCEP has an advanced set of regulations covering rules of origin, specifically in trade in goods. This regulatory treatment has the potential to create trade diversification between RCEP members and the EU. Potentially, frictions could emerge over trade flow diversion as a result of rules of origin and the ensuing preference margins. Closer coordination is needed and elimination of differentiated treatment of individual RCEP members on behalf of the EU. All of this will affect global supply chain flow volumes as Southeast and Northeast Asia may continue to be major suppliers of products and services to Europe and North American markets.

The third report from PA Consulting (2017) suggested there are four individually and combined impacts in the UK and EU automotive sector: *margin erosion, added cost, longer lead times* and *higher vehicle prices*. They believed added costs due to tariffs and longer lead times would provide the most significant impact in all three scenarios, with margin erosion and higher vehicle price having less of an impact.

The key risks from these three reports that would impact a firm with dramatic changes in its external environment appear to be costs related to labour, operations including procurement and production, and changes in rules and regulations. In a logistics and SCM context we believe these reduce direct labour costs, rules and regulations as regards tariffs/customs costs, and operations as regards direct fuel costs. We further added currency or financial costs, which was not specifically noted in the foregoing three reports but may have been implicit in several factors.

Risk registers have long been used in project management to identify, quantify and evaluate risks in terms of likelihood and potential impact (see, for example, Williams, 1994). To operationalize our framework, we produced a simple risk register, shown in Table 22.2, with three potential effect choices in the fourth column, a positive effect, no or a neutral effect, and a negative effect, to demonstrate our framework for considering deglobalization risks. Due to space restrictions for this chapter we only show transport as one area of logistical and supply chain activities, and only consider ocean shipping and road freight as two prime modes in the supply chain. Table 22.2 is based on our intuitive views from the inductive research approach. Our four factors of cost and two additional features of modality capacity and infrastructure comprise risk factors derived from Bello and the three reports and using Peck's model for endogeneity and exogeneity.

Table 22.2 Example of a transport risk register due to deglobalization

Transport Activity	Description	Likely Risk	Potential Effect (+positive, =neutral, -- negative)
Ocean Freight	Currency costs	Increase across borders without control	--
	Customs and regulatory costs	Increase due to reduced trade agreements	--
	Labour costs	Neutral or lower due to domestic sources	+
	Fuel costs	Increase due to purchasing abroad	--
	Modality capacity	Container availability	+

Table 22.2 *continued*

Transport Activity	Description	Likely Risk	Potential Effect (+positive, =neutral, -- negative)
	Infrastructure	Ports accessibility and control of infrastructure	+
Overall Effect			≈ =
Air Freight	Currency costs	Increase across borders without control	--
	Customs and regulatory costs	Increase due to reduced trade agreements	--
	Labour costs	Neutral or lower due to domestic sources	+
	Fuel costs	Increase due to purchasing abroad	--
	Environmental costs	Increase due to air traffic and pollution effects	--
Overall Effect			≈ =
Road Freight	Currency costs	No real effect within country but possible effect across borders	≈ -- → =
	Customs and regulatory costs	No real effect within country but possible effect across borders	≈ -- → =
	Labour costs	No real effect within country but possible slight effect across borders	≈ -- → =
	Fuel costs	Increase due to purchasing abroad	--

Table 22.2   *continued*

Transport Activity	Description	Likely Risk	Potential Effect (+positive, =neutral, -- negative)
	Environmental costs	Increase due to traffic and pollution effects	--
Overall Effect			≈ =
Rail Freight	Currency costs	No real effect within country but possible effect across borders	≈ -- → =
	Customs and regulatory costs	No real effect within country but possible effect across borders	≈ -- → =
	Labour costs	No real effect within country but possible slight effect across borders	≈ -- → =
	Fuel costs	Increase due to purchasing abroad if diesel	--
	Infrastructure utilization	Authorization of track use and logistics issue of intermodal transport functions	--
Overall Effect			≈ -- → =

SOURCE Grant, Menachof and Bovis (2017)

Conclusions

We began this chapter with an assertion that we are currently living in a nationalistic/populist and risky world where deglobalization of logistics and supply chains and related activities is a real concern that must be addressed.

Pivotal to this debate is the promulgation of new regulatory systems which could strike a meaningful and workable balance between free trade and national concerns and embrace the positive dynamics of fit-for-purpose industrial policies. The need to install such systems balancing the facilitation of free trade whilst protecting national interests is imperative, although such a balance is difficult to strike because its inherent features run against the grain of international normative and political dogma over the last century.

The fundamental thesis of this chapter is that we have been witnessing a dilution of globalization, in the same pattern and analogy of having witnessed global warming and its effects on the environment. Although the fundamental principle of free trade is paramount to the world's political and economic systems, priorities of national or even regional systems will attempt to balance the positive effects of free trade with any adverse effects arising out of uninhibited market access to trade. How can this be achieved?

We offer a two-fold approach. First, free trade is only one dimension of globalization. Free trade allocates resources where this is most beneficial to the owners of production factors. On the other hand, free trade opens numerous possibilities for economic growth based on diversification, mobility and policy intervention. The latter epitomizes the need to instigate contemporary industrial policies. This approach aims at creating framework conditions under which improvement of national or regional competitiveness would compensate where necessary for market failure.

Secondly, a responsive and responsible political and economic leadership will provide contemporary and fit-for-purpose industrial policies across the world to harness the benefits of free trade whilst balancing negativities from ensuing industrial reorganization. Such policies should be interoperable and aim at several tasks. The first is to set out boundaries within which industry and enterprise can flourish. The second task is to ensure that conditions are present for industry to develop and to realize its competitive potential. Finally, the third task is to ensure that the frameworks, institutions and instruments that are necessary for the business environment and for industry are able and capable to accommodate contemporary societal needs and requirements.

Our proposed deglobalization risk framework provides a useful approach for logistics and SCM practitioners to address this paradigmatic shift over the coming decades and provides guidance for strategic management and decision making related to the deglobalization phenomenon and its associated risks. Further, we provide five research suggestions to guide logistics and SCM researchers with a set of issues to refine and evaluate to prove this framework's efficacy and usefulness:

- Our lack of empirical evidence leads to our first suggestion that empirical research should be conducted on levels of business and risk both domestically and abroad for both SMEs and MNEs, including operations in the other two quadrants, to validate our intuitive assertions.

- Our second suggestion is to investigate those costs as they relate to deglobalization in logistics and supply chains to verify and validate their appropriateness and impact.

- Our third suggestion is for researchers to develop and empirically test our framework for all logistical and supply chain activities, building on findings from the second suggestion to verify and validate costs.

- Our fourth suggestion is for researchers to investigate the nature and impact of deglobalization on supply chain relationships in domestic and international markets from both a short-term and long-term perspective.

- Finally, and in concert with our fourth suggestion, our fifth suggestion is to undertake interdisciplinary and international research to investigate legal implications affecting various international trade agreement blocs such as the TPP, RECP, ASEAN, EU, and the North American Free Trade Agreement (NAFTA) as amended by the United States, Mexico and Canada; international business implications affecting inward or foreign direct investment, mergers and acquisitions and international market access; national, regional and international economic system trade-offs affecting regional/free trade and their effects on industrial policy; and operational, cost and structural implications affecting domestic/international supply chains, strategic procurement, local content and regional trade agreements.

There are some limitations to our discussions and qualitative research. As noted, this chapter lacks supporting evidence due to this topic being nascent; however, our research suggestions above will enable researchers to address same. Further, our views may not be shared by the mainstream of logistics and supply chain researchers as there has been a critical mass related to globalization and its impetus due to global supply chains – hence our views may challenge orthodoxy and not be fully appreciated by colleagues. We cannot suggest much here other than to ask practitioners, academics and colleagues to adopt an open mind to these issues and the real evidence underlying some of them.

Finally, this work was undertaken before the coronavirus or Covid-19 pandemic took hold across the globe in 2020. Farrell and Newman (2020) believe it to be an enormous stress test for globalization and will force a major re-evaluation of the interconnected global economy. They argue globalization has allowed for the rapid spread of contagious diseases and has fostered deep interdependence between firms and nations that makes them more vulnerable to unexpected shocks and discovering just how vulnerable they are. They conclude that the lesson of the Covid-19 pandemic is not that globalization failed, but that it is fragile, despite or even because of its benefits.

Sigala *et al* (2020), in an EU Horizon 2020 funded research project entitled *Health Emergency Response in Interconnected Systems* (HERoS), identified disruptions in medical supply chains relating to the Covid-19 pandemic caused by consumer behaviour, capacity limitations and legislation; in particular, the production, logistics and cargo transport, fulfilment and delivery of medical supplies orders to health professional and patients. They suggested reshaping medical supply chains to be more flexible, responsive and agile to mitigate disruptions through *inter alia* switching from single sourcing to multiple sourcing strategies, pre-positioning of medical supplies, private–public sector collaboration, as well as standardization of medical supplies, visibility of end-to-end supply chains and forecasting of financial needs.

In other words, collaboration and risk management are as important in global medical supply chains and pandemics as in other sectors, as evidenced by shortages of quality personal protective equipment (PPE) and consumer hoarding of items such as toilet paper during the outset of the Covid-19 pandemic. Accordingly, we conclude by suggesting firms using our framework must consider those additional risk factors affecting supply chain vulnerability and resilience within Peck's level 4 wider environment that go beyond what she notes are 'integrated supply chain management, business continuity planning, commercial corporate risk management or an amalgamation of all of these...' (Peck, 2005, p 225).

References

Altomonte, C and Ottaviano, GIP (2009) Resilient to the crisis? Global supply chains and trade flows, in *The Great Trade Collapse: Causes, consequences and prospects*, ed R Baldwin, pp 95–100, Centre for Economic Policy Research (CEPR), London

Balsa-Barreiro, J, Vié, A, Morales, AJ and Cebrián, M (2020) Deglobalization in a hyper-connected world, *Palgrave Communications*, 6 (28), doi.org/10.1057/s41599-020-0403-x (archived at https://perma.cc/538H-BKPK)

Bello, W (2002) *Deglobalization: Ideas for a new world economy*, Zed Books Ltd, London

Bovis, CH (2015a) *The Law of EU Public Procurement*, 2nd edn, Oxford University Press, Oxford UK

Bovis, CH (2015b) The governance of public-private partnerships, *European Court of Auditors Journal*, OJ-AD-14-011-2A-C

Bovis, CH (2015c) Risk in public-private partnerships and critical infrastructure, *European Journal of Risk Regulation*, 6 (2), pp 200–207, heinonline.org/ HOL/Page?handle=hein.journals/ejrr2015&div=31&g_sent=1&casa_ token=&collection=journals (archived at https://perma.cc/LPB9-UXEL)

Delis, A (2017) Six graphs showing the state of the UK economy a year after Brexit, *The Conversation*, 22 June, theconversation.com/six-graphs-showing- the-state-of-the-uk-economy-a-year-after-brexit-referendum-79598 (archived at https://perma.cc/ZPJ6-6KTM)

Eber, L, Vega, D and Grant, DB (2019) Using key supplier relationship management to enable supply chain risk management in the automotive industry, *Journal of Supply Chain Management: Research & Practice*, 13 (1), pp 14–26, jscm.au.edu/index.php/jscm/article/view/164 (archived at https://perma.cc/3GJN-T2NZ)

Escaith, H (2009) *Trade collapse, trade relapse and global production networks: Supply chain in the great recession*, Munich Personal RePec Archive (MPRA) Paper No. 18433, mpra.ub.uni-muenchen.de/18433/ (archived at https://perma.cc/LZ6K-GNMQ)

Farrell, H and Newman, A (2020) Will the coronavirus end globalization as we know it? *Foreign Affairs*, 16 March, www-foreignaffairs-com.cdn.ampproject. org/c/s/www.foreignaffairs.com/articles/2020-03-16/will-coronavirus-end- globalization-we-know-it?amp (archived at https://perma.cc/EB6L-4HT8)

FrontierStrategyGroup (2016) Manufacturing Attractiveness Index of the ASEAN countries, frontierview.com/ (archived at https://perma.cc/XY5L-SXCL)

Grant, DB (2005) The transaction/relationship dichotomy in logistics and supply chain management, *Supply Chain Forum: An International Journal*, 6 (2), pp 38–48, doi.org/10.1080/16258312.2005.11517146 (archived at https://perma.cc/MY8U-369L)

Grant, DB (2017) *Deglobalization of supply chain in an increasingly nationalist world*, Invited presentation at the Changing Marketplace for Logistics Session at Multimodal, 4 April, NEC, Birmingham, UK

Grant, DB, Menachof, D and Bovis, C (2017) *Supply chain deglobalization in an increasingly nationalistic world*, Proceedings of the 22nd Annual Logistics Research Network (LRN) Conference, 6–8 September, Southampton Solent University, e-proceedings

Guardian (2016) You're wrong Michael Gove – experts are trusted far more than you, *The Guardian*, Opinion, 9 June, www.theguardian.com/

commentisfree/2016/jun/09/michael-gove-experts-academics-vote (archived at https://perma.cc/743Z-7UNL)

Hingley, M, Lindgreen, A and Grant, DB (2015) Intermediaries in power-laden retail supply chains: An opportunity to improve buyer-supplier relationships and collaboration, *Industrial Marketing Management*, 50, pp 78–84, dx.doi.org/ 10.1016/j.indmarman.2015.05.025 (archived at https://perma.cc/M8TN-65DX)

Lewis, MK (2013) The TPP and the RCEP (ASEAN + 6) as potential paths toward deeper Asian economic integration, *Asian Journal of WTO & International Health Law and Policy*, 8 (2), pp 359–78, heinonline.org/HOL/Page?handle= hein.journals/aihlp8&div=17&g_sent=1&casa_token=&collection=journals (archived at https://perma.cc/MX2R-EPAZ)

Mandják, T, Wimmer, Á and Durrieu, F (2017) The influence of economic crises on network behaviour, *Journal of Business and Industrial Marketing*, 32 (3), pp 445–56, dx.doi.org/10.1108/JBIM-07-2015-0126

Mangan, J (2017) Global supply chains – have they reached a limit? Proceedings of the 22nd Annual Logistics Research Network (LRN) Conference, 6–8 September, Southampton Solent University, e-proceedings

Mangan, DJ and McKinnon, A (2019) Review of trends in manufacturing and global supply chains, and their impact on UK freight, *Foresight Future of Mobility: Evidence Review*, Government Office for Science, London, https://www.gov.uk/government/organisations/government-office-for-science (archived at https://perma.cc/BR6B-6SKR)

Menachof, D (2017a) SCL Hub Supply Chain and Logistics Conference for Industry Leaders, 6 June, Hilton Waldorf Hotel, London

Menachof, D (2017b) Council of Supply Chain Management Professionals (CSCMP) Academic Research Symposium, CSCMP Annual Conference, 24 September, Georgia World Congress Center, Atlanta

Menachof, D and Grant, DB (2016) Does the concept of 'nearporting' provide a pathway to better logistics sustainability? *Journal of Supply Chain Management: Research & Practice*, 10 (1), pp 1–11, jscm.au.edu/index.php/jscm/article/view/124 (archived at https://perma.cc/8C6P-G6CA)

PA Consulting (2017) Brexit: The impact on the automotive supply chain, PA Consulting, March, www.paconsulting.com (archived at https://perma.cc/ 3U8P-UYSU)

Peck, H (2005) Drivers of supply chain vulnerability: an integrated framework, *International Journal of Physical Distribution and Logistics Management*, 35 (4), pp 210–32, www.emeraldinsight.com/doi/full/10.1108/09600030510599904 (archived at https://perma.cc/YTJ9-PW55)

Postelnicu, C, Dinu, V and Dabija, D-C (2015) Economic deglobalization – from hypothesis to reality, *Ekonomie a Management*, 18 (2), pp 4–14, dx.doi.org/ 10.15240/tul/001/2015-2-001 (archived at https://perma.cc/5R3V-T62Y)

Rafi-Ul-Shan, PM, Grant, DN and Perry, P (2020) Are fashion supply chains capable of co-opetition? An exploratory study in the UK, *International Journal of Logistics: Research and Applications*, forthcoming at doi.org/10.1080/13675 567.2020.1784118 (archived at https://perma.cc/J3FZ-43N9)

Rahman, MM and Ara, LA (2015) TPP, TTIP and RCEP: Implications for South Asian economies, *South Asia Economic Journal*, **16** (1), pp 27–45, doi.org/ 10.1177/1391561415575126 (archived at https://perma.cc/462C-MZY4)

Sigala, IF, Kovács, G, Alani, H, Smith, B, Xu, J, Wu, G, Rollio, A, Cicchetta, G, Boersma, K, Grant, DB, Riipi, T and Wang, K-M (2020) D.1 Gap analysis and recommendations for securing medical supplies for the Covid-19 response, *Health Emergency Response in Interconnected Systems*, www.heros-project.eu/ output/deliverables/ (archived at https://perma.cc/7FLX-WRG5)

Steenkamp, J-B (2019) The uncertain future of globalization, *Industrial Marketing Review*, **36** (2), pp 527–35, doi.org/10.1108/IMR-12-2018-0355 (archived at https://perma.cc/3W5D-UYVU)

Sutherland, B (2020) Maybe global supply chains were a bad idea, Bloomberg Online, 21 February, www.bloomberg.com/opinion/articles/2020-02-21/ coronavirus-forces-a-rethinking-of-supply-chains (archived at https://perma.cc/ YE3A-GQUM)

Teller, C, Kotzab, H, Grant, DB and Holweg, C (2016) The importance of key supplier relationship management in supply chains, *International Journal of Retail and Distribution Management*, **44** (2), pp 109–123, doi.org/10.1108/ IJRDM-05-2015-0072 (archived at https://perma.cc/TWN9-GKNT)

Wee, H (2017) Fighting for jobs in America's former 'Sock Capital of the World', LinkedIn, www.linkedin.com/pulse/fighting-jobs-americas-former-sock-capital-world-heesun-wee (archived at https://perma.cc/8Z2M-KG2W)

Williams, TM (1994) Using a risk register to integrate risk management in project definition, *International Journal of Project Management*, **12** (1), pp 17–22, doi.org/10.1016/0263-7863 (archived at https://perma.cc/TP8W-UBBY) (94)90005-1

Witt, MA (2019) De-globalization: Theories, predictions, and opportunities for international business research, *Journal of International Business Studies*, 50, pp 1063–77, doi.org/10.1057/s41267-019-00219-7 (archived at https://perma.cc/R9AH-8ZN9)

INDEX

Note: Acronyms are filed as presented; numbers are filed as spelled out. Page locators in *italics* denote information within a figure or table.

abatement potential 253
Accounting Standards Authority 392
active responsibility *318, 319, 327*
adaptivity (flexibility) 5–7, 10–11, 148,
        169, 171, 211, 213–14, 228
additive manufacturing (3D printing) 105,
        158, 204, 206, 264, 343, 363
    adoption rate 368, *369*, 371, *372*
Africa 65, 134, *166*, 167, 173, 179, 313
agility 3–4, 24, 144–45, *278, 279*, 347
air pollution 246, 247–49, 255, 265
Airbus 258
airfreight 66, 210, *250, 251*, 261, 401, *439*
Alphabet 104
Amazon 90, 104, 105, 154, 157, 159, 318
AP Moller-Maersk 75, 192
Apple 32, 104, 212, 226, 228, 313
artificial intelligence (AI) 33, 74, 105–06,
        108, 136, 343, *361*, 362, 372
    adoption of 185, 368, *369*, 370
Asda 156
ASOS 90, 147, 154, *155*
assets review 6–7
Association of Southeast Asian Nations
        (ASEAN) 435–37, 442
attitude-behaviour gap 315–16
Auchan 157
automation 105–06, 109, 173, 204, 206,
        208, 260, 363, 370, 384
automotive (car) sector 144, *167, 168*,
        313–14, 437
see also BMW; Ford Motor Company;
        Honda; Land Rover; Toyota

B&Q 194–95, *196, 197*
backloading 124, 127, 130, 131, 132
balanced scorecard 395, 397–98, *411*
barcode scanning 181, 360, *361*
battery technology 256, *257, 258*
Belt and Road Initiative 173, 180, 437
benchmarking *25*, 86–87, 122, 152, 234, 393
Benetton 147, 148, 150–51
big data 33, 74, 103, 136, *361*, 362, 368,
        369, 386, 413
    see also cost-to-serve analytics
biodiesel 255
biofuels 242, 256, 258
biomethane 255
black carbon 251–52
black swan events 52–53
blockchain 33, 109, 204–05, 368, *369*, 371

BMW 75–77
board responsibilities 65, 198, 208, 290,
        404, 408
Boeing 7–8, 215
Boohoo 154, 160, 306–07, 320–27
Bosch 40, 41, 46
BP Macondo Well disaster 72
Brexit 58, 77, 429–30, 432
B2B (business-to-business) 96, 105, 165,
        235, 316
B2C 104, 105, 165
budgeting 22, 374
bullwhip effect 1, 5, 349
Burberry 150, 160
business-as-usual 275, *278*
business cases 29
business-*not*-as-usual 99, 100, 108–12
business planning 179, 397
business process re-design 414
business strategy 103, 190, 225–26, 300, 433
buyer power (ethics) 314

Campaign™ SC model *278, 279*
capacity utilization *19*, 121
capital employed 16, *17, 19*, 394
car manufacturing *see* automotive (car)
        sector
carbon dioxide (CO_2) emissions 52, 124,
        130, 151, 193, 246, *250*–55, 308
carbon offsetting *252*, 254
carbon pricing 254
cash 394
cash-to-cash (C2C) cycle 16, 18, 24, 26–28,
        29, *30*, 31, 42, 393–94
Castorama 194–95
Caterpillar 73, 207
cell system manufacturing 395
centralization 2, 9–10, 23, 105–06, 178,
        217, 264–65
champions 301
change 2, 100, 102, 378
Chief Customer Supply Chain Officer 283
Chief Supply Chain Officer 286
China 173, 185, 437
    see also Belt and Road Initiative
circular economy 103, 105, 110, 132, 231,
        264
civil society 317, 324, 325
click-and-collect 91, 155, 157
climate change (emergency) 8, *54–55*, 60,
        99, 102, 249–50, 265, 429

cloud computing 11, 33, 136, 360, *361*, 368, *369*, 371, 372, 376
CMT units 325
collaboration 153, 171, 181, 235–38, 346, 352, 384–85
  see also horizontal collaboration; vertical collaboration (integration)
collaborative customer segments *274*, 276
collaborative investments 43–44, 46–48
collaborative procurement 104–05, 106, 109, 346–47, 352
Collaborative™ SC model *278*, *279*
collaborative transportation 131, 261–62
Collect+ 157
collection and delivery points 125, 157
communications 200, 224–25, 301, 302
Companies Act (2006) 290–91, 301
competitive advantage 20, 48, 81, 146–48, 212–13, 420
complaint handling (analysis) 81, 85–86, 88–89
complexity 168–69, *170*, 211, *375*
Comprehensive and Progressive Trade Agreement for Trans-Pacific Partnership 436
compressed natural gas 255
computer systems 23–24, 71, 414
conceptual innovation 297
concurrent engineering 419–20
consensus building 179, 303
consequentialist reasoning 312–13
container shipping 124, 127, 133, 135–36, 137, 210, *251*, 260
contingency plans 57, 60, 68–69, 70, 71, 72
continuous improvement 28, 144, 398, 406–07
control risk 8, 71–72, 73, 226–27
control towers 8, 12, 74, 236, 280, 288, 408, 412–13
cooperation 38, *42*, 44, 105, 110, 131, *176*, 183, 229
cooperative game theory 36, 48
coopetition 109
coordination 8, 44, 171, 374
core competence focus 144, 148, 212, 214–15, 217, 228, 229
Corporate Governance Code (2018) 290, 301
Corporate Human Rights Benchmark 152
corporate probability of default *43*
corporate social responsibility (CSR) 101–02, 110, 142, 151–53, *176*, 197–98, 234, 309
cost analytics 179–80, 182
cost pressure (reduction) 26–27, 28, *170*, 171–72, 373
cost-to-serve analytics *176*, 182, 202–03, 275, 277, 285, 395, 400, *402*
CO_2 (carbon dioxide) emissions 52, 124, 130, 151, 193, 246, 250–55, 308

Council of Logistics Management 178
Covid-19 pandemic *52*–57, 60, 102, 198–99, 203–04, 285, 349–52, 391–92, 443
  retail logistics 142, 151, 158–60
  stock market response to 62, *63*
credit rating 46, 49
credit risk 42, 132
critical incident technique 89
critical incidents 85–86
cross-contamination matrices 126
C2C (cash-to-cash) cycle 16, 18, 24, 26–28, 29, *30*, 31, 42, 393–94
cube-outs 122, *123*, 126
cubefill indices 123
culture *170*
  organizational 61, 175, 177, 187, 298
customer expectations 169, *170*, 183–84
customer responsibility 313–14, 317–20, 324
customer segmentation 273–75
customer service 79–94, *145*, *410*
cyber security 181, 374, *375*, 376, 379

data-driven supply chains 33, 104–05, 108, 109, 144, 181, 185–87, 363–64
  see also big data
data protection 374, 376
data source 108, 386
decentralization 105, 106, 136, 149, 177, 265, 341, 382
decision-making 4, 65–66, 109, 110, *176*, 177, 302–04, 350–51
Deepwater Horizon disaster 72
deglobalization 429–32, 434–35
delivery, recording and governance model 406–08
delivery reliability 125, *128*, 169, 183–85, *186*, 188
demand (demand fluctuations) 3, 5, 69–70, 125, *126*, *128*, *145*, 146
dematerialization 264
deontic reasoning 312
design for manufacturing 419–20
developing countries 178–79, 192, 194, 232, 239, 244, 428
digital divide 371
digitalization 11, 74–77, 103–09, 136–37, 185, 187, 204–06, 277–80, *281*, 358–90
digitalization barriers 373–75
Direct Sourcing Group 197
disaster recovery 75
disruption 8–9, 62–65, 66, 71, *170*
  see also Covid-19 pandemic
distribution centre metrics 11, 147, 155, 256, *410*, 411
Dow Jones Industrial companies 29, *30*
Dow Jones Sustainability Indices 235
Dreamliner 7–8
drones 91, 157–58, 343, 370

dual sourcing 65, 69, 70, 215
Dynamic Alignment™ business model
        271–73, 283–85
dynamic customer segments 274, 276
Dyson 197

e-commerce (online retail) 80, 82, 84–86,
        89–91, 153–58, 159, 168, 171,
        184, 387
    see also Amazon; ASOS; Boohoo
economic profit value see EVA (EVA impact
        matrix)
economic risk 58, 59
economic sustainability 233, 234
ecosystem-centred view 109, 236, 270, 422
efficiency 2, 23–24, 106, 107, 144
electronic data interchange 215, 361
electronic physical distribution service
        quality framework 89–90
emerging markets 136, 184
empowerment 178, 181, 294, 295, 301, 304
empty running 119, 123–25, 131, 136, 262
end-to-end digitalization 277–80, 288, 379
end-to-end planning 4–5
end-to-end supply chain integration 176,
        182, 183, 193–94
endogenous risks 43, 44–45, 433
energy efficiency 253, 259–61
Energy Efficiency Index 260
engagement teams 301
engine idling 260
entrepreneurship 144, 154, 231, 290, 373
environmental responsibility (sustainability)
        101–02, 103, 107, 110, 129, 151,
        232–34, 238, 241–42, 309
environmental risk 58, 59, 70–71, 99
Erdoğan, President 392
Ericsson 37–38, 39, 40, 41, 62
ERP (enterprise resourcing planning) systems
        4, 205, 360, 361, 362, 368, 370
ESG approach 317
ethical shopping 315–17
ethics 306–37
Euro VI 248
Euro Stoxx 50 companies 29, 30
EVA (EVA impact matrix) 15–19, 28–29
event management 75, 278, 413
exogenous risks 44–46, 433
expenses accounting 22, 393
extrinsic motivation 295

Facebook 104
Factory Act (1833) 296
Fashion Revolution 152
fashion sector 142, 147, 149–55, 157–60,
        193–94, 239–40, 320
fast fashion 147–48, 150, 152, 160, 193,
        321, 324–25
fast-moving consumer goods (FMCG) 127,
        130, 143–44, 167, 168, 172,
        183–84, 411

feedback 23, 75, 77, 182, 254, 398
fight or flight 303–04
financial crisis (2008/9) 9, 52, 190–91, 429,
        430, 431
financial investments 43–44, 46–49
financial performance 14–35, 42, 392–94
financial risk 41–46, 49
5W1H method 101
fixed asset turnover 16, 24, 26–27, 29, 30,
        299
fixed assets reduction 26–27
flexibility (adaptivity) 5–7, 10–11, 148,
        169, 171, 211, 213–14, 228
focused factories 10
foldable ISO containers 133
Ford Motor Company 210, 215
forecasting 3, 5, 145, 410, 411–12
free trade 428, 429, 441
free trade agreements 436–37, 442
freight flow imbalances 127, 128
Fukushima disaster (Japanese earthquake)
        38, 41, 65, 73, 75
Fully Flex™ SC 278, 279
functional leadership 302
functional metrics 408–09

garment (textile) sector 21, 147, 151, 153,
        167, 172–73, 193, 239, 320,
        321–22
Garment without Guilt initiative 153
geopolitical risk 8–9, 52, 55, 58, 59, 149,
        192
Gini coefficient 436
Global Reporting Initiative 234
global risks 54–55, 62–63
global sourcing 9, 39–40, 97, 106, 170,
        172–73, 190–209, 285, 286,
        320–21
global supply planning 179–80
global warming potential 52, 203, 246,
        251, 255
globalization 210, 428–29, 430
goal setting 402–06
Google (Google Maps) 76, 77, 104, 432
governance 64–65, 109, 152, 176, 177–78,
        226–27, 404, 406–08
    see also Corporate Governance Code
        (2018)
green gold measures 253
green hydrogen 257–58
green (greening of) supply chains 21,
        240–42, 246–69
greenhouse gas emissions 54, 193, 246,
        249–69
greenwashing 152, 198, 315
grey hydrogen 257
grocery sector 81, 133, 146, 155–60, 213

Halfords 157
handling equipment 123, 126, 128, 135–36
HCVs 133–34

health and safety regulations *123*, 126, *128*
Heathrow 60
heavy fuel oil (HFO) 248, 251, 255, 258
Hermes 160
Honda 65, 73, 216
honeycomb of supply chain resilience model 68–72, 74
horizontal collaboration 129–30, *176*, 183, 211–12, 213, 283–85
horizontal time 146
humanitarian relief 338–57
humanitarian relief consolidation 346–47
hydrocarbons 248
hydrofluorocarbon (HFC123) 251

Icelandic volcano disruption *63*, 66, 73
ICT *see* technology (ICT)
impact 57
imperfect supply chain obligations 314, 315
improved business-as-usual 100–07, 111
inclusivity 297, 300, 301
incoterms 200
Inditex 23, 27, 321
industrial dynamics 1
industrial marketing 143–44
Industry 4.0 103, 360, 362, 382–90
information 'backbone' 204–05, *413*
inland waterways 258, 263, 264
innovation 98, 103, 105, 109, 155, 187, 296–300, 386–87
innovation barriers 298–99
innovation enables 299
innovative customer segments *274*
input measures 394–95, *396*, 397, 411
instinctive (intuitive) decision-making 303–04
inter-operability (modularization) 11, 103, 107, 135, 137
intermodal transport 263–64
International Energy Agency 256, 261
International Maritime Organization 248–49, 260–61
internationalization 142, 149–51
internet 84, 137, 204, 205, 385, 412–13
Internet of Things (IoT) 8, 33, 74, 204, 206, 280, *361*, 362, 368, *369*
intrinsic motivation 295
inventory buffers 5, 9
inventory holding costs 22, 23–24, 202–03
invoicing 132, 409
ISO standards 234

Japanese earthquake (Fukushima disaster) 38, 41, 65, 73, 75
joint ventures 157, 286
just-in-time (JIT) practices 2, 9, 125, 128, 148

Kellogg's 130
Kimberly-Clark 130

Kipling method 101
known knowns 53, *56*
known unknowns 53, *56*

labour conditions 435
labour costs 151, 172, 173, 206, 240
Land Rover 66
last-mile logistics 85, 156, 157, 349, 387
layers and pillars model 200, 202–03
lead time management *145*, 146–48, 185
leadership 286–87, 289–305, 378–79
leagile approach 144–45
lean supply chains 2, 9, 144–45, *278*, *279*
least-developed countries (LDCs) 248, 428
Leclerc 157
legislation 312, 317, *375*, 394
    see also Companies Act (2006); Factory Act (1833); Sarbanes-Oxley Act (2002)
Levitt report 306–07, 320, 323–24, 325, 326–27
LHVs 133–34
Li & Fung *150*, 197
lightweighting 134–35, 259, 261, 264
liquid natural gas (LNG) 255
liquidity risks 44, 46
load-matching 136
loading methods 135–36
localization 159–60, 169, 171, 173, 177–78, 180, 217
logistics, defined 39, 143, 359
logistics costs 82, 172
Logistics 4.0 (smart logistics) 382–83, 385–89
logistics service providers (LSPs) 167, 168, 171, 184, 216, 218–22
    and digitalization 372–73, *375*, 382–83, 386, 387–89
    retail sector 90
    and sustainability 236, 238, 241–42
long-term supply chain relationships 218–22
Louis Vuitton 160
luxury fashion sector 150, 160

machine learning 12, 136, 371
maintenance efficiencies 260, 363
managed reporting 392, 394
management determinants 401, *402*
manual stacking 135
manufacturing processes 105, 395, *410*, 418–26
manufacturing readiness 422–23, *424*
manufacturing sector 71, 167, *191*, *434*, 435–36
margin 393
marginal abatement cost analysis 253
maritime freight 119–20, 124, 127, 248–49, 255, 258, 260–61
    see also container shipping; ocean freight

market dynamics 110
marketing 79–94, 143, 144
Marks and Spencer 321
maturity models 178
medical devices sector 215, 349
methane 251, 255
metrics (measurement) 4, 222–27, 391–417
    financial performance 14–35, 42
    freight transport 120–25
    supply chain disruption 62–65
    sustainability 234–35
mid-market fashion retailers 150, 159
millennial employees 242
mitigation phase, disaster relief 344
mitigation risk 72
mobile computing (devices) 136, 368, 369,
    371, 372
modern slavery 194, 203, 307, 311, 312,
    317, 323, 325
'modern truck scenario' 261
modularization 11, 103, 107, 135, 137
moral organization 297
most favoured nation principle 428
motivational leadership 295
multi-channel models 90, 158, 345
Multi-Fibre Arrangement, abolition of 320
multinational companies (MNCs) 149,
    171, 207, 307, 358, 373, 377,
    434–35

nationalism 429
natural disasters 54–55, 71, 77, 102, 198,
    287, 338, 339–40
natural gas 251, 255–56, 257
natural resource scarcity 98, 105, 106, 110,
    232, 233, 346
near-shoring 69, 160, 182, 203, 206–08,
    264, 431
Nestlé 130, 262
network forces 169–72
network optimization technologies 181,
    278, 279
network organizations 148
networked economy 169–71
networks 182–83, 414
    see also collaboration; cooperation;
        near-shoring; network
        forces; network optimization
        technologies; outsourcing
new modular loading unit 135
Next 155, 159
Nike 319
nitrogen oxide (NOx) 246, 247–48, 255
nitrous oxide 251
Nokia 62
nominated day delivery systems 132

objectification 103
objective setting 217–22, 225–26
Ocado 158
ocean freight 438–39

see also container shipping; maritime
    freight; sea freight
offshoring 9, 142, 147, 148, 149, 150, 160,
    180, 217, 321
omni-channel models 154–55, 168
online procurement 127, 136, 137
online retail see e-commerce (online retail)
onward delivery system 131
open innovation 105, 187
open systems 6
operational decision-making 66, 350–51
operational risk 43, 45, 59
order fulfilment process 84–85, 97, 98, 132,
    155–57, 349
organization design (structure) 4, 178, 200,
    202, 279, 280–85, 286, 414–15
organizational culture 61, 175, 177, 187,
    298
output measures 394–95, 396, 397
outsourcing 2, 7–8, 9, 98, 171, 182,
    239–40
    retail sector 23, 142, 148, 149–51
    see also logistics service providers (LSPs)

packaging 123, 132, 316
pallets 122, 123, 127, 135, 218, 221, 222,
    223
pandemic see Covid-19 pandemic
Pandemic Supply Chain Network 350–52
    see also Covid-19 pandemic
Paris Climate Agreement (2015) 249
particulate matter 246, 247
partnerships 109, 171, 176, 184, 321
passive complicity 318–19, 327
Patagonia 153
payload weights 121
PDCA (plan-do-check-act) cycle 406–07
people strategies 175–77, 270–88, 295–96
PepsiCo 262
perfect supply chain obligations 314
performance management (measurement)
    391–417
    financial 14–35, 42
Philips Microchip 37–38, 62
'phoenix system' 322
physical internet 137, 385
physical organization 297
physical resource management 346
picking-centre fulfilment 155–56, 158
pilot projects 257, 370–71
pipeline maps 146–47
planning processes 179–80
playbooks 178
pollution 151, 198, 234, 246–49, 255, 265
populism 429, 432
postponement strategy 23, 202–03, 341,
    343
power shifts 99, 314
powertrain 259
Prada 150, 160
Premier Inns 60

preparedness phase, disaster relief 341–42
pricing 89, 197, 315
probability 57
probability of default 42–44, 46, 49
process (processes) 177–80
process risk 71, 72, 73
Procter & Gamble 123, 215
procurement 95–118, 127, 285–87,
    346–49, 352
    online 136, 137
procurement mapping 96, 101
procurement research 96–98
product design 123, 153, 419, 420, 425
product development 97, 153, 182, 195,
    227, 419–20
product life cycle 14, 145, 174, 199–200,
    206, 382, 420
product-service bundles (servitization)
    102–03, 105, 107
product variety 145
profit margins 16, 21, 24, 29, 30, 145, 156,
    218
profitability 82, 393
project accumulation customer segments
    274, 276
project plans 29
Provenance 309
Provision 172(1) (Companies Act) 291
purchasing policy 145
push-back racking 221, 222

qualitative metrics 224–25
quantitative metrics 223–24

Race to Zero 249–50
racking systems 127, 135, 221–22
rail freight 123–24, 173, 250, 251, 256,
    261, 263–64, 440
Rana Plaza factory collapse 73, 151, 240, 320
Rank A Brand 152
ratings agencies 41
re-shoring 69, 106, 160, 204, 206–08, 264,
    287
real options decision-making 6
reciprocal cooperation 110
recovery 10, 85
recovery phase, disaster relief 344
Regional Comprehensive Economic
    Partnership 436–37
regionalization 106, 131, 155, 178, 179,
    264, 341
regulation 133, 152, 170, 174–75, 310–11,
    394, 428, 436
    health and safety 123, 126, 128
renewable energy 256, 258, 259, 263
reserve-and-collect 157
resistance 10, 243, 374, 375, 378, 429
resource-based theory (resources
    management) 148, 346
response phase, disaster relief 343

retail sector 71, 84–85, 142–63, 167, 168,
    172, 194–95, 372, 387
    see also B&Q; fashion sector; Marks
    and Spencer; Tesco; Walmart
return on capital employed (ROCE) 16,
    26–27, 29, 394
return on investment 220, 394
return on shareholders' fund 394
returns policy (reverse logistics) 90, 91,
    132, 142, 155
revenue growth 26–27, 29, 30
RFID tags 360, 361, 370
risk 8–10, 38, 41–46, 57–60, 66–73, 98,
    170, 203–04, 375, 433
    control 226–27
    credit 132
    financial 49
    geopolitical 52, 55, 149, 192
    global 54–55, 62–63
risk levels 433–35
risk management 38–39, 56, 57, 60–62,
    202, 347
risk monitoring 61
risk registers 438–40
road freight 119, 122–23, 133, 246–47,
    250, 257, 259, 261–63, 439–40
robotics 33, 180, 204, 206, 207, 368, 369,
    370, 371
ROCE (return on capital employed) 16,
    26–27, 29, 394
roll-cages 122, 126, 128, 135
rolling credit 132
RoRo ferries 251, 258
Ryanair 212, 228

safety stock 9, 18, 19, 24, 71
Sainsbury's 156, 315
sales growth 294, 393
Sarbanes-Oxley Act (2002) 37, 64–65
SARS epidemic 52, 53, 56, 57
scaling up 102
scenario modelling 29, 180, 280, 288,
    371
Science Based Target Initiative 253
SCOR model 24, 86
sea freight 124, 127, 193, 250, 258, 263
    see also container shipping; maritime
    freight; ocean freight
seasonal teams 91
Securities and Exchange Commission 392
sensor technology 75–77, 280, 281, 360,
    370, 386
service level agreements 402–06, 408, 414
service quality (gaps) model 87–88
services 80, 81, 85
servitization (product-service bundles)
    102–03, 105, 107
shadow boards 296
shareholder value 15, 16, 18–20, 24–30,
    64, 311, 393, 398

sharing economy 7
Ship Energy Efficiency Management Plans
    260–61
Silk Road initiative 173, 190
silo mentality 4, 11, 127, 200, 280, 285, *375*
single sourcing *9*, *65*, 73, 215
skills development 74, 106, 148, 176, *202*,
    211–12, 220, 342, 378, 415
slip sheets 135
slow steaming 260
smart logistics (Logistics 4.0) 382–83,
    385–89
SMEs (small & medium sized
    enterprises) *358*, 364, 373, 377,
    387, 434–35
social sustainability 233, 234, 238, 240, 311
software integration 135–36, 370
South Africa 65, 134, 192
special and differential treatment 428
stackability 122, *123*, 133, 135
stakeholder mapping 301
stakeholders 80, 82, 187, 301, 302, 311,
    378, 392, 424
standardization (standards) 135, 177–79,
    299, 347, 374, 377
'Starfish' project 130
start-ups 103, 136, *154*, 187
stock metrics *410*
stock-outs *19*, 24, 82, *145*
storage 127, *128*, 131, 219, 352, 359
store-based fulfilment 155–57
Strategic Crystal 414–16
strategic decision-making 65
strategic planning 300, 342, 345–46, 350,
    352
strategic procurement 95, 98, 101–02
strategic suppliers (single sourcing) *9*, 65,
    73, 215
strategy 103, 190, 225–26, 300, 301, 433
    postponement 23, 202–03, 341, 343
structural culpability *318*, 319, *327*
structural determinants 401, *402*
structural flexibility 6–7, 10
sub-optimization 228, 400, 408, 412
subsidiarity 416, *434*
sulphur dioxide (SOx) 246, 248–49, 255
supplier metrics *410*
supplier relationship management 23,
    98, 104–05, 148, 153, 210–30,
    240–42, 325–26, 431
    see also strategic suppliers (single
        sourcing)
supplier segmentation 286, 287
supply chain integration 21, 22–23, 39, 44,
    143–44, *176*, 177–78, 236–38,
    359, 414–16
    end-to-end 182, 183, 193–94
supply chain management 1–2, 36, 41,
    143–44, 146, 210, 212, 213–14,
    360, 399–400

supply chain mapping 74, 425
supply chain orchestration 8, *96*, 360, 382,
    385
supply chain planning 174, 345–46, 347–49
supply chain probability of default *43*
supply chain readiness 423–24
supply chain resilience 10–12, 52–78, 102,
    107, 287–88, 347, *348*
supply chain risk management 36–51,
    60–62, 202, 347
supply risk 70, 73
support infrastructure 436
sustainability 83, 98, 109, 151–53, *154*,
    170, 197–99, 231–45, 314–15
sustainability advantage 111
Sustainable Development Goals (SDGs) 99,
    101, 108, 198–99, 233
Symrise 184
synchromodality 263
systems thinking 103, 213–14, 228

tactical decision-making 65–66
talent management *170*, 174, 175–77,
    292–93, 374, 378–79
Tata 212, 213
team-based organizations 4
technology audit assessments 421–22
technology (ICT) 24, 33, 98, *99*, *170*, 176,
    180–82, 210–11, 418–26, *434*
    battery 256, 257, 258
    humanitarian relief 343, 347
    network optimization *278*, *279*
    sensor 75–77, 280, *281*, 360, 370, 386
    see also additive manufacturing (3D
        printing); artificial intelligence
        (AI); automation; barcode
        scanning; blockchain; cloud
        computing; computer systems;
        cyber security; digitalization;
        drones; electronic data
        interchange; ERP (enterprise
        resource planning) systems;
        information 'backbone'; internet;
        Internet of Things (IoT); machine
        learning; mobile computing
        (devices); RFID tags; robotics;
        software integration; virtual
        reality
technology readiness levels 421–22, 424
technology risk *58*, *59*
technology roadmaps 181, 422
10C framework 252–54
tensegrity 271–73
Tesco 144, 149, 156, 157, 212, 213, 226,
    228, 314
textile (garment) sector 21, 147, 151, 153,
    167, 172–73, 193, 239, 320,
    321–22
3-dimensional concurrent engineering
    420

3D printing *see* additive manufacturing (3D printing)
Timberland 153
time-based competition 146–48
Tod's 150
total shareholder return 15
toxic leadership 294
Toyota 73, 216, 226, 227
trade conditions 436
trade policy *434*
training 61, 72, 176–77, 346
transactional customer segments *274, 276*
transparency 11–12, 104, 152–53, 187, 238
transportation 22, 119–41, 184, 210, *237*, 238, 241, 435, 438–40
    digitalization of *359, 375*
    green logistics 246–51, 255–65, 410–12
    see also airfreight; maritime freight; ocean freight; rail freight; road freight; sea freight; trucks
triangulation 127
triple bottom line 198
truck dimensions 133–34
trucks 120–28, 131, 133–36, 246–48, *251*, 256–63
TUB Logistics Navigator 179–80

Ulula 309
unattended delivery 90–91
uncertainty 38
Unilever 314, 315
United Biscuits 130
United Nations (UN) 152
    framework convention on climate change (UNFCC) 249–50, 251
    Sustainable Development Goals (SDGs) 99, 101, 108, 198–99, 233
    World Food Programme (WFP) 339

unitized freight (loading) 122, 135–36
unknown unknowns 53

value gaps 24–28
velocity 3, 393–94
vendor-managed inventory 9, 131, *145*
vertical collaboration (integration) 9, 23, 131, *176*, 183, 210–11, 228, 280, *282, 286*
    retail sector 147, 148, 150
vertical time 146
virtual reality 368, *369*, 373
visibility 3, 4–5, 8, 11–12, 61, 108, 136, 137, *176*, 181
volatile organic compounds 248
volatility 5, *170*, 173, 174–75, 184, 203
volatility management performance tool 175
volume metrics 122–23
voting (decision-making) 303

Waitrose 133
Walmart 23–24, 26–27, 149, 195, 197, 213, 215, 226, 314
waste 2, *145*, 193, 194
weigh-outs 123, 126
weight metrics 121, 123, 133–35
Whitbread 60
win-lose initiatives 32
win-win initiatives 32–33
work flow (event) management 75, *278*, 413
working capital 16, 26, 27, 31–32, 37, 172, 180, 215, 394
World Health Organization 247, 350, *351*
World Trade Organization (WTO) 190–92, 428, 432, 436

Zara 23, 26–27, 28–29, 147, 148, 150–51, 321, 325

www.ingramcontent.com/pod-product-compliance
Lightning Source LLC
Jackson TN
JSHW071947131224
75385JS00017B/385